THE EMERGENCE OF
RUSSIAN PANSLAVISM
1856-1870

Studies of the Russian Institute of Columbia University

THE EMERGENCE OF RUSSIAN PANSLAVISM 1856-1870

by Michael Boro Petrovich

1956

COLUMBIA UNIVERSITY PRESS, *New York*

THE TRANSLITERATION SYSTEM USED IN THIS SERIES
IS BASED ON THE LIBRARY OF CONGRESS SYSTEM WITH
SOME MODIFICATIONS

LIBRARY OF CONGRESS CATALOG CARD NUMBER: 56-5880

© 1956 COLUMBIA UNIVERSITY PRESS, NEW YORK

PUBLISHED IN GREAT BRITAIN, CANADA, INDIA, AND PAKISTAN
BY GEOFFREY CUMBERLEGE: OXFORD UNIVERSITY PRESS
LONDON, TORONTO, BOMBAY, AND KARACHI

MANUFACTURED IN THE UNITED STATES OF AMERICA

D
377
.P4

THE RUSSIAN INSTITUTE OF COLUMBIA UNIVERSITY

THE RUSSIAN INSTITUTE was established by Columbia University in 1946 to serve two major objectives: the training of a limited number of well-qualified Americans for scholarly and professional careers in the field of Russian studies and the development of research in the social sciences and the humanities as they relate to Russia and the Soviet Union. The research program of the Russian Institute is conducted through the efforts of its faculty members, of scholars invited to participate as Senior Fellows in its program, and of candidates for the Certificate of the Institute and for the degree of Doctor of Philosophy. Some of the results of the research program are presented in the Studies of the Russian Institute of Columbia University. The faculty of the Institute, without necessarily agreeing with the conclusions reached in the Studies, believe that their publication advances the difficult task of promoting systematic research on Russia and the Soviet Union and public understanding of the problems involved.

The faculty of the Russian Institute are grateful to the Rockefeller Foundation for the financial assistance which it has given to the program of research and publication.

62543

STUDIES OF THE

RUSSIAN INSTITUTE

OF COLUMBIA UNIVERSITY

Soviet National Income and Product in 1937
By Abram Bergson

Through the Glass of Soviet Literature: Views of Russian Society
Edited by Ernest J. Simmons

The Proletarian Episode in Russian Literature, 1928-1932
By Edward J. Brown

Management of the Industrial Firm in the USSR: A Study in Soviet Economic Planning
By David Granick

Soviet Policies in China, 1917-1924
By Allen S. Whiting

Ukrainian Nationalism, 1939-1945
By John A. Armstrong

Polish Postwar Economy
By Thad Paul Alton

Literary Politics in the Soviet Ukraine, 1917-1934
By George S. N. Luckyj

The Emergence of Russian Panslavism, 1856-1870
By Michael Boro Petrovich

To
the memory of
my Father

PREFACE

SOME TWO MONTHS after Hitler attacked the Soviet Union, the Kremlin resurrected the Panslavic idea. A Panslavic Committee met in Moscow on August 10, 1941, to call upon Slavs everywhere, about two hundred million of them, to unite against the German aggressors. Less than four years later, the Kremlin again put Panslavism to use in seeking to consolidate its new dominion over Eastern Europe.

The author was in a position to watch both the defensive and the aggressive aspects of Soviet Panslavism at close range. In April, 1942, he attended the American Slav Congress in Detroit as a private observer. He again saw Panslavism operate in Yugoslavia in 1944-46 while a member of the OSS American Military Mission to Marshal Tito. More recently he observed its workings in Czechoslovakia in 1948-49 while engaged in research for this study. It was this experience, coupled with an awareness of the increasingly important role of the Slavic peoples in modern history, which prompted the present work.

Nevertheless, in writing the pages which follow, the author has made an effort not to intrude the present upon the past. Parallels between Tsarist and Soviet Panslavism will no doubt suggest themselves to the reader. Yet, like all past phenomena, Russian Panslavism of the nineteenth century must be studied for its own sake, and not as a "precursor," if it is to be understood.

By Panslavism is meant the historic tendency of the Slavic peoples to manifest in some tangible way, whether cultural or political, their consciousness of ethnic kinship. Far from being an isolated phenomenon, Panslavism has its roots in the same soil which nourished its Western counterparts—Pan-Germanism, Pan-Latinism, and similar patterns of thought and action. If the term "Panslavism" has been used somewhat loosely, not only by the protagonists and the enemies of this movement, but even by scholars, it is because the movement itself has consisted of scattered and sometimes mutually hostile forms. Manifestations ranging from vague expressions of Slavic cultural solidarity to more or less specific programs for the political unification either of all the Slavs (plus certain non-Slavs) or of a regional grouping of several Slavic peoples have all been generally regarded as "Panslavic." In the nineteenth century these forms included Austro-Slavism, an idea fostered especially by various Czech and Slovak leaders; Polish Messianism; the Illyrian movement of the South Slavs; Slavic federalism as advocated by certain Ukrainian patriots; and Great Russian Panslavism. This study is limited to the last of these, and then only to the period of its emergence as a developed ideology and movement. This work is intended to be chiefly a contribution to the history of ideas rather than to the history of Russian foreign policy. The author hopes to describe the further course of Russian Panslavism in a subsequent volume.

The structure of the present work requires some explanation. The opening chapter presents a survey of Panslavic manifestations in Russia before the reign of Alexander II, that is, before Russian Panslavism became a public movement with a distinct program. A chapter on Slavophilism in the 1840's offers an introduction to the philosophical origins of the Russian Panslavic ideology. The third chapter deals with the general concepts of the Panslavist ideology itself. The following chapters are devoted to more specific and practical ideas of Russian Panslavism or to organizations and activities directed to putting these ideas into effect.

The author belongs to a generation of young American students of Russian history which has not had access to Soviet libraries. Especially frustrating was his inability to make use of Panslavist archives in the Lenin Library—materials which the Institute of Slavic Studies of the Soviet Academy of Sciences has only recently begun to gather and to classify. Despite this handicap, over three quarters of the many sources used in the following study consist of the public writings and private correspondence of Russian Panslavists and their contemporaries. Most of these works were found in this country, though the author was fortunate in being able to use the resources of both the Russian Archive and the Slavic Library in Prague. Thus while the present work cannot hope to be definitive, it does aspire to present the most complete study of Russian Panslavism in the 1850's and 1860's which can now be published on the basis of the available materials.

ACKNOWLEDGMENTS

IT WOULD BE IMPOSSIBLE to thank all who have helped this volume reach completion. I am especially grateful to Professors Geroid T. Robinson and Philip E. Mosely, of the Russian Institute of Columbia University, not only for invaluable guidance, but for a patience and sympathy which exceeded the bounds of duty. The shortcomings of this work can be attributed only to the author's stubbornness in not heeding the counsels of these advisers. I am also indebted to the Rockefeller Foundation, which enabled me to attend the Russian Institute from 1946 through 1948, and to the Social Science Research Council, which made possible a year's research in Prague in 1948-49. This study could never have been carried to fruition without the help of the staffs of the Russian Archive and the Slavic Library of Charles University in Prague, the Library of Congress, Butler Library of Columbia University, the New York Public Library, and the Library of the University of Wisconsin. The encouragement and assistance given me by my colleagues in the History Department of the University of Wisconsin, as well as by Professor Robert Lee Wolff of Harvard University, Mr. William M. Kirsch of Madison, Mr. D. B. Tripp of New York, Mr. Jacob B. Hoptner, formerly of the Mid-European Studies Center of the National Committee for a Free Europe, Harriett Scantland, and numerous others, will always be appreciated. To John P. Spielman, Jr., and William P. Kaldis of the University of Wisconsin, as well as to Nancy and George Deptula, go my thanks for their help in preparing the manuscript.

I also wish to thank the following publishers for permission to quote material from these copyrighted works: Pitirim Sorokin, *Social Philosophies in an Age of Crisis*, Beacon Press; Hans Kohn, *The Twentieth Century*, Macmillan Company; Alexander Herzen, *My Past and Thoughts*, translated by Constance Garnett, Chatto and Windus, Ltd.; the translation of four lines of a poem by

Tiutchev cited by Professor W. Lednicki in his article "Panslavism" in *European Ideologies*, edited by Feliks Gross, Philosophical Library.

Madison, Wisconsin   M. B. P.

NOTE ON THE SPELLING
OF PROPER NAMES

THE TRANSLITERATION OF Russian proper names in this study follows the system used by the Russian Institute of Columbia University, which is in turn a slight modification of the Library of Congress system. An effort has been made to distinguish between the old and the new Russian orthography and to transliterate titles according to the orthographic system in which they were written. Where Russian Christian names had English equivalents, these were used—though the author could not bring himself to use John, George, and Theodore for such typically Russian forms as Ivan, Iurii, and Fëdor. All non-Russian Slavic names and titles have been transliterated according to the Library of Congress system. Slavic names and titles originally written in the Latin alphabet have been preserved in their native form.

CONTENTS

THE EMERGENCE OF
RUSSIAN PANSLAVISM
1856-1870

RUSSIA AND THE PANSLAVIC IDEA BEFORE 1856

*Très-peu de personnes savent comprendre
avec délicatesse ces sortes de questions
relatives à l'esprit des races.*

ERNEST RENAN

THE TERM "PANSLAVISM" has been generally used to denote the historic tendency of the Slavic peoples to manifest in any tangible way, whether cultural or political, their consciousness of ethnic kinship.

As a movement, Panslavism was a product of modern times. The word itself did not enter political parlance until about 1830. The term "Panslavism" was first used by a Slovak, Ján Herkel, in a work published in Budapest in 1826 which was entitled *Elementa universalis linguae slavicae e vivis dialectis eruta et sanis logicae principiis suffulta*.[1] It is noteworthy that the word was coined by a Western Slav rather than by a Russian, and that it was first employed in a work on Slavic linguistics rather than politics. It is also rather typical of early nineteenth-century Panslavism that this work should have been published in a non-Slavic language and in a non-Slavic city.

Panslavism as a public movement did not assert itself in Russia until the Crimean War and the beginning of Alexander II's reign in 1855. Although Russian Panslavists attempted to create the impression that Russians had long been Panslavists at heart, history hardly bears them out in this claim.

It is true, however, judging by their earliest records, that the

---

[1] See Louis Léger, "Panslavisme," *La Grande Encyclopédie*, XXV (Paris, n.d.), 954; also Walter Schubart, *Europa und die Seele des Ostens* (Lucerne, 1938), p. 206; also A. N. Pypin, "Panslavizm," *Viestnik Evropy* (October, 1878), p. 314.

Russians have known from their beginnings as a nation that they were Slavs and that they constituted a part of a larger cultural family of Slavic peoples. The author of the Russian Primary Chronicle—whom V. O. Kliuchevskii, the famed Russian historian, somewhat playfully dubbed a Panslavist[2]—recorded in the first years of the twelfth century that "the Slavic race is derived from the line of Japheth" and that this race included Moravians, Czechs, White Croats, Serbs, Carinthians, Liakhs (Poles), and the various tribes of the Russian land. "Thus the Slavic race was divided," wrote the medieval Russian chronicler, "and its language was known as Slavic."[3] It must be noted, however, that the compiler of the chronicle was rather vague in his knowledge of the other Slavs. Though he lists the various Slavic peoples several times, no single list is complete, and no two lists are identical.[4]

Even on the threshold of their modern history the Russians of Muscovy knew hardly more about the non-Russian Slavs than did their earliest chroniclers. As late as 1674 a compendium published in Kiev which was entitled *Sinopsis ili kratkoe sobranie ot raznykh lietopistsev o nachalie slaviano-rossiiskago naroda* (Synopsis or a Short Collection from Divers Chroniclers concerning the Beginnings of the Slavo-Russian People) claimed that all the Slavic peoples—"all, as many as there be to whom the use of the Slavic tongue is natural" —possessed a single sire, namely, "Mosokh, the sixth son of Japheth, grandson of Noah."[5] The Russians of seventeenth-century Muscovy had so little idea of the other Slavs that they called their own countrymen of Western *Rus'* "Lithuanians" and those of the Ukraine "Circassians."[6]

While the very existence of monkish tales and folk legends concerning the common origin of the Slavs indicates that the

---

[2] V. O. Kliuchevskii, *Kurs russkoi istorii*, I (Petrograd, 1918), 121.

[3] Samuel H. Cross, *The Russian Primary Chronicle* (Cambridge, Mass., 1930), pp. 137-38.

[4] George Vernadsky and Michael Karpovich, *A History of Russia*, Vol. I: George Vernadsky, *Ancient Russia* (New Haven, 1943), pp. 308 ff.

[5] Cited by Josef Perwolf, "Slavianskaia vzaimnost' s drevnieishikh vremen do XVIII vieka," *Zhurnal Ministerstva Narodnago Prosvieshcheniia*, CLXXI (1874), 161-62.

[6] A. N. Pypin, "Obzor russkikh izuchenii Slavianstva," *Viestnik Evropy* (April, 1889), p. 589.

Russians have long possessed a conception of Slavic kinship, there is no evidence that this conception motivated them, until the eighteenth and especially the nineteenth century, to undertake concerted action of any kind with other Slavs in the name of their ethnic kinship. On the contrary, the history of the relations between the Russians and their closest Slavic neighbors, the Poles, has been one of mutual hostility.

In the centuries preceding the rise of modern nationalism, Russia's attitude with respect to the other Slavs was more affected by religious than by ethnic considerations. Even throughout the nineteenth century the Russian people and their government showed a much greater interest in the Orthodox Slavs than in their Roman Catholic or Protestant kinsmen. This was all the more natural in view of the fact that Russia's traditional political interests as well as earliest cultural ties lay precisely in the Orthodox Balkans.

It was out of the historic contacts between Russia and the Orthodox Balkans that one of the chief components of later Russian Panslavism emerged—messianism. Russian messianism rested originally on the claim that Russia was the true heir of Byzantium and the sole protector of Orthodox Christendom. The messianic strain has been a powerful undercurrent in Russian history. It began to take hold of Russian minds when Isidor, the Greek Metropolitan of Moscow, returned from the Council of Florence-Ferrara in 1439 to report to an indignant Muscovy that the Greeks (including himself) had signed an ecclesiastical union with the hated Latins in the hope of gaining Western aid against the Turks. So wrathful were the Russians that Isidor found it necessary to flee the country. The fall of Constantinople in 1453 shook Holy Russia, but the news seemed hardly surprising. It was obvious to the devout Muscovites that God had but used the Turk as the instrument of His chastisement against the apostate Greeks. Yet what a terrible punishment it was for all the Orthodox to be deprived of an empire without which the very existence of Orthodox Christendom was hardly conceivable.

It was with the marriage of Ivan III with Zoë Paleologus, the niece of the last emperor of Constantinople, on June 1, 1472, that Muscovy began to think of itself as the only true heir of Byzantium.

That conviction received its outward manifestation when the Grand Prince of Muscovy placed the double-headed eagle of Byzantium on his escutcheon and assumed the title of caesar or tsar. This claim to the imperial dignity bore with it the sacred obligation of assuming the protection and deliverance of all Orthodox Christians.

With its own final liberation from the Tartar yoke in 1480, Muscovy began to take its messianic role with even greater seriousness. Eager to have Moscow proclaimed the ecumenical See of the Orthodox world, the Russian clergy gave currency to the idea that the Russian capital was the Third Rome. This claim was given classic expression by the abbot of a monastery near Pskov, Philotheus, who wrote to the Tsar:

The Church of the Old Rome fell because of the infidelity of the Apollinarian heresy. The Second Rome—the Church of Constantinople —was hewn down by the axes of the sons of Hagar. And now this Third Rome of thy mighty kingdom—the holy catholic and apostolic Church— will illumine the whole universe like the sun. . . . Know and accept, O pious Tsar, that all the Christian kingdoms have come together into thine own, that two Romes have fallen, and that a third stands, while a fourth there shall not be: thy Christian kingdom shall fall to no other.[7]

And thus Russian national ambitions became coupled with a sacred mission, a feeling of vocation which was to be frequently invoked in Russian foreign policy down the ages.

That this Russian messianism was for some five centuries predominantly a religious conception is well illustrated by the failure of Juraj Križanić's mission in seventeenth-century Muscovy. Russian Panslavists of the nineteenth century hailed Križanić as a progenitor of Russian Panslavism, a title which he richly deserved. Yet the career of this remarkable man reveals how indifferent the Russia of his time was to any Panslavic idea.

To begin with, this father of Russian Panslavism was not a Russian. He was a Croat and a Roman Catholic priest who came to Muscovy in 1659 during the reign of Alexis hoping to effect a

[7] P. Miliukov, *Ocherki po istorii russkoi kultury*, I (2d ed., St. Petersburg, 1905), 23.

union between the Russian Church and the Papacy. By an imperial decree of January 8, 1661, Križanić was exiled to Siberia, and during his fifteen years at Tobol'sk, from 1661 to 1676, he wrote some nine works on religion, philosophy, linguistics, and government, largely in a hybrid Slavic language of his own invention. It was in his treatise, *Razgovory ob vladatelstvu* (Discourses on Government), that Križanić urged the unification of all the Slavic peoples under the aegis of the Russian Tsar. Despite the inhospitable welcome which he had received in Russia, Križanić was a passionate Russophile and looked upon Russia as the only hope of a much-divided Slav world.

He believed wholeheartedly that the Slavs had at one time been a single entity and that Russia had been their primeval home prior to the dispersion. He blamed the dispersion of the Slavs on their neighbors, especially the Germans. Križanić appealed to Tsar Alexis, "Thou, O Tsar, art now alone of God given to succor the Trans-Danubians, Poles, and Czechs, to begin to know their oppressed and shameful state and to think about the enlightenment of the people that they might take the German yoke from off their necks."[8]

How did Križanić envisage Russia's role in this liberation and unification of the Slavs? He wrote:

The Trans-Danubian Slavs (Bulgars, Serbs, and Croats) have long since lost not only their kingdoms, but all power, and language, and reason, so that they do not understand what is honor or freedom and no longer think upon them. They cannot help themselves, but a force from without is needed to set them again on their feet and to reinstate them among the number of peoples. If thou, O Tsar, canst not in these difficult times make possible their victory nor reestablish their ancient kingdoms, thou canst correct the Slavic language in books and enlighten and open the spiritual eyes of those peoples through wise books so that they may come to know honor and to think of their resurgence.[9]

Križanić undoubtedly regarded force as the only means of liberating

---

[8] Juraj Križanić, *Razgovory ob vladatelstvu*, in P. Bezsonov's edition, *Russkoe gosudarstvo v polovinie XVII vieka* (Moscow, 1859), I, Part LI, 115.
[9] *Ibid.*

the Slavs, and therefore he called on the Russians as the most powerful of the Slavic peoples to achieve this liberation. Yet he certainly
did not envisage this liberation as a step toward the absorption of
all the Slavs by the Russians. On the contrary, he expressly appealed to the Tsar to "reinstate them among the number of peoples,"
that is, as separate national entities, though under Russian protection. Until such time as Russia should find itself able to accom-
plish this mission, Križanić proposed that it undertake what
amounted to a program of cultural Panslavism. His hybrid Slavic
language was designed to be a concrete contribution to the linguistic
"reunification" of the Slavs. As for religious differences among the
Slavs, the Roman Catholic priest suggested a compromise by which
all the Slavs would recognize papal supremacy while Rome in turn
would recognize the right of the Slavs to worship in their own
tongue and in their own way.

This first program of Panslavism found no fertile soil at all in
the tsar's domains. Križanić's idea was completely ignored in
Russia for two whole centuries, until the long-forgotten manuscript
was resurrected in 1859 by a Russian Panslavist, P. A. Bezsonov.

On the other hand, the Russians did evince an interest in those
Slavs who were their coreligionists. Especially since the elevation
of Moscow to the rank of a patriarchal See in 1589 and with the
end of the Time of Troubles, Eastern Christendom came to look
upon Holy Russia as the only free center of Orthodoxy as well as
the most powerful one. With the founding of the Romanov dynasty
in 1613, a stream of suppliant Balkan Orthodox clergy coursed to
Moscow in hope of Russian aid. It was during Sophia's regency,
while the young Peter I was still coruler with his brother Ivan, that
the great Serbian Patriarch, Arsenius III Čarnojević, called upon the
young Tsars to send an army to the Danube where, he promised,
they would be joined by the Serbs, Bulgars, and Moldavians, and
thus be given "a way to Constantinople without hindrance." The
deposed Patriarch of Constantinople, Dionysius, also exhorted the
corulers on behalf of the Greeks, Serbs, Bulgars, and Vlakhs:
"Arise, come and save us!"[10]

[10] Aleksije Jelačić, *Rusija i Balkan; pregled političkih i kulturnih veza Rusije
i balkanskih zemalja 866-1940* (Belgrade, 1940), pp. 23-24.

While Muscovite Russia maintained precarious relations with the Orthodox Slavs of the Balkans, it had hardly any intercourse at all with the Roman Catholic or Protestant Slavs. The one tragic exception was the Poles—whom the Russians knew all too intimately. Attempts by various Slavic historians to trace the relations between Russia and the Czechs, Slovaks, Slovenes, or Croats in fact succeed only in showing how scant these relations really were.[11] Thus by the time of Peter the Great, and for some time thereafter, few even well-educated Russians knew very much about these schismatic kinsmen of theirs in Central Europe.

It was not until Peter's accession to sole power in 1689 that practical interests involving Russian national ambitions combined with traditional religious sympathies to inaugurate a period of closer relations between the Balkan Orthodox Slavs and Russia. Peter's desire to establish contact with the Balkan Christians arose from his hope that they would rebel against their Turkish masters and support Russia in its war with the Porte. This hope was fed by increased appeals for help from the Balkans after the turn of the century. Between 1704 and 1710 alone at least four Serbian leaders journeyed to Moscow to knit connections, solicit funds, and at least in one case to offer the services of the Serbs to "their Orthodox tsar . . . for in faith and tongue we have no other tsar than God in heaven and on earth the most orthodox tsar Peter."[12] It is significant that these appeals now came from secular as well as from spiritual leaders in the Balkans. Perhaps the most famous Serb in Peter's Russia was the Hercegovinian Sava Vladislavić, whom Peter eventually honored with the title of Count Raguzinskii (that is, of Ragusa) for his distinguished services to the Russian Crown. It was probably he who framed Peter's proclamation of 1711 to the Orthodox Slavs of Serbia, Slavonia, Macedonia, Bosnia and Hercegovina which called upon them to join Russia against their common enemy—the infidel Turk.

---

[11] See especially Josef Perwolf, *Slaviane, ikh vzaimnyia otnosheniia i sviazi* (Warsaw, 1886), and his *Vývin idey vzájemnosti u národův slovanských* (Prague, 1867); also Josef Jirásek, *Rusko a my; dějiny vztahů československo-ruských od nejstarších dob až do roku 1914,* 4 vols. (2d ed., Brno, 1946).

[12] Cited by B. H. Sumner, *Peter the Great and the Ottoman Empire* (Oxford, 1949), p. 45.

Although Russia continued to regard Orthodoxy as its most binding tie with the Balkan Slavs, even during and long after Peter's reign, eighteenth-century Russia began to take note also of the ethnic affinity between itself and the Balkan Slavs, to an extent difficult to determine. It can hardly be maintained that Panslavic feelings played any real role in Russian policy at this time when nobody in Peter's Russia could even enumerate all of the Slavic peoples and point out on the map where they lived.[13] It was this Russian ignorance of some of the other Slavs which forced Peter to commission studies which would provide simple background information for himself and his diplomats. The Emperor himself requested Sava Vladislavić to translate into Russian a work published in 1601 by the Ragusan abbot, Mavro Orbini, entitled *Il Regno degli Slavi* (The Realm of the Slavs). So eager was Peter to obtain this book that he had it sent to him all the way to Astrakhan, where he was engaged in a campaign at the time.[14] By a decree of October 2, 1697, Peter ordered one of his "fledglings," Ostrovskii, to the "Sclavonian land" to discover who lived there, what kind of government the people had, whether they were seafarers or landsmen, and whether a Russian could understand their tongue. The order was never carried out. Peter was forced to establish a special commission to collect foreign works about the Slavs. And when he commanded it to engage someone to write a work "concerning the beginnings of the Slavic people and their language," the commission turned to the German philosopher Leibniz.[15]

Peter's venture in the Balkans came to naught. Only the doughty Montenegrins and some of the Serbs raised the banner of revolt against the Turks after encouragement from Russian emissaries, and this action achieved nothing. Yet Peter's relations with the Balkan Slavs did serve to awaken Russian interest in these little known coreligionists and to lay a foundation for further mutual contact. However, while the Russian government and church

[13] A. N. Pypin, "Russkoe slavianoviedenie v XIX-m stolietii," *Viestnik Evropy*, IV (1889), 239.

[14] S. M. Soloviëv, *Istoriia Rossii s drevnieishikh vremen*, XVIII (2d ed., St. Petersburg, n.d.), 802.

[15] *Ibid.*, XVII, 638.

showed an interest in the Balkan Slavs, it was fully a century before
Russian scholars or Russian society paid any attention to them.

Russia's war with Turkey in 1735-39 and its gains on the Black
Sea brought Russia closer to the Balkans, while Russian victories
inspired growing hopes among the Balkan Christians. Elizabeth's
ambassador to the Porte, Veshniakov, reported from Constantinople: "All the wretched Christians await liberation by Your
Imperial Majesty. A Russian army has but to appear suddenly on
the Danube and in a short time it will be increased tenfold. Let it
only carry weapons in reserve. Moldavia, Wallachia, Bulgaria,
Serbia, Slavonia, Dalmatia, Montenegro, Albania, all Greece, the
islands, and Constantinople itself will simultaneously take up the
Cross and come to the aid of Your Majesty."[16] Elizabeth did not
share her ambassador's optimism. She did, however, aid many
Balkan Slavs, especially the Serbs of Vojvodina, by permitting them
to migrate to southern Russia. There these colonists founded New
Serbia and Slaveno-Serbia, which eventually became the province
of Novorossiia. These migrations continued in the reign of Catherine II and eventually provided Russia with some of her most
distinguished citizens.

Catherine's political designs in the Balkans definitely gave precedence to religious solidarity over Russian ethnic ties with the
Balkan peoples. It was as the champion of Orthodoxy rather than
as the protector of Slavdom that she intended to exert Russian
influence in the Ottoman Empire. This was the intent of that
fateful clause in the Treaty of Küchük-Kainardji in 1774 by which
Russia claimed a spiritual protectorate over the Orthodox subjects
of the Sultan. Catherine's "Greek Project" of 1782 proved that she
was far more interested in making Russia the physical as well as
the spiritual heir of the Byzantine Empire than she was in establishing a free Slavdom. Her readiness to sacrifice all of Serbia and
Bosnia-Hercegovina to Austria that her felicitously named grandson, Constantine, might sit on the throne of the Paleologi indicated
how little Catherine cared for ethnic ties. Certainly her partitions
of Poland indicated even more forcefully that Russian national
interests took little account of racial ties in this period.

[16] Jelačić, *Rusija i Balkan*, p. 33.

Official Russia evinced a renewed interest in the Balkan Slavs during the reign of Alexander I. Again this interest arose from practical considerations of foreign policy.

In 1804 and 1807 the Russian Foreign Ministry received two noteworthy memoranda which are modest milestones in the history of early Russian Panslavism. The first was by the liberal philanthropist V. N. Karazin (1773-1842), who achieved fame as a writer and especially as the founder of the University of Kharkov. His interest in the Balkan Slavs may be attributed in some measure to the fact that his grandfather was a Serb. In a letter of November 21, 1804, written in French and addressed to Prince Czartoryski, Alexander's Foreign Minister, Karazin made an impassioned plea for Russian aid to the other Slavs. "Can the illustrious leader of the free tribes of the Slavs, the only Supreme Leader of their Church, allow these unfortunate brethren to fall prey to the most disastrous calamities?" he asked. "Will his magnanimous heart be capable of refusing all assistance and of destroying at one blow the hope of millions of men whose eyes are turned to Him as to a Divine Liberator whom they already worship as the Messiah whom they have so vainly expected during the centuries?"

In a supplementary letter of November 27, 1804, Karazin proposed to Czartoryski the establishment of "a Slavic kingdom with one of Alexander's august brothers placed on the throne" and assured the Foreign Minister that "Providence has already prepared everything for this." He included in this Slavic kingdom Bulgaria and most of the provinces of modern Yugoslavia. Karazin was certain that this kingdom, tied to Russia by religion, consanguinity, a dynastic bond, and gratitude, would become Russia's "market and natural point of support in all undertakings and in all relations with Europe as well as with Africa."[17]

The idea of a vast Slavic federation under Russia's protection found a champion in Vladimir Bogdanovich Bronevskii (1784-1835), a Russian naval officer who served under Admiral Seniavin in the Mediterranean from 1805 to 1810. In a memorandum addressed to the Russian Foreign Ministry just before the peace at Tilsit, Bronevskii urged his government to help the Slavs of both

[17] V. N. Karazin, *Sochineniia, pis'ma i bumagi* (Kharkov, 1910), pp. 37 ff.

Turkey and Austria to establish their own federation under Russia's patronage. Such a federation, he wrote, could be used as a counterweight to any Western European coalition, particularly Napoleon's imperial system.[18]

Apart from this secret memorandum, Bronevskii deserves to be remembered also for popularizing the other Slavs among his own countrymen in two books. The first, published in St. Petersburg in 1818-19 and again in 1836, contained an account of his experiences in the Mediterranean campaign under Admiral Seniavin. The other was a description of his journey in 1810 from Trieste to St. Petersburg via Slovenia, Croatia, Hungary, Poland, and White Russia.[19]

As during the time of Peter the Great, Balkan Slavic leaders appealed to Alexander for aid. In 1804 the archimandrite of the monastery of Piva in Hercegovina, Arsenius Gagović, came to St. Petersburg to propose the restoration of the medieval Serbian Empire under a Russian prince. On January 14, 1804, Jovan Jovanović, Bishop of Bačka, wrote the Metropolitan of St. Petersburg imploring him to intervene at the Imperial Court on behalf of the Serbs. On June 1 of the same year the famed Metropolitan of Karlovci, Stevan Stratimirović, sent a memorandum to Alexander I urging the unification of the Serbian lands, Srem, and southern Dalmatia under a Russian prince. "There is not a people under heaven," wrote the ranking Serbian prelate in Austria, "that loves the Russians and the Russian rulers as much as the Serbs."[20]

In September, 1804, three Serbian emissaries—Archpriest Matija Nenadović, Jovan Protić, and Petar Novaković-Čardaklija—left for Russia on a mission from Karadjordje, the leader of the Serbian insurrection against the Turks. On St. Demetrius Day, October 26, they arrived in the Tsar's capital, where they were received by Adam Czartoryski. The Serbian Orthodox priest had the strange experience of trying to convince a Roman Catholic Polish aristocrat that Holy Russia was Orthodox Serbia's only hope. "Fine," said

[18] A. N. Pypin, "Panslavizm," *Viestnik Evropy*, LXXIII (May, 1878), 744-45.
[19] The titles of V. B. Bronevskii's books are *Zapiski morskago ofitsera, v prodolzhenii kampanii na Sredizemnom morie pod nachalstvom vitse-admirala Dmitriia Nikolaevicha Seniavina ot 1805 po 1810 god* (St. Petersburg, 1818-19, and 2d ed., St. Petersburg, 1836) and *Puteshestvie ot Triesta do S.-Peterburga v 1810 godu* (Moscow, 1828).
[20] Jelačić, *Rusija i Balkan*, p. 44.

Czartoryski, according to Nenadović's touching account, "but Serbia is far away from Russia, and we are friends with the Turks." And so each of the emissaries was given some money and sent home. Nenadović did not have the heart to disillusion his country-men, and so he told them that great Mother Russia had promised its help.[21]

Actually, with the outbreak of hostilities between Russia and Turkey in 1807, the Tsar did aid Karadjordje with funds, diplomatic recognition, and troops. On May 28, 1812, however, in anticipation of Napoleon's invasion of its own soil, Russia concluded the Treaty of Bucharest with the Porte, by which the Sultan was enjoined to extend an amnesty to the Serbs.

Misfortune awaited the Serbs, however, when the Russian government decided to make further use of the Balkan Slavs. When Admiral Chichagov had been named commander-in-chief of the Russian armies in Moldavia in 1811-12, he had been instructed "to make use of the martial spirit of the peoples of Slavic origin—the Serbs, Bosnians, Dalmatians, Montenegrins, Croats, and Illyrians"—to divert Napoleon's forces. Chichagov had been further advised, should the occasion arise, "to promise independence, the establishment of a Slavic kingdom." He did indeed find a response to these promises, especially among the Serbs ("This people is a treasure for us," he reported).[22] On Chancellor Rumiantsev's advice, Alexander I issued a proclamation to all the Balkan Slavs stating that France's war against Russia was also a war against them inasmuch as the same blood flowed in the veins of the Russians and the other Slavs.[23] But the fortunes of war drove Chichagov's armies from the Danube to the Berezina to save the Russian homeland from the French Antichrist. "Beloved brother, George Petrović," began a letter from Alexander I to Karadjordje, "I exceedingly regret that Russia is now forced to leave Serbia. . . . God grant that Russia may save itself and remain whole—it will not abandon Serbia."[24]

Needless to say, left to their own resources, the Serbs were

---

[21] *Ibid.*, p. 45.

[22] Pypin, "Panslavizm," *Viestnik Evropy*, LXXIII (May, 1878), 745-46.

[23] Alfred Fischel, *Der Panslawismus bis zum Weltkrieg* (Stuttgart and Berlin, 1919), p. 173.

[24] Jelačić, *Rusija i Balkan*, p. 51.

crushed by the Sultan and their lands were devastated by Turkish punitive expeditions. Again Russian national interests perforce took precedence over religious or ethnic solidarity with the other Slavs. After the Congress of Vienna, Alexander was deaf to any pleas from the rebel Slavs of the Balkans. The sanctity of legitimate thrones, including that of the Sultan, and the friendship of Metternich became more important to him.

It was in this forbidding climate which pervaded the last decade of Alexander's reign that Russian society first showed some interest in the idea of Slavic solidarity. Romantic liberal nationalism from the West fired some of the Russian petty nobility and intelligentsia with the same zest for rebellion against authority and for secret societies that inspired their contemporaries in the West. This period saw the formation of the first two Panslavic organizations in Russia—a Masonic lodge called Les Slaves réunis (a Panslavic society with a French name!) and another secret organization called the Society of United Slavs (Obshchestvo soedinënnykh Slavian). It is not known whether these two societies were connected in any way. It is certain, however, that both were founded by young Russian liberals, many of them army officers who had participated in the Napoleonic wars and had thus come directly into contact with Western romantic nationalism.

The Masonic lodge was founded in Kiev on March 12, 1818, with fifty-three members, largely Polish in nationality, of whom nine were "members in absentia" and nineteen were "honorary" members. Its seal consisted of a Cross Formée with two clasped hands and an inscription in Polish—Jedność Słowiańska (Slavic Unity). An almanac of the Masonic Grand Lodge Astrée of St. Petersburg for 1820-21 listed the lodge as number 17 of some twenty-four affiliated lodges throughout Russia. Nothing is known about its activities except that its members were not involved in the Decembrist movement, as were the members of the Society of United Slavs.[25]

More is known of the Society of United Slavs because of its implication in the revolt of December 14, 1825. The society was

[25] D. L. Mordovtsev, "Razvitie slavianskoi idei v russkom obshchestvie XVII-XIX vv.," *Russkaia Starina*, XXI (1878), 187-89.

founded in 1823 by two artillery officers, the brothers Peter and
Andrew Borisov, after an earlier secret society of theirs, the Friends
of Nature, had dissolved. The new society's members were largely
of the poorer nobility and the classless intelligentsia.[26] Originally
it counted some thirty-six members.[27] Its program transcended
Russian nationalism by calling for a democratic federation of all
the Slavic peoples. Each member was required to take the following oath: "I shall endure a thousand deaths, a thousand obstacles
shall I endure and devote my last breath to the freedom and
fraternal union of the noble Slavs."[28] The so-called Catechism of
the society consisted of seventeen articles, all phrased in the language of rationalism and enlightened liberalism. The first fourteen
articles were simply rules of behavior and general declarations of
belief. The final three articles read as follows:

XV. Thou are a Slav, and in thy land on the shores of the seas which
surround it, thou shalt establish four fleets: the Black, White, Dalmatian and Arctic [*sic*], and amid them thou shalt raise up [sign for "a
city"] and in it thou shalt establish the goddess of Enlightenment
whom thou shalt place on the throne by thy might. Thence shalt thou
receive Justice for thyself. . . .

XVI. In thy [sign for "ports"], O Slav, trade and sea power shall
flourish, and in [sign for "the city"] in the midst of thy land, justice
shall begin to dwell with thee.

XVII. Thou desirest to have this? Unite with thy brethren, from
whom the ignorance of thy forbears has separated thee. Thou desirest
to have all this? Thou shalt sacrifice a tenth portion of thy yearly
income and shalt dwell in the hearts of thy comrades. . . .[29]

While the United Slavs aimed at the establishment of a democratic republic in a Russia in which serfdom would be abolished,
they also dreamed of the liberation of all the Slavs and of their
unification into a single federal state in which each national unit
would be autonomous. The seal of the society consisted of an
octagon with the name of a Slavic land inscribed on each side:

---

[26] Anatole G. Mazour, *The First Russian Revolution* (Berkeley, 1937), p. 145.
[27] Pypin, "Panslavizm," *Viestnik Evropy*, LXXIII (May, 1878), 749.
[28] Militsa V. Nechkina, *Obshchestvo Soedinennykh Slavian* (Moscow, 1927),
pp. 94-95.
[29] *Ibid.*, pp. 97-98.

Russia, Poland, Serbia, Moravia, Dalmatia, Bohemia, Croatia, and Hungary (meaning Slovakia?). The center of the octagon bore the numeral *I* while four sides bore anchors representing the four "Slavic" seas, which were enumerated with a rather typical disregard for accuracy as "the Black, White, Dalmatian, and Arctic" —the Baltic being omitted altogether![30]

Arguing that one had to liberate Russia before one could liberate the other Slavs, Sergiei Muraviev-Apostol and Michael Bestuzhev-Riumin persuaded the United Slavs to join Paul Pestel's Southern Society in 1825. The alliance between the two societies was a most uneasy one, especially since the United Slavs were far more democratic in membership and views. At any rate, both shared the same fate at the hands of Nicholas I as a result of the failure of the uprising of December, 1825.

II

Associated as it had become with liberal nationalism, political Panslavism was anathema in the Russia of Nicholas I. In his fanatical devotion to the cause of legitimate monarchy, Nicholas equated the idea of Slavic liberation with sedition. He had no sympathy for the rebellious subjects of his brother rulers, the Emperor of Austria and the Sultan of Turkey. He regarded all Russians who showed any interest in the plight of the other Slavs as potentially dangerous troublemakers. Yet not even his autocracy could seal off Russia from the powerful current of romantic nationalism which was sweeping over all of Europe. Though he effectively prevented political Panslavism from raising its head within his borders, it was in his stifling reign that Russian scholars laid the foundations of cultural Panslavism in Russia.

Cultural Panslavism had its origin in that remarkable national awakening of the Slavs in the dawn of the nineteenth century. Submerged for centuries by their masters, the Czechs, Slovaks, Poles, Slovenes, Croats, Serbs, and Bulgars were roused to a renewed awareness of their national identities—not by their political leaders, since political activity was made impossible by their rulers, but by their cultural leaders. Deprived for the present of their

[30] *Ibid.*, p. 111.

national dignity, these Western and Southern Slavs nourished their hopes in the future by seeking to revive the faded memories of a glorious past. In so doing, they discovered that they were brothers bound not only by a common misfortune but by a vast cultural heritage.

It was their men of learning and the arts—their philologists, archaeologists, historians, folklorists, and poets—that these submerged Slavic nationalities had to thank for their cultural rebirth. Josef Dobrovský (1753-1829), Czech founder of Slavic philological studies, demonstrated in his *Institutiones Linguae Slavicae Veteris* (Institutions of the Old Slavic Tongue) that the Slavs had no need of relying on myths to show their common origin when their languages offered scientific proof of their kinship. His compatriot and colleague, Josef Jungmann (1773-1847), was an ardent Panslavist who, despite the great love which he bore his native Czech tongue, pleaded the cause of a common Slavic language. The Slovak poet who wrote in Czech, Ján Kollár (1793-1852), thrilled Slavs everywhere with his great ode to Slavic unity, *Slavy Dcera* (Daughter of Glory), and by his program of cultural Panslavism, *Ueber die litterarische Wechselseitigkeit zwischen den verschiedenen Stämmen und Mundarten der Slawischen Nation* (Concerning Literary Reciprocity between the Various Branches and Dialects of the Slavic Nation). Another Slovak, Pavel Josef Šafařík (1795-1861), laid the groundwork for the study of a common Slavic past in his *Slovanské starožitnosti* (Slavic Antiquities). The great Serbian folklorist and lexicographer, Vuk Karadžić (1787-1864), captivated all of romantic Europe with his collection of Serbian folk poetry. The Serbian poet Dositej Obradović (1739-1811) sang paeans to Slavic unity. When the Croatian founder of the "Illyrian" movement, Ljudevit Gaj (1809-72), referred to "our people," he meant all the Slavs. The Slovene poets France Prešern (1800-1849) and Stanko Vraz (1810-51) praised Slavia with their lyrics. Next to the first Bulgarian historian, Father Paissii (1722-98), the Ruthenian Iurii Venelin (1802-39) was the greatest awakener of the Bulgarian people, thanks to his historical research and collection of Bulgarian folklore. That immortal trio of Polish Romanticism—Adam Mickiewicz (1798-1855), Julius Słowacki

(1800-1849), and Zygmunt Krasiński (1812-58)—inspired their compatriots with a messianic idea that was to provide Russian Panslavism with a serious competitor.

All of these great cultural leaders, and many others, helped to awaken national movements among their countrymen which sought primarily to establish the individuality and cultural worth of each Slavic people. Yet these romantic movements all propagated in various ways and degrees the ideal of a Slavic unity which had been lost in the past through foreign oppression and which was to be resurrected with the end of that oppression. Panslavism as a cultural and even as a political ideal arose not in Russia but among the Western and Southern Slavs, those dispossessed and humiliated peoples that had far more need of unity and mutual help than did the mighty Russian Empire. It was with the rise of Romanticism among the Slavs of Austria and the Balkans that Russian society became interested in Slavdom.

It is a paradox that the Slavic cultural renascence as a whole owed much to non-Slavic Western and particularly to German scholarship. Just as the Western Slavs owe a debt to Johann Gottfried von Herder (1744-1803) for his early recognition of Slavic cultural unity and potentialities, so Russian Slavic studies owe a similar debt to August Ludwig von Schlözer (1735-1809). This pioneer of modern Russian historiography was the first in Russia to substitute for medieval legends surrounding the ethnogenesis and kinship of the Slavs the findings of scientific historical research. In his *Probe russischer Annalen* (Review of Russian Annals), published in 1768, Schlözer began by asking who the Russians were. His reply was that they were Slavs, kinsmen of the Poles, Czechs, Croats, and other Slavs, as the similarity of their languages very clearly showed. Schlözer began his *Allgemeine nordische Geschichte* (General Nordic History), published in 1771, by describing the Slavs as "that great, renowned, ancient, mighty race which spreads so vastly in the North and about which we know so little." He divided the Slavs into nine chief dialects (*Hauptdialekte*): Russian, Polish, Bohemian, Polabian, Wendish (i.e., Slovenian, in his terminology), Croatian, Bosnian (Serbian?), Bulgarian, and Lusatian. Despite the crudity of this listing, it is remarkable that this German recognized the Bulgarians as a Slavic people when Šafařík, the Slav, omitted them entirely from his list of Slavs several decades later! In 1767, upon becoming a member of the Russian Academy of Sciences, Schlözer had edited a critical edition of the Chronicle of Nestor. In 1802, near the close of his life, he published a study of this work in which he wrote, "Hardly has any other people on earth extended its rule or its language over so much of the world as have the Slavs. From Ragusa on the Adriatic Sea northward to the Baltic and the Arctic and eastward to Kamchatka in the neighborhood of Japan, one can find Slavic peoples everywhere."[31]

The first native Russian scholarship in Slavic or even in Russian history did not really develop until the reign of Alexander I. One of the earliest notable Russian historians, Nicholas M. Karamzin (1766-1826), described the Slavs as follows, in his monumental *Istoriia gosudarstva rossiiskago* (History of the Russian State):

Disseminated over Europe, encircled by other peoples, and often subjugated by them, the Slavic peoples lost their unity of language and, in the course of time, their dialects came into being, of which the main ones are the following: Russian . . . Polish . . . Czech . . . Illyrian, that is, Bulgarian—the coarsest of all the Slavic tongues, . . . Bosnian, Serbian—the most pleasant to the ear, as many find—Slavonian and Dalmatian . . . Croatian, similar to Wendish in Styria, Carinthia, Krain, as well as in Lusatia.[32]

It is noteworthy that like the first medieval Russian chronicler, Karamzin postulated a prehistoric Slavic unity based on language, and blamed the loss of this unity on foreign subjugation. It is no less interesting that Karamzin's list of Slavs was hardly an improvement over the list of the first monkish chronicler.

With the founding of the Moscow Society of History and Antiquities in 1804, and especially with the impetus given to research by Count Nicholas P. Rumiantsev's generous support of a project to collect historical documents, interest in early Russian history and literature grew markedly. It was this preoccupation

[31] Cited by Fischel, *Der Panslawismus,* p. 33.
[32] N. M. Karamzin, *Istoriia gosudarstva rossiiskago* (3d ed., St. Petersburg, 1830), pp. 121-22.

with their own country's past and language rather than any special interest in their Slavic kinsmen that inspired Russian scholars such as M. G. Kachenovskii, A. Kh. Vostokov, K. F. Kalaidovich, and P. I. Köppen to undertake Slavic studies in this early period. This interest multiplied under the nationalistic impact of the Napoleonic wars. Russian "thick journals," especially the *Viestnik Evropy* (European Herald), which was edited by Kachenovskii, began to feature the linguistic and historical studies of such scholars as Dobrovský, Lelewel, Maciejowski, and others. Köppen's learned journal, *Bibliograficheskiia Listy* (Bibliographical Notes), included contributions by a whole pleiad of foreign Slavic scholars— Dobrovský and Hanka of Prague, Kopitar and Karadžić of Vienna, Ján Kollár of Budapest, Šafařík of Novi Sad, Bandtke of Cracow, and Linde and Mrongowius of Warsaw. A lively private correspondence was begun between Russian scholars in the field of Slavic studies and their colleagues in other Slavic lands. These scholars visited one another's countries with an ease which can only excite the envy of the modern student of Eastern European affairs.

In 1822 when A. S. Shishkov, president of the Russian Academy, considered publishing a monumental comparative lexicon of all the Slavic tongues, the Czech Slavist, Václav Hanka, proposed that the Academy bring to Russia several Slavic scholars from abroad. After Shishkov was made Minister of Public Education, the subject of inviting foreign Slavic scholars into Russia was brought up again in 1826—this time in connection with the establishment of regular chairs of Slavic studies at Russian universities. Hanka, Šafařík, and Čelakovský—all Czechs—were considered. However, Nicholas I was persuaded that the government ought to train native Russians for the posts.[33] In 1835 the Ministry of Public Education proposed to the universities of Moscow, St. Petersburg, Kharkov, and Kazan that they select promising young scholars who might be sent to study in the Slav lands across the border.

This decision gave birth to the first generation of native Russian specialists in Slavic studies: P. I. Preis (1810-46), I. I. Sreznevskii (1812-80), V. I. Grigorovich (1815-76), and O. M. Bodianskii

---

[33] See V. I. Jagić (Iagich), *Istoriia slavianskoi filologii* (St. Petersburg, 1910), pp. 283-93, for a full account of this episode.

(1803-76). Although only the last three of these men later became adherents of the Russian Panslavic cause, all of them contributed indirectly to making such a cause possible merely by acquainting Russian society with the other Slavs. "It is strange to say," wrote one of their most distinguished successors, Professor A. N. Pypin, "but only from that time hence, that is, only from the forties did Russian learning receive the first exact information about the whole group of related peoples to the south and west."[34] Many a distinguished Russian Panslavist of Alexander II's reign had his first interest in the non-Russian Slavs aroused by these pioneers of Slavic studies at the universities of Moscow, St. Petersburg, Kharkov, and Kazan.

III

Political Panslavism, what there was of it, hit upon a bad time in the reign of Nicholas "the Club." Though Russian national interests led Nicholas, as they did Peter, Catherine, and Alexander before him, to cross the Danube and to make war on the Turks (in 1828), this campaign was relatively devoid of references to Russia's role as the protector of Orthodox Christians and Slavs in the Balkans. Nicholas disliked the idea of rebellion against legitimate monarchs, even when those monarchs were his enemies. While the Slavic sympathies of the Russian public found expression in Pushkin's *Piesni zapadnykh Slavian* (Songs of the Western Slavs), the Russian government remained silent about Russia's kinship with the Slavs. Indeed, references to Slavic kinship became tantamount to treason when in 1830 and 1831 Nicholas's own Polish subjects raised the banner of revolt. When in 1832 Alexis S. Khomiakov, the Slavophile lay theologian and poet, wrote an ode to Slavdom, *Orël* (The Eagle), in which he depicted the Russian imperial eagle spreading its protective wings over the Slavs of Germany, Austria, and Turkey, the work was promptly banned.

With the Polish revolt there began a marked intensification of repressive measures designed to cut off Russian society from the West and to prevent any deviation from the official creed of

[34] Pypin, "Russkoe slavianoviedenie," *Viestnik Evropy*, V (August, 1889), 728.

Nationalism-Orthodoxy-Autocracy. Insofar as Panslavism aimed at the cultural freedom and political liberation of the Slavs, Nicholas regarded it as seditious and would have none of it. His hostility to Panslavism was not unfounded.

Despite the sad fate which had befallen the Society of United Slavs in December, 1825, another generation took its place in Nicholas's reign—and again in Kiev. The unrecognized capital of a submerged Ukraine, Kiev was geographically exposed and culturally receptive to the romantic Panslavism in full swing across the border. Had Ukrainian scholars and artists been free to find satisfaction of their nationalistic impulses in the cultural field, they might not have found it necessary to resort to illegal political activity. Yet St. Petersburg offered them nothing but hostility. This went so far, for example, that when in 1839 the University of Kiev requested permission to establish a chair of Slavic studies along with its sister institutions of Great Russia, the government rejected the request.[35]

In 1846 a small group of Ukrainian patriots—including the historian N. I. Kostomarov, the poet Taras Shevchenko, the ethnographer and writer Kulish, and others—founded the Brotherhood of Saints Cyril and Methodius. Its aims were much like those of the ill-fated Society of United Slavs. The program of the Brotherhood included the following tenets:

1. We hold that the spiritual and political unification of the Slavs is their true destiny toward which they should aspire.

2. We hold that with their unification, each Slavic people should have its independence, and we recognize as such peoples the South Russians, the North Russians together with the White Russians, the Poles, the Czechs together with the Slovaks, the Lusatians, the Illyro-Serbs together with the Carinthians, and the Bulgars.

3. We hold that each people should have a popular government, and that it should preserve the complete native equality of its citizens, respecting the Christian religion and their station.

4. We hold that government, legislation, the right of property and education among the Slavs should be founded on the holy religion of our Lord Jesus Christ.

[35] V. I. Semevskii, "Nikolai Ivanovich Kostomarov, 1817-1885," *Russkaia Starina* (January, 1886), p. 187.

5. We hold that with such equality, education and a pure morality should serve as conditions for participation in government.

6. We hold that there should exist a general Slavic assembly composed of the representatives of all [Slavic] lands.[36]

As one of the society's chief founders, Kostomarov, later recalled, Kiev was proposed as the capital of the Slavic federation and was therefore to have the status of an all-Slavic city belonging to no national unit. While this was not definitely decided, the consensus of these Ukrainian patriots was that Great Russian be adopted as the common language of the Slavic federation, though each member nation would preserve its own national tongue. The federation was to be republican in form. Each autonomous unit was to elect its own president and assembly. All were to elect a president and assembly for the entire federation every four years. The federal president was to be assisted by a minister for foreign affairs and a minister of the interior.[37]

The Brotherhood lasted for only a few months before the Third Section of His Imperial Majesty's Chancery caught up with it. Though the Ukrainian society espoused only peaceful means to achieve its ends, the government at St. Petersburg regarded it as dangerous and punished the ringleaders with arrest, exile, and army service. The official attitude of the government was summed up in a memorandum which Count Uvarov, Minister of Public Education, directed to his agency in Moscow at the time:

The question of Slavdom, as it concerns us [he wrote], presents two sides: one which malicious men could use to incite minds and spread dangerous propaganda, criminal and provocative; the other side embodies the sanctity of our beliefs, our originality, our national spirit, within the limits of the law, and has an indisputable right to the solicitude of the government. Russian Slavophilism in its purity should express unconditional loyalty to Orthodoxy and autocracy, but everything which transgresses these limits is an admixture of alien concepts,

---

[36] "M. K.," "K sviedieniiam ob ukraino-slavianskom obshchestvie," *Russkii Arkhiv*, No. 7 (1893), pp. 399-400.

[37] Semevskii, "Nikolai Ivanovich Kostomarov, 1817-1885," *Russkaia Starina* (January, 1886), pp. 187-88, citing the unpublished part of Kostomarov's autobiography as dictated by Kostomarov to N. Bielozerskaia.

the play of phantasy or a mask which conceals a malicious desire to take advantage of inexperience and to attract visionaries.[38]

Despite Uvarov's approval of "Russian Slavophilism in its purity," the fact of the matter was that the government found actual Russian Slavophilism far from "pure." Nicholas was outraged by the events of 1848 in Europe. The specter of revolution loomed everywhere as shaky thrones toppled one by one. Though hardly the sole cause of their monarch's troubles, the Slavs of Austria took advantage of the general confusion to forward their own cause. Confronted by a German-minded Vor-Parliament in Frankfurt, the Austrian Slavs held a congress of their own in Prague during the hectic June days of 1848. Had Nicholas been favorably disposed toward these Slavs, he might have brought about the complete dissolution of the Austrian Empire. Instead, he saved the Hapsburg throne by sending a punitive expedition into Hungary.

It was this official Russian hostility to the idea of Slavic liberation that lay behind the arrest in 1849 of two prominent members of the Slavophile circle in Moscow, Ivan S. Aksakov and Iurii F. Samarin. The government apparently suspected that Russians who were called "Slavophiles" were probably harboring dangerous sympathies for the rebellious Slavs across the border. Both Aksakov and Samarin assured the Third Section, Nicholas's security police, that the Slavophile circle of Moscow maintained no relations whatsoever with the non-Russian Slavs even though they felt a sincere compassion for their brethren by blood and faith. Evidently satisfied that the Slavophiles did not constitute a clear and present danger, Nicholas had both men released soon after their arrest. His marginal notes to their depositions indicated clearly, however, his distaste for their views. "Under the guise of compassion for the supposed oppression of the Slavic peoples," he wrote, "there is concealed the idea of rebellion against the legitimate authority of neighboring and, in part, allied states, as well as the idea of a general unification which they expect to gain not through God's

[38] Cited by A. N. Pypin, "Iz istorii panslavizma," *Viestnik Evropy*, CLXIII (May, 1893), 274-75.

will but through disorder, which would be ruinous for Russia."[39]

There was, however, one Russian Panslavist who enjoyed the confidence of Nicholas's government, the distinguished historian of the Russian people, Michael Petrovich Pogodin (1800-1875). Pogodin achieved this distinction by assiduously advertising his loyalty to what Uvarov, and many since, mistakenly regarded as "pure" Slavophilism—that is, Nationalism-Orthodoxy-Autocracy as conceived by the government. Pogodin's interest in the non-Russian Slavs was first awakened by his reading of Schlözer's study on the Chronicle of Nestor. In this work, following the section on Saints Cyril and Methodius, the Apostles to the Slavs, Schlözer had advised young scholars desirous of knowing more about their own people's history to study the history and languages of the other Slavs. An entry which Pogodin made in his diary at the age of twenty-one shows how taken he was by the idea of a united Slavdom. "Spoke with Kubarev," he wrote, "on the unification of all the Slavic peoples into one whole, one single state. If another Peter be found—and he finds another Suvorov, the game is up."[40]

As a student, Pogodin attracted the attention of that Maecenas of Russian historiography, Count Rumiantsev, who encouraged him to translate Josef Dobrovský's work on Saints Cyril and Methodius from the German. This he did in 1825, though not with conspicuous success. In 1826 Pogodin and his lifelong friend and colleague, Stephen Petrovich Shevyrëv (1806-64), embarked on a translation of Dobrovský's *Institutiones*. This, too, was such a poor translation that it was not published until 1833 after much revision. In 1840 Pogodin and Samarin published in the *Otechestvennyia Zapiski* (Notes of the Fatherland) another badly mauled translation, that of Ján Kollár's work on Slavic reciprocity, *Ueber die litterarische Wechselseitigkeit* (On Literary Reciprocity).

After ten years of theoretical study, Pogodin decided in 1835 to become personally acquainted with the Slavs across the border. In that year he made the first of his six trips to the Slavic West before the Crimean War. Through his travels Pogodin came to know

[39] *Ibid.*, p. 285.
[40] Cited by N. P. Barsukov, *Zhizn' i trudy M. P. Pogodina*, I (St. Petersburg, 1886), 56.

more influential Slavic cultural leaders than any other Russian of his time. He counted among his acquaintances and friends Šafařík, Hanka, Jungmann, Palacký, Čelakovský, Kollár, Karadžić, Kopitar, Venelin, Bouček, Linde, Maciejowski, Miklošič, Štúr, and many others.

Unable to contain his enthusiasm for the cause of Slavic unification, and yet unable to make public his views in Russia, Pogodin decided to exert what influence he could on his government in a long series of confidential memoranda to the Minister of Public Education. Thoroughly devoted to the Russian autocracy, Pogodin made it his task to convince the imperial government that instead of opposing Panslavism as a revolutionary doctrine, it should convert this idea to its own ends.

In his memorandum of 1838 he stressed the idea that history advanced by means of a succession of chosen peoples, to which he added the corollary that the future belonged to the Slavs.

But which people among the Slavs [he asked rhetorically] now holds first place? Which people can by its composition, language, and totality of traits be called the representative of the whole Slavic world? Which has the greatest guaranty in its present position and past history for a future of greatness? Which is closer than all the rest to this lofty goal? Which has the most visible means of attaining it? Which? . . . The heart trembles with gladness. . . . O Russia, O my fatherland! Is it not thou! . . . O, if only thou! Thou, thou are fated to fulfill, to crown the development of mankind.[41]

Probably despairing that Nicholas would have a change of heart, Pogodin sought especially to influence the heir to the throne, Nicholas's son, Alexander. In his history of Russia, which Pogodin wrote in 1838 expressly for the instruction of the Heir Apparent, he presented the picture of a Slavdom united by Russia—a vast empire forming one ninth of mankind.

Is not the political fate of Europe, and therefore of the world [he asked], in our hands? Emperor Nicholas, quietly sitting in Tsarskoye Selo, is nearer the realization of Charles V and Napoleon's dream of a universal empire than the two ever were at the zenith of their fame.

[41] M. P. Pogodin, *Istoriko-politicheskiia pis'ma i zapiski M. P. Pogodina* (Moscow, 1874), pp. 1-14.

But another and more desirable honor awaits Russia. The time of European nations is past, their strength runs out. They can produce nothing higher in religion, law, science or art, nor have they carried mankind to its moral goal. Now the future belongs to the Slavs who will serve mankind. Russia, as the representative of the Slav race, will fuse ancient and modern civilization, reconcile heart and head, establish everywhere law and peace, and prove that mankind's goal is not only liberty, art, and science, or industry and wealth, but something higher—the true enlightenment in the spirit of Christianity, the guidance by God's word which is assurance of all happiness.[42]

Following his second trip to the Slav lands of Austria in 1839, Pogodin wrote another private memorandum to the government in which he predicted the rise of a Slavic empire from the Adriatic to the Pacific. He emphasized that Russia had no real friends in Europe save the Slavs. Pogodin warned particularly against Austria and regarded the accord between Russia and that country as a most unnatural one. This was to be the leitmotif which would pervade all of his subsequent memoranda. Pogodin was certain that both Austria and Turkey were on the brink of dissolution, and that the first major war in which either engaged would wreck that country. Meanwhile he urged the Russian government to demonstrate its interest in the Slavs of these two crumbling empires and to gain their support, especially since these Slavs had been embittered by Russia's apparent indifference to their fate.[43]

Nicholas's government showed a willingness to listen to such private advice, as long as it was private, but Pogodin's Panslavic ideas could not overcome the hostility of Russian officialdom. The Russian scholar then tried to arouse the interest of Russian society in at least the culture of the non-Russian Slavs if not in their political plight, by founding a newspaper in 1841 called the *Moskvitianin* (Muscovite). He found the apathy of the Russian reading public even harder to crack than the suspicion of the government. It took a cataclysm from without to shake both the Russian government

[42] Cited and translated by Hans Kohn, *The Twentieth Century* (New York, 1949), p. 103.
[43] See Pogodin's memoranda of 1839 and 1842 in his *Istoriko-politicheskiia pis'ma*, pp. 15-45 and pp. 46-64.

and Russian society out of their stagnation. That cataclysm came in 1853.

With the outbreak of war with Turkey in 1853 and with the formation of a European coalition against Russia, the Russians discovered that they did not have a reliable friend in all of Europe. Even Austria, which had ample reason to be grateful for Nicholas's suppression of the Hungarian revolt in 1849, repaid her debt with a menacing and malevolent neutrality. The Crimean War was a sobering experience for Russians. It destroyed the entire concept of European solidarity upon which Nicholas had based his foreign policy. It also dispelled the officially cultivated lethargy of the Russian public. Pogodin found his opportunity.

In 1853 and 1854 he bombarded the government with one Panslavic memorandum after another, nearly all in answer to the same desperate question: "Where are we to look for allies?" He replied:

Our only, and most hopeful, and most powerful allies in Europe are the Slavs, our kinsmen by blood, tongue, heart, history, and faith, and there are ten million in Turkey and twenty million in Austria. . . . Here are our natural allies! Show them the fine, sacred cause of freedom from the intolerable foreign yoke under which they have been groaning for four hundred years, be capable of directing their living, mighty, enthusiastic forces, and you will see the wonders which they will perform.[44]

In the year 1854 alone Pogodin wrote fourteen such memoranda. It was in his memorandum of May 27, 1854, that Pogodin specifically proposed that Russia liberate all the Slavs and create a Slavic union which would be similar in intent, he suggested, to the Rhenish Confederation which France had established as a buffer.

Pogodin was both vague and contradictory in his description of the proposed Slavic federation. "Call the new union the Danubian, the Slavic, or the Southeastern European union," he wrote, "with its capital in Constantinople, and under the presidency and protection of—you think Russia? No, not Russia: Russia seeks no conquests." Who, then, did Pogodin think was going to head the union? The Poles? There were only ten million of them, he pro-

---

[44] Pogodin, *Istoriko-politicheskiia pis'ma*, p. 78, memorandum of December 7, 1853, to Countess A. Bludova.

tested. The Serbs? Only eight million. The Bulgars? Only five million. And thus, with a superb indifference to his earlier disclaimer,
Pogodin concluded that only the Russians with their fifty million
people possessed the numerical strength to undertake such a task.
"Fifty million—do you hear?" he exclaimed in exultation. "Who
has more? Czechs, Slovenes, Montenegrins! All are silent, none has
more. Consequently Russia should become the head of the Slavic
union, not by its own wish, not arbitrarily, nor out of ambition
and love of power, but out of necessity, in the very nature of
things."[45]

Pogodin's Slavic union was to include not only the Slavic peoples
but other East Europeans as well. He mentioned specifically
Greece, Hungary, Moldavia, Wallachia, and Transylvania as constituent member states. He professed to see no reason why these
lands would object to being included as long as they were granted
complete autonomy in their domestic affairs.

The common business of the entire confederation was to be
entrusted to a parliament meeting in Constantinople as well as to
the head of the confederation, the Russian emperor. "This will
be the inevitable result of the present war," Pogodin prophesied,
"sooner or later, no matter what anyone may say or do."[46]

In another long and passionate memorandum, that of July, 1854,
Pogodin argued that Russian interests had converged on Constantinople from the dawn of Russian history. The Russian state had
been founded on the water-road from Novgorod to Constantinople.
Olga had been baptized in the Byzantine capital, and Vladimir had
received Christianity from the great imperial city. It was Constantinople that had sent Saints Cyril and Methodius to the Slavs.
It was from Constantinople that the Russian tsars had inherited
their imperial title and historic mission. Napoleon was right,
Pogodin insisted, when he called Constantinople the capital of the
world. "It must belong," he declared, "or rather it cannot belong
to anyone but to the East, and the representative of the East is
Russia."[47]

[45] *Ibid.*, pp. 119-20.
[46] *Ibid.*, p. 120.
[47] *Ibid.*, p. 191.

As for official fears that to encourage the liberation of the Slavs would mean to abet revolution in Europe, Pogodin boldly declared that the other Slavs had as much right to rise up against their Turkish and Austrian oppressors as the Russians had in rising up against the Tartars.[48] To say this to the government of Nicholas I took some courage. However, it was all in vain. Nothing came of Pogodin's memoranda—although the present historian may admit that his prophecies have not been entirely unfulfilled. Even if Nicholas had been disposed to follow Pogodin's advice in 1854, he was hardly in a position to do so without bringing Austria down upon his western flank. The Emperor expressed his appreciation of Pogodin's devotion, but he found that "these views and ideas are not entirely well founded and do not easily lend themselves to practical fulfillment."[49] The most Nicholas was willing to do was to proclaim his country's traditional role as protector of Orthodoxy and to appeal to the Orthodox Christians of Turkey to rise up in common defense of their religion—but not in defense of Slavdom. On February 19, 1855, Nicholas I died in bitter humiliation, and a whole period of Russian history died with him.

It was in the national predicament arising out of the Crimean debacle that Russian Panslavism emerged from the realm of vague sentiment, secret societies, private memoranda, and seminar rooms to become a public movement in Russian society. After Crimea, national self-interest prompted Russians to seek protection in new allies. A messianic tradition coupled with religious sentiment already bound Russians to the Balkan Slavs. Romantic nationalism and the attendant rise of Slavic studies in Russia brought Russians into cultural contact with the Western Slavs as well. The Panslavic movements and Russophilia of the Austrian and Balkan Slavs appeared to hold great promise for future collaboration between them and their Russian kinsmen. The unification movements of the Germans and the Italians made Slavic desires for unification seem all the more justifiable. What was needed to join all of these factors into a full-fledged movement was a Russian Panslavic ideology and its propagation by a concrete organization.

---

[48] *Ibid.*, p. 199.
[49] Cited by Barsukov, *Zhizn' i trudy M. P. Pogodina*, XIII, 118.

2

THE SLAVOPHILE BACKGROUND

Oh, East is East, and West is West,
And never the twain shall meet.

RUDYARD KIPLING

One has only to understand that West is West,
and East is East!   MICHAEL POGODIN

To ESTABLISH THE INTELLECTUAL paternity of any political or cultural movement is a notoriously delicate task. While physical fatherhood is a singular proposition, brain children can claim a bewildering plurality of putative sires. Russian Panslavism offers a welcome exception. Although its genealogy is an ancient one, its immediate progenitor is clearly identifiable. Russian Panslavism was the ideological heir of Russian Slavophilism. Indeed, it may be stated that Russian Panslavism was the practical extension of the Slavophile idea in the field of Russian political and cultural relations with the other Slavs.

The bond between Slavophilism and Russian Panslavism was not only an ideological one. When the first post-Crimean Panslavic organization in Russia—the Moscow Slavic Benevolent Committee —was founded in 1858, its thirty-one charter members included such distinguished Slavophiles as Khomiakov, Samarin, Koshelëv, and Constantine Aksakov. Ivan Aksakov was its secretary-treasurer from the first and, on Pogodin's death in 1875, became its president. He held this post until the dissolution of the society in 1878. Thus there was even a personal tie between Slavophilism and Panslavism.

Various Russian Panslavists themselves proudly and gratefully acknowledged their filial debt to the Slavophiles. "All of us members of the Slavic Committee," declared Professor M. D. Koialovich in his eulogy to Iurii Samarin in 1876, "are in greater or lesser measure and more or less consciously Slavophiles."[1] In a eulogy to another Slavophile leader, Alexis Khomiakov, A. V. Vasiliev told the St. Petersburg Section of the Slavic Benevolent Committee in 1877, "We think that it is not enough for anyone who wishes to be an active member of the Committee to be just a man, a humanitarian, but it is indispensable that he be a Slavophile, that is, it is indispensable that he confess and adhere firmly to the principles of Slavophile teaching."[2]

To establish the relationship of Slavophilism and Panslavism is no problem. On the contrary, the bond between them was so close that some have found it difficult to distinguish between them. "Men who are little acquainted with the matter," wrote a Russian student of Khomiakov, "believed and still believe that, in accord with the appellation, the whole essence of Slavophilism lies in sympathy with the Slavs abroad, in Panslavism."[3] Yet to identify Slavophilism with Panslavism is to confuse two different generations, two movements whose aims and methods were distinct. Slavophilism was a system of thought which grew out of Russia's rather tardy and short-lived Romantic period. Its greatest original productivity fell almost entirely within the reign of Nicholas I. Of the very small circle of Slavophiles, Ivan and Peter Kirieevskii died in 1856, Khomiakov and Constantine Aksakov died in 1860. Their passing not only ended the creative period of Slavophilism but coincided with a general change of season in Russian intellectual history. In a touching eulogy to his deceased friends and opponents, the self-exiled Herzen observed in his *Kolokol* (The Bell), "The Kirieevskiis, Khomiakov, and Aksakov *have accomplished their task*. . . . With their end begins a turning point in Russian thought."[4]

---

[1] *V pamiat' Iu. F. Samarina; riechi proiznesënnyia v Peterburgie i v Moskvie po povodu ego konchiny* (St. Petersburg, 1876), p. 26.

[2] *Pervyia 15 liet sushchestvovaniia S.-Peterburgskago Slavianskago blagotvoritel'-nago obshchestva* (St. Petersburg, 1883), p. 415; minutes for the session of January 23, 1877.

[3] V. N. Liaskovskii, "Aleksiei Stepanovich Khomiakov; ego biografiia i uchenie," *Russkii Arkhiv*, III (1896), 338.

[4] A. Herzen (Gertsen), "Konstantin Sergieevich Aksakov," *Kolokol*, No. 90 (January 15, 1861), p. 1. The italics are Herzen's.

Unlike Slavophilism, Panslavism was primarily a program of action. It fell almost entirely within the reign of Alexander II— from the Crimean War to the Russo-Turkish War and the Berlin fiasco of 1878. Yet despite the qualitative differences between Slavophilism and Panslavism, the latter movement can scarcely be imagined without the ideological foundation provided by the former. Slavophilism was the very soul of the Panslavic body, and once Panslavism as a program of action succumbed to ends and means that were not in keeping with the spiritual principles upon which it had been founded, it suffered dissolution.

Not a few observers, both Russian and foreign, have remarked on the dissimilarities between Slavophilism and Panslavism. "The name Slavophilism itself has nothing in common with sympathies for the contemporary Slavs," Paul Miliukov observed in a study on Slavophilism.[5] That indefatigable Amazon of the Panslavic cause in England, Olga Novikova—called "the M.P. for Russia"—explained to her English readers, "The Slavophiles are also well-wishers of the Slavs, but their first and chief interest is domestic, and aims at the restoration of primitive ideas, customs and institutions."[6] The eminent French student of Russian affairs, Anatole Leroy-Beaulieu, remarked in an article written in 1876, "There is a group of distinguished men there to whom for some thirty years the name Slavophiles (*slavianofily*) has been applied; but what does this name or this sobriquet mean? Does it have any connection with foreign policy and the Slavs of Turkey? Not at all: it is only an allusion to internal policy and to the Russian or Muscovite tendencies, if you will, of a certain school. . . . This term Slavophile does not at all correspond to the word Panslavist."[7] A more recent English student of Russia, Sir Bernard Pares, similarly concluded, "Slavophilism is in no way to be identified with Pan-Slavism; the first is a sincere product of Russian thought; the second is a weapon in the armoury of Russian foreign policy."[8]

[5] P. Miliukov, "Slavianofil'stvo," *Entsiklopedicheskii Slovar'* (Brockhaus i Efron), XXX, 307.
[6] Olga Novikova, *Skobeleff and the Slavonic Cause* (London, 1883), pp. 235-36.
[7] Anatole Leroy-Beaulieu, "Les réformes de la Turquie: la politique russe et le panslavisme," *La Revue des deux mondes* (December, 1876), pp. 526-27.
[8] Sir Bernard Pares, *Russia* (Washington–New York, Penguin Books), p. 72.

Nevertheless, the Slavophile philosophy exerted an enormous influence on the Panslavists. The Slavophiles formulated nearly every basic tenet of the Russian Panslavic ideology. It was the Slavophiles who transmitted to the Panslavists the theory of chosen peoples succeeding each other to primacy in world history—an idea that later Panslavists such as Danilevskii were to attempt to invest with the authority of scientific truth. Probably the main contribution which Slavophilism made to Panslavism was its division of mankind by cultures and its postulate of a Slavic culture—original, independent, and self-contained—whose basic principles were not only distinct from, but opposed to, the basic principles of the Romano-Germanic culture. Slavophile doctrine provided the Panslavists with a delineation of a Slavic way of life which they were to use in judging their brethren abroad. The Slavophile insistence that Orthodoxy was the only true faith was to saddle Russian Panslavism with one of its most unrealistic and disunifying tenets. Slavophile predictions of "the rotting of the West" and of Russia's future supremacy imbued the Panslavists with a zealous messianism. Finally, the Slavophiles left a legacy of ideals—ultimate allegiance to a universal culture, the quest for inner justice rather than legal form, the stress on natural development rather than coercion, the preference for social rather than political solutions, the insistence on the right of each historic people to cultural self-determination —ideals which the earlier Panslavists accepted in the realm of theory and which the later Panslavists largely abandoned in practice.

It is not within the scope of this work to describe all aspects of the Slavophile doctrine, but an understanding of Slavophilism is essential in order to grasp the significance of Russian Panslavic ideology.

II

Slavophilism was but one expression of Russian Romanticism— a movement which came to Russia in the fury of the storm which the French Revolution and Napoleon's legions unleashed over all Europe. The Napoleonic wars were a catalyst which set off vital changes in the intellectual climate not only of Western Europe but of Russia as well. The flames over venerable "Moscow the White-stoned" burned deep into the Russian consciousness. The Grand Army's dramatic retreat from Holy Russia in 1812 and Russian participation in the final defeat of the French "Antichrist" endowed Russians with a renewed awareness of their own strength and meaning as a nation. On the other hand, Russian officers who had watered their horses in the Spree and the Seine and had witnessed the marvels of Western Europe returned to their homeland with a disturbing realization of the gulf which separated Western culture and the Russian way of life. It was altogether in the spirit of the times that Romanticism should have flown to Russia on the wings of a contradiction—the simultaneous awareness of Russia's might and Russia's backwardness.

Once again in their tumultuous history Russians sought a purpose that would give their national existence that significance of which they believed it to be worthy. In this quest Russian intellectuals were beset by a compelling need to define their nation's place in the world. In effect, this meant to determine Russia's place in Europe itself. The basic problem was not a material but a spiritual one. However enthusiastically or reluctantly, some Russians had long recognized the necessity—even before Peter the Great—of drawing on the material achievements of the West. More fundamental was the problem of evaluating the intrinsic character and worth of Russian culture, in the broadest sense, and its role in the development of modern civilization. As one of Russia's leading intellectuals and statesmen, Iurii Samarin, was to put the question, "Should Russian culture be increasingly influenced not only by the external achievements but also by the very principles of Western European culture, or, inasmuch as it is influenced more profoundly by its own original Russian Orthodox spiritual way of life, should it recognize therein the principles of a new future phase of the universal culture?"[9] It was not an easy question to answer. Intelligent Russians could not but recognize their debt to European culture. Yet a newly dedicated national pride could hardly reject Russia's heritage. It was natural that the ambivalent attitude of the Russian intelligentsia should have crystallized into two schools

[9] Cited by N. L. Brodskii, *Rannie slavianofily* (Moscow, 1910), p. xli.

of thought within Russian society: the Slavophiles and the Westernizers.

III

Though earlier traces of Slavophile doctrine could be found in Russia, it was in 1839, with the appearance of two articles, that Slavophilism as a system of ideas became established. Neither article was published at the time, but each found a private audience in the salons of the Elagins and the Sverbeevs. The first was A. S. Khomiakov's "O starom i novom" (On the Old and the New); the second was I. V. Kirieevskii's reply, "V otviet A. S. Khomiakovu" (In Reply to A. S. Khomiakov).[10]

The first leading lights of the Moscow circle were Alexis S. Khomiakov, who was acclaimed as the movement's greatest ideologist, and Ivan V. Kirieevskii, whose particular contribution was his comparison and contrasting of Western European culture with Russia's Slavic culture. In the period from 1841 to 1843 two additional adherents were recruited—Iurii F. Samarin and Constantine S. Aksakov, both of whom helped to define the relative roles of state and society in Slavic culture and posed the question of the Slavic peasant commune or the *obshchina*. In 1847 and 1848 Ivan Kirieevskii's brother, Peter, and A. I. Koshelëv made their adherence to Slavophilism complete. Not until 1848 did Constantine Aksakov's brother, Ivan, join. Yet no Slavophile was to publicize the Slavophile point of view with as much ardor and to such effect as Ivan Aksakov did during nearly four decades of editorial activity. Prince V. A. Cherkasskii joined the Slavophile circle in the 1850's, more out of political than philosophical reasons. He himself called his adherence a *mariage de raison*.[11] Other Slavophiles included Professor I. D. Beliaev, Professor N. A. Popov, F. V. Chizhov, V. A. Panov, and others.

[10] S. Dmitriev, "Slavianofily i slavianofil'stvo," *Istorik-Marksist*, LXXXIX, No. 1 (1940), 87. For Khomiakov's article, "O starom i novom," see his *Polnoe sobranie sochinenii*, III (Moscow, 1900), 11-29. For Ivan Kirieevskii's reply, "V otviet A. S. Khomiakovu," see his *Polnoe sobranie sochinenii*, I (Moscow, 1911), 109-20.

[11] Dmitriev, "Slavianofily i slavianofil'stvo," *Istorik-Marksist*, LXXXIX, No. 1 (1940), 88.

The total number of avowed and active Slavophiles was never large. Ivan Aksakov once told the story of a Frenchman who visited Russia during the reign of Nicholas I and confidentially whispered into the ear of a Slavophile, "Combien êtes-vous?" The Slavophile smiled, seeing that the Frenchman was thinking in the numerical terms of a party, and replied, "There are three, four, five of us, and not at all in agreement: you yourself have been a witness to our quarrels."[12] The Slavophiles were not a party; they were a philosophical school, a coterie of intellectuals. Their strength was not in numbers, simply because their world was one of ideas and not of action.

The designation "Slavophile" means literally one who loves the Slavs. Yet an examination of the voluminous writings of the Slavophile theoreticians will show that these men rarely wrote of the non-Russian Slavic peoples as concrete political or national entities. The reader will find ample reference to Slavic philology, mythology, and ancient institutions in the Slavophile scriptures. It is difficult, however, to find specific references to the non-Russian Slavs and their contemporary problems in the works of Khomiakov, the Kirieevskiis, Constantine Aksakov, or Iurii Samarin. Not until the Crimean War did some of the Slavophiles devote any real attention to the non-Russian Slavs.

It is true that even before this time Khomiakov and the great Slavophile poet Tiutchev addressed a few of their numerous poems to their Slavic brethren abroad—especially during the Russo-Turkish War in 1828 and the Polish insurrection of 1830. It is also known that Peter V. Kirieevskii visited Bohemia, and that Khomiakov had some correspondence with the Czech Slavist, Václav Hanka. Tiutchev also took some interest in the Czechs, though he had no great understanding of the Czech people.[13]

One of the most prominent Slavophile ideologists, Constantine Aksakov, showed no especial interest in the other Slavs until the last few months of his life while on a trip through the lands of the West and South Slavs—a trip taken primarily to restore his

[12] Ivan Aksakov, *Sochineniia*, Vol. II: *Slavianofil'stvo i zapadnichestvo, 1860-1886* (St. Petersburg, 1891), p. 56; *Den'* editorial for March 24, 1862.
[13] Josef Jirásek, *Rusko a my; dějiny vztahů československo-ruských od nejstarších dob až do roku 1914*, II (Brno, 1946), 57.

rapidly failing health. His brother and companion, Ivan, wrote with touching enthusiasm in the fall of 1860, "Before, in Moscow, Constantine was rather indifferent to the Slavs, but now, face to face with them, he has felt all of the moral obligation which rests on Russia with respect to the Slavs, and has given himself over ardently to this emotion."[14] But not for long. Two and a half months later Constantine Aksakov was dead.

In his inaugural lecture at the University of St. Petersburg in 1865, Professor Vladimir Lamanskii, one of the most active Panslavic disciples of the Slavophiles, admitted, "Khomiakov, Kirieevskii, C. Aksakov and others did not themselves leave any strictly academic works in the field of Slavic studies."[15] He did, however, express gratitude for the inspiration which the Slavophiles afforded later scholars.

Why did the Slavophiles have so little interest in their Slavic contemporaries abroad? It is true that the regime of Nicholas I hardly encouraged Russians to concern themselves with foreign affairs. Indeed, that monarch's fanatical championship of legitimate monarchy in the Concert of Europe made it decidedly dangerous for Russian subjects to speculate openly about the liberation of their Slavic kinsmen. Nevertheless, a prudent desire to avoid the confines of the Peter and Paul Fortress does not in itself explain Slavophile indifference to the contemporary affairs of the non-Russian Slavs.

The main reason lies in the fact that the Slavophiles were philosophers, amateur philologists and folklorists, men of letters. For their limited Moscow circle Slavdom was an abstraction, a cultural principle, a way of life rooted in prehistory. If they attempted to describe and to interpret this way of life, if they urged its maintenance or restoration, it was primarily because they saw in this way of life, as interpreted by themselves, Russia's only solution of its inner contradictions. Thus the Slavophiles addressed themselves not to their Slavic kinsmen across the border but to their own fellow countrymen. Even after the hurly-burly of Panslavism

[14] Ivan Aksakov, *Ivan Sergieevich Aksakov v ego pismakh*, III (Moscow, 1892), 496-97; letter of Friday, September 30, 1860.
[15] V. I. Lamanskii, "Vstupitel'noe chtenie Dotsenta Peterburgskago universiteta V. I. Lamanskago," *Den'*, No. 50-51 (December 11, 1865), p. 1199.

was done, A. I. Koshelëv recalled in his memoirs that he and his Slavophile comrades were given that name "even though sympathy and love for the Slavs was never the most essential feature of our outlook."[16]

Whence, then, came the designation "Slavophile"? Originally the name was applied to Admiral A. S. Shishkov and other staunch advocates of Church Slavonic influence on the Russian language during the first years of the reign of Alexander I.[17] Thanks to Shishkov's progressive literary opponents, the term *slavianofil'stvo* (Slavophilism) was from the first endowed with a rather disreputable meaning. Vasilii Pushkin is credited with having first used the word "Slavophile" as a term of disapprobation. Another writer of the time, Makarov, wrote a comedy entitled *Obrashchennyi slavianofil* (The Converted Slavophile) in which the character "Slavophile" was portrayed as a reactionary fool.[18]

When the epithet was resurrected in the following reign, to be applied to the Moscow circle, it continued to have a derogatory flavor. Writing in the *Moskovskii Sbornik* (Moscow Review) in 1847, Khomiakov observed, "Some periodicals mockingly call us Slavophiles, a name constructed on a foreign model, which in the Russian translation would mean Slav-lovers. For my own part I am prepared to accept this title and confess it proudly: I do love the Slavs."[19] This confession of love notwithstanding, the early Slavophiles felt that they had been saddled with a name which was neither of their own choosing nor representative of their primary aim.

When Iurii Samarin and Ivan Aksakov were arrested in 1849 by the Third Section, the security police of Nicholas I, Aksakov especially was asked to explain for His Imperial Majesty's benefit the precise meaning of Slavophilism and what relation it might have to Panslavism. On the first point Aksakov replied:

Men who were devoted to Russia with all their might and all the power

[16] A. I. Koshelëv, *Zapiski* (Berlin, 1884), p. 126.
[17] Liaskovskii, "Aleksiei Stepanovich Khomiakov," *Russkii Arkhiv*, III (1896), 374. Also T. G. Masaryk, *Rusko a Evropa* (2d ed., Prague, 1930), I, 406.
[18] V. I. Jagić (Iagich), *Istoriia Slavianskoi filologii* (St. Petersburg, 1910), p. 160.
[19] A. S. Khomiakov, "O vozmozhnosti Russkoi khudozhestvennoi shkoly," *Polnoe sobranie sochinenii*, I (Moscow, 1900), 96-97.

of their soul, who humbly studied the treasures of spiritual wealth of the people, who piously revered the basic principles of their way of life, inseparable from Orthodoxy,—these men were dubbed, God knows why, Slavophiles, even though in their relation to the Western Slavs there was only a sincere compassion for the position of their brethren by blood and faith.

In answer to a query regarding the possible Panslavic tendencies of the Slavophiles, Ivan Aksakov replied with a conviction that transcended the natural desire for self-preservation:

We do not believe in Panslavism and consider it impossible: 1) because unity of religion of the Slavic peoples would be indispensable for this, whereas the Catholicism of Bohemia and Poland constitutes a hostile and alien element which is incompatible with the element of Orthodoxy among the other Slavs; 2) all the separate elements of the Slavic nationalities might be dissolved and merged into a whole only in another mightier, more integrated, more powerful element, that is, the Russian; 3) the greater part of the Slavic peoples are already infected by the influence of barren Western liberalism which is contrary to the spirit of the Russian people and which can never be grafted onto it. I admit that Russia [*Rus'*] interests me much more than all the other Slavs, while my brother Constantine is even reproached for complete indifference to all the Slavs except those of Russia, and then not all but particularly those of Great Russia.

Evidently mollified by Aksakov's replies, the Emperor wrote to his chief of the Third Section, Count Orlov, the terse instructions, "Summon, read, instruct, release." On March 22, 1849, after having been his sovereign's involuntary guest for four days, Aksakov was summoned, read to, instructed, and released. This was not the end of Aksakov's career as a Panslavist, however, but the beginning.[20]

If Nicholas feared that the Slavophiles advocated the liberation and unification of the Slavs, then this fear must have been based on evidence not available to posterity. It is true that the private letters of Ivan Aksakov to his family betrayed the hope that the Austrian Slavs might gain more recognition after the events of 1848. Of all the Moscow Slavophile circle, Ivan Aksakov probably showed the most active interest in foreign affairs and current events in the

[20] The entire episode of Ivan Aksakov's arrest is described by A. N. Pypin in his "Iz istorii panslavizma," *Viestnik Evropy*, CLXIII, Book 5 (1893), 285-86.

Slavic lands across the border. Perhaps this may be partly explained by the fact that in this period, at least, he was not a theoretician of Slavophilism but a younger disciple. Yet there is no evidence to show that even he, much less the leading ideologists of Slavophilism, expressed even private hopes of the political unification of the Slavic peoples under Russia's aegis, either before 1849 or for some years thereafter.

What connection, then, did the Slavophiles have with the Slavs as a whole? The Slavophiles were interested in the Slavic race as the bearer of a separate culture in world history. As A. D. Gradovskii pointed out, "The Slavophiles proclaimed the right of the Slavs . . . to play a role in universal history; . . . they demonstrated the cultural worth of those principles which make up the individuality of the Slavic race."[21]

The Slavophiles deduced these principles not so much from the contemporary life of the various Slavic peoples as from their own interpretation of the Slavic, and especially the Russian, past. In so doing they were very prone to describe as typically "Slavic" what was, in fact, typically Russian—a Slavophile failing which the Panslavists were also to adopt. The Slavophiles' view of what was typically Russian was in turn markedly colored by their own personal social background. The great majority of the Moscow Slavophiles were reared in the patriarchal spirit of ancestral homesteads. Of their families a Russian historian observed, "Like spreading oaks, these families grew in the easy soil of serfdom, their roots invisibly intertwined with the life of the people and drawing life from its waters, while their topmost branches reached up into the atmosphere of European culture."[22] These Slavophiles were provincial gentry who were generally closer to the traditions of the Russian peasantry than were most of the Westernizers. To a man like Khomiakov, who accepted not only the philosophy of the Greek Fathers of the Church but the rites and fasts of Orthodoxy as well, the religion of the masses meant much more than to the Westernizers. Till the end of his days, Constantine Aksakov kissed

[21] A. D. Gradovskii, "Pervyie Slavianofily," *Sobranie sochinenii*, VI (St. Petersburg, 1901), 162.
[22] M. Gershenzon, *Istoricheskie Zapiski* (2d ed., Berlin, 1923), pp. 44-45.

his father's hand on each greeting, even before guests. The fact that some of the Slavophiles sported Russian native costumes, instead of the Western dress which the law required their social class to wear, has become more notorious than understood. Herzen poked good-natured fun at the Slavophiles by claiming that they were the only people in all Russia who wore the *murmolka* or outmoded peasant fur cap. Chaadaev quipped that Constantine Aksakov wore a costume which was so national that the peasants in the street took him for a Persian![23] It must indeed be admitted that there was something of Don Quixote about these knights-errant of Slavophilism who thus dramatized their defiance of both the government and the Westernizers. "Mais montrez-nous donc vos Slaves," fashionable visitors from St. Petersburg and abroad would eagerly ask their Muscovite friends, and their hosts would point out the Slavophiles as in a zoo.[24]

It was natural for men who had been reared in such devotion to Holy Russia to desire its perpetuation. They labored for this aim not only in the face of ridicule but of hostility, both on the part of the Imperial government and the Westernizers, neither of whom really understood them. Even as friendly and as wise a critic as Granovskii cried out against the Slavophiles in a fitful moment, "These men are as repulsive to me as graves! They exude the odor of carrion. Their opposition is sterile, for it is founded only on a rejection of that which has been accomplished here during over a century and a half of our history."[25] This judgment still hangs over the heads of the Slavophiles.

IV

The Slavophile doctrine was never enshrined in any single work. It developed piecemeal in the writings of various men whose interests were not at all as similar as their social background and their philosophical outlook. It is no easy task to synthesize this doctrine

[23] A. Herzen, *My Past and Thoughts*, trans. Constance Garnett (New York, 1924), II, 273.
[24] E. A. Dmitriev-Mamonov, "Slavianofily," *Russkii Arkhiv* (1873), p. 2495.
[25] Cited by G. K. Gradovskii, "Retsidiv slavianofil'stva," *Obrazovanie*, No. 3 (St. Petersburg, 1909), p. 57.

—and only a very few have tried it with any degree of success. In the heat of battle with their opponents, the Slavophiles were often wont to express their theories in their most extreme form. Furthermore, Slavophile doctrine not only lacked clarity; it even contained contradictions.[26] It is small wonder, then, that Slavophilism has been ill understood.

It is even less wonder when one realizes how badly Slavophilism was misrepresented—not only by the Westernizers themselves, who were equally susceptible to the fury of the fray, but by the intellectual progeny of the Westernizers. The fact that the censors and even the Third Section of His Imperial Majesty's Chancery hounded the Slavophiles did not prevent some Westernizers from accusing their opponents of being apologists for the reactionary regime of Nicholas I. Commenting on the incompatibility of Slavophile views with those of Nicholas's government, Paul Miliukov remarked, "This difference, which was unknown to the public at large and ignored in the polemics of the press, was understood quite well by the censorship, and even before Slavophilism became known in the press, it was already suspect in the eyes of the government."[27] Nevertheless, Herzen recalled, speaking for the Westernizers, "We saw in their doctrines [of the Slavophiles] fresh oil for anointing the Tsar, new chains laid upon thought, new subordination of conscience to the slavish Byzantine Church."[28]

The Westernizers and the Slavophiles waged intellectual war on one another with the passion of a fratricidal vendetta. Indeed, it seemed on occasion that their war of words would turn into a physical contest. Peter Kirieevskii and Granovskii were deterred from engaging in a duel only by the energetic intervention of their friends.[29] "Who plucked out your eye?" a grim Slavic folk tale asks, and the reply is, "My brother." The Westernizers and their Slavophile opponents (*"nos amis les ennemis,* or more correctly, *les ennemis nos amis,"* Herzen called them[30]) were indeed breth-

[26] The friendly critic A. N. Pypin points out some contradictions in his article, "Eshche nieskol'ko slov po iuzhno-slavianskomu voprosu," *Viestnik Evropy,* II (March, 1877), 357-87.

[27] Miliukov, "Slavianofil'stvo," *Entsiklopedicheskii Slovar',* XXX, 309.

[28] Herzen, *My Past and Thoughts,* p. 254.

[29] *Ibid.,* p. 299.

[30] *Ibid.,* p. 254.

ren. "Like Janus, or the two-headed eagle," Herzen recalled in his memoirs, "we looked in different directions while one heart throbbed within us."[31] There are few scenes in all fiction as touching as Herzen's last embrace with Constantine Aksakov at the time of their final break in 1844.[32] As closely knit members of the same intimate Russian intellectual class, Slavophiles and Westernizers shared the same academic milieu. Indeed, both camps subscribed basically to the same ideological premises. They were the heirs and disciples of German nationalism, Romanticism, and Idealism. Whereas most Western Europeans ordinarily approached the problems posed by these trends with a critical intellect, the Russian intelligentsia—hungry for a *Weltanschauung* it could swallow whole—embraced these ideas with the fervor of religious converts. This was especially true of the Slavophiles, who were less attracted by cold Kantian critique and the abstractions of the godless Fichte than by the emotional mysticism of Schelling and the cosmic vision of Hegel.[33]

Both the Westernizers and the Slavophiles took as their starting point the Hegelian concept that the history of mankind is but the gradual revelation in this world of a universal absolute idea which is borne in successive stages by various peoples and in consecutive epochs.[34] This theory looked to the eventual establishment of a universal culture. Hegel believed that his own German people were to realize the crowning fulfillment of human history.

The Westernizers came to hold the view that Russians should reject all in their way of life which did not conform to this universal culture, as it was being advanced by Western civilization. Men such as Bielinskii, Herzen, and Granovskii urged their countrymen to learn from the West, since it was there that the absolute idea was achieving its most complete expression. "The mistake of the Slavophiles lies in their imagining that Russia once had an individual culture, obscured by various events and finally by the Petersburg period," Herzen proclaimed, and then added, "Russia

---

[31] *Ibid.*, p. 302.
[32] *Ibid.*, pp. 193-94.
[33] F. Steppun, "Niemetskii romantizm i russkoe slavianofil'stvo," *Russkaia Mysl'* (March, 1910), pp. 65-91 *passim*.
[34] Gradovskii, "Pervyie Slavianofily," *Sobranie sochinenii*, VI, 163-64.

never had this culture, never could have had it. . . . Only the mighty thought of the West to which all its long history has led is able to fertilize the seeds slumbering in the patriarchal mode of life of the Slavs."[35] Russia, the Westernizers held, could play a significant role in universal history only to the extent that the Russian people became a part of Western European culture. This meant that "backward" Russia had to renounce its "Asiatic" heritage in order that it might pass as quickly as possible through all the stages of development already experienced by Western Europe. At least this is what many Westernizers believed before they experienced their own personal disappointment in Western Europe—especially after 1848.

Accepting the same basic premise of successive stages of development toward a universal culture, the Slavophiles reached quite another conclusion. Adopting the concept of the chosen people, they simply transferred the mantle of the elect from German to Slavic shoulders.[36] They certainly disagreed profoundly with Hegel's judgment that the Slavs were a dark mass of nationalities lacking in energy and that any epoch belonging to the Slavs would be a terrible one. Thus by their acceptance of Hegel's philosophy of history and by their rejection of his conclusions, the Slavophiles established one of the cardinal tenets of the future Russian Panslavic movement.

The greatest single contribution of Slavophilism to the Panslavic ideology was the concept that Russia possessed a separate, original, independent, and self-contained culture based on a Slavic way of life which was not only different from that of the Romano-Germanic world but was incompatible with it. "Russia is a land with a way of life all its own, not at all similar to that of European states and lands," wrote Constantine Aksakov. "Those who ascribe to it European views, and judge it on that basis, are very mistaken."[37] The great poet of Slavophilism, Fëdor Tiutchev, enshrined this declaration in the famous lines:

[35] Herzen, *My Past and Thoughts*, pp. 274-75.
[36] V. Z. Zavitnevich, *Russkie slavianofily i ikh znachenie v dielie uiasneniia idei narodnosti i samobytnosti* (Kiev, 1915), pp. 26-27.
[37] Constantine Aksakov, "O tom zhe," *Sochineniia istoricheskiia*, in *Polnoe sobranie sochinenii*, I (Moscow, 1889), 16.

> Russia is not revealed by mind,
> Nor by common standards understood;
> Distinct her destiny in mankind,
> And faith alone discerns her mood.[38]

To be sure, the Slavophiles were neither first nor alone in suggesting that Russia belonged to a civilization apart. There was P. I. Chaadaev's famous lamentation in his *Philosophical Letters*, for which Nicholas I had him declared insane in the eyes of the law:

We have never walked hand in hand with other nations. We do not belong to any of the great families of mankind, either to the West or to the East, we do not have the tradition of either. We exist as if beyond the limits of time and as if we were never touched by the universal education of humanity.[39]

It is worth while to indicate here one important difference (among many) between Chaadaev and the Slavophiles. Whereas the bitter Chaadaev cried out in hopeless despair, the Slavophiles had a philosophy which gave them an abiding faith in the salvation of the Russian people.

The Slavophiles significantly advanced the concept of Slavic Russia's peculiarity (*samobytnost'*) by attempting to demonstrate that the difference between Western European and Russian culture was not only a matter of degree but of character and principle.[40] In trying to prove this proposition, the Slavophiles stressed principally the differences between Western and Russian concepts of religion, the sources of their intellectual life, and the principles underlying the social organization and government of each.

Western Christianity, the Slavophiles asserted, consisted of a Roman Catholicism and a Germanic Protestantism, both of which were but two sides of the same counterfeit coin—rationalism. It

[38] F. I. Tiutchev, *Stikhotvoreniia* (Moscow, 1935). I am indebted for the above translation to an anonymous translator, "E. M. K.," who jotted down this English version on the flyleaf of the copy in the Butler Library of Columbia University.

[39] The above translation is found in George Kennan's article, "Russia and the United States," *New Republic*, June 26, 1950. The article was also published in its unabridged form in a private edition by George Kennan.

[40] See especially I. V. Kirieevskii's article, "O kharaktere prosvieshcheniia Evropy i o ego otnoshenii k prosvieshcheniiu Rossii," *Polnoe sobranie sochinenii*, I (Moscow, 1911), 174-222. The article was first published in 1852 in the form of an open letter to Count E. E. Komarovskii in the *Moskvitianin*.

was especially A. S. Khomiakov who, as the leading Russian lay theologian of his time, dissected Western Christianity—not from the dogmatic point of view, for Roman and Greek dogma are essentially one, but from the social and philosophical points of view. "The Roman heresy was not directed against God or Christ; it was a heresy against Christian fellowship; it was a social heresy, and therefore it affected mainly the corporate life of Western society, encouraging the growth of pride, aggressive individualism, and exaggerated rationalism. Khomiakov saw the first signs of this social disease already in the early stages of Latin Christianity."[41]

"Once a living community governed by the free consent of its members," Khomiakov declared, "the Church became a state; lay members became obedient subjects, and the hierarchy their rulers."[42] And thus, he concluded, error took root when pride replaced Christian fellowship, and material power replaced spirituality. Having lost contact with the wellspring of faith, the Church turned to coercion, militant discipline, and the subjection of the divine mysteries to the barren rationalistic formulae of Aquinas and the Scholastics. Khomiakov regarded the Protestant revolt not as a genuine break with Roman error but as a logical extension of it. The anarchic individualism of Protestantism, he held, was the inevitable outcome of Roman rationalism. The main conflict to which the Reformation gave vent was that of individual rationalism against an authoritarian ecclesiastical rationalism. Khomiakov and his Slavophile comrades regarded both individualism and sacerdotal authoritarianism as crimes against Christian ecumenical fellowship, and they abhorred rationalism as the chief enemy of faith.

Western intellectual development was rooted, in the Slavophile view, in the classical heritage of Rome. Here was the real source of the West's false worship of formalism, legalism, scholasticism— all of which were more concerned with external appearance, external justice, and external truth than with the inner essence of reality. So ingrained had these attitudes become in the Western

[41] Nicolas Zernov, *Three Russian Prophets: Khomiakov, Dostoevsky, Soloviev* (London, 1944), pp. 64-65.
[42] Khomiakov, *Polnoe sobranie sochinenii*, VII, 448.

mind, Ivan Kirieevskii claimed, that not even the injection of Greek humanism from an overrun Constantinople in the fifteenth century could exert a lasting effect. Rationalism triumphed, and by the eighteenth century Europe's faith had been destroyed. What was Europe to do? It could not go back. And so each European began to search his own reason for new principles of life. Out of this desperate quest, the Slavophiles pointed out, have come all of those "isms" which have pecked and gnawed away at a dismembered Western society.

As for Western government and social organization, the Slavophiles saw only coercion at the foundation. From the tyrannical anarchy of the feudal barons to the organized despotism of even the most democratic modern states, Western governments were allegedly based on conquest and legalized brute force. Ivan Kirieevskii pointed to the Holy Roman Empire as the first great synthesis of the three false foundations of Western society: an authoritarian church, a legal system which denied natural rights, and a statism based on conquest and oppression. It is little wonder, Kirieevskii observed, that such artificial unity could not long endure, no matter into what new shapes the unholy amalgam might be cast. The only way in which Western society has sought deliverance, he claimed, was by still another curse—revolution. Not wishing to recognize that violent change was the necessary outcome of basic faults in the culture, the West deified revolution and dubbed it *Progress.*[43]

Meanwhile, lacking the true solidarity of a natural and truly Christian social order, the Slavophiles claimed, the West was doomed to rot away. It was destined to disintegrate in the face of its internal contradictions—thanks to rationalism, skepticism, authoritarianism, individualism, secularism, indifferentism, materialism, socialism, cosmopolitanism, statism, and a host of other destructive agents. "We Russians do not belong to this doomed world," wrote Khomiakov, "and we can say so while yet paying due respect to all that is great in European achievements in art, science, and history."[44]

---

[43] Kirieevskii, "O kharakterie prosvieshcheniia Evropy i o ego otnoshenii k prosvieshcheniiu Rossii," *Polnoe sobranie sochinenii,* I, 182-90 *passim.*
[44] Cited by Zernov, *Three Russian Prophets,* p. 69.

How did the Russian Slavophiles portray their own culture? It has become almost commonplace to claim that the Slavophiles based Russia's peculiarly Slavic culture on Nationalism, Autocracy, and Orthodoxy—the trinity which the reactionary Minister of Education, Count Uvarov, proclaimed as the pillars of Nicholas I's absolutism. This is not the place to examine the sources of this confusion, but even a cursory examination of Slavophile writings would be sufficient to dispel it.

As the disciples of Schelling and Schlegel, not to speak of the Fathers of the Greek Church, the Russian Slavophiles attached primary importance to religious feeling. Like their German mentors, they regarded religion not as a part of culture but as its very core. Faith was for them the mainspring of human existence. They could not conceive of religion as simply a compartment of life when all of life was sustained by man's fundamental beliefs. When the Slavophiles spoke of the Church, they meant a mystical union in Christ of all true believers—the living, the dead, and those yet to be born. This was what they meant by *sobornost'* or catholicity.[45] They certainly did not mean the Most Holy Synod of the Russian Orthodox Church. Indeed, their great complaint against Western Christianity was that religion had become separated from actual life by an overemphasis on its institutional form. Russia, however, had kept the true faith, they proudly maintained—not an irrational but a suprarational faith transcending the limits of human reason and temporal institutions. Orthodoxy, they believed, sought the inner understanding of the soul's depth, that true harmony of mind and spirit which lay at the very basis of the integrity of personality.

Men with such a viewpoint—whatever one may think of them—could scarcely agree with Uvarov's concept of a State Church. "It were better," wrote Khomiakov dryly, "if we had rather less of official religion."[46] The Slavophiles yearned for one holy, catholic, and apostolic church of a spiritually reunited Christendom. Schelling once expressed the desire to see Peter (Roman Catholi-

---

[45] The term *sobornost'* is almost impossible to translate. The concept includes all that is denoted by the words catholicity, ecumenicity, or fellowship. Orthodox Slavs use the word *sobornost'* in its adjectival form in the Church Slavonic translation of the Nicean Creed when they affirm their belief in the catholic church.

[46] Cited by Brodskii, *Rannie slavianofily*, p. lvii.

cism) and Paul (Protestantism) brought together by John in a true communion of love.[47] The Slavophiles maintained with fervor that it was in Holy Russia that John's church existed. Certainly the Slavophile view of Orthodoxy was no less dogmatic than Uvarov's. It did not, however, at all resemble the concept that sought to degrade the church to the position of an agency of the St. Petersburg government.

It was the Slavophiles who transmitted to the Panslavists the dogma that Greek Christianity as preserved by the Orthodox Slavs was the true religion of Slavdom. Orthodoxy was the true ecumenical faith which the Slavs as a whole had received in its purity, the Slavophiles maintained, though not all the Slavs had been able to keep the true faith as the result of Western coercion. Only in the freedom inherent in Orthodoxy, they held, could the Slavs maintain and develop their ancient social institutions, notably the agrarian commune or *obshchina*. "That is why a Slav cannot fully be a Slav outside of Orthodoxy," Khomiakov insisted. "It is bitter for us to reflect that not all the Slavs are Orthodox. We believe that they, too, will in time all be enlightened by the truth; we love them with all our soul and are ever ready to extend to them the hand of brotherhood and help against all."[48] The Slavophiles deeply regretted the religious separation which divided the Slavs into Orthodox, Uniat, Roman Catholic, Protestant, and Moslem. They hoped for the spiritual unification of the Slavs in Orthodoxy. That they envisaged any forcible conversion of the non-Orthodox Slavs is unthinkable. As Khomiakov, the greatest of the Slavophile lay theologians, proclaimed, "Let all have full freedom of religion and its confession!"[49]

As for the concept of nationalism, a whole world stood between the official nationalism fostered by Nicholas I and the populist nationalism preached by the Slavophiles. To identify the two is to submit to the tyranny of words. "It is positively fortunate," Tiutchev once wrote to Foreign Minister Prince Gorchakov, "that there is in the Russian language only one and the same word to

---

[47] Masaryk, *Rusko a Evropa*, I, 417.
[48] Khomiakov, *Polnoe sobranie sochinenii*, I, 387.
[49] *Ibid.*, p. 386.

express two concepts: *populaire* and *national*. That word is *narodyni*."[50] Tiutchev's satisfaction is, in this case, the historian's despair. To call the Slavophiles "nationalists" is to put them in Uvarov's camp. To call them "populists" is to trespass on the realm of the later Narodniki. Perhaps the best course is to forget labels and to examine the contents.

Official Russian nationalism was based on the concept of the state (*gosudarstvo*); Slavophile nationalism was based on the land (*zemlia*) in the sense of "country." While official nationalism glorified a Russian Empire which was designated on the map as *Rossiia*, the Slavophiles owed their allegiance to Holy Russia, *sviataia Rus'*. The difference between *Rossiia* and *Rus'* cannot be translated; it involves a whole concept of life. Official nationalism was embodied in the government (*pravitel'stvo*) with its apparatus of a standing army of soldiers, a sitting army of bureaucrats, a kneeling army of priests, and a crawling army of spies—to borrow a characterization of the Austrian Empire. Slavophile nationalism was personified in the people (*narod*)—not the public or "society" (*obshchestvo*) which had divorced itself from the real people to become the slaves of Westernism—but the Russian peasantry, the common folk. Official nationalism commanded obedience to an emperor (*imperator*). Slavophile nationalism yearned for a tsar.

The Slavophiles frankly regarded the state as an evil, perhaps historically necessary, but nonetheless sinful. The sin lay in coercion. Whatever justification the state had for its existence reposed on the need for justice. But there was a difference, the Slavophiles argued, between external and inner justice. The former was based on force, the latter on harmony. The very existence of a state signified to the Slavophiles an admission of an imperfect society in which conflict was present. Where social contracts and constitutions were needed, the Slavophiles warned, one could be certain that there was something basically amiss.

The Slavophiles insisted that whereas the states of Romano-Germanic Europe were founded on conquest and coercion, the Russian state emerged as the result of an invitation from the people

[50] Cited by K. Pigarev, "F. I. Tiutchev i problemy vneshnei politiki tsarskoi Rossii," *Literaturnoe Nasledstvo*, XX (1935), 226.

of *Rus'* to the Varangians to come and to rule over them. Constantine Aksakov and Ivan Kirieevskii took quite literally the Primary Chronicle's story of the invitation because it seemed so logical to them. The true Slavic way of life knew no political coercion, they held. The early Slavs constituted a homogeneous yet scattered society of patriarchal households and self-governing communes. When the danger of invasion from without pressed upon the Russian Slavs, rather than violate the harmony of their society they called upon foreigners to fulfill the functions of the state—protection and arbitration. The foreigners were paid for these external services in taxes.[51] "The essence of my brother's (and Khomiakov's) view consists of the following," Ivan Aksakov wrote in a private letter, "that the Russian people is apolitical, that it never rebelled for its political rights, but that it is a social people having to fulfill the tasks of the inner life, the life of the land. Its ideal is not governmental perfection but the establishment of a Christian society."[52]

In their dual capacities, the Slavophiles held, the state and the land acted in harmony—thanks to a common recognition of certain basic principles—until Russia's forcible Westernization in the eighteenth century. The grand princes of Kiev and the tsars of Muscovy consulted with their land assembly (*zemskii sobor*) and council (*vieche*). With the accession of the first Russian emperor, Peter I, this old way of life was interrupted. The contradictions arising from the violent revolution which disrupted ancient principles necessarily resulted in the introduction of Western absolutism in the government of Russia.

The Slavophiles dramatized the schism within the Russian Slavic soul, torn between loyalty to its own pristine Slavic principles and the desire to imitate the West, by pointing to Moscow as the embodiment of the Russian tradition and to St. Petersburg as the den of Westernism. To the Slavophiles Peter's capital—which bore the

[51] Constantine Aksakov, *Polnoe sobranie sochinenii*, Vol. I, especially these articles: "Ob osnovnykh nachalakh russkoi istorii," "O tom zhe," "O russkoi istorii," and "Nieskol'ko slov o russkoi istorii, vozbuzhdennykh istorieiu g. Solovieva," *passim*.

[52] Ivan Aksakov, *Ivan Sergieevich Aksakov v ego pis'makh*, III, 228. Letter of January 15/16, 1862, to Countess Antonina Bludova.

foreign name of *Sankt Peterburg*—stood for all those Western errors which were corrupting Russia and turning it away from the path of its Slavic fathers. On the other hand, Moscow the White-stoned, with its forty times forty churches, was hailed by the Slavophiles as the true and only capital of the Russian folk. Constantine Aksakov used to say, "Moscow is the capital of the Russian people, while Petersburg is only the residence of the Emperor." To which Herzen wittily replied, "And observe to what lengths the distinction goes—in Moscow they invariably put you in the lock-up, while in Petersburg they take you to the *Hauptwacht*."[53] So bitter were the Slavophile denunciations of St. Petersburg that at least one distinguished resident of that maligned capital, Alexander V. Nikitenko, was goaded into complaining to his diary, "They nurture hatred and contempt for Petersburg, and regard its governmental significance as pure usurpation. One has only to live in Petersburg, in their opinion, to lose all patriotic feeling for Russia."[54] Petersburghers were right when they sneeringly called Moscow a big village, Ivan Aksakov once wrote in an editorial, for Moscow was truly close to the countryside and the country folk.[55] St. Petersburg prattled of Western democracy, he continued, but it actually regarded the Russian land as a *tabula rasa* on which it could scrawl whatever it wished. Ivan Aksakov reminded his readers that Moscow's Russia consisted of millions and millions of people who governed themselves according to ancient custom and forms which had never been incorporated in the Code of Laws which St. Petersburg worshipped.[56] St. Petersburg governed by one law; the people abided by another. Slavophile nationalism called on St. Petersburg to heal the breach by returning to the national principles it had forsaken.

As for Count Uvarov's concept of autocracy, the Slavophile

[53] Herzen, *My Past and Thoughts*, II, 293.

[54] Aleksandr Vasilievich Nikitenko, *Zapiski i dnevnik, 1804-1877*, II (St. Petersburg, 1904-5), 195.

[55] Ivan Aksakov (unsigned), lead editorial in *Den'*, March 21, 1864, p. 1. Compare this with Herzen's description, "Life in Moscow is more like life in the country than in the town, the only difference is that the houses are nearer each other." (*My Past and Thoughts*, II, 280-81.)

[56] Ivan Aksakov (unsigned), lead editorial in *Den'*, June 20, 1864, p. 3.

circle of Moscow had little liking for the institution of absolute monarchy, already outmoded in the West, but still entrenched in St. Petersburg. The Slavophiles evoked from their country's past an idealized portrait of the benign patriarchal tsar, the loving father of his people, who sat in consultation with the people's representatives in the assembly of the land.

Napoleon is credited with the remark that all Alexander I had to do to defeat him was to grow a beard. This shrewd observation well illustrated the hope of the Slavophiles. If the Russian emperor would only become tsar once again and call his people to him in a land assembly, then, the Slavophiles maintained, Holy Russia would rediscover its strength. The beardless emperors—Peter and his successors—like Samson of old, had lost their strength when they set themselves up against God's way and the way of their people.[57]

Having no hope in the regeneration of Nicholas I, the Slavophiles nurtured the faith that his successor might be made to see the way. When Alexander II came to the throne in 1855, Constantine Aksakov used the good services of Count D. N. Bludov to submit a memorandum in which he attempted to enlighten the Emperor with regard to allegedly traditional principles of Russian government. "The Russian people does not wish to rule," Aksakov assured the new monarch. The people cared little for political participation, secure in the knowledge that there is no power but of God ("niest' vlast' ashche ne ot Boga"). The tsar had always held exclusive *political* power, Aksakov conceded, but the people have the natural right to think and to speak. Aksakov reminded Alexander II that his Muscovite predecessors did not fear the opinion of the people but invited the expression of popular opinion in the land assemblies. He urged the view that just as the state possessed full power in its own political sphere, so the people possessed rights within their own social sphere—and that these two spheres should

[57] Concerning the whole question of beards, it is interesting to note Herzen's remark, "Slavism, or Russianism, not as a theory, not as a doctrine, but as a wounded national feeling, as an obscure tradition and a true instinct, as antagonism to an exclusively foreign influence, has existed ever since Peter the Great cut off the first Russian beard." (*My Past and Thoughts*, II, 257.)

be connected by mutual trust, consultation, and nonintervention.[58]

True, the Slavophile concept of the historic monarchy was very far from English or French parliamentarianism, which the Slavophiles rejected as unsuited to Russian society, but it was also sufficiently removed from the official Russian autocracy to bring down on the heads of the Slavophiles the wrath of the government in St. Petersburg.

Slavophile nationalism regarded the folk with a truly mystical awe. "Outside the national soil there is no foundation," wrote Ivan Aksakov, "outside the people there is nothing real, vital, and any goodly thought, any institution which is not rooted in the national soil or which does not grow out of it organically will not bear fruit but will turn into rubbish."[59] He and his Slavophile preceptors decried the artificiality of the Western state. They denounced it as a mere mechanism, an apparatus in which codes of law replaced conscience and discipline took the place of inner conviction. For the Slavophile, freedom of speech, press, and conscience were not just legal rights; they were the necessary means by which each individual fulfilled his natural obligation to the community.

The Slavophiles saw all of Russian history as the record of the relations between the Russian state or government on the one hand and the Russian land or people on the other.[60] There is a striking divergence between the views of Granovskii, a leading Westernizer, and Khomiakov with regard to the role of the people in history. Wrote Granovskii:

The masses, like nature or the Scandinavian Thor, are either senselessly cruel or senselessly good-natured. They stagnate under the burden of historical and natural determinism from which only the separate individual can free himself intellectually. It is in this disintegration of the masses by the intellect that the process of history consists.[61]

[58] K. P. Petrov, "Slavianofil'skoe uchenie," *Istoricheskii Viestnik,* LXXXV (1901), 908. The memorandum is also discussed in A. A. Kornilov, *Obshchestvennoe dvizhenie pri Aleksandrie II, 1855-1881* (Moscow, 1909), p. 29. The memorandum was published in *Rus'*, Nos. 26-28 (May 9, May 16, May 23, 1881).
[59] Ivan Aksakov, *Sochineniia,* Vol. II: *Slavianofil'stvo i zapadnichestvo, 1860-1886,* pp. 3-4; *Den'* editorial of October 14, 1861.
[60] Masaryk, *Rusko a Evropa,* I, 441.
[61] Cited by Brodskii, *Rannie slavianofily,* p. lxi.

How different a view is expressed in the following passage by Khomiakov:

Peoples mean everything, and the ideas which they direct or which are embodied in them. . . . The great phenomena of history are produced by the general aspiration of the whole people.[62]

Following the teachings of his brother, Constantine, of Khomiakov, and of the Kirieevskii brothers, Ivan Aksakov wrote the following confession of faith:

The state is, of course, necessary, but it does not follow that one should believe in it as the only aim and highest standard of man. Man's social and personal ideals stand higher than the most perfect government, just as conscience and inner truth stand higher than law and external truth. The ideal may be unattainable, as man's perfection is generally unattainable, but it must be constantly held up before man and it must inspire him to go forward toward its attainment and realization.[63]

Whereas Count Uvarov's official nationalism regarded the state and its head as the starting point, Slavophile nationalism rested on the masses and their primary social institutions—the family and the agrarian commune or *obshchina* (also called the *mir*). "For the Russian peasant," wrote Khomiakov, "the commune is the very embodiment of his social conscience."[64] In the commune the Slavophiles found the Slavic institution par excellence, one which both preceded the influence of the Orthodox religion on the Slavs and was more widespread among them. In their glorification of the commune the Slavophiles were not interested primarily in proving the cultural bond between Russians and other Slavs, for they took this for granted. Rather they wished to stress the social, as distinct from the political, nature of the Russian people in order to justify their own quest for social liberties and home rule by local communities.

The importance which Slavophile nationalism assigned the people

---

[62] *Ibid.*

[63] Ivan Aksakov, *Sochineniia*, Vol. II: *Slavianofil'stvo i zapadnichestvo, 1860-1886*, p. 19, *Den'* editorial of November 11, 1861.

[64] Cited by Brodskii, *Rannie slavianofily*, p. liii.

(*narod*) assumed metaphysical aspects. To the Slavophiles, peoples were links in the chain of universal history. To be sure, the Slavophiles regarded humanity as a higher category and ideal than nationality, but they also believed that the universal absolute idea was advanced by separate nationalities. To be the vessel of such a sacred calling, they insisted, each people had to be true to itself, that is, to the basic principles of its own culture. "Just as a man cannot be without his own individuality," wrote Constantine Aksakov, "so a people cannot be without its own nationality."[65] It was each nation's obligation to the universal idea to preserve its own originality (*samobytnost'* in Russian, *Eigenart* in German), its own consciousness of self (*samosoznanie*, *Selbstbewusstsein*), for only thus could it make its own specific contribution to the progress of mankind.

From this basic proposition there emerged a corollary: each nation had its own merit, inasmuch as each contributed to the progress of the universal idea. Therefore each nation had a natural right to cultural self-determination.

This did not mean, however, that the Slavophiles were committed to the belief that all groups of humans had an equal right to existence and development as nations. Since national ideas differed from one another, the Slavophiles saw no reason for not grading them as superior or inferior ideas. Their criterion was the advancement of the universal absolute idea. "What is nationality," asked Samarin in 1847, "but the universal principle whose development has been entrusted to a certain people in preference to others as the result of a special affinity between this principle and the natural characteristics of that people?"[66]

The Slavophiles differentiated, for instance, between historic and nonhistoric peoples, that is, between nations and tribal societies with no clear consciousness of a national existence, culture, or mission. The Slavophiles also judged between historic nations which were the bearers of "true" ideas and those which were the vessels of "false" ideas. Thus if the Greco-Slavic world was next in succession to act as the torchbearer of the universal absolute

---

[65] *Ibid.*, p. lxii.
[66] Cited by Miliukov, "Slavianofil'stvo," *Entsiklopedicheskii Slovar'*, XXX, 50.

idea, and if the Romano-Germanic world stood in the way, this was for the Slavophiles a clear conflict between truth and falsehood. Also the Slavophile circle distinguished between nations which by virtue of size and importance were able to fulfill their universal mission and those that were not. Despite the Slavophile avowal of respect for all nations, their loyalty to the idea of a universal culture caused them to reject the claims of small nations to self-determination as cultural entities on the grounds that these nations did not possess the material means necessary to fulfill a national mission.[67]

V

Such were the basic dogmas of the Moscow Slavophiles. To say that these were the principles which the Slavophiles *transmitted* to the Panslavists is to imply an intent which the Slavophiles could not have had. Certainly the Slavophiles of the 1840's could not foresee that their philosophical viewpoints would be adopted by a later group with an intent that was not theirs. The Slavophiles sympathized with the lot of their Slavic brethren across the border, but their main concern was Russia's own national problem—a concern which was so absorbing as to leave the Slavophiles little interest in the practical affairs of the non-Russian Slavs. Constantine Aksakov, Ivan and Peter Kirieevskii, and even Khomiakov were quietistic religious philosophers who, despite their pleas for more freedom and light, were both politically disinterested and socially conservative.

Nevertheless, it was from the Slavophiles that the Russian Panslavists took their view of world history, their postulate of a mutually incompatible Romano-Germanic world, in decadence, and an ascendant self-contained Slavic world, and their belief in Russia's historic mission as the leading representative of Slavdom.

For the Slavophiles, mankind and a universal culture were higher goals than Russia and the Slavic culture. Slavophile doctrine denounced coercion and all its works, accepting only what came

[67] N. Ustrialov, "Natsional'naia problema u pervykh slavianofilov," *Russkaia Mysl'*, No. 10 (1916), pp. 1-22 *passim*.

about naturally as the result of harmony and inner justice. Slavophilism preached the sanctity of historic nations and the inviolable freedom of individuals bound to one another by a community of interests and by love. Russian Panslavism was to confront the problem of reconciling its own aims with the means which Slavophilism regarded as essential to success.

3

RUSSIAN PANSLAVIST IDEOLOGY

Like leaves on trees the race of
*   man is found,*
Now green in youth, now
*   with'ring on the ground;*
Another   race   the   foll'wing
*   spring supplies,*
They fall successive and succes-
*   sive rise.*

HOMER, *Iliad*, VI
(Pope's translation)

RUSSIAN PANSLAVIST IDEOLOGY rested largely on the writings of Michael P. Pogodin, Ivan S. Aksakov, Iurii F. Samarin, Vladimir I. Lamanskii, Alexander F. Hilferding, and Nicholas Ia. Danilevskii. It was these men and their Panslavic colleagues who developed a pietistic, introspective, romantic philosophy into a militant program of foreign intervention in an age of Materialism and Realism.

Michael Petrovich Pogodin (1800-1875) deserves the title of modern Russia's first real Panslavist. His practical interest in the non-Russian Slavic peoples as concrete entities with concrete problems antedated by over a decade and a half the Slavophiles' abstract preoccupation with a postulated Slavic way of life. His four trips to the lands of the Austrian and Balkan Slavs between 1835 and 1848, his newspaper, *Moskvitianin* (Muscovite), which he published from 1841 to 1856, and the many memoranda which he addressed to Nicholas's government on the Slavic Question, especially during the Crimean War, offer ample evidence of his active interest in the Slavic peoples. As a publisher and editor, Pogodin possessed the means to spread the Slavic cause. As professor of

Russian history at the University of Moscow, Pogodin occupied a public tribune from which he was able to influence his students, notably Samarin, and his colleagues—Shevyrëv, Maksimovich, and others—to espouse Panslavism. Probably no Russian Panslavist of his time matched Pogodin's personal acquaintance with the leading figures of the Slavic world. Although not strictly a Slavophile, Pogodin shared many Slavophile views on the nature of the Slavic culture and especially on the opposition of the Romano-Germanic world to Slavic Russia. His views on Nationalism, Autocracy, and Orthodoxy, however, coincided with the official interpretation rather than with the considerably more liberal Slavophile view. As a result, Pogodin had an entrée with the ministries of Foreign Affairs and Public Education which his Slavophile comrades lacked. Like Ivan Aksakov, Pogodin was especially active as a propagator of Panslavist aims.

Without doubt the most forceful and prolific popularizer of Russian Panslavism was Ivan Sergieevich Aksakov (1823-86). A member of the original Slavophile circle in Moscow and, in a sense, its spiritual heir, Ivan Aksakov did more than anyone else to transform the tenets of Slavophilism and to harness them to the practical exigencies of Panslavism. Like his famous father, Sergiei T. Aksakov, the author of the beloved *Family Chronicle*, Ivan possessed a brilliant mastery of the Russian language. Like his equally famous brother, Constantine, he nurtured a mystical love for the Russian people and a fanatical belief in Russia's mission in world history. Unlike his father or his brother, Ivan was not so much the writer or the thinker as he was the champion of celebrated causes—not only of Panslavism, but of emancipation of the serfs, land reform, abolition of censorship, judicial reforms, and other enlightened domestic improvements. He was a fearless polemicist and an indefatigable ringer of tocsins. Seven thick tomes of his collected works and three volumes of his correspondence testify to his breadth of interest, sincerity, command of language, and tireless zeal. As publisher and editor of a whole series of periodicals, notably *Den'* (Day), Aksakov influenced public opinion as did few of his fellow Panslavists. Neither a philosopher nor a scholar, Ivan Aksakov did not codify his ideology into a system. It is to his multitude of editorials and letters that one must look for his thoughts on Panslavism. And because his literary activities spanned some four decades, Ivan Aksakov himself constituted a living bridge between the Slavophile philosophy of the forties and the Panslavic program of the sixties and seventies.

Another prominent member of the original circle of Slavophiles, Iurii Fëdorovich Samarin (1819-76), also formed an important link between Slavophilism and Russian Panslavism. Though he achieved fame as a statesman and as an administrator, Samarin was actually a meditative man—"an incorrigible Slavophile," as he used to call himself. His government service under both Nicholas I and Alexander II brought him into direct contact with those "fringe-lands" of the Russian Empire in which the conflict between Western and Eastern European culture appeared in its sharpest form—in the Baltic region and Congress Poland. Ardently Russian and Orthodox, Samarin developed a profound hatred for Western-ism as a concept which he saw personified politically in the Ger-mans and ecclesiastically in the Jesuits. Samarin's emphasis on peasantism as the very basis of the true Slavic way of life was reflected in his active participation in the land reforms during the first decade of Alexander II's reign. After the Polish insurrection of 1863, he joined N. A. Miliutin in Poland to carry out land reforms there and thus drive a wedge between Poland's gentry and peasantry. More the Slavophile than the Panslavist, Samarin showed considerably less interest in the Slavs beyond Russia's borders than in the Slavs of the Russian Empire.

Vladimir Ivanovich Lamanskii (1833-1914), too young to have been a member of the Slavophile circle, was, however, one of St. Petersburg's leading disciples of the Moscow philosophy. Lamanskii's interest in the Slavs was awakened by his studies of Slavic history and philology at the University of St. Petersburg, where I. I. Sreznevskii was his principal professor. His master's essay, *O slavianakh v Maloi Azii, Afrikie i Ispanii* (On the Slavs in Asia Minor, Africa, and Spain), published in 1859, is a most original study. Following that work, Lamanskii undertook the first of many trips to the Slavic lands outside Russia. *Zaria* (Dawn) published in 1871 what was perhaps his major contribution to Panslavism as an ideology, his doctoral dissertation, *Ob istoricheskom izuchenii greko-slavianskago mira v Evropie* (On the Historical Study of the Greco-Slavic World in Europe). According to Lamanskii, the Greco-Slavic world was a cultural unit which should be studied as a separate and independent historical entity. As a Panslavist, Lamanskii marks the break with Slavophilism as an abstract philosophy, and the turn to Panslavism as a source of action rather than contemplation. Whereas in 1840 Pogodin and Samarin had together translated Ján Kollár's romantic treatise on Slavic *reciprocity*, in 1867 Lamanskii chose to translate L'udovít Štúr's rigorous appeal for Slavic *unification* under Russian hegemony.

Like Lamanskii, Alexander Fëdorovich Hilferding (1831-72), a younger disciple of the Slavophiles, and especially of Khomiakov, belonged to the same generation of Realists. His zest for Slavic studies was stimulated by O. M. Bodianskii, at the University of Moscow. Curiously enough, though he was to become a leading ideologist of Russian Panslavism and president of the St. Petersburg Section of the Slavic Benevolent Committee from its founding in 1863 to his death, Hilferding was not a Slav by ethnic background! In a eulogy of Hilferding delivered in 1873, Ivan Aksakov recalled that Hilferding had been born in Warsaw of a Lutheran father of Dutch origin and a Catholic mother born in Ceylon.[1] Writing for Pogodin's *Russkii* (Russian), Peter Lavrov reported that Hilferding's family had moved from Germany to Russia in the beginning of the eighteenth century and that his father was a Catholic converted to Orthodoxy.[2] Hilferding's failure to be elected a member of the Russian Academy of Sciences in 1869 was ascribed by some to the animosity of its German members, who allegedly looked upon Hilferding as a renegade! Sharp-witted Tiutchev took this opportunity to write a public letter to Hilferding in *Golos* (The Voice) in which he exclaimed, "I hasten to congratulate you on your failure! It was a brilliant success." How could the invincible German garrison which commanded the Academy of Sciences

[1] Ivan S. Aksakov, "Riech' o A. F. Gil'ferdingie," *Obshcheevropeiskaia politika, 1860-1886*, in *Sochineniia*, VII (Moscow, 1887), 789.

[2] *Russkii biograficheskii slovar'*, V, 195. Lavrov cited as his source the article on Hilferding in F. Rieger's *Naučný Slovník*.

allow Hilferding within the walls of their citadel, Tiutchev asked![3]

As a student Hilferding saw much of the Moscow Slavophile circle. In 1853 the Russian section of the Academy of Sciences published his essay "On the Relationship of the Slavic Language [*sic*] to Sanskrit," and then his master's essay, "On the Relationship of the Slavic Language [*sic*] to Related Languages." Both works clearly showed Khomiakov's influence, so much so that Bodianskii, who distrusted Khomiakov's scholarship, would not have accepted the essay had he not liked the young scholar.[4] In 1855 he published his study *Istoriia baltiiskikh Slavian* (History of the Baltic Slavs). Appointed to the Ministry of Foreign Affairs in 1852, in 1856 he became Russian consul in Bosnia and Hercegovina, where he became known as a champion of the Serbs. From this experience came his articles in *Moskovskiia Viedomosti* (Moscow News) and *Russkaia Besieda* (Russian Discourse) from 1856 to 1859 on the history of the Serbs and Bulgars. His work *Les Slaves occidentaux* (The Western Slavs) was published anonymously in Paris in 1859. That same year Hilferding became a desk chief in the Asiatic Department of the Foreign Ministry—a department which, despite its name, included the Balkans. Returned to St. Petersburg, Hilferding again turned his interest on the Balkan Slavs and in 1862 published a study on the Kashubs entitled *Ostatki slavian na iuzhnom beregu Baltiiskago moria* (Remnants of the Slavs on the Southern Coast of the Baltic Sea).

After the outbreak of the Polish uprising, Miliutin invited Hilferding, among others, to work with him on an official committee for Polish affairs, and Hilferding wrote several apologias for the Russian case in Poland. In 1868 he became first president of the St. Petersburg Section of the Slavic Benevolent Committee. The greater part of his Panslavic ideology is to be found not in his scholarly works but in the many newspaper and magazine articles which he wrote on the Slavic Question.

The greatest single contribution to the Panslavist ideology was undoubtedly made by Nicholas Iakovlevich Danilevskii (1822-85)

[3] *Golos*, No. 357 (December 17, 1869), cited by the *Russkii biograficheskii slovar'*, V, 195.
[4] A. N. Pypin, "Russkoe slavianoviedenie v XIX-m stolietii," *Viestnik Evropy*, IV-V (September, 1889), 264.

in his remarkable book, *Rossiia i Evropa: vzgliad na kul'turnyia i politicheskiia otnosheniia slavianskago mira k germano-romanskomu* (Russia and Europe: A View of the Cultural and Political Relations of the Slavic with the Germano-Roman World). First published as a series of articles in 1869 in the newly founded monthly *Zaria*, this lengthy exposition of Russia's Panslavic mission exerted a vast influence on Russian Panslavic thought. *Rossiia i Evropa* first appeared in book form in 1871. The first edition sold only twelve hundred copies. It was not until the appearance of its third edition in March, 1888, that Danilevskii's work became truly popular, owing to the greatly increased interest of the Russian public in the rest of Slavic Europe as a result of the Russo-Turkish War of 1877-78. It was in this period that Danilevskii's *Rossiia i Evropa* achieved both fame and notoriety as the Bible of Russian Panslavism. Danilevskii transformed the Slavophile mystique into a would-be scientific theory and developed from it a frankly hegemonistic political program of Slavic unification under Russian supremacy. In an age when science was held in almost superstitious awe, Danilevskii gave the Panslavic view of history great appeal by claiming for it, through applying superficially impressive but incredibly crude analogy, the validity of an axiom of natural science.

By training Danilevskii was certainly better prepared to deal with the phenomena of natural science than with socio-historic facts and concepts. Born in 1822, the son of a Russian brigadier general, Danilevskii received an excellent education, first in the lycée of Tsarskoe Selo, and later at the University of St. Petersburg as a specialist in botany. He spent most of his professional career as a government ichthyologist, in which capacity he engaged in nine major ichthyological expeditions between 1853 and his death in 1885. It was during the winter of 1865, between two such expeditions, that Danilevskii wrote *Rossiia i Evropa*. The only other major work for which he is known is a two-volume critique of Darwinism published in 1885.[5] There is no evidence

---

[5] N. N. Strakhov, "Zhizn' i trudy N. Ia. Danilevskago," publisher's preface to the fifth edition of *Rossiia i Evropa; vzgliad na kul'turnyia i politicheskiia otnosheniia slavianskago mira k germano-romanskomu* (St. Petersburg, 1895), pp. ix-xxi *passim*.

that Danilevskii possessed any training in the social sciences aside from his general education. His efforts at historiography must, therefore, be considered the work of an intelligent amateur.

Other Russians might be cited for their writings on Panslavism: Orest Fëdorovich Miller (1833-89), professor of the history of Slavic literature at the University of St. Petersburg; Peter Aleksieevich Bezsonov (1828-98), librarian at the University of Moscow, 1867-79, and professor of Slavic studies at the University of Kharkov as of 1879; Michael Nikiforovich Katkov (1818-87), editor of *Moskovskiia Viedomosti* and publisher of the *Russkii Viestnik* (Russian Herald); Alexander Ivanovich Koshelëv (1806-83), ardent Slavophile and editor of *Russkaia Besieda*; Nil Aleksandrovich Popov (1833-91), Slavic scholar and professor of Russian history at the University of Moscow; Anton Semënovich Budilovich (1846-1908), professor of Russian and Church Slavonic at the University of Warsaw; and others. Most of these and other Panslavists, however, largely followed the line set by Ivan Aksakov, Pogodin, Samarin, Lamanskii, Hilferding, and Danilevskii.

II

Russian Panslavist ideology rested on the Slavophile premise that Europe was divided into two incompatible "worlds"—the Romano-Germanic and the Greco-Slavic. For its Slavophile proponents this dogma of two worlds was vitally important because it proclaimed that history had separated Western and Eastern Europe by a difference not only in degree but in kind. Therefore, they argued, it was unnatural for Russia, as a part of the Greco-Slavic world, to imitate a rotting West when Russia's strength lay in its own Slavic way of life. In essence, their central point was that Slavic Russia possessed an independent culture which was more worthy of fulfilling a universal role than was the culture of the West. Leading Panslavists took the dogma of "two worlds" a step forward by their insistence that Romano-Germanic Europe was not only basically different from Greco-Slavic Europe but that the former was unalterably inimical to the latter by a historic necessity transcending the human will.

"It is time we understood," wrote Ivan Aksakov in the first issue of his *Den'* in October, 1861, "that the often instinctive hatred of the West for the Slavic Orthodox world springs [not from transient political rivalries but] from other deeply hidden causes. These causes lie in the antagonism of two antithetical spiritual and moral principles and in the envy of a senescent world toward a new world to which belongs the future."[6] This is why, Aksakov charged, a spent West which has already fulfilled its glorious mission in world history could now only try to obstruct Russia's material and moral might in the hope of thereby preventing the rise of a new world in Eastern Europe. Where but in this deep-seated hatred could one find a rational explanation, he demanded, for Europe's cold indifference to the fate of Orthodox Christians in the Balkans who were defending their faith and freedom against the barbarism and tyranny of Islam?[7] Western Europeans did not regard "the Slavic nationality" as an entity worthy of respect, Aksakov declared in his newspaper *Moskva* (Moscow) in 1866. Rather they looked down upon the Slav as an *anima vilis*, as the plebeian of European mankind and mere *Düngmittel* (fertilizer) for the civilizing mission of the Romano-Germanic spirit. As for Russia itself, Aksakov wrote in his short-lived newspaper *Moskvich* (Muscovite), "The very fact of its existence is considered a fault, a sin, a crime against Europe."[8]

The Panslavist poet Tiutchev warned in 1864:

Between Russia and the West there can be no alliance, either on the basis of interest or for the sake of any principle. . . . There does not exist in the whole West a single interest, a single principle which does not plot evil against Russia, especially against its future, and which would not attempt to do it harm. And this is why the only, the *only*, policy for Russia with respect to the Western states is not an alliance with this or that state, but disunion, a divorce from them.

[6] Ivan Aksakov, *Sochineniia*, Vol. I: *Slavianskii vopros, 1860-1886* (Moscow, 1886), p. 5.

[7] Cited by Nil Popov, *Istoriia Slavianskago blagotvoritel'nago komiteta v Moskvie: vtoroe piatilietie, 1863-1867* (Moscow, 1872), p. 200. Originally published in *Den'*, No. 35, 1862.

[8] Ivan Aksakov, *Sochineniia*, Vol. VII: *Obshcheevropeiskaia politika, 1860-1886* (Moscow, 1887), p. 180. Originally published in *Moskvich*, January 26, 1868.

This policy was described by Tuitchev as "malevolent neutrality."[9]

"The mutual hatred [between West and East] is so profound," wrote Vladimir Lamanskii, "their principles and interests so incompatible, that reconciliation and agreement between the two enemy camps may not be expected until after a struggle and the decisive defeat of one of the adversaries."[10]

Nicholas Danilevskii's entire work *Rossiia i Evropa* was an attempt to answer the question asked at the beginning of his book: "Why is Europe inimical to Russia?" The immediate circumstance which gave Danilevskii the occasion to pose this question was the Prussian war with Denmark over Schleswig-Holstein in 1864. Danilevskii perceived a painful paradox in the reluctance of the European Concert to protect little Denmark from the unwarranted aggression of Prussia and their enthusiasm in rushing to Turkey's aid in 1853 when Russia had gone to war, he said, to preserve the sanctity of treaties and the religious freedom of Orthodox Christians. "Whence this indifference towards a humane, liberal Denmark and that sympathy for a barbaric and despotic Turkey?" Danilevskii wondered, and then concluded, "This is not just an accident, nor a journalistic escapade, nor the striving of some particular faction, but the collective diplomatic action of all Europe."[11] Prussia's war with Denmark was for the Western Europeans but a family quarrel; the war with Turkey involved Russia, an outsider to which Europe was inimical.

Danilevskii professed failure to see how Russia could have provoked such unfriendliness. He so generously justified the actions of his own country that he found it impossible to accept any of the conventional reasons for Western Europe's animosity. He insisted that the Romano-Germanic West could not really fear Russian

[9] Cited by K. Pigarev, "F. I. Tiutchev i problemy vneshnei politiki tsarskoi Rossii," *Literaturnoe Nasledstvo*, XX (1935), 205-6, from an unpublished letter written by Tiutchev to his daughter, Anna, on June 26, 1864, and which was found in the Muranovskii archives. Anna was Ivan Aksakov's wife.

[10] Cited by G. Kniazev, "Slavianskii 'vostochnyi' vopros v opredielenii V. I. Lamanskago," *Zhurnal Ministerstva Narodnago Prosvieshcheniia* (September, 1916), pp. 4-5.

[11] N. Ia. Danilevskii, *Rossiia i Evropa: vzgliad na kul'turnyia i politicheskiia otnosheniia slavianskago mira k germano-romanskomu* (5th ed., St. Petersburg, 1895), p. 3.

aggression, since in Europe Russian armies had consistently fought for European and not Russian interests, notably in the Napoleonic wars and the revolution of 1848 in Austria. Nor could he discover in Russian imperialism an adequate cause for Europe's hostility, since Russia took only its due on time-honored grounds of ethnic kinship, settlement, compensation, security, or civilizing mission! Certainly, Danilevskii argued, the Russian conscience was clearer than that of any Western empire. Refuting the Western charge that Russia was the foe of freedom and enlightenment, Danilevskii pointed to Catherine II and Alexander I as the most enlightened monarchs of Europe. Did anyone suppose, he asked, that the abolition of serfdom in Russia had made Europe any more kindly disposed toward Russia? Finally, there was the excuse of Western Europeans that they did not know or understand Russia. For this argument the proud Russian had only sarcasm. "Why is it," he asked in mock wonder, "that Europe—which knows everything from the Sanscrit language to Iroquois dialects, from the law of the division of constellations to the constitution of microscopic organisms—is ignorant only of Russia? . . . Europe does not know because she does not wish to know."

What, then, was the real reason for Western Europe's hatred of Russia?

The fact is that Europe does not recognize us for her own. She sees in Russia and generally in the Slavs something alien to her and at the same time something which she cannot use as mere raw material which she could exploit for profit as she does in China, India, Africa, the greater part of the Americas, and so on—material which could be formed and shaped in her own form and image.[12]

Thus it was not in wars, imperialism, balance of power, or the suppression of liberty that the reason for European enmity toward Russia lay, Danilevskii concluded. The real reason lay "in the unknown depths of those flaming sympathies and antipathies which constitute the historic instinct of nations, leading them . . . to an aim unknown even to themselves."[13]

Western Europe hated Russia, Pogodin believed, precisely be-

[12] *Ibid.*, p. 50.
[13] *Ibid.*

cause they were two worlds apart. "One must only understand that West is West, and East is East!" he exclaimed at the beginning of the Crimean War, a year before Rudyard Kipling was born! "Our climate is different from that of the West, we have a different terrain, a different temperament, character, different blood, different physiognomy, different outlook, different ways of thinking, different beliefs, hopes, desires, pleasures, different relationships, different conditions, a different history, everything different!"[14]

"East and West—these are not geographical terms," wrote Ivan Aksakov, "but qualitative terms which denote a difference in cultural principles which have become active forces in the history of mankind."[15]

"Is Russia European?" Danilevskii asked in the title to the third chapter of his *Rossiia i Evropa*, and replied, "Unfortunately or fortunately, for better or worse, no, it is not." Like Aksakov, he pointed out that the question had nothing to do with geography, that the Ural boundary was just a convenient metaphor, and that science knew only a Eurasia. "Europe is the arena of Germano-Latin civilization. The words are synonymous."[16] The Russian people took no part, he said, in the development of feudalism, Roman Catholicism, Scholasticism, the Reformation or the Counter-Reformation, or any of the great currents which swept across the history of Western Europe. Sharing neither in the benefits nor in the vices springing from these currents, Danilevskii asserted, Russia neither belonged to Europe nor did it have reason to entertain any such pretensions. He expressed only scorn for those of his compatriots who, out of a false feeling of inferiority, claimed that Russia was European by adoption if not by birthright. In rebuttal he professed his inability to detect any trace of parental tenderness in Europe's relations with Russia, nor did he consider Europeanization by adoption possible for Russia. East could not become West because they were separated by historicultural principles which were stronger than the human will, principles which shaped the human will.

[14] M. P. Pogodin, *Sobranie sochinenii*, Vol. III: *Istoriko-politicheskiia pis'ma i zapiski v prodolzhenii krymskoi voiny, 1853-1856* (Moscow, 1874), pp. 252-53.
[15] Aksakov, *Sochineniia*, I, 176.
[16] Danilevskii, *Rossiia i Evropa*, p. 58.

Before Danilevskii, Panslavists, like the Slavophiles, had expressed the difference between Western and Eastern Europe by calling them separate "worlds." In their vocabulary a "world" denoted a cultural system which, with all its inner diversity, nevertheless constituted a whole made up of interrelated and connected parts, the sum total of which were self-contained and distinct from other cultural systems.[17] Lamanskii was vague as to the number of such "worlds" in existence, but, having inherited the Slavophile emphasis on religion, he was inclined to identify culture with religion. Hence he spoke of the "Confucian, Buddhist, Shamanist and Moslem East" as being four "individual, independent worlds."[18]

As to how these "worlds" came about and developed, even before Danilevskii, a few Panslavists of the Slavophile tradition had expressed the belief that the process involved was not a fortuitous one. "We are bound to recognize the fundamental and indubitable truth," wrote Alexander Hilferding in 1862, "that history is not a simple combination of accidents. . . . Directly or indirectly, the history of a people is created by its own organic laws which directly determine its inner development."[19] Aksakov observed similarly, "just as a philologist who studies the language of a people is made aware of unconscious laws which govern a folk language, so the historian can find laws in the historical development of a people."[20] Neither Panslavist ever formulated the historical laws in whose existence he professed to believe.

It was Nicholas Danilevskii who gave the Russian Panslavist ideology its first and only systematic formulation in his book *Rossiia i Evropa*, first published in serial form in 1869. In a heroic effort to endow Panslavism with that feeling of certainty which stems from the belief that one is allied to Eternity, Danilevskii worked out a remarkable pseudo-scientific theory. Taking his cue from the field of natural science, in which he could claim some competence, the zealous Panslavist developed a theory of human

[17] A. D. Gradovskii, "Pervyie Slavianofily," *Sobranie sochinenii*, VI (St. Petersburg, 1901), 180.

[18] Kniazev, "Slavianskii 'vostochnyi' vopros v opredielenii V. I. Lamanskago," *Zhurnal Ministerstva Narodnago Prosvieshcheniia*, p. 26.

[19] A. F. Hilferding, *Sobranie sochinenii*, Vol. I: *Ocherk istorii Chekhii* (St. Petersburg, 1868), p. 345.

[20] Aksakov, *Sochineniia*, I, 180.

civilizations classed according to entities which he called "cultural-historical types."

Danilevskii rejected the Hegelian basis of Slavophilism which regarded universal history as the unilinear development of an Absolute Idea through successive stages. Commenting on this aspect of Danilevksii's theory, Pitirim A. Sorokin observed:

Just as botany and zoology gave up the artificial unilinear classification of plants and animals and replaced it by natural classification into a number of different types (genera and species) of organisms, each of which represents not a step in a unilinear hierarchic development on the ladder of gradual perfection of organisms, but rather entirely different plans of organization, each perfect in its own way; just as there are not one but many architectural styles each of which is perfect in its own manner; so also there are not one but many civilizations or historico-cultural types, each perfect in its own way and all together manifesting the infinitely rich creative genius of humanity.[21]

It was not mere chance which prompted Danilevskii to borrow the terminology of botany and zoology in explaining his theory. He actually believed that there was a parallel between individual living organisms and human societies, as he made clear in the following remarkable passage:

All living things, individually and collectively . . . are given a certain span of life subject to an exhaustion from which they must die. Geology and paleontology demonstrate that for various species, genera and orders of living things there was a time of genesis, highest development, gradual decline and, finally, complete disappearance. How and why this occurs no one knows, though various explanations have been sought. In substance, this aging, this process of senescence experienced by species, genera and orders is no more wondrous than the death of separate individuals, the real cause of which also nobody knows or understands. History speaks the same for peoples: they too are born, achieve various degrees of development, grow old, become senile, and die—not only of external causes. External causes, as in individual persons, in most cases only hasten the death of the ill and weakened body

---

[21] Pitirim A. Sorokin, *Social Philosophies of an Age of Crisis* (Boston, 1950), p. 56. Sorokin's third chapter, which he devotes entirely to Danilevskii, provides a very convenient summary of Danilevskii's social theories.

which, if in possession of its strength, its youth or virility, would very well have withstood their harmful effects.[22]

The modern reader will readily recognize the similarity between Danilevskii's organismic explanation of the rise and decline of human societies and the better known theories of Oswald Spengler and Arnold J. Toynbee's interpretation of the genesis, growth, breakdown, and disintegration of civilizations.[23]

By Danilevskii's definition, "cultural-historical types correspond to the great linguistic-ethnographic families or races of mankind,"[24] of which he recognized ten major divisions: (1) Egyptian, (2) Chinese, (3) Assyro-Babylonian-Phoenician, Chaldean, or Ancient-Semitic, (4) Hindu, (5) Iranian, (6) Hebrew, (7) Greek, (8) Roman, (9) Neo-Semitic or Arabic, and (10) Germano-Latin or European. Oddly enough, Danilevskii failed to include the Slavic cultural-historical type, probably because he believed that it had not yet come into its own in world history. Although he recognized the existence of other cultural types in history, he dismissed the two early American civilizations—the Aztec and the Inca—as having died a violent death, whereas the Huns, Mongols, and Turks were described as "negative agencies," mere comets in this historical solar system which, having helped dying civilizations to pass from the scene, returned to the nothingness from which they came.[25] All other inhabitants of the earth were, for Danilevskii, only "ethnographic material," nonhistorical peoples which played neither a positive nor a negative role in world history, possessing no historical individuality or having lost it as remnants of decayed civilizations.

True to his scientific inclinations, though not at all to his scientific training, Danilevskii devised five "laws" which offer a convenient summary of his views:

[22] Danilevskii, *Rossiia i Evropa*, pp. 76-77.
[23] The writer has been able to find no evidence that Danilevskii's theories directly influenced either Spengler or Toynbee, or any of their sources of inspiration. The German translation of *Rossiia i Evropa* was published by H. Köhler as *Russland und Europa* in Jena in 1917. Another German translation was published under the same title by K. Nötzel in Stuttgart in 1920.
[24] Danilevskii, *Rossiia i Evropa*, p. 130.
[25] *Ibid.*, pp. 91 ff.

Law I. Every race or family of peoples identified by a separate language or by a group of languages sufficiently similar so that their kinship may be directly perceived without profound philological research constitutes an original cultural-historical type if it is generally capable of historic development in accord with its own spiritual tasks and has already emerged from infancy.

Law II. In order that the civilization which is peculiar to an original cultural-historical type may actually be born and develop, it is necessary that the peoples belonging to it enjoy political independence.

Law III. The basic principles of the civilization of one cultural-historical type are not transmissible to the peoples of another type. Each type creates these for itself, under the greater or lesser influence of preceding or contemporary alien civilizations.

Law IV. The civilization peculiar to each cultural-historical type achieves completeness, variety, and richness only when the various ethnographic elements which make it up comprise a federation or a political system of states, without being absorbed by a single political body but rather availing themselves of their independence.

Law V. The course of development of cultural-historical types is very similar to that of those perennial monocarpic plants whose period of growth lasts indefinitely, but whose period of florescence and fruition is relatively short and exhausts their vital forces once and for all time.[26]

When stripped of their scientific verbiage, these laws converge upon the simple idea that peoples whose cultural kinship is demonstrated by the cognate character of their languages should form a political federation which will preserve inner diversity within a general cultural unity. Danilevskii left no doubt that these laws governing cultural-historical types were for him no mere statements of scientific observation but a concrete proposal for bringing to the fore the one cultural-historical type which had not yet had its day on the stage of history—the Slavic. He set out to demonstrate with the authority of science what the Slavophiles before him had already proclaimed with the voice of philosophy—that the Romano-Germanic civilization of contemporary Western Europe was in the final stages of dissolution, and that the Slavs were on the threshold of a glorious future.

[26] *Ibid.,* pp. 95-96.

To be sure, the Russian prophets of Western doom could well be embarrassed by the obvious fact that the Europe of their time appeared to be far from the point of death. Danilevskii argued, however, that new civilizations always arose precisely at the time when the light of the older civilizations which they were to replace was shining most brilliantly. "The very abundance of the achievements of European civilization in our nineteenth century," he confidently proclaimed, "is a sign that the creative power which produced them has already begun to wane and to drift downward in its course."[27] Having disposed of his Western European rival, the Panslavist declared, "Thus I conclude that the development of an independent Slavic culture is not only generally necessary, but now expressly timely."[28]

Danilevskii's use of the word "necessary" must be noted here. As in English, so in Russian the word "necessary" (*neobkhodimo*) can mean either something predetermined or something which is highly desirable but dependent upon human choice and human will for its achievement. Taken in the context of Danilevskii's five "laws" on cultural-historical types, Danilevskii's statement that the development of an independent Slavic culture was "necessary" would mean that he regarded such a development as historically predetermined. Yet his emphasis on a program of Slavic unification, which will be discussed in the final chapter of this study, suggests that he believed that human choice and human will were required to realize his cherished aim. One may therefore conclude that Danilevskii's scheme of history was a confused mixture of deterministic and voluntaristic elements.

Danilevskii urged his fellow Slavs to understand that they were on the threshold of their glory. If the Slavs failed now to take up their mission and to assume their rightful place in world history, Danilevskii warned, then their chance would be gone forever, and the "thousand years of ethnographic preparation" by a Russia which had maintained its own state existence and had achieved national might at such historic sacrifices would all have been in vain, a "soap bubble." "And thus," the Russian Panslavist solemnly

[27] *Ibid.*, p. 180.
[28] *Ibid.*, p. 183.

announced, *"for every Slav: Russian, Czech, Serb, Croat, Slovene, Bulgar (I should also like to include the Pole)—after God and His holy Church—the idea of Slavdom should constitute a lofty ideal, above freedom, above science, above learning, above all worldly riches*, for not one of these will be achieved without the realization . . . of a spiritually, nationally and politically autochthonic, independent Slavdom."[29]

III

It is a legitimate cause for wonderment that, in the face of Slavic disunity, the Russian Panslavists could have fabricated an ideology on the basis of such a chimera as the unity of the Slavic world. A program of frank Russian imperialism defended in the terms of any of the traditional justifications—security against a hostile West, the protection of Orthodox Christians, the need for outlets such as the Dardanelles—would have been at least understandable. While the Russian Panslavists abandoned none of these arguments, they steadfastly maintained with unmistakable sincerity that the Slavic world ought to be one politically because it was, supposedly, one culturally.

To recount the many differences which mark off the peoples of Eastern Europe one from another would be an unedifying tale, and Russian Panslavists were painfully conscious of these differences. How, then, was it possible for a Russian Panslavist to maintain that Eastern Europe constituted a natural and separate entity? As Danilevskii, for one, readily admitted, it was most difficult to ascertain the distinguishing features of any cultural-historical type inasmuch as these features were qualitative and not quantitative. Moreover, though they might characterize the type, these features would not necessarily hold true of all the individuals within that type. Some features found in one cultural-historical type might also be encountered in another such type. The only workable approach, Danilevskii claimed, was to concentrate on those distinctive features which were characteristic of a given cultural-historical type throughout its history. Only then could one be

[29] *Ibid.*, p. 133. The italics are Danilevskii's.

reasonably certain that a given feature was characteristic of the type as a whole and that individual divergences constituted exceptions; that this feature was independent of temporary or fortuitous circumstances characteristic of only one period of development; and that this feature was materially significant as a distinguishing factor.[30]

There was one approach to this problem which Danilevskii and his fellow Panslavists rejected: any of the various theories of biological racial classification coupled with the concept of racial superiority, which were to have a serious influence on Western thought, particularly after the mid-nineteenth century. While, it is true, some Panslavist comments implied that the Slavs as a whole belonged to a single physical group, this contention is met with only rarely.[31]

The leading representative of the Slavophiles, Ivan Aksakov, dismissed the importance of physical or racial kinship, as is evident from a letter to the Czech leader, František Rieger. "Not the physiological characteristics alone of the stock, or even language, constitutes nationality and the right to an independent existence," Aksakov wrote. "Nationality in history is a predominantly moral and spiritual conception. What is the good of preserving physiological distinctions if the distinctiveness of the spirit has not been preserved, if the people lacks a moral personality?"[32] In this apparent reproach to the Germanized Czechs what Aksakov rejected was not the existence of a Slavic physical unity but the importance of such a unity.

Nicholas Danilevskii's lengthy *Rossiia i Evropa* devoted only five pages to the question of physical or racial kinship, and these five pages dealt solely with his adverse criticism of the Retzius classification.[33] The author was particularly sensitive to the impli-

---

[30] *Ibid.*, p. 190.

[31] For example, in his "Epistle to the Serbs," published in 1860, A. S. Khomiakov assured the Serbian people, "Dear to us is your external appearance, which witnesses to your blood kinship with us." See "K Serbam poslanie iz Moskvy," *Russkii Arkhiv*, III (1876), 104.

[32] Aksakov, *Sochineniia*, I, 311.

[33] The Swedish scientist Anders Adolf Retzius devised an anthropological classification which was in great vogue in mid-nineteenth century Europe. He grouped all humans according to head form and facial angle.

cation (not Retzius's) that the Slavs, being of the brachycephalic or short-headed group, were less capable of achieving a high culture than the dolichocephalic or long-headed group, to which most of the Aryan peoples belonged. The short-heads, he maintained, had been erroneously considered inferior perhaps simply because circumstances had not favored the establishment by them of a more advanced culture. Danilevskii advanced three contentions with respect to the Retzius classification, any one of which, he declared, would be acceptable to Slavic *amour-propre*: the Retzius system was artificial, being based on an insufficient number of criteria; the Slavs actually belonged at the top of the racial hierarchy by virtue of being straight-jawed short-heads (the orthognathic brachycephalic group); or the Retzius system did not really establish a vertical hierarchy at all, but rather a horizontal arrangement of races.[34] One need not go into Danilevskii's reasoning here. From the general tone of his argument, it may be taken that Danilevskii favored the first of these three propositions, threw in the second as a challenge rather than as a personal belief, and added the third just to be on the safe side of science.

Undoubtedly one of the reasons why some Russian Panslavists found the argument of physical or racial kinship distasteful was because the Russians themselves were the victims of propaganda, particularly Polish propaganda, based on this very theory. Certain Polish scholars, notably F. H. Duchiński, had no little success in Western Europe with the charge that the "Muscovites" were really a Slavic-speaking mélange of Slavs, Mongols, and Finns, whereas the real Russian Slavs were the Ukrainians and the White Russians.[35] This so-called Turanian Theory gave vogue to the adage, "Scratch a Russian, and find a Tartar."

This Polish contention provoked a rather curious bit of retaliation on the part of at least two Russian Panslavists. During the Polish insurrection of 1863 Professor Pogodin asserted that the

[34] Danilevskii, *Rossiia i Evropa*, p. 189.

[35] Alfred Fischel, *Der Panslawismus bis zum Weltkrieg* (Stuttgart and Berlin, 1919), p. 371. Note F. H. Duchiński's book, *Pologne et Ruthénie, origines slaves*, published in 1861; also E. Rykaczewski's preface to the French translation of Joachim Lelewel's *Histoire de la Lithuanie et de la Ruthénie jusqu'à leur union définitive avec la Pologne conclue à Lublin en 1569* (Paris and Leipzig, 1861), pp. v-vi, for Polish statements of the Turanian Theory.

Polish gentry were really of Celtic or Latin origin and had never
united racially with the Polish Slavs.[36] Professor Orest Miller
advanced the opinion that the Polish gentry were possibly of
Sarmatian origin and claimed to discern a noticeable difference in
external physical appearance between the Polish gentry and the
Polish peasantry. This is an inverse parallel to de Gobineau's theory
of the Germanic origin of the French nobility. Whereas de Gobineau was trying to prove the superiority of his Frankish patrician
stock, the Russian Panslavists were seeking to explain why the
Polish gentry used their own peasantry so cruelly. While de Gobineau postulated the innate superiority of the Teutonic race, Pogodin
and Miller were not seeking to prove the superiority or inferiority
of anyone. Pogodin and Miller were merely trying to "prove" that
there was a difference in the ethnic origin of the Polish nobility and
Polish people which might explain why the former were leading
the latter to ruin. It is noteworthy that other Russian Panslavists
ignored this argument.

What criteria, then, did various Russian Panslavists employ in
their attempt to demonstrate the unity of the Slavic "world" or
the Slavic "cultural-historical type"? However much they differed
in their emphasis on this or that criterion, all of them, before and
after Danilevskii, agreed that racial unity was a cultural concept
based largely on spiritual and social homogeneity.

When Hilferding, for example, spoke of the "moral unity" of
the Slavs, he was not referring to national characteristics in the
ordinary and vulgarized sense. He was indignant at publicists, especially German publicists, who attributed to races such supposedly
popular traits as courage, parsimony, love of strong drink, or talent
for music. Hilferding insisted that racial character was determined
not by such qualities but by fundamental spiritual and social concepts. "Moral qualities change (through the influence of education
and so on)," he wrote, "but these concepts are constant."[37] In a
eulogy of Hilferding delivered before the St. Petersburg Section

---

[36] M. P. Pogodin, "Pol'skii vopros," *Stat'i politicheskiia i Pol'skii vopros, 1856-
1867* (Moscow, 1876), p. 330.

[37] *Pervyia 15 liet sushchestvovaniia S.-Peterburgskago Slavianskago blagotvoritel'nago obshchestva* (St. Petersburg, 1883), p. 219; originally published in *Golos*,
No. 54, 1873.

of the Slavic Benevolent Committee in 1873, Bestuzhev-Riumin made the following comment with respect to Hilferding's point: "Certainly everything changes in the course of time: customs, morals, and economic relations, but nevertheless there remains a certain something [*chto-to takoe*] which constitutes the essence of a people's life, and that is a concept which expresses itself in one way or another, despite all the changes in the fortunes of any people."[38]

Danilevskii also tried his hand at defining the ingredients which went into the composition of national character. Though his classification had the merit of orderliness, it hardly added any substance. All cultural-historical types, he asserted, could be differentiated one from another on the basis of three criteria: the peculiar ethnic characteristics which expressed themselves in the life of a given cultural-historical type; the "higher moral principle by which alone the fruitful development of any civilization is able to take place" and on which the learning, art, and social and political order of that civilization are based; and the historical experience peculiar to the peoples belonging to a given cultural-historical type.[39]

Hilferding was an especially active exponent of the idea that the distinctive feature of the true Slavic order was communality based on an agrarian way of life. He pointed to the Russian and Balkan peasant communes (the *obshchina* and the *zadruga*), to the similarity of kinship terms denoting the various members of the large complex family, as well as to the similarity of words dealing with local government in all the Slavic languages, as evidence of a common primitive social order. Hilferding thought of the peasant commune as a moral union ideally founded on the equality and the harmony of all of its members. Inasmuch as the land was owned cooperatively by the commune, the Slavic peasant was supposed to have enjoyed a material security which endowed him from time immemorial with what Hilferding described as "the consciousness of moral independence and the feeling of human dignity."[40] The

[38] *Ibid.*

[39] Danilevskii, *Rossiia i Evropa*, p. 104.

[40] A. F. Hilferding, *Sobranie sochinenii*, Vol. II: *Stat'i po sovremennym voprosam slavianskim* (St. Petersburg, 1868), p. 460.

Slavic peasant commune, he claimed, preserved the sanctity of Slavic family life and safeguarded true Slavic social democracy. The commune solved one of man's oldest problems—the conflict between the natural freedom of each individual and the social authority which limited that freedom. "The Slavic race did not wish to limit personal freedom by the authority of the aristocratic preeminence of some members of society, as did the Germanic peoples," Hilferding claimed, "but sought to limit the personal freedom of each member of society through the moral authority of the unanimous will of all of its members. Freedom and unanimity, this is the real essence of Slavic life."[41]

Hilferding chose especially the Germans to demonstrate the fundamental divergences between Western and Slavic social principles. Whereas the prehistoric Slavic family lived together (as proved by the use of patronymics as place names) and owned land in common, he argued, the German family group lived not in a collective village but in scattered homesteads. Whereas the land belonged to the commune among the Slavs, the Germans had very early adopted the principle of personal private property, and out of this emerged the practice of inheritance by primogeniture, which was unknown in the Slavic East.[42] Thus inequalities arose in the Western social structure, and harmony of purpose turned to competition. Unanimity vanished, and brute force was elevated to a social principle under feudalism. Later in parliamentary governments force was given legal form as the rule of the majority—and the majority itself was ruled by an aristocracy based on wealth, while everybody was ruled by the principle of individual self-interest.

Out of Western individualism there had emerged what Danilevskii called one of the most characteristic principles of the Romano-Germanic cultural-historical type—force (Danilevskii used the German expression, *Gewaltsamkeit*)—which rested on the premise that one individual was superior to another. In Western political life, he charged, this principle had led to the oppression of one

---

[41] A. F. Hilferding, *Chiem podderzhivaetsia pravoslavnaia viera u iuzhnykh slavian?* (Moscow, 1861), p. 21.

[42] A. F. Hilferding, *Sobranie sochinenii*, Vol. IV: *Istoriia Baltiiskikh Slavian* (St. Petersburg, 1874), pp. 68-69.

people by another. In Western social life, it resulted in a hierarchy in which the upper classes ruled over the lower classes. In Western religious life, it led either to the authoritarianism of the Vatican or to the anarchic individualism of Protestantism. Just as Western Christendom began its existence as a separate body by papal usurpation of the prerogatives of the entire ecumenical Church, Danilevskii charged, so the Western body politic, the Holy Roman Empire, began with Charlemagne's usurpation of the prerogatives of the Roman emperor who was even then sitting on his rightful throne in Constantinople. And both Western Christendom and the Western body politic had since continued in their application of force as a basic principle—as the Waldensians and Albigensians, the victims of St. Bartholomew's Eve, Michael Servetus, the negroes of Africa, the victims of the guillotine, and countless others would testify at the Last Judgment.[43] In the West, Danilevskii continued, all progress comes as the result of conflict between opposing parties—whether that conflict be a peaceful one, as in parliamentary states, or a violent one, as during the Reformation or the French Revolution.[44]

Not so in the Orthodox Slavic East, Danilevskii claimed. The Slavs did not need the Philosophes of eighteenth-century France to persuade them to be tolerant. The Slavs were naturally tolerant because their social order was based on the equality of all its members. Even the non-Orthodox Czechs have always been the victims and not the perpetrators of intolerant acts. The only "sad exception" in the Slavic world, Danilevskii contended, were the Westernized Poles. It is interesting to note how Danilevskii glossed over religious and political intolerance in Russia. He insisted that acts of persecution against Old Believers and sectarians in Russia were but "pale copies" of the Western European auto-da-fé and witchhunt. Furthermore, he maintained, this example of Russian intolerance had two separate phases: the religious phase before Peter, and the political phase which began with that monarch. Danilevskii explained the religious phase by attributing it to the influence of the Westernized Kievan clergy which then predominated in

---

[43] Danilevskii, *Rossiia i Evropa*, p. 191.
[44] *Ibid.*, p. 202.

Moscow. He attributed the political phase to the Westernization of Russia's government under Peter and his Germanized successors, who disliked the Old Believers' opposition to their alien innovations. In both cases the source of the evil lay in the West.[45] It must be noted that Danilevskii ignored the question of the status of the subject nationalities of the Russian Empire in his discussion of Russian intolerance.

As for Slavic social equality, Professor Michael Pogodin took pride in the fact that there were in the Russia of his day only about three hundred titled families, of which hardly one twentieth were of pre-Petrine stock. "All of us have an equal voice," he confidently proclaimed, "we all have equal rights, each of us can tomorrow assume the highest post in the government on the same level with the beloved descendants of Rurik and Gedimin."[46] His colleague, Orest Miller, took pride in Khomiakov's declaration: "We shall be, as we always have been, the democrats among the other families of Europe." True, Russia also suffered from certain social inequalities imported from the West, Khomiakov admitted, but nobody would ever succeed in infecting the Russian people with a spirit of contempt for their fellow men or with the feeling of superiority over other peoples.[47]

Another cornerstone of the Panslavist ideology was the dogma that only the Orthodox Church was truly consonant with the Slavic way of life. Undoubtedly this was one of the most troublesome legacies which Panslavism received from Slavophilism. The Slavophiles' primary emphasis on Orthodoxy is comparatively easy to understand. Their principal concern was Russia, and Russia was Orthodox. The Panslavists' insistence on Orthodoxy is more difficult to explain. One would have expected them to avoid applying this Slavophile tenet of the romantic forties to a program which looked to the unification of all Slavs, whether Orthodox or not. After all, according to the statistics of the Panslavists, there were 19,628,442 Roman Catholic Slavs, 3,147,429 Greek Catholic or

[45] *Ibid.*, p. 200.
[46] M. P. Pogodin, *Russkii*, Nos. 5-6, March 27, 1867, p. 66.
[47] Cited by Orest Miller, "Osnovy ucheniia pervonachal'nykh slavianofilov," *Russkaia Mysl'*, Book 3 (March, 1880), p. 27.

Uniat Slavs, 1,436,000 Protestant Slavs, and 900,000 Moslem Slavs in the 1870's.[48] From a practical viewpoint alone—not to speak of the tolerance which was supposed to be a natural characteristic of the Slavs—it would seem that a program of Slavic unification would have attempted to avoid the inclusion of religious unity as a plank in its platform. Such was not the case.

"The Eastern world is the Orthodox-Slavic world, whose representative is Russia," Ivan Aksakov declared with finality.[49] "To be a Latin means to belong to the Latin Church, to have Rome as one's spiritual fatherland, to be in spiritual union with the whole Latin Western world, to be joined, to a certain extent, with its moral and historic destiny. To be Orthodox means to be in spiritual union with the Eastern Church, with the Greco-Slavic world. Through the force of this deep spiritual difference the European world is divided into two halves—East and West."[50] To Iurii Samarin it was equally clear that "Catholicism is undoubtedly as much a manifestation of the Latin element in the realm of religion as Protestantism is a Germanic manifestation."[51] Vladimir Lamanskii defined Western Europe as a land mass which he divided into six general areas: of these he designated three—Scandinavia, Great Britain, and Germany with Holland—as Protestant, and three—Italy, France with Belgium, and Spain with Portugal—as Roman Catholic. For him as well, Slavic Europe was Orthodox Europe.[52] Danilevskii was no less adamant on this point. "The difference in the cultural principles of the Russian people and the majority of the other Slavic peoples [*sic*] from the Germano-Roman peoples consists of the fact," he stated, "that the former confess Orthodoxy and the latter confess Roman Catholicism or Protestantism."[53]

[48] A. S. Budilovich, "Statisticheskiia tablitsy raspredieleniia Slavian," *Slavianskii ezhegodnik; Kalendar' na 1876 god (visokosnyi)*, ed. by N. P. Zaderatskii (Kiev, 1876), pp. 237-39.

[49] Aksakov, *Sochineniia*, I, 176.

[50] *Ibid.*, p. 175.

[51] Iurii F. Samarin, "Dva slova o narodnosti v naukie," *Russkaia Besieda*, I (1856), 37.

[52] Vladimir Lamanskii, *Ob istoricheskom izuchenii Greko-slavianskago mira v Evropie* (St. Petersburg, 1871), p. 42.

[53] Danilevskii, *Rossiia i Evropa*, p. 212.

Lamanskii claimed that only ecumenical, conciliar Orthodoxy coincided with the natural principles of the Slavic society. As he pointed out:

The predominance of the rural commune and the peasantry among the Slavs is not to be explained by ethnographic characteristics alone, though they may have some influence, but it is founded chiefly on the uniqueness of the cultural order of the Greco-Slavic world, on the Orthodox teachings regarding the Church which are in such profound disagreement with the Romano-Germanic or Catholic-Protestant teachings. With the triumph of Romanism among the Western Slavs, the rural commune and the peasantry declined. In purely Orthodox countries an aristocracy cannot long survive, let alone develop.[54]

Hilferding expressed the same opinion in May, 1860:

In my opinion, the strength of the Orthodox faith among the Southern Slavs lies in the fact that the very essence of Orthodoxy is fully in accord with the essence of the Slavic spirit and way of life. . . . Wherein lies the essence and peculiar character of the organization of the Orthodox Church if not in the fact that it recognizes human freedom within itself? It limits that freedom and preserves unity not by the force of an external authority, but by the natural force of the unanimity and consent of all of its members.[55]

The historical argument in favor of Orthodoxy as the true Slavic religion postulated that all of the Slavic peoples (with the possible exception of the Poles) had received Christianity from Orthodox Byzantium; only subsequently had some of them fallen under the sway of Roman Catholicism, later of Protestantism or Islam. "In the domain of religion," A. S. Budilovich declared, "the unity of the Slavs had already once been nearly achieved. There once existed an all-Slavic Church, but not all had remained faithful to it."[56]

To buttress this conception the Russian Panslavists propagated

[54] Lamanskii, *Ob istoricheskom*, p. 47.

[55] A. F. Hilferding, "Chiem podderzhivaetsia pravoslavnaia viera u iuzhnykh slavian?" *Stat'i po sovremennym voprosam slavianskim*, in *Sobranie sochinenii*, II, 191 ff. Also published as a separate brochure in Moscow, 1861.

[56] A. S. Budilovich, "O sovremennom polozhenii i vzaimnykh otnosheniiakh Zapadnykh i Iuzhnykh Slavian," included in the minutes for November 3, 1874, of the St. Petersburg Section of the Slavic Benevolent Committee in *Pervyia 15 liet*, p. 273. Also published in the *Slavianskii Sbornik*, I (1875), 585-604.

a veritable cult of Saints Cyril and Methodius, "the Protopraeceptors of the Slavs." In these two Greek brothers from Salonica and in their conversion of Slavs of the Balkans and of the Great Moravian Empire, the Russian Panslavists found historical allies. Thanks to the efforts especially of Michael Pogodin and Ivan Aksakov as well as to the blessings of the Most Holy Synod of the Russian Orthodox Church, the first in a series of annual commemorations of the "Apostles to the Slavs" was observed on May 11, 1862, in the chapel of the University of Moscow. It was ironic that the Moscow Panslavist sponsors could not find a single icon of Saints Cyril and Methodius in all Russia and had to rummage through piles of medieval manuscripts before unearthing a liturgy to the two saints, in a twelfth-century service book. Not since medieval times had Slavic Russia observed the feast of the Protopraeceptors of the Slavs and the Equals of the Apostles![57]

The Panslavic character of this religious ceremony was greatly enhanced by the presence of a most significant relic—a finger of St. Cyril, presumably from the hand that had written out for the illiterate Slavs their first alphabet. Through this symbol the Russian Panslavists emphasized the linguistic unity of the Slavs.[58]

Russian Panslavists made much of the cult of Saints Cyril and Methodius. "Cyril and Methodius," wrote Hilferding in 1862, "have had the remarkable fate of not yet having been relegated to the *past* even after a thousand years. . . . Standing at the threshold of the historical life of the Slavic race, these men were the heralds of its spiritual unification. . . . For both the Southern and the Western Slavs they are more than historical figures, the founders of their culture; they are also a symbol of Slavic self-awareness and unity."[59]

[57] Aksakov, *Sochineniia*, I, 13 and 17.

[58] Josef Jirásek, *Rusko a my; dějiny vztahů československo-ruských od nejstarších dob až do roku 1914* (Brno, 1946), I, 66. The relic had been presented to Michael Pogodin in 1835 by Canon Pěšina in the Cathedral of St. Vitus in Prague during a ceremony attended by three outstanding figures of the Slavic renascence, Hanka, Šafařík, and Kollár. Pogodin had in turn presented the relic to the University of Moscow on its centenary in 1855; N. P. Barsukov, *Zhizn' i trudy M. P. Pogodina* (St. Petersburg, 1905), XIX, 92.

[59] Hilferding, "Kak otnosiatsia k Kirillu i Mefodii sovremennyie Slaviane," *Sobranie sochinenii*, I, 331 ff.

"As modest as was the ceremony of May 11," Ivan Aksakov reported in *Den'*, "it constituted an expression not only of a tardily awakened recognition of the creators of Slavic letters, but also of a consciousness of the idea of a Slavdom which is arising in our society. This holiday serves as a pledge of the future *spiritual* unification of all the Slavs, a link binding estranged brethren."[60] In 1869 Pogodin echoed the same sentiment before the Moscow Slavic Benevolent Committee, following a solemn service to Saints Cyril and Methodius. "Cyril and Methodius—the first and, alas, till now the last true Panslavists—should be a symbol of a common renascence." He asked the Committee, of which he was then president, to pray for the realization of "one flock and one shepherd."[61]

Russian Panslavists were ever on the lookout for traces of loyalty to a "Slavic Church" among the non-Orthodox Slavs. One such sign was the local use of Church Slavonic in the Roman Mass and the preservation of the Glagolitic alphabet as a hieratic script by the Dalmatian Croats. Another such sign Panslavists found, oddly enough, in the Hussite movement among the Czechs, traditionally regarded by the West as a precursor of Protestantism. A modest body of writings, purporting to show a connection between Orthodoxy and Hussitism, contended that Cyril and Methodius had brought to the Czechs the Orthodox Christianity of the Greeks and the Byzantine rite in the Slavic tongue.[62] Saint Václav (the "Good King Wenceslas," martyred in 929 A.D.) had been reared in the Slavic orthodoxy of his sainted mother, Ludmila, and even though he later propagated Roman Catholicism, the Czech people allegedly remembered him as a Slavic martyr of Orthodox origin.

---

[60] Aksakov, *Sochineniia*, I, 13.

[61] M. P. Pogodin, "Riech' proiznesennaia v sobranii Slavianskago blagotvoritel'nago komiteta 1869 goda, fevralia 11 dnia," *Riechi proiznesennyia M. P. Pogodinym v torzhestvennykh i prochikh sobraniiakh, 1830-1872* (Moscow, 1872), pp. 455-56. It might be noted that the Roman Catholic Church was also sponsoring a cult of Saints Cyril and Methodius. For a Russian Panslavist's description of this movement and reaction to it see Hilferding, *Sobranie sochinenii*, I, 333 ff.

[62] E. Novikov's *Pravoslavie u Chekhov* (Orthodoxy among the Czechs), Moscow, 1848; V. Elagin's article, *Ob istorii Chekhii Fr. Palatskago* (On the History of Bohemia by Fr. Palacký), 1848; E. Novikov's *Gus i Luter* (Hus and Luther), Moscow, 1859; Fëdor Tiutchev, *Chekham v godovshchinu Gusa* (To the Czechs on the Anniversary of Hus) and *Gus na kostre* (Hus at the Stake).

Bořivoj had been consecrated a bishop of the Greek rite. The reason St. Adalbert left Bohemia for Poland was that he had lost his battle against Greek Orthodoxy in the Czech lands. That most popular of all Czech religious hymns, the medieval "Hospodine pomilui ny" (Lord, have mercy upon us), attributed to Adalbert, was really an Eastern Orthodox chant. The monastery of Sazava was long a stronghold of Slavic Orthodoxy in Bohemia, even after Rome's triumph, and Slavic Orthodoxy continued to be a living tradition in fourteenth-century Bohemia under Charles IV. It was because John Hus had belonged to this tradition of Cyril and Methodius, Russian Panslavists maintained, that he had been martyred at Constance by the anti-Slavic and anti-Greek Western Church.[63]

In his works on Hussitism Novikov[64] portrayed Hus as an Orthodox martyr, and Hilferding published a treatise by a Patriarch of Constantinople which argued in favor of this claim. Pogodin lauded especially Hus's insistence on the supremacy of a church council over papal prerogative and pointed out that the demand of the Hussite Calixtines or Utraquists for communion in both kinds for laity as well as clergy was but a reflection of an earlier Orthodox tradition in Bohemia. So, too, was their demand to put an end to the compulsory celibacy of the clergy and their approval of offering small children the communion. Pogodin also made much of the fact that Hus's comrade, Jerome of Prague, had actually sought communion in a Russian Orthodox Church.[65]

When in 1869 a solemn commemoration of Hus's martyrdom was held in Prague, the Moscow Slavic Benevolent Committee resolved to send a chalice as a reminder to the Czech people of their historic bond with Slavic Orthodoxy.[66] In a lengthy poem written for the occasion Tiutchev hailed the chalice as "a pledge of love and unity," calling upon the Czechs to accept "that which was

[63] See Jirásek, *Rusko a my*, I, 67 ff., for a concise statement of Russian Panslavist attitudes toward John Hus.

[64] Eugene Petrovich Novikov became Secretary of the Russian Embassy in Constantinople, Russian Minister to Greece, and Ambassador to Austria-Hungary.

[65] M. P. Pogodin, "Pri prazdnovanii piatisetlietnei godovshchiny Gusovoi," *Sobranie statei, pisem i riechei po povodu Slavianskago voprosa* (Moscow, 1878), p. 141.

[66] *Ibid.*, p. 150.

once yours, which the ancient Czech family had bought at such a price."[67] In another poem, entitled "Hus at the Stake," Tiutchev exclaimed:

> O land of Czechs, O native kin,
> Do not reject your legacy;
> Complete your sacred task, and win
> The triumph of our unity.[68]

The plea did not fall on entirely deaf ears, for there were supporters of a "Slavic Church"—at least in the form of national Catholic bodies—in Slavic Central Europe. Nevertheless the Russian Panslavist cults of Saints Cyril and Methodius and John Hus accomplished little or nothing.

Ivan Aksakov warned in an editorial in 1867:

Now or never, if the Slavs wish to remain Slavs, and not only to remain Slavs, but to deliver themselves from the clutches of the spiritual captivity which binds them to the destinies of the Latin world, they must give a decisive and direct answer to the question with which contemporary history confronts them. They must repudiate Rome and all its works, publicly and clearly, without quibbling or evasion. The Slavs stand at the crossroads: either the road to the West or the road to the East, the road of Latinity or the road of Orthodoxy, union either with the destinies of the Western European world or the destinies of the Greco-Slavic world—for the ruling faith of Slavdom, even by the number of the faithful alone, not to speak of its identity with the Slavic ethnic being, is the Orthodox faith. . . . Choose, Czechs, Moravians, Croats, Slovenes![69]

Ivan Aksakov hoped that the Catholic Slavs would renounce Romanism, unite with Orthodoxy, "resurrect" the Slavic liturgy of their fathers, and erect Orthodox churches in Prague, Brno, and other non-Orthodox capitals. Other Panslavists were more circumspect, but there was none who did not harbor this hope.

Why did the Russian Panslavists insist on the religious unity of the Slavs under the banner of Orthodoxy, when the chances of

---

[67] "Chekham v godovshchinu Gusa," *F. I. Tiutchev, stikhotvoreniia,* edited by K. Pigarev (Moscow, 1945), p. 276.

[68] "Gus na Kostre," *ibid.,* p. 275.

[69] Aksakov, *Sochineniia,* I, 177. The omission of the Poles is noteworthy.

achieving it were so slight? Most of them did not, in fact, insist on religious unity in actual practice. When one compares their actual program with their ideological utterances, one is struck by an unexpected divergence. Committed in theory to the proposition that Orthodoxy was the true Slavic religion, the Russian Panslavists exhibited relative tact and restraint in their relations with the Catholic Slavs, with the exception of the Poles. At the Moscow Congress of 1867, Michael Pogodin struck a keynote with his statement that "we Great Russians ask no one who he is and what his faith—Catholic, Protestant, Uniat, Orthodox: this does not prevent us from loving them all and wishing them well."[70] Nowhere in Russian Panslavist literature does one find the slightest hint that Catholic, Protestant, or Moslem Slavs ought to be converted to Orthodoxy by any means other than persuasion and by their own free will. In practice Russian Panslavic organizations showed almost no interest in actively encouraging the conversion of non-Orthodox Slavs outside Russia, except for the erection of an Orthodox church in Prague in 1874. Even this project was conceived and financed largely by Russian nobles living abroad who felt that if Paris, London, Carlsbad, Nice, and Dresden had Russian Orthodox churches for Russian travelers, Prague ought to have one also. Apparently the Prague church of St. Nicholas was intended to be more of a showpiece than a headquarters for an Orthodox mission.[71] Russian Panslavic organizations were, on the other hand, interested in persuading Uniat White Russians and Ukrainians to accept Orthodoxy. They considered this conversion, however, simply an attempt to restore the pre-1596 situation.

By logical necessity Russian Panslavists insisted on Slavic religious unity within Orthodoxy as a tenet of their ideology. Having

---

[70] M. P. Pogodin, "Nieskol'ko zamietok o Velikorusskom plemeni, sravnitel'no s prochimi slavianskimi plemenami," *Sobranie statei, pisem i riechei*, p. 48.
[71] For the Slavic Benevolent Committee's role in founding the Orthodox church of St. Nicholas in Prague, see *Pervyia 15 liet sushchestvovaniia S.-Peterburgskago Slavianskago blagotvoritel'nago obshchestva*, especially the minutes for the meetings of May 11, 1871; September 19, 1871; October 7, 1873; March 4, 1873; and May 11, 1875. See also M. P. Pogodin, "Slavianskiia nuzhdy," *Sobranie statei, pisem i riechei*, p. 80. See also F. M. Istomin, *Kratkii ocherk dieiatel'nosti S.-Peterburgskago Slavianskago Blagotvoritel'nago Obshchestva za 25 liet ego sushchestvovaniia, 1868-1893* (St. Petersburg, 1893), p. 19.

accepted in other matters the Slavophile definition of the ideal Slavic way of life, they had to accept the religious criterion as well, or else abandon the entire Slavophile outlook, a conclusion which was unthinkable for them. To Panslavist and Slavophile alike, religion was not a compartment of a civilization but its very core. Even a hardened realist like Danilevskii asked, "How can a government be free . . . from Christ?"[72] And Ivan Aksakov held that "religion is a way of life which permeates the entire existence of a people like the very air, and determines, sometimes consciously and sometimes unconsciously, its character and the direction of its historic destiny as well as the conduct of its life, spiritual and—in part—material, social as well as political."[73] He found it impossible to ignore the religious element in his thought simply because to do so might seem a more practical course. "There is nothing more pernicious to the true rebirth of the Slavic nationality," he warned indignantly, "than the false idea that nationality stands above faith, that religion is only a matter of personal conscience, and that Slavic patriots should be indifferent to it."[74] It was this adamant attitude which brought Russian Panslavists face to face with a dilemma which remained unresolved.

Russian Panslavists were on safer ground in vaunting the linguistic unity of the Slavic peoples. They made much of the fact that despite the vicissitudes of over a thousand years of recorded history, the Slavs were linguistically so much akin that their languages could be regarded as dialects of a Proto-Slavic tongue. The part that Slavic linguistic unity played in the Russian Panslavist ideology is treated separately in the following chapter.

IV

Little is more significant of the nature of Russian Panslavism and its values than the opinions of leading Russian Panslavists regarding the various Slavic peoples. Applying the yardstick of their ideology, Russian Panslavists evolved a veritable hierarchy of

[72] Danilevskii, *Rossiia i Evropa*, p. 223.
[73] Cited by A. N. Pypin, "Slavianskii vopros po vzgliadam Iv. Aksakova," *Viestnik Evropy*, IV (1886), 768.
[74] Aksakov, *Sochineniia*, I, 175.

the Slavic peoples based on the degree to which each conformed to an ideal Slavic way of life.

Beyond doubt, the Russian Panslavists regarded the Poles as the most disturbing element in their idyllic picture of Slavic unity. By their very existence as a subject nation, in part held captive by the Russian Empire, the Poles constituted a living refutation of the Russian Panslavist claim that Russia was the true guardian of the Slavic way of life and the champion of Slavic liberation. So challenging was the Polish problem that the Russian Panslavists produced an extensive apologetical literature which explained and justified their position with respect to the Poles. Since the Panslavist attitude toward Poland is the subject of a separate chapter, it is enough here to mention briefly why the Russian Panslavist leaders relegated the Poles to the lowest position on their scale. Historically, Poland was Russia's traditional enemy. The Poles had shed Russian blood on Russian soil. For centuries they had held millions of Russians in physical and spiritual subjection. Furthermore, Poland was Roman Catholic, not in the same way as the other Roman Catholic Slavs, but with all of the fervor of a Jesuit-inspired Ultramontanism. Not for nothing had the Vatican bestowed upon its beloved Slavic bastion the title of *Polonia fidelis*. Though a Slavic country, Poland was thoroughly infected with the poison of Westernism through a Latin clergy, a feudal aristocracy, and a bourgeois intelligentsia. The Poland of these three segments of society was no pitiable victim of Western aggression; it was a "fawning renegade" from Slavdom which had repeatedly demonstrated its eagerness to spread the poison of the West "with fire and sword."

Hilferding believed that the Roman Catholic and Protestant Slavs of Austria-Hungary, apart from the Poles, were more to be pitied than censured. Undeniably victims of Western imperialism, these Slavs had preserved their Slavic identities, though somewhat damaged, against great odds. Hilferding regarded the brilliant resurgence of their national movements in the beginning of the century as proof of the strength of their Slavic character. This strength lay in the common people. "The only preservers of the Slavic nationality in the Austrian domains," Hilferding pronounced, "are tillers of the soil and craftsmen. Their representatives in the intellectual field are the lower clergy and the village teachers."[75] In them alone lay the salvation of the Slavic spirit in Central Europe, he observed, for they did not fear the police and were immune to the influence of alien culture.[76] Hilferding found the absence of a native aristocracy among the Austrian Slavs gratifying. He exulted that in this the new Bohemia differed from the old. "The Czech state perished under the full sway of its aristocracy," he observed. "The new Bohemia will rise again from the midst of the common people."[77]

Despite these and other redeeming features, especially the existence of Protestantism among Czechs, Slovaks, and Slovenes, the Austrian Slavs were subjected to ideological criticism by Russian Panslavists. Much of this criticism came from precisely those Panslavists—Hilferding, Lamanskii, Ivan Aksakov, Pogodin, and others —who had taken the trouble to tour the Slavic lands outside Russia and who could therefore submit their ideology to the test of reality. The lessons of such trips were not always comforting. An example is Lamanskii's experience of Bohemia in 1862. Adolf Patera, a young scholar of Slavic studies, later to become Hanka's successor as curator of the Czech Museum Library, took Lamanskii to his native village near Beroun. The Russian made the following observations in a letter to his family:

In the outward lay of the land and its appearance [the village] preserves many purely Slavic traits which vividly recall our Russian villages, but as far as internal organization is concerned, it has already been overtaken by dreadful disfiguration. Not only is there no communal ownership of the land, but there is no sort of communal government.[78]

The closest this Bohemian village came to any communal action,

[75] Hilferding, "Razvitie narodnosti u zapadnykh Slavian," *Stat'i po sovremennym voprosam slavianskim*, in *Sobranie sochinenii*, II, 62. Originally published in the *Russkaia Besieda*, 1856, as well as in a French translation entitled *Les Slaves occidentaux*. The article was based on Hilferding's observations during a trip through the Slavic lands of Austria in 1856-58.

[76] *Ibid.*, p. 109.

[77] Hilferding, *Sobranie sochinenii*, Vol. I: *Ocherk istorii Chekhii*, p. 411.

[78] B. D. Grekov (ed.), *Dokumenty k istorii slavianovedeniia v Rossii, 1850-1912* (Moscow and Leningrad, 1948), p. 38; letter of June 9/21, 1862.

Lamanskii sadly observed, was in collecting a certain amount of wheat for the village schoolteacher. He was amazed that the villagers had no way of punishing evil-doers in their midst, as in Russia, by having them sent off to the army, but were forced, over the smallest offense, to go to the local police station. He observed two distinct classes among the villagers: the propertied *sedlák*, and the poor *domkář* who possessed nothing but his hut and had no vote, though his class was in the majority. "Our [Westernized Russian] economists say this is fine," Lamanskii complained, "for this has already become the European style. We [Russians] supposedly have nothing but a vestige of Asiatism. . . . You must see to what direful humiliation the Slavic nationality has come; you would see that it would have died out completely had not these vestiges of Asiatism survived." "The difference between ourselves and the Western Slavs," Lamanskii concluded, "lies in the fact that we have better preserved all the old, the basic, the Slavic ways. Here [in Bohemia] the gentry have become completely Germanized and have become traitors and enemies of the people. With us it is only half so."[79]

Hilferding's comments on his trip through the Czech lands reflected the importance which Panslavists attached to the peasantry as the bearers of the Slavic way of life. Comparing urbanized Bohemia with Moravia, he pointed out that "in Moravia . . . the towns are almost entirely German, but most of the villages are purely Slavic. The Moravians have preserved the ancient Slavic character and customs better [than the Bohemians], but for the most part they are simple villagers, poorly developed, poor in historic memories." Hilferding also expressed regret over their conservative Catholicism.[80]

Hilferding's chief complaint was leveled at the Slavic intelligentsia of Central Europe. "What is nationality as understood by the Western Slavs?" Hilferding asked. "It is the right," he replied, "of each people to its own individual existence, the right to be one's self, that is, to speak and to write in one's own language, to

[79] *Ibid.*
[80] Hilferding, "Razvitie narodnosti u zapadnykh Slavian," *Sobranie sochinenii,* II, 76.

adhere to one's own traditions, and to be administered as a separate people. For the Western Slavs the idea of nationality does not constitute anything more; they perceive in it no other principle." He castigated this concept as being superficial and negative. What "vital principles" distinguished these Western Slavs from their non-Slavic neighbors? These were questions, Hilferding charged, about which the Western Slavic intelligentsia did not think, and for which they had no answer. True, this intelligentsia had preserved the outward manifestations of their race—language, customs, and traditions. However, in the social, religious, and intellectual spheres, Hilferding charged, they belonged to a foreign world, which, having destroyed in them the "organic development of Slavic life," had given them in return more conventional forms. The struggle of the intelligentsia among the Western Slavs for the preservation of their own Slavic languages was well and good, Hilferding stated, but cultural independence required much more. What good was it to have one's own language, when one had nothing to say from his own heart and mind, but merely echoed the learning of the West?[81]

Not even the Orthodox Slavs of the Balkans were exempt from the ideological lapses of their brethren in Austria. Russian Panslavists nurtured a special tenderness for the Balkan Slavs. "To be sure—and we have no desire to conceal it," Ivan Aksakov admitted, "Russians find it easier to comprehend particularly that fraternal tie which is founded not on blood kinship alone, but on spiritual kinship as well. It is easier for them to recognize as brethren those branches of the Slavic race which, together with them, have kept faith with the traditions of the ancient Ecumenical Church, rather than the Latinized Slavs, whose spiritual center is Rome."[82] And yet Russian Panslavists found grounds for complaint even among these Orthodox kinsmen.

The criticisms of the Balkan Slavs by the Russian Panslavists received classical expression in their joint "Epistle from Moscow to the Serbs"—an all-too-much neglected document in the history

[81] *Ibid.*, pp. 84 ff.
[82] Aksakov, *Sochineniia*, I, 313.

of both Slavophilism and Panslavism. Written by Alexis S. Khomiakov a few months before his death in 1860, this Epistle was the
Slavophile leader's last important work, in a sense, his last testament. Khomiakov's Epistle was signed by ten of the Panslavists.[83]
Most of these were devotees of the Moscow Slavophile circle, and
all were members of the Moscow Slavic Benevolent Committee,
formed two years earlier. Although it bore no reference to the
Moscow Slavic Benevolent Committee, the Epistle in fact represented its views.

The "Epistle from Moscow to the Serbs" was in several ways a
unique document.[84] It was the only joint statement of their beliefs
ever issued by the Slavophiles. It was also the first concrete attempt
by Russian Panslavists to intervene in the internal affairs of non-
Russian Slavs. The document was likewise a significant link between

[83] A. S. Khomiakov, "K Serbam; Poslanie iz Moskvy," *Polnoe sobranie sochinenii*
(3d enlarged edition, Moscow, 1900), I, 377-408. The signatures on the last page
include the following: A. S. Khomiakov, M. P. Pogodin, A. Koshelëv, I. Bieliaev,
N. Elagin, Iu. Samarin, P. Bezsonov, C. S. Aksakov, P. Bartenev, F. Chizhov, and
I. S. Aksakov. All eleven names appear in their Serbian form in *Ivan Sergieevich
Aksakov v ego pis'makh*, IV (Moscow, 1892), 239, footnote. A complete but unsigned Russian text of the Epistle may also be found in the *Russkii Arkhiv*, III
(1876), 104-27. The Serbian text may be found in *Srpska Kraljevska Akademija:
Posebna izdanja*, LIV (Sremski Karlovci, 1925), 266-89.

[84] Ivan Aksakov, then secretary-treasurer of the Moscow Slavic Benevolent
Committee, took it upon himself to publish the work—on whose funds, it is not
known. Aksakov was chosen since he was abroad at the time, and could therefore
publish the work where it would be beyond the reach of Russian censors. At first
Aksakov intended to print the Epistle in Belgrade, which he was visiting at the
time, but his Serbian friends advised him against this. "As far as our epistle to
the Serbs is concerned," Aksakov wrote to his family on August 7, 1860, "everyone to whom I have read it has been sent into ecstasy, and on the advice of the
Metropolitan [Michael] and all my friends, I will have it published in Leipzig in
Russian and in Serbian, as it cannot be published here in Belgrade. The censorship
will not allow it, and it would be rather unpleasant for both princes [Miloš
Obrenović and his son, Michael]. And no press will print such a thing secretly."
(*Ivan Sergieevich Aksakov v ego pis'makh*, III, 477.) And thus, ironically enough,
this fraternal message from the Russian Panslavists to their Serbian kinsmen could
not be published either in Russia or in Serbia at the time, but could be in Leipzig!
The Epistle was printed in both Russian and Serbian (the Serbian title, *Srbljima
poslanie iz Moskve*, and text bearing the strong influence of the Russian-inspired
"Slavo-Serbian" literary language and old orthography which Vuk Karadžić and
his followers had replaced with the Serbian vernacular and reformed orthography),
and "thousands of copies" were sent to the Serbian Balkans. E. L. Mijatovics,
"Panslavism; Its Rise and Decline," *Fortnightly Review*, XIV, New Series
(1873), 107.

Slavophilism and Panslavism. And, since both Khomiakov and Constantine Aksakov died before the year was out, it stands at the
bounds between Slavophilism and Panslavism.

The Epistle was a piece of rather highhanded and unsolicited
advice, as well as a confession of faith couched in the stern but
consciously benign language of a New Testament epistle. It is
important for the history of Slavophilism because of its castigation
of Westernism within Russia. Its importance in the history of
Panslavism lay in its claim to judge other Slavs in the light of a
peculiarly Russian ideology. *"There is nothing political here,"* Ivan
Aksakov underscored in a letter to his friend at the Imperial Court,
Countess Antonina Bludova. "The aim of the letter is to present to
the Serbs in good time our own bitter experience, that they may
not fall into the same errors. It is not meant particularly for sale,
but is meant to be read by the Serbs, to whom it will be sent in
honest frankness. . . . It has the character of a completely spiritual
epistle."[85] This disavowal notwithstanding, the Epistle arose from
the Russian Panslavists' deep dissatisfaction with the turn of political events in the Principality of Serbia. Under Prince Alexander
Karadjordjević, Serbia had maintained a careful neutrality during
the Crimean War, to the Russians' great chagrin. In return, Serbia
had received guarantees from the Concert of Europe, which
weakened Russian influence over it. The deposition of Alexander
in January, 1859, and the return of old Miloš Obrenović to the
Serbian throne promised better relations with Russia, but these
hopes were not fulfilled. Miloš's death before the end of 1860
brought to the fore a new course. His son, Michael, a highly educated European gentleman, early evinced an ambition to make
peace with his powerful neighbors to the north and south and to
institute a modern administrative régime in a Serbia free of foreign
influences. There ensued what Russian Panslavists considered the
pernicious Westernization of Serbia, especially with the influx of
Austrian-educated Serbian officials into the government. Serbian
culture was undergoing a parallel process. Russian Panslavists came
to fear that the political and cultural ties which had once bound

---

[85] Ivan S. Aksakov, "Pis'mo k grafinie A. D. Bludovoi," *Russkii Arkhiv*, VI
(Book II, 1915), 131.

Serbia to Russia were growing steadily weaker under this Western impact. The Epistle aimed at recalling the Serbs to their native path, so to speak. Despite Aksakov's naively enthusiastic reports, it left a very poor impression on leading Serbs.[86]

The "Epistle from Moscow" was written in the rhetorical style of an apostolic missive to the Corinthians, but with little of the apostle's humility. Although addressed to "temporal brothers by blood and spiritual brothers in Christ," this epistle from the latter-day apostles of Russian Panslavism read more like the authoritative advice of a sinful yet omniscient paterfamilias. After assuring the Orthodox Serbs of the special love which Russia bore them, the Epistle observed that the Serbs had "made a good beginning" but that new trials awaited them in their hour of freedom. "Therefore let it be permitted to us, your brethren," Khomiakov and the ten urged, "who love you with a profound and sincere love and who are spiritually pained at the very thought of any evil befalling you, to turn to you with some warnings and counsels. We are older than you in recorded history [*sic!*]. We have passed through more varied if not more difficult trials than you, and we beseech God that our experience, bought at so exorbitant a price, may serve the need of our brethren."

Against what were the Serbs warned? "The first and greatest danger, which always accompanies glory and success," the Epistle pointed out, "consists of pride." Khomiakov urged the Serbs not to become puffed up with pride because of their successes and not to exalt themselves above their Slavic brethren. The Serbs were also cautioned against imitating the spiritual pride of the Greeks or the intellectual pride of the Western nations, especially the latter. In an effort to impress the Serbs with the humility and sincerity of his own intentions, Khomiakov thereupon recited in true Slavophile fashion the evils which Westernism had brought to Russia.

What, then, did the Russian Panslavists advise the Serbs to do? First, to preserve their Orthodox religion, "the apple of the inner

[86] An especially useful review of the Serbian cultural and, to a lesser extent, political background to the Epistle may be found in Julius Heidenreich (Dolanský), *Ruské základy srbského realismu* (Prague, 1933).

62543

EMORY & HENRY LIBRARY

and spiritual eye." The Epistle warned the Serbs against being intolerant toward non-Orthodox Serbs, but nevertheless counseled them to exclude such compatriots from public office. The Serbs were also advised against permitting social inequalities to arise in their midst. "You are happy above other peoples," they were assured, "because every Serb looks upon a Serb as a brother equal to himself, and there is among you none superior or inferior except in the service of society." The Epistle held up the Poles as an example of the tragedy which could befall a society based on the aristocratic principle. The Serbs were further warned against putting too much stock in foreign learning. The Epistle conceded that they still had much to learn from others, including Westerners, but were asked to remember that knowledge was still not true enlightenment. Here again Khomiakov went into a lengthy recital of Russia's self-abasement before the culture of the West. "The foreign intellect should arouse within you the activity of your own intellect," he advised, "and you will heighten this activity more and more. You should not, however, graft on to yourselves a foreign way of life, because by doing so you will be inoculated, not with foreign health but with foreign disease." Khomiakov insisted that he did not hold everything Western to be pernicious. He did believe, however, that "that which is in good order and harmonious in one (because it is in harmony with its own being) becomes the beginning of disorder and disharmony when grafted on to another whose being is based on another law."

The Serbs were also warned against losing the purity of their language. "Call the holy faith [by the Latin word] 'religion,' " Khomiakov declared, "and you disfigure Orthodoxy itself." As to the Serb who chose to speak a foreign tongue in his own society, the Epistle advised that he be treated with "the same respect that one would accord a parrot." The Epistle counseled the Serbs on matters of dress. "Changes in the national costume and preference for Western dress emanate from an evil source," it charged, "from contempt for one's own, and servility before what is alien." The Epistle also condemned the propriety of conferring medals, of encouraging luxury in private life ("the velvets and brocades of the Polish gentry reduced Poland to tatters"), of adopting the

Western "double standard" in private morality, of introducing capital punishment, and the like. The Serbs were advised to maintain the principle of unanimity in all decisions of a public nature, to support local justice on the communal level, to avoid giving too much power to officials or to priests at the expense of social freedom, and to establish popular education. "Perhaps we have left much unsaid," the Epistle concluded, "or have said it not clearly, or even with errors. You, brethren, add what has not been said, understand what has not been said clearly, correct the errors, and receive our words, words which come of the heart and of love, with love and good will."[87]

The "Epistle from Moscow to the Serbs" was not the only expression of Russian Panslavist concern over the state of affairs in the Slavic Balkans. Ivan Aksakov returned from his trip to Serbia and Montenegro with many of his beliefs in the Slavic purity and simplicity of the Serbs rather shaken by what he had observed. "Serbia has, in our opinion, been taking a rather false path of development in recent times," he observed in a *Den'* editorial in

[87] The "Epistle from Moscow" brought a sharp reaction from the Serbs. Indeed, it produced a polemic in the Serbian press between the Russophiles and the Nationalists. The chief protagonists of the former party were the politician and historian, Djura Vukičević and the young Serbian Slavophile, Jovan Ilijć [*sic*]. The latter party was represented by the Serbian philologist, Djuro Daničić, and the leading Serbian historian of the time, Stojan Novaković. Daničić denounced the Epistle—"the new Muscovite gospel," as he scornfully called it—as the work of fanatics who "either do not know what they want, or else do not know what they are saying." (Djuro Daničić, "Dopis," *Danica*, No. 5, February 20, 1861, republished in "Sitniji spisi Dj. Daničića," *Srpska Kraljevska Akademija: Posebna Izdanja*, LIV [Sremski Karlovci, 1925], 289-92.) Novaković declared, "It is the aspiration of the modern age that all peoples gain independence for themselves and for their own nationality. All the Slavic peoples must pursue this primarily, each in its own way." The question was, he argued, whether the Slavic peoples could look upon Russia as a true helper in this task, or whether Russia was seeking merely to impose its hegemony on all the Slavs. The answer, he said, was to be found in Ivan Aksakov's editorial in the first issue of *Den'* on October 15, 1861, which he cited in the Russian original: "To liberate the Slavic peoples from material and spiritual oppression and to grant them the gift of an independent spiritual and, if you please, political existence under the shade of the mighty wings of the Russian eagle—here is Russia's political calling, its moral right, and its obligation." Novaković commented, "For my own part, I would not say that the Slavic peoples will ever liberate themselves if what Mr. Aksakov desires is Russia's calling and if it is realized. I cannot understand why precisely 'the mighty wings of the Russian eagle' connotitute the condition of their independence." (Stojan Novaković, "Dopis," *Danica*, No. 1, January 10, 1862, republished in *Srpska Kraljevska Akademija: Posebna Izdanja*, LIV, 304-5.)

1862. "Instead of directing all of its forces and thoughts to the attainment of a single aim, that is, the liberation of the entire Serbian people, Serbia—or rather its government—has undertaken to assume quickly the external forms of the European bourgeoisie and to take on the aspect of a well-ordered and well-knit government." Aksakov deplored this trend as most "premature" and openly regretted that the Europeanized Prince Michael was not like his father, "old Miloš," whose directness tolerated no bureaucratic and diplomatic procedures.[88] Aksakov expressed similar disappointments with Montenegro, where Prince Danilo had broken with the primitive traditions of government under the prince-bishops.[89] His private letters in which he described his impressions of Montenegro during his trip there in 1860 were full of biting contempt for the Francomania of the Prince's Court, and for the Europeanized bureaucratic government which was being imposed on a proud warrior people.[90]

Vladimir Lamanskii also deplored Western influence in the Slavic Balkans. In his inaugural lecture at the University of St. Petersburg in 1865, he openly criticized the "Parisians" and the "Schwabs" (Austrian-educated Serbs) of the Serbian Principality, and the "Magyarones" (Magyarized Serbs) in the Hungarian-administered province of Vojvodina.[91]

As for the Bulgars, Pogodin and Ivan Aksakov in particular expressed concern over the tendency of some Bulgar leaders to look westward for help against both the Turks and the Greeks. Aksakov complained that for every young Bulgar sent to Russia for an education, hundreds were being sent to French and German schools.[92] Russian Panslavists were particularly troubled by the appearance of a Uniat movement among the Bulgars. One of the reasons for founding the Moscow Slavic Benevolent Committee in 1858 was to counteract the attraction of Roman Catholic propaganda in Bulgaria and to convince Bulgars that subservience to

[88] Aksakov, *Sochineniia*, I, 23.

[89] *Ibid.*, pp. 44-87 *passim.*

[90] *Ivan Sergieevich Aksakov v ego pis'makh*, Vol. III *passim.*

[91] Vladimir I. Lamanskii, "Vstupitel'noe chtenie Dotsenta Peterburgskago universiteta V. I. Lamanskago," *Den'*, No. 52, December 18, 1865, p. 1241.

[92] M. N. Pokrovskii, "Vostochnyi vopros ot parizhskago mira do berlinskago kongressa (1856-1878)," *Istoriia Rossii v XIX viekie* (St. Petersburg, n.d.), p. 7.

Rome was in no sense preferable to subservience to Constantinople.[93]

While Russian Panslavists did not hesitate to excoriate Russian society for its Westernism, they nevertheless clung to the conviction that Holy Russia was the truest repository of the Slavic ideal. The Russian Panslavist ideology was based on the premise that Russia held a position of primacy among the Slavic nations, and that Fate had predestined the Russian Empire to unite all the Slavs under its protection.

[93] S. A. Nikitin, "Vozniknovenie Moskovskogo slavianskogo komiteta (Iz istorii russko-bolgarskikh sviazei posle Krymskoi voiny)," *Voprosy Istorii* (August, 1947), pp. 63-64.

4

THE PANSLAVIC PRESS
IN RUSSIA

In the beginning was the word . . .
GOSPEL OF SAINT JOHN

THE GREAT AWAKENING of the Slavs in the early nineteenth century was accompanied by the realization that the Slavic peoples knew each other very little after centuries of political and cultural separation. The first prerequisite for any sort of Slavic solidarity was for the Slavs to become mutually acquainted. The earliest Russian periodicals with an all-Slavic orientation had as their primary task to acquaint the Russians with their Slavic brethren.

The reign of Nicholas I was hardly an auspicious time for newspapers, especially for those that dared to show any interest in foreign affairs. Nevertheless, the last fifteen years of his regime saw the rise and fall of four journalistic enterprises which were devoted wholly or in part to the Slavic world: M. P. Pogodin's *Moskvitianin* (Muscovite), 1841-56; P. P. Dubrovskii's *Dennitsa-Jutrzenka* (Morning Star), 1842-43; D. A. Valuev's *Sbornik* (Review), 1845; and its successor, the Slavophile *Moskovskii Sbornik* (Moscow Review), 1852-53. None of these publications espoused the cause of Slavic political unification. Yet they were pioneers in the development of Russian Panslavism in that they fostered Russian sympathetic interest in the other Slavs—an interest which eventually led to the founding of the first Russian Panslavic organization in 1858.

Undoubtedly the most influential of these four publications, and the most long-lived, was the *Moskvitianin* of M. P. Pogodin and S. P. Shevyrëv, "the Siamese twins of Moscow journalism," as Herzen dubbed them. Their newspaper was founded primarily to do battle for the sacred traditions of Holy Russia against the

Westernizers. It was because of this that Nicholas I granted his reluctant permission to issue the new journal. "Agreed," he scrawled tersely in the margin of the enabling document, "but with strict supervision."[1] He need not have feared. Herzen did not exaggerate when he portrayed Pogodin and Shevyrëv as "conscientiously servile."[2]

The two partners did not make immediate use of their sovereign's permission. In 1838 both received official leave to travel abroad for reasons of health. Each took this opportunity to visit Slavic centers abroad and to become personally acquainted with the most distinguished scholars and writers of the Slavic renascence.[3] This experience left a deep impression on both.

Thanks to Count Uvarov's personal assurances of his "more than official cooperation" as Minister of Education, Pogodin and Shevyrëv published the first issue of *Moskvitianin* in January, 1841.[4] Pogodin was the general editor; Shevyrëv took charge of the literary section.

Moskvitianin consisted of seven sections, only one of which, a relatively small one, dealt with the Slavs. Yet *Moskvitianin* devoted more space to the non-Russian Slavs than did any other journal in Russia at the time. It brought its readers reviews of the latest non-Russian Slavic books and periodicals, reports on the activities of learned societies in the various Slavic centers abroad, notices on the travels of distinguished Slavic personages such as Vuk Karadžić or on the lectures of Mickiewicz in Paris, letters from Slavic scholars such as Šafařík, and general articles on the Slavic Question. *Moskvitianin*'s Slavic section depended especially on the valuable contacts which Pogodin and Shevyrëv had made with many Slavic political and literary leaders.

[1] A. G. Dementiev, *Ocherki po istorii russkoi zhurnalistiki, 1840-1850 gg.* (Moscow-Leningrad, 1951), p. 186.

[2] A. Herzen, *My Past and Thoughts*, trans. Constance Garnett (New York, 1924), II, 295. Herzen also recalled that one of Shevyrëv's ancestors had allegedly sung psalms of praise to Ivan the Terrible even as he was being tortured by that autocrat!

[3] Pogodin's travels to the Slavic lands have been discussed elsewhere in this work. For a sketch of Shevyrëv's academic career and travels, see V. I. Jagić (Iagich), *Istoriia Slavianskoi filologii* (St. Petersburg, 1910), pp. 660-61.

[4] N. P. Barsukov, *Zhizn' i trudy M. P. Pogodina* (St. Petersburg, 1905), V, 487-91 *passim*.

Moskvitianin propagated the Panslavic cause as much as it dared. Despite his caution, Pogodin evidently caused some to think that this newspaper was politically dangerous, judging by an official report which Uvarov received in early 1842. The report read as follows:

In recent years several newspapers, especially *Moskvitianin*, have adopted as their special task to present the Slavs who are living under the rule of Turkey and of Austria as suffering special oppression, and to foretell their imminent deliverance from their foreign yokes. . . . To encourage meddling in the political lot of certain Slavic peoples, to represent Russia as a leader from which they can expect the best direction of their future, and publicly to applaud their passion for liberation —such propaganda can hardly be considered harmless.[5]

There is no record that Uvarov ever did anything about the report.

Moskvitianin maintained a rather precarious existence for sixteen years, from 1841 to 1856. Except for the first two years, the journal fared badly. It certainly never came close to providing competition for that noted journal of the Westernizers, *Otechestvennyia Zapiski* (Notes of the Fatherland). In 1846, when the latter journal had some 3,000 subscribers, *Moskvitianin* had only one tenth of that number.[6] In 1855 Pogodin finally wrote an "Epilogue" to his venture, though he continued to publish for another year. The last issue of *Moskvitianin* provided a sad record of its decline. After a supreme effort, Pogodin somehow managed, by the end of 1857, to send his few subscribers the final issue for 1856, and bade *Moskvitianin's* loyal friends farewell. The spring of Alexander II's reign inaugurated a brilliant period in Russian letters and journalism in which *Moskvitianin* could not hold its own.

Inasmuch as *Moskvitianin* was a general periodical in which Slavic news formed but a small part of each issue, the successes or failures of that journal were hardly decisive for the Slavic cause.

---

[5] Cited by A. M. Skabichevskii, *Ocherki istorii russkoi tsenzury, 1700-1863* (St. Petersburg, 1892), pp. 326-27. Unfortunately, the author of the report does not specify which newspapers other than *Moskvitianin* were involved.

[6] "Moskvitianin," *Novyi Entsiklopedicheskii Slovar'*, XXVII (Petrograd, n.d.), 312. The Soviet scholar A. G. Dementiev placed the number of *Moskvitianin's* subscribers in 1846 at 200; see his *Ocherki po istorii russkoi zhurnalistiki*, p. 217.

However, the fact remains that *Moskvitianin* played an important role in the emergence of Russian Panslavism. Throughout sixteen difficult years it endeavored to bring a knowledge of the other Slavs to an apathetic Russian public. In this period Slavic intellectuals abroad came to look upon it as a real friend in need. Many of them mistook its voice for the voice of official Russia and of the Russian people, and long found comfort in this error. L'udovít Štúr, the Slovak author of one of the strongest statements of Panslavism ever penned, *Das Slawenthum und die Welt der Zukunft* (Slavdom and the World of the Future), specifically acknowledged his debt of gratitude to *Moskvitianin*.[7] The many letters which Pogodin received from his Slavic friends abroad witnessed to the influence which he and his journal exerted beyond the borders of the Russian Empire.[8] Indeed, one of the tragedies of Michael Pogodin and other Russian Panslavists was that their Panslavism was always taken more seriously abroad than by their own countrymen.

II

The first newspaper in the Russian Empire to be wholly devoted to the Slavic world was the bilingual *Dennitsa-Jutrzenka* (Morning Star), founded in Warsaw in 1842 by P. P. Dubrovskii. Its Russian founder was at the time a professor at the Warsaw Gymnasium. The newspaper carried articles written either in Russian or in Polish. Its masthead proclaimed it to be "a literary periodical devoted to Slavic affairs." The editor chose as his motto the words "Slavus sum, nihil slavici a me alienum puto." Thoroughly imbued with the idea of Kollár's Slavic reciprocity, Dubrovskii hoped that an all-Slavic newspaper might bring the Slavs closer to one another.

[7] See the first Russian edition of this work: L'udovit Štúr (Liudevit Shtur), "Slavianstvo i mir budushchago; Poslanie Slavianam s beregov Dunaia," trans. V. I. Lamanskii, in *Chteniia Imperatorskago Obshchestva Istorii i Drevnosti Rossiiskikh pri Moskovskom Universitetie*, III, Materialy slavianskie, Books 1-3 (1867), p. 169.

[8] See *Pis'ma k M. P. Pogodinu iz Slavianskikh zemel' 1835-1861*, edited by Nil Popov, in *Chteniia Imperatorskago Obshchestva Istorii i Drevnosti Rossiiskikh pri Moskovskom Universitetie*, Book 4 (1879), pp. 137-448; Book 1 (1880), pp. 449-746.

He desired especially to facilitate a rapprochement between Russians and Poles after the ill-fated Polish insurrection of 1830-31. *Dennitsa-Jutrzenka* first appeared in January, 1942, as a fortnightly.

In his ideology Dubrovskii shared two basic tenets of the Moscow Slavophiles: the "originality" of the Slavic culture (*samobytnost'*— or *rodowość* as *Dennitsa-Jutrzenka* rendered this term in Polish), and the future mission of the Slavs. Dubrovskii prophesied a new era for the Slavic peoples—hence the name *Dennitsa-Jutrzenka* or *Morning Star*—and he called upon the West to take serious note of Slavic history and learning. In his political views, Dubrovskii generally agreed with M. P. Pogodin, though the censorship of Nicholas I made it equally difficult for either publicly to express his hope for the political liberation of the Slavs of Central and Southern Europe.

Dennitsa-Jutrzenka survived only two years. Inasmuch as its public consisted of little more than a handful of subscribers (only twenty-five in 1842!), most of them Slavic scholars scattered over hundreds of miles of wretched postal communications and across hostile political frontiers, the newspaper was doomed to financial death. Nevertheless, in its two years of existence, Dubrovskii brought before his limited reading public the works of some of the leading figures of the Slavic intellectual world.[9] Yet his newspaper's failure to arouse the interest of the Russian public provides further evidence that the Panslavic cause enjoyed almost no popularity in the Russia of Nicholas I.

III

The first journal specifically devoted to the Slavs as a whole to be published in Russia proper was Valuev's *Sbornik istoricheskikh i statisticheskikh sviedienii o Rossii i narodakh ei iedinoviernykh i iedinoplemennykh* (Review of Historical and Statistical Information on Russia and Coreligious and Coracial Peoples), whose first and only issue was published in 1845 in Moscow. Dmitrii A. Valuev

---

[9] This account of the *Dennitsa-Jutrzenka* is based largely on an article by Jiří Horák, "P. P. Dubrovského Dennica-Jutrzenka," *Z dějin literatur slovanských* (Prague, 1948), pp. 340-49.

(1820-45) was an early member of the Slavophile circle. While a student at the University of Moscow, he fell under the influence of Professor S. P. Shevyrëv. Despite his youth, Valuev was the first member of the Slavophile circle to undertake the systematic publication of its views. His journal was also the first public indication that the Slavophiles had any interest in Russia's Slavic kinsmen across the border.

"Until Russian learning masters all that is related to the Russian world," the program of the first *Sbornik* proclaimed, "it will never possess a vital and complete knowledge of Russia itself, in the way that the Romano-Germanic world knows itself. Therefore . . . we are determined above all to become acquainted insofar as possible with the current position and the history of all the lands and peoples which are of the same faith and race as Russia."[10] It will be noted that this Slavophile program characteristically stressed knowledge of Russia as the prime purpose of becoming acquainted with the other Slavs. Also noteworthy is the program's declared emphasis on Orthodoxy rather than on Slavdom, an emphasis which was fully consonant with the Slavophile belief in the primacy of religion in human existence.[11]

Despite the magazine's professed interest in the "current position" of the other Slavs, none of its articles touched on current politics. However, *Sbornik* contained several serious studies, largely historical, on the social, cultural, and legal institutions of the Slavic peoples as well as a very informative statistical survey on "The Slavic and Orthodox Population of Austria" written by Valuev himself.

Unfortunately *Sbornik's* young editor did not live to continue the work begun with such enthusiasm. Even its one issue did something to make known the philosophy of the Slavophiles and to encourage an interest by Russians in the Western and Southern Slavs. Like Dubrovskii's newspaper, Valuev's *Sbornik* proclaimed the future mission of the Slavs in world civilization. As Khomiakov wrote in its first article, "Long-suffering but finally delivered in a

---

[10] D. A. Valuev, "Predislovie," *Sbornih istoricheshihh i statistioheskikh suiedenii o Rossii i narodakh ei iedinoviernykh i iedinoplemennykh*, I (Moscow, 1845), 18.
[11] *Ibid.*, pp. 18-19.

fateful struggle, its communities all more or less tarnished by a foreign admixture but nowhere stamped by an inherited stigma of crime and unjust gain, the Slavic world preserves for mankind, if not the germ, then certainly the possibility, of renewal."[12]

After Valuev's untimely death, the Slavophiles continued the work of *Sbornik* in the annual *Moskovskii Sbornik* (Moscow Review), published in 1846 and 1847. Its chief contributors were younger Slavophiles such as Iurii Samarin, Constantin Aksakov, A. N. Popov, F. V. Chizhov, Ivan Aksakov, and N. A. Rigel'man. Their academic allies included Professors M. A. Maksimovich, V. I. Dal', I. I. Sreznevskii, and S. M. Soloviëv.[13] The 1846 and the 1847 annual carried fewer articles on the non-Russian Slavs than had Valuev's *Sbornik*. The few noteworthy studies included Sreznevskii's article on Vuk Karadžić, Pogodin's report from Prague, and Rigel'man's survey of the literature of the Western Slavs.

The fateful year 1848 brought a temporary halt to the publication of *Moskovskii Sbornik*, for revolution in Western Europe made Nicholas I all the more determined to clamp down on public opinion at home. Two of its most active supporters, Ivan Aksakov and Iurii Samarin, were arrested briefly in 1848. As the foreign crisis which led up to the Crimean War loomed larger, however, the pressure of outside events appeared to some contemporaries to soften domestic oppression. "It seemed," A. I. Koshelëv, the Moscow Slavophile, wrote in his memoirs, "as if out of a depressing, dark dungeon we were emerging if not into God's light, at least into an ante-chamber where we could sense refreshing air."[14]

In mid-1851 Koshelëv persuaded Ivan Aksakov not to seek a post in the government and, instead, to revive *Moskovskii Sbornik* along broader, less exclusive lines. The first of four new issues, which appeared on April 21, 1852, was almost exclusively a Slavophile performance. It included very little about the non-Russian Slavs, a great deal about the conflict between Western and Russian culture. *Moskovskii Sbornik* soon became involved in so many diffi-

[12] A. S. Khomiakov, "Stat'ia pervaia, vmiesto vvedeniia," *Sbornik*, I, 7.
[13] Barsukov, *Zhizn' i trudy M. P. Pogodina*, VIII, 313.
[14] Cited by Alexander Kornilov, *Modern Russian History* (New York, 1943), I, 307.

culties with the censorship that the Slavophiles decided against publishing a periodical of their own for the remainder of Nicholas's reign.[15] This meant, in effect, that Pogodin's failing *Moskvitianin* was left as the only Russian periodical with any significant interest in the Slavs and the Slavic cause.

IV

With the accession of Alexander II, in 1855, and an apparent relaxation of censorship rules, two famous Russian journals saw the light of day—Katkov's *Russkii Viestnik* (Russian Herald) and the Slavophile *Russkaia Besieda* (Russian Discourse). From 1856 to 1860, *Besieda* was the only periodical in all Russia to bring before the Russian public a regular flow of significant articles on the Slavic world. For the Slavs across the border, *Russkaia Besieda* replaced *Moskvitianin* as a tangible mark of Russian interest in their destinies.

The idea of *Russkaia Besieda* originated with A. I. Koshelëv and A. S. Khomiakov, who desired to revive a Slavophile organ and to continue their battle with the Westernizers in the greater freedom of the new reign. *Besieda* proclaimed as its principal aim "to study Russian life," and in foreign affairs its chief interest lay in the Slavic Question. As Khomiakov declared in his introduction to the first issue:

In those days when all Europe loudly proclaimed its furious hatred against us, when all breathed with malice, the only voice of sympathy which we heard came from our blood brothers—the Slavs, and our brothers in the faith—the Greeks. . . . In accord with the interest of the fatherland, *Russkaia Besieda* will devote particular attention to all that concerns the life of the Slavic peoples and the Greek people.[16]

In its four years of publication there was hardly an issue of *Russkaia Besieda* but which contained at least one article about the non-Russian Slavs. Though most of its articles dealt with history,

---

[15] For descriptions of *Moskovskii Sbornik* and its troubles with the censorship, see especially Ivan S. Aksakov, *Ivan Sergieevich Aksakov v ego pis'makh*, III (Moscow, 1892), Appendix, pp. 14-15; Skabichevskii, *Ocherki istorii russkoi tsenzury*, pp. 365 ff.; and M. K. Lemke, *Ocherki po istorii russkoi tsenzury i zhurnalistiki XIX stolietiia* (St. Petersburg, 1904), pp. 284 ff.

[16] A. S. Khomiakov, "Liubeznyi chitatel'!" *Russkaia Besieda*, No. 1 (1856), p. v.

ethnography, and literature, *Russkaia Besieda* also managed to
include several significant articles on the current political position
of the non-Russian Slavs.[17] It also opened its columns to Slavic
authors outside Russia.[18]

Despite the excellence of its contents, *Russkaia Besieda* did not
enjoy great popularity with the Russian reading public at large.
The limited number of its subscribers gave further proof that the
so-called Slavic Question did not greatly interest the Russian intelligentsia. After all, there were many other important issues to think
about, issues closer to home, such as the liberation of the serfs and
other much-needed reforms. Even at its height Slavophilism was
never popular. Awakened from the torpor of Nicholas's regime,
the progressive elements of Russian society could not believe that
the Slavophiles had much to offer in the creation of a better future.

In 1858, upon his return from a trip abroad, Ivan Aksakov was
persuaded to become editor of *Russkaia Besieda*. Koshelëv, however, continued to bear the title of managing editor for official
purposes because Aksakov had been under a ban since 1853. It was
Aksakov's great hope to emphasize the Panslavic tendencies of the
journal. He had felt from the first that its Slavic section was too
academic and aimless. "This question must be made as popular as

[17] For example, Alexander Hilferding contributed an unending stream of studies
—on the national cultural movement of the Lusatian Serbs in Saxony, on Russian
cultural influences in Galicia, the mutual relations of Saint Vladimir and Boleslaw
the Brave, Southern Slav folk tales, travels through Bosnia, Saints Cyril and
Methodius, the history of the Serbs and Bulgars, and others. E. P. Kovalevskii,
chief of the Asiatic Department of the Foreign Ministry (which desk included the
Balkans), Prince P. A. Viazemskii, F. V. Chizhov, and A. I. Koshelëv himself
contributed accounts of their travels through the Slavic lands of the Hapsburgs
and the Sultan. M. A. Maksimovich and P. A. Kulish wrote on Ukrainian themes.
E. P. Novikov contributed a study on Hus and Luther. P. A. Bezsonov published
several significant studies on early Slavic manuscripts, including Juraj Križanić's
seventeenth-century work *Ob vladatelstvu* (On Government). Vladimir Lamanskii
wrote a study on Russian-Greek relations. V. I. Veselovskii wrote a review of
contemporary Polish literature and the Polish press. Especially noteworthy political
articles were Prince V. A. Cherkasskii's "Two Words regarding the Eastern
Question" and Michael Pogodin's excerpts from his memoranda to the Minister
of Public Education. Both articles stressed Russia's need to rely on the non-Russian
Slavs in the achievement of its historic aims.
[18] For example, the Czech writer Karel Jaromír Erben contributed a study on
Slavic mythology. The fiery Bulgarian patriot Khristo Daskalov published a bold
defense of the Bulgarian movement for national liberation. The Polish scholar
V. A. Maciejowski wrote on the peasant commune, etc.

possible," he wrote to Prince Cherkasskii. "It must be taken out of the field of archaeology and brought to life, endowed with political significance, etc."[19] Aksakov expressed optimism over what appeared to him to be a growing interest on the part of the Russian public in the Slavic Question, thanks to the efforts of *Russkaia Besieda*. Even the St. Petersburg press, he exulted, was becoming interested in the foreign Slavs. Aksakov had concrete plans of setting up as an adjunct to *Russkaia Besieda* a Slavic Bureau (Slavian-skaia Kontora), an office which would maintain regular connections with the non-Russian Slavs and act as a clearinghouse for donations, shipments of books, and the like. "In a word," he wrote to Cherkasskii, "*Besieda* would be a political center for the Slavs and a real prime-mover."[20]

In 1860 Ivan Aksakov went abroad as a companion to his seriously ailing brother, Constantine. Meanwhile, for lack of subscribers, *Russkaia Besieda* fell on bad days while in Koshelëv's hands. In a letter to his family from Belgrade on July 20, 1860, Ivan Aksakov wrote, "A. I. Koshelëv writes that he is definitely going to discontinue the *Besieda*. I have already replied that to discontinue *Besieda* was simply a moral impossibility, more impossible than any physical impossibility; on the other hand, inasmuch as it would be simply dishonorable to insist on further financial aid on his part, I asked only that he not announce in print that *Besieda* would be discontinued, as I would look for funds."[21] Aksakov intended to appeal to that part of the Russian non-peasant society that was ideologically most acceptable to him as a Slavophile, the tradition-bound merchant class. He hoped especially to raise a "Slavic fund" which would not only make possible further publication of *Russkaia Besieda*, as a newspaper rather than as a journal, but would enable his proposed "Slavic Bureau" to make contributions to the non-Russian Slavs. But such optimistic planning in Belgrade did not help Koshelëv in Moscow. An attempt was made to transfer *Russkaia Besieda* completely to Aksakov, but it ended

[19] O. Trubetskaia, *Materialy dlia biografii kn. V. A. Cherkasskago*, I (Moscow, 1901), 124, Aksakov's letter of July 17, 1858, to Cherkasskii.
[20] *Ibid.*
[21] Aksakov, *Ivan Sergieevich Aksakov v ego pis'makh*, III, 468, letter of July 20, 1860, from Belgrade to his parents.

in failure. *Russkaia Besieda* closed publication with the second number in 1860.

Even before his departure abroad, Ivan Aksakov had written an "epilogue" for the sixth and last issue of 1859—what amounted to a valedictory of *Russkaia Besieda*. He wrote:

We have succeeded in extricating the Slavic Question from the realm of archaeological interest and in bringing it into the realm of a living, active sympathy, and have brought to life an intellectual movement in the circle of our literary Slavic brethren. Circumstances beyond our control prevented us from enlarging the scope of our relations and from establishing, as an adjunct to *Russkaia Besieda*, a Slavic Bureau, which is so necessary to both the Russians and the [other] Slavs. Nevertheless, we have been repaid by the warm sympathies of our suffering kinsmen even for the little that we have done. We know that the discontinuation of *Besieda* will resound grievously in all the Slavic lands of Austria and of Turkey, but we beg our Slavic brethren not to be troubled, first, because many of our newspapers and magazines— even those in St. Petersburg—now admit articles on the Slavic Question to their pages and express sympathy for Slavic nationalism . . .; and second, because we are interrupting our activity only temporarily, and we hope to avail ourselves in the interval of greater means for undertaking a more active service in the Slavic cause. We are happy to have succeeded apparently in dispelling misconceptions such as existed among us as well as among the [other] Slavs concerning Russian Panslavism and in convincing our brethren that our sympathy is alien to any encroachment on their independent development. The recognition of the right of every Slavic nationality to an independent way of life has always been the slogan of Russian Slavophilism.[22]

V

Convinced of the necessity of maintaining a Russian Panslavic journal or newspaper, Ivan Aksakov could not permit his cause to remain without a voice after the demise of *Russkaia Besieda*. In the decade from 1859 to 1869 Russian Panslavism found its principal and almost only journalistic outlet in four of Aksakov's

[22] Ivan S. Aksakov, "Zakliuchitel'noe slovo," *Russkaia Besieda*, No. 6 (1859), pp. vi-vii.

periodicals: *Parus* (The Sail), 1859; *Den'* (Day), 1861-65; *Moskva* (Moscow), 1867; and *Moskvich* (Muscovite), 1867-68.

While serving as actual though unofficial editor of *Russkaia Besieda*, Ivan Aksakov had made every effort to have the old ban on his literary activity lifted, and in mid-1858 he was released from the dead hand of Nicholas I. Now free to write in his own name, the Panslavist immediately set about to realize plans for a weekly newspaper which he intended to call *Parus*. He had felt for some time that a "thick journal" such as *Russkaia Besieda* could at best reach but a limited public. "At present you and I have no ground under our feet in our sympathy for the Slavs," he wrote to Vladimir Lamanskii in this period, "that is, the Slavic Question does not extend to the people's midst, it is alien to them. One of *Parus*'s tasks, among other things, will be to popularize the Slavic Question as much as possible."[23] Ivan Aksakov believed that only a lively newspaper could do the job. He was encouraged in this ambition by a noticeable relaxation in the censorship. "At present," Aksakov reported in June, 1858, to that notable friend of Panslavism, Michael F. Raevskii, protopresbyter of the Russian Embassy church in Vienna, "the censorship is not restricting us in discussions on politics or, at least, very little. One is permitted to revile Austria as much as one likes."[24]

As a matter of fact, Ivan Aksakov received direct encouragement to start *Parus* from Egor Petrovich Kovalevskii, then chief of the Asiatic Department of the Foreign Ministry. Such support was significant especially since the "Asiatic" Department included the Balkans in its field of interest. The extent of Kovalevskii's support cannot be determined from presently available sources. It is certain, however, that he proposed the publication of *Parus* and gave Aksakov at least his advice from the beginning.[25]

[23] O. V. Pokrovskaia Lamanskaia (ed.), "Perepiska dvukh slavianofilov," *Russkaia Mysl'* (September, 1916), p. 3, letter of September 3, 1858, from Ivan Aksakov to Vladimir Lamanskii.

[24] Aksakov, *Ivan Sergieevich Aksakov v ego pis'makh*, IV, 2, letter no. 1 of June 22, 1858, from Ivan Aksakov in Moscow to M. F. Raevskii in Vienna.

[25] "I should tell you," Ivan Aksakov wrote to Pogodin, "that in proposing that we publish a newspaper, E. P. Kovalevskii urgently requested that at first . . . neither your name nor mine should appear—two names which St. Petersburg stomachs find irritating and somewhat indigestible." Barsukov, *Zhizn' i trudy M. P. Pogodina*, XVI, 306.

On the other hand, it would be incorrect to infer that encouragement from Kovalevskii endowed *Parus* with official protection. As Aksakov informed Pogodin on November 30, 1858, after the appearance of *Parus* had been publicly announced, "*Parus* is badly off; orders have been issued that it be watched very strictly, and all three agencies—the Ministry of Public Education, the Foreign Ministry, and the Third Section—are infuriated."[26] Their fury was aroused by an incident which got the enthusiastic editor of *Parus* into hot water before the publication of a single issue. The Slavic Question provided the cause.

In late 1858 Aksakov drafted a circular announcing the establishment of a Slavic Bureau as an adjunct of *Parus*. The circular was cleared by the Moscow censors. It was then translated into Serbian, Czech, Polish, and Bulgarian. Two hundred copies in each language were sent abroad. Immediately both Kovalevskii brothers, the Minister of Public Education and the head of the Asiatic Department, descended upon Aksakov. The Minister, Evgraf Kovalevskii, "strongly censured" the Moscow censors, N. P. Giliarov-Platonov and N. F. von Kruse, for dereliction of duty.[27] Egor Kovalevskii reproved Aksakov for interfering as a private citizen in foreign relations without permission of the Foreign Ministry. Aksakov was reminded that the original program of *Parus*, which the censorship administration had approved, made no mention at all of the word "Slavic." Therefore *Parus* could not be permitted to print articles about the non-Russian Slavs, at least not in a special section of the newspaper. The distraught Aksakov complained to Prince Cherkasskii, "This really upsets me inasmuch as I have organized correspondents everywhere, and just now, when the Slavic Question is to the fore and will perhaps soon become the most vital issue in European politics, these lively dispatches from Athens, Constantinople, Zagreb, the Ionian Isles, and

---

[26] *Ibid.*, p. 311.

[27] In his article, "Sorok liet tomu nazad," *Viestnik Evropy*, IV (August, 1904), F. Voroponov described the former censor as follows on page 445: "N. P. Giliarov-Platonov (then censor)—a man with an outlook of his own, but sympathetic in much to and approaching Slavophilism." Nicholas F. von Kruse was one of the thirty-one charter members of the Moscow Slavic Benevolent Committee.

elsewhere would have given the newspaper a current political interest."[28]

Thus on the very threshold of his new enterprise, Aksakov discovered that his *Parus* could have neither a Slavic Bureau nor a section devoted specifically to news from the Slavic lands. He submitted to this decision only because he believed that by a little subterfuge he could organize informally what would amount to a *de facto* Slavic Bureau. As for the Slavic news section, he decided that he would print reports from the Slavic lands under the headings "news from Austria" or "news from Turkey."

Egor P. Kovalevskii of the Asiatic Department and Hilferding, then an official of the Foreign Ministry, assured their friend Ivan Aksakov that the prohibition on the Slavic Bureau and the Slavic news section did not stem from the Foreign Ministry. The Foreign Ministry had merely felt justified in reprimanding Aksakov for ignoring it in what it regarded as a delicate aspect of foreign relations. Both officials were, however, quite disappointed, especially in view of their own Panslavic sympathies, that Aksakov's range of activity had been so severely curtailed.[29]

Despite these ominous storm clouds, *Parus* appeared for the first time on January 3, 1859. A. S. Khomiakov greeted the new venture and its Slavic mission with an allegorical poem in the first issue:

> The Sail is set; the winds are full,
> The ropes are taut,
> The mast rides high
> Across the roaring waves.
>
> The Sail is Russian. O'er the waves
> The ship sails proud,
> And set to join
> Its brother skiffs to its mighty sides.[30]

The ship was not to sail for long. *Parus* was banned after its second issue, thanks to four articles which ran afoul of the censorship.

[28] Trubetskaia, *Materialy dlia biografii kn. V. A. Cherkasskago*, I, 241.
[29] Aksakov, *Ivan Sergieevich Aksakov v ego pis'makh*, IV, 18, letter no. 10 of April 13, 1859, from Ivan Aksakov to M. F. Raevskii in Vienna.
[30] Cited by Barsukov, *Zhizn' i trudy M. P. Pogodina*, XVI, 306.

Three of these dealt with Russian domestic affairs: the censorship, serfdom, and laws affecting the urban class. The fourth article— Pogodin's review entitled "The Past Year in Russian Life"—dealt with Russia's position in the Slavic world.

Pogodin's article was a bitter critique of Russian foreign policy in Eastern Europe. It deplored Russia's passivity toward the Slavs of Austria and the Balkans in the face of Western hostility toward these peoples. Pogodin's indignation exceeded the bounds of dignity. "Do you wish to hear my opinion concerning the Eastern Question?" he asked, and then replied, "The Eastern Question— ha, ha, ha!" He portrayed especially the plight of the Ottoman Slavs with great emotion. "For the sake of the balance of Europe," he wrote, "ten million Slavs must groan, suffer, and agonize under the yoke of the most savage despotism, the most unbridled fanaticism, and the most desperate ignorance."[31] As for the Austrian Slavs, he wrote:

In Austria there are five million Germans and twenty million Slavs who are alien to the former in language, creed, and history, and who cannot tolerate the former, but rather hope against hope for a chance to free themselves. Austria cannot sleep a single peaceful night at home without making fast all her doors, without tightly closing all the windows, without posting sentries everywhere, without surrounding herself with all kinds of guards—and it is this Austria, if you please, which feels an invincible vocation to gather into her arms ten million more Slavs in the East who are even more alien to herself. . . . And Russia, which includes sixty million Slavs, kinsmen of the Austrian and Turkish Slavs, is told, in the words of the German publicists: mind your own affairs and do not even think of turning your eyes toward the East! Such is the role which the benevolent Germans relinquish to Russia. What is Russia itself doing in the arena of European politics? She keeps silent.[32]

The censors castigated Pogodin's article as "a caustic disparagement of our foreign policy . . . and forbidden interference by a private person in the views and deliberations of the government."[33]

Pogodin was given the impression that his article had proved to

[31] *Ibid.*, p. 450.
[32] *Ibid.*, pp. 331-32.
[33] Skabichevskii, *Ocherki istorii russkoi tsenzury*, p. 451.

be more damaging than the three other offending articles. Even before the ban on *Parus* was announced, he received a letter from P. I. Mel'nikov of St. Petersburg, which reported, "Your article in *Parus* has caused everyone to rear up on his haunches, and the outcome will be such that we shall recall with envy Buturlin's literary reign of terror. At the session of the Geographic Society on January 15 it was loudly said that *Parus* was being banned not for its lead article but for yours."[34] Pogodin received confirmation of this view from Countess Antonina D. Bludova, the extremely well-informed lady-in-waiting to the Empress. "The finishing blow to the already dying *Parus* came precisely as the result of your article," she wrote two weeks after the ban, "but it did not come at all from the Foreign Ministry."[35] She chided the Panslavists for provoking dullards in government circles against the Slavic cause and thus inviting the administration to revert to ever more stringent restrictions of the press.

Pogodin was deeply wounded by the entire affair. He had been not only loyal to the government but even servile. When Pogodin received a copy of the ban from Ivan Aksakov, he recorded in his diary on February 5, "I fell into a rage and wrote a thunderous letter to the Minister."[36] He read the first draft of the letter to many of his friends, and even sent a copy to Ivan Aksakov, with whom he was no longer on speaking terms, ostensibly because the latter had made some unauthorized editorial alterations of his article. Most of his friends cautioned Pogodin to omit the thunder, which he did. The end product was a tediously long apologia which ran the gamut from abject protestations of loyalty to a dramatic effusion of wounded feelings.[37]

Having banned *Parus*, the government immediately found cause to regret its action. Prince A. M. Gorchakov, the Foreign Minister, objected to the ban at a time when Russian policy dictated the encouragement of Slavic sympathies for Russia. He insisted that it was bad form for the Tsar's government to ban *Parus* at precisely the same time as the Austrian government had prohibited its

[34] Barsukov, *Zhizn' i trudy M. P. Pogodina*, XVI, 338.
[35] *Ibid.*, p. 345.
[36] *Ibid.*, p. 348.
[37] See Skabichevskii, *Ocherki istorii russkoi tsenzury*, pp. 451-53, for the text.

importation into the Hapsburg lands. Gorchakov's chief of the Asiatic Department, Egor P. Kovalevskii, spoke to the Empress on behalf of a pro-Slavic newspaper in Russia. She in turn interceded with the Emperor who, according to Aksakov, as usual stated that he had always thought such a newspaper should exist! Alexander II ordered Egor Kovalevskii to seek a way out of the dilemma. The simplest solution would have been, of course, to lift the ban, but the Emperor would not agree to this. A second alternative was chosen—to inaugurate another newspaper. Kovalevskii sent Hilferding to Moscow to negotiate with the Slavophiles. Koshelëv refused on the grounds that he was too much occupied with the land reforms. Chizhov agreed to lend his name to such a newspaper on the condition that Ivan Aksakov provide the funds and in fact edit it. Meanwhile Aksakov was asked not to make public any notice of *Parus*'s demise, so that the projected newspaper could avail itself of the same subscribers. After remonstrance from Chizhov, he agreed to edit such a newspaper behind Chizhov's name.

"Well now, isn't that a comedy?" Aksakov exclaimed in an account of the entire matter to Raevskii in Vienna. "Two months ago *Parus* was forbidden to write about the Slavs, the censors were sternly reprimanded for allowing my circulars to go into print—I stubbornly violated the prohibition, which they had already forgotten about, then they banned *Parus* itself, and now they write —'save the idea of *Parus*!' "[38] As though to revenge himself on the government, Aksakov proposed that the new newspaper be called *Parokhod* (The Steamboat)—a fitting successor to *Parus* (The Sail)! Partly because for political reasons he disliked the obvious play on words, and partly because he wished to direct *Parus*'s successor along specifically Slavic lines, the Emperor himself proposed the name of *Slavianskii Viestnik* (Slavic Herald).

During these negotiations, the enemies of such a venture joined forces. Foreign Minister Gorchakov himself turned against the idea his Ministry had inaugurated because he resented Egor Kovalevskii's having by-passed him in going to the Imperial family. Besides, Gorchakov had wished merely to escape an embarrassing situation

---

[38] Aksakov, *Ivan Sergieevich Aksakov v ego pis'makh*, IV, 20.

—the coincidence of Austria's and Russia's ban on *Parus*—and not to start a Panslavic crusade in Russia through a government-sponsored organ. Gorchakov had always been contemptuous of the Panslavic program. "I find it difficult to believe," he once remarked, "in the sympathy of the Slav peoples for autocratic Russia." As a diplomat he was a realist of the Western school who was not easily swayed by mystical and grand projects. Therefore he urged on the Emperor that the entire matter be reviewed by the Council of Ministers, where Gorchakov could count on Timashev, Dolgorukii, Mukhanov, Panin, and others to kill the project. Meanwhile Gorchakov's brother, the Viceroy of the Polish Kingdom, who was then visiting St. Petersburg, added his senile voice to the ministerial outcry against Aksakov. The Viceroy proclaimed that *Parus* was harmful to Russia's interests. To bring the Slavic idea to the Poles, he insisted, was tantamount to inciting rebellion. The Slavs of the Austrian Empire were already so Germanized, he declared, that they were beyond hope. As for the Balkan Slavs of the Ottoman Empire, they were for Russia not because of race but because of the Orthodox religion.

The strength of the opposition plus the apparent logic of the Viceroy's arguments forced the Emperor to compromise. A new session of the Council of Ministers was called. Its members agreed to the projected newspaper on three principal conditions: that it make no mention of an independent Slavic way of life, that it avoid politics altogether but confine itself to academic subjects, and that it make no reference whatsoever to *Parus*. "Of course," Ivan Aksakov reported to Father Raevskii, "we refused."[39]

The government thereupon proposed to the *Sankt-Peterburgskiia Viedomosti* (Saint Petersburg News) that it inaugurate a Slavic section in its pages. Although that newspaper had never shown any particular interest in the non-Russian Slavs, its editor, Kraevskii, proved obedient to the government's wishes. The government went so far as to ask Aksakov to deliver to Kraevskii's office all articles on Slavic affairs that had been meant for *Parus*. Aksakov refused. He was bitterly opposed to the *Sankt-Peterburgskiia*

[39] *Ibid.*, p. 21. The text of the government's decision is to be found in Skabichev-skii, *Ocherki istorii russkoi tsenzury*, p. 454.

Viedomosti inasmuch as it expressed official rather than public
opinion. Aksakov warned Raevskii in Vienna against collaborating
with Kraevskii. If official policy should demand a reconciliation
with Austria, Aksakov predicted, that would be the end of Kraevskii's Slavic section.[40]

Following these bitter experiences, Ivan Aksakov left Russia to
accompany his ailing brother Constantine on a tour of Europe in
the hope of restoring him to health. The two brothers decided to
visit the Slav lands of Austria and of the Balkans. In the course
of these travels of 1860, Ivan Aksakov became more convinced
than ever of the necessity of publishing a Panslavic newspaper in
Russia.[41]

While still on the journey, Constantine Aksakov died on the
Ionian island of Zante. Ivan brought his brother's body back to the
Russian soil which they worshipped. After having buried his
brother, Ivan took up the task of realizing his plans for another
newspaper which would be devoted to the Slavic cause. This new
effort led to the establishment of the newspaper *Den'*, without
doubt his most brilliant journalistic enterprise and the most influential instrument of the Russian Panslavic movement.

VI

In mid-1861 Aksakov submitted to the Minister of Public Education, Evgraf P. Kovalevskii, a formal application for permission
to publish a newspaper. To it he attached the most innocent statement of editorial policy that he could write. Indeed, he did not
even request the right to publish a special section on politics for he
was afraid of creating difficulties. After much wrangling in the
censorship board, Aksakov's petition was referred to the Emperor
and to the Council of Ministers, who gave their approval.[42]

"My newspaper is called the *Day*," Aksakov wrote in a private

[40] Aksakov, *Ivan Sergieevich Aksakov v ego pis'makh*, IV, 23.

[41] *Ibid.*, III, see especially pp. 435, 447, 453-54.

[42] For descriptions of the troubles which Aksakov experienced in inaugurating
the *Den'*, see especially the following: *Ivan Sergieevich Aksakov v ego pis'makh*,
III, 112, and IV, 57, 183-85; Barsukov, *Zhizn' i trudy M. P. Pogodina*, XVIII,
469 ff.; A. V. Nikitenko, *Zapiski i dnevnik, 1804-1877* (St. Petersburg, 1904-5),
II, 12.

letter. "This name has no special significance."[43] Others, however, attached more meaning to the name. "Aksakov is publishing the *Day*," Pogodin wrote to his comrade Shevyrëv with more than a touch of malice, "and whether he will have long to spend the time of day or whether he will be forced to seek a lodging for the night is not known."[44] Apparently Aksakov himself had the time of day on his mind when he began his first editorial in *Den'* as follows: "A light rain drizzles without surcease; it is raw, wet, slippery; a gray cloud lies like felt across the sky; the air is heavy and stifling."[45] There were many gray days ahead, days so hazy that one branch of the government could not see where the other was trying to go.

Den' lasted some four years—from October 13, 1861, to the end of 1865, when its editor closed it down for personal reasons. The newspaper enjoyed the collaboration of the old Moscow Slavophiles, and especially that of the Panslavic circles of Moscow and St. Petersburg. In its first six months *Den'* counted about three thousand subscribers.[46] By the end of the first year it had nearly four thousand.[47] The following year the figure fell to 2,500, and there it remained. Aksakov attributed the decline to two reasons: the apathy of the Russian public for the Slavic cause, and the anger of the gentry over *Den'*'s championing of the liberation of the serfs.[48]

The year 1862 was a disastrous one for the entire nonofficial Russian press. *Den'* had more than its share of troubles with the censors. In June, 1862, Aksakov was forced to withdraw as editor when he refused to divulge the name of the author of a letter to the editor. From that time until October 15, 1862, Iurii Samarin's

---

[43] Aksakov, *Ivan Sergieevich Aksakov v ego pis'makh*, III, letter of June 11, 1861.

[44] Cited by Barsukov, *Zhizn' i trudy M. P. Pogodina*, XVIII, 472.

[45] Ivan S. Aksakov, "Moskva, 14-go oktiabria 1861 g.," in *Slavianofil'stvo i zapadnichestvo, 1860-1886*, in *Sochineniia*, II (St. Petersburg, 1891), 3.

[46] Aksakov, *Ivan Sergieevich Aksakov v ego pis'makh*, IV, 86, letter no. 49 of December 21, 1864, to M. F. Raevskii in Vienna.

[47] "Ivan Sergieevich Aksakov," *Biograficheskii Slovar'*, I, 98. M. K. Lemke claimed that by 1862, *Den'* acquired 7,750 subscribers, or as many as Katkov's *Moskovskiia Viedomosti*. See his *Epokha tsenzurnykh reform, 1859-1865* (St. Petersburg, 1904), p. 192, footnote. This figure is not borne out by Ivan Aksakov himself.

[48] Aksakov, *Ivan Sergieevich Aksakov v ego pis'makh*, IV, see letter no. 27 of May 10, 1861, and letter no. 49 of December 21, 1864, both to M. F. Raevskii.

name appeared on the masthead as responsible editor. During this period Samarin did his best to placate the authorities through his private intervention.[49] Despite Samarin's overtures, by the thirty-fourth weekly issue in 1862, the government decided that it could no longer tolerate Aksakov's newspaper. Publication of *Den'* was completely banned by order of the Emperor, who had himself taken time from the weighty affairs of state to censor some of Aksakov's articles. The details of the banning are not germane here. It is important to note, however, that Aksakov's troubles with the government in this period had nothing to do with the Slavic question. "As long as *Den'* exists," its editor once declared, "it will devote itself primarily to our own Russian domestic questions, compared to which Slavic affairs have but a secondary interest."[50] It was undoubtedly *Den'*'s outspoken stand on behalf of the great reforms, especially its insistence on the abolition of censorship, that earned it the hostility of the bureaucracy. Yet just as in the case of *Parus*, the very fact that a newspaper which was so wholeheartedly devoted to the Slavic cause should have been subjected to constant assaults by the Imperial government created an embarrassing dilemma.

Despite his past differences with Ivan Aksakov, that indefatigable champion of the Slavs, Michael Pogodin, made every possible use of this dilemma to rescue *Den'*. In another of his famous memoranda to the Minister of Public Education, he indignantly expostulated against the government's action. "All the Slavic peoples looked upon *Den'* as their own faithful friend, helper, and mediator, which has taken their fate to heart," Pogodin argued, "which sincerely wishes them well, assiduously seeking all means to help them. This was a natural tie, the strongest Russia has had with the

---

[49] In a letter to A. V. Golovnin, the Minister of Public Education, Samarin characterized *Den'* as "the only publication founded upon the principle of a vital conservatism." Hoping to spare *Den'* further difficulties, he added, "You must decide what is better: to preserve a sincere and promising ally as it is, with all its faults, sharpness, enthusiasm, etc., or to reject it . . . and remain defenseless against *Kolokol, Sovremennik,* and *Russkoe Slovo.*" (Cited by N. Sladkevich, "K voprosu o polemike N. G. Chernyshevskogo so slavianofil'skoi publitsistikoi," *Voprosy Istorii* (June, 1948), p. 78, on the basis of an unpublished letter in the Samarin Collection of the Moscow Lenin Library.)

[50] Aksakov, *Ivan Sergieevich Aksakov v ego pis'makh,* IV, 238, letter no. 38 of February 5-6, 1862, to Countess Antonina Bludova in St. Petersburg.

Slavs. The ban on *Den'* constitutes proof to them of the government's disfavor with regard to their situation, it will arouse their dissatisfaction, whereas we should seek their friendly feelings and win them to our side in any case." Pogodin had a second argument. *Den'*'s open war on Polish pretensions to the Ukraine and to White Russia was extremely useful. By banning *Den'*, Pogodin suggested, the government was playing into the hands of the Polish party.[51]

How much weight such arguments carried cannot be judged. However, *Den'* was not only allowed to resume publication with the issue of October 15, 1862, but Aksakov was fully reinstated as responsible editor. *Den'* carried on without interruption until 1865.

During its brief career it maintained a real tie between Russia and the other Slavs. Through its columns the Russian public became better acquainted than ever before with their "Slavic brethren." Ivan Aksakov kept alive the Slavophile creed by extricating it from the realm of the abstract and by applying it to two causes: the great reforms at home, and the union of the Slavs. Unlike earlier Slavophile publications, *Den'* reflected a far more active interest in the current political position of the non-Russian Slavs. It preached the eventual unification of all the Slavic peoples, a union of brotherhood under mighty Russia's aegis. It was for others to define that union and to suggest means of realizing it. *Den'*'s indisputable contribution to the Panslavic cause was to nurture and to develop Russian public interest in that cause until the great crisis and the final triumph which *Den'*'s editor believed to be inevitable.

In the autumn of 1865 Ivan S. Aksakov married Anna Fëdorovna Tiutcheva, daughter of the Slavophile poet and a lady-in-waiting to the Empress. In order to devote himself to improving his own financial situation so that he might meet his new responsibilities as a family man, Aksakov discontinued *Den'*. It was perhaps a measure of the Russian public's continued apathy to the Panslavic cause that *Den'* ended its days with a deficit of from one to three thousand rubles.[52] Yet such would be a poor measure of its significance as a leavener.

[51] Cited by Barsukov, *Zhizn' i trudy M. P. Pogodina*, XIX, 417-18.
[52] Nikitenko, *Zapiski i dnevnik*, II, 254, entry of October 23, 1865.

VII

Ivan Aksakov could not long content himself to be without a newspaper. By the fall of 1866 he was again in the market for a new journalistic venture. He managed to scrape up enough money from his merchant friends in Moscow after promising them that out of the twenty-four columns of his newspaper, two would be devoted to commerce, and that a weekly editorial would deal with this subject. On January 1, 1867, just a year and a quarter after the end of *Den'*, its successor, *Moskva* (Moscow), made its appearance as a weekly political, economic, and literary review.

Moskva continued the interest of its predecessor in the Slavic Question. As its editor reported to Raevskii in Vienna, "Of course, the Eastern and Slavic Questions will occupy one of the most prominent places in it." Aksakov begged Raevskii for more news from the Slav lands—not long articles, but real news dispatches. "Slavdom is now no longer just an archeological interest," Aksakov confidently proclaimed, as though to reassure himself, "but a live contemporary interest."[53]

Aksakov made it clear from the beginning that he meant to continue his war on the censorship, and it would be tedious to record in detail the punishments meted out to the editor of *Moskva*. It is enough to say that during its brief existence from January 1, 1867, to October 21, 1868, *Moskva* received nine official reprimands from the censorship and three bans—on March 26, 1867, for three months; on November 29, 1867, for four months; and finally on October 21, 1868, for six months.[54] The last ban was ordered personally by the Emperor because he objected to *Moskva*'s polemic with the ultraconservative newspaper *Viest'* (News).[55] The official reasons for those actions included charges that *Moskva* had encouraged "lack of confidence and respect" toward the government, that its articles contained "indecorous

[53] Aksakov, *Ivan Sergieevich Aksakov v ego pis'makh*, IV, 91, letter no. 53 of October 13, 1866, to M. F. Raevskii in Vienna.
[54] K. Arseniev, "Russkie zakony o pechati," *Viestnik Evropy* (April, 1869), p. 804.
[55] S. M. Sukhotin, "Iz pamiatnykh tetradei S. M. Sukhotina, 1867-i god," *Russkii Arkhiv*, I (1894), 605.

expressions with respect to the acts of the government authorities"
and "sharp expressions against the actions of the government."[56]

A contemporary student of the Russian press, K. Arseniev,
offered more specific reasons. Of the three main reasons given, two
touched on the Slavic question. The first reason for the ban was
that the *Moskva*'s editor had flagrantly defied the laws on the press.
The second reason involved the newspaper's stand on the so-called
Ostsee Question. *Moskva* was charged with inciting the hatred of
one part of the population against another by supporting the cause
of Orthodoxy against the Lutheran Germans in the Baltic provinces. The third reason involved *Moskva*'s resolute defense of the
Bulgars in their struggle with the Patriarch of Constantinople for
the independence of their own Orthodox Church. According to
the censors, *Moskva* was guilty of an improper discussion of the
relations between Church and State in Russia and the relation of
other churches to each other.[57]

In order to circumvent the final ban, Aksakov resorted to founding another newspaper called *Moskvich* (Muscovite). Published
under the nominal editorship of P. Andreev, it was in fact edited
by Aksakov. More defiant than ever, Aksakov took pains to indicate that *Moskvich* was but a revived version of *Moskva*, even in
external appearance.[58] This brazen attitude aroused Pogodin to
remark that both Aksakov brothers were wont to throw themselves against the knife, but whereas Constantine had done so
blindly, Ivan did it with his eyes open![59] As was generally expected,
Moskvich was permanently banned on February 13, 1869. Meanwhile *Moskva*, which had been consigned to the limbo of a temporary ban during this period, was also permanently banned by a
decision of the State Council. Neither *Moskva* nor *Moskvich* was
as important to the Panslavic movement as *Den'* had been. Nevertheless, their demise offered only further proof to the Slavs outside
of Russia that the country of the Tsar-Liberator did not speak
with one voice.

[56] Vladimir Rozenberg, *Russkaia pechat' i tsenzura v proshlom i nastoiashchem*
(Moscow, 1905), pp. 234-35.
[57] Arseniev, "Russkïe zakony o pechati," *Viestnik Evropy* (April, 1869), p. 804.
[58] Nikitenko, *Zapiski i dnevnik*, II, 357.
[59] *Ibid.*, p. 385.

The history of the Russian Panslavic press up to 1870 should certainly indicate that in this period the Russian government and the Panslavic movement hardly constituted a hand-in-glove conspiracy. Yet the clumsy and halfhearted attempts of the Russian Foreign Ministry, especially its Asiatic Department, to attract the sympathies of Russia's Slavic kinsmen as a useful instrument in the conduct of its foreign policy was, after all, a far cry from Nicholas I's opposition to the rebellious subjects of his imperial neighbors, the Hapsburg Emperor and the Sultan. The Russian Panslavic press kindled and tended a low-burning flame which was to flare up fiercely on more than one occasion in the half-century to come.

5

PANSLAVIC ORGANIZATION IN RUSSIA

As an organized public movement Russian Panslavism received its first impetus from the Crimean War. Russia's military and diplomatic defeat led a growing number of educated Russians to realize that the internal order they had so dearly paid for in liberty resulted in weakness rather than in strength. The international security which had been bought from the Concert of Europe at the degrading price of serving as Metternich's gendarme turned to bitter disillusionment when that Concert of Europe attacked Russia.

It was natural that in its disillusionment and isolation Russia should have turned to setting its own internal affairs in better order, and under Alexander II Russia directed its attention to long-overdue reforms. With greater freedom of movement and thought permitted by the new reign, a segment of Russian society could strongly express its feeling that now was the time for Russia to erect a buffer against the hostile West.

The Crimean War had brought not only official Russia but also educated Russians in general into close contact with the Balkan Slavs. While Pushkin's generation had applauded the daring exploits of the Serbian rebels against the infidel Turk, the Russian public of the mid-century was interested chiefly in the plight of the hitherto almost unknown Bulgars.

Taking advantage of this interest, the Bulgarian merchant colony in Odessa organized in 1854 a society for popularizing the Bulgarian cause in Russia. At first the Odessa group had no official standing in the eyes of the Russian government, but it did what it could privately to gain support and raise money for Bulgarian popular organizations and schools.[1] Throughout the war its most active representative, Nikola Palauzov, maintained relations with a wide

---

[1] Nikola Bobchev, "Slavianofilskoto dvizhenie v Rusiia i novobŭlgarskoto obrazovanie," *Proslava na osvoboditelnata voina 1877-1878 g.* (Sofia, 1929), pp. 192 ff.

circle of Russian officials and public figures. Especially important among the latter was Professor Michael Pogodin.[2]

Following the Crimean War, the Bulgars in Russia continued their activities. They were particularly eager to gain support for the Bulgarian Church and for the education of young Bulgars in Russia. One of the most active members of the Bulgarian group was Naiden Gerov. A graduate of the Richelieu Lycée in Odessa and later Russian consular agent in Plovdiv in his own country, Gerov spent most of 1856 in Russia working for the Bulgarian cause. During that time he wrote a stream of memoranda on Russo-Bulgarian relations which he addressed to the Russian Foreign Ministry as well as to any Russian of note who would listen.[3] On March 23, 1856, Gerov sent Egor Kovalevskii, of the Foreign Ministry, a memorandum on the need for church books in Bulgaria and urged the Russian government to make such books available to the Bulgars at a low price. On April 11 Gerov sent another letter to Foreign Minister Gorchakov in which he complained of the Russian government's inactivity in the Balkans. It was in this letter that the Russian government first heard a proposal for establishing a private society in Russia which would maintain relations with the Slavs outside Russia.

Perhaps [Gerov wrote] the government does not desire to expend sums for the support of students from the Slavic nations and to maintain more extensive relations with them, or it finds this difficult for some reason. In this case it would do our coreligionists in Turkey a great favor were it to permit the establishment of a society for the support of the Church, for the development of education, and for helping our poor kinsmen.[4]

[2] S. A. Nikitin, "Vozniknovenie Moskovskogo slavianskogo komiteta," *Voprosy Istorii*, No. 8 (August, 1947), p. 51. Pogodin's correspondence shows that he maintained ties with the Odessa Bulgars through Savva Vŭlchev Filaretov, then a Bulgarian stipendiary at the University of Moscow. See *Pis'ma M. P. Pogodina iz slavianskikh zemel' 1835-1861*, ed. by Nil Popov, in *Chteniia v Imperatorskom Obshchestvie istorii i drevnostei rossiiskikh*, Vol. 112 (January-March, 1880), pp. 718-41 *passim*.

[3] Nikitin, "Vozniknovenie Moskovskogo slavianskogo komiteta," *Voprosy Istorii*, No. 8 (August, 1947), p. 53.

[4] Bŭlgarskata Akademiia na naukitie, *Arkhiv na Naiden Gerov (1871-1876)*, ed. by M. G. Popruzhenko and T. Panchev, in *Dokumenti za bulgarskata istoriia* (Sofia, 1932), II, 474.

Similar letters were written to Kovalevskii, General Vasil'chikov, and other Russian officials by Gerov and his compatriots.

The efforts of the Bulgars were directed not only at the Russian government but at Russian high society. They found the Slavophile circle of Moscow especially responsive. Gerov came to Moscow in early May, 1856, and made the personal acquaintance of some of the Slavophile leaders through Professor Pogodin. In a letter of May 24 to a compatriot, Gerov described the Slavophiles as "men with a Slavic tendency who are disposed to be useful to us." He added, "True, there are not many of them, but their possibilities are great, their intention firm, and their zeal limitless."[5] Gerov reported that some of the Moscow Slavophiles were planning to petition the government for permission to found a society for aiding Orthodox Christians in Turkey. He considered Ivan S. Aksakov to be "the heart" of the circle, and he frequently mentioned Hilferding and Pogodin.

It was not the Moscow Slavophiles, however, but St. Petersburg high society that established the first Russian organization on behalf of the Balkan Slavs. In 1856 three prominent titled ladies in capital society founded a philanthropic society with the aim of sending books and supplies to Orthodox churches and schools throughout the Balkans. The founders were Princess T. V. Vasil'chikova, the wife of the general, Countess N. D. Protasova, wife of the Procurator of the Holy Synod, and Countess Antonina Bludova, lady-in-waiting to the Empress. Their founding manifesto made no mention whatsoever of Slavic solidarity but, in consonance with an earlier Russian tradition, stressed the bond of Orthodoxy.[6] The ladies collected and sent significant sums of money to Orthodox religious establishments in Adrianople, Constantinople, Prizren, Sarajevo, Mount Athos, the Orthodox monasteries of Dalmatia and

---

[5] *Ibid.*, pp. 397-98, letter of May 24, 1856, from Gerov to S. M. Toshkovich in Odessa.

[6] Rather indicative not only of Gorchakov's humor but of his contemptuous attitude toward Slavophilism was his quip at the expense of Countess Bludova: "Celle-là ne restera pas tranquille jusqu'à ce qu'elle n'ait le c—— bien assis sur le croissant de la Sainte Sophie." In the company of ladies this last was softened to "jusqu'à ce qu'elle ne soit assise à califourchon," etc. See Iu. S. Kartsov, "Za kulisami diplomatii," *Russkaia Starina*, Vol. 133 (January, 1908), p. 96.

Hercegovina, and elsewhere. Their activities were limited to the religious and educational sphere.[7]

II

It was in Moscow, nevertheless, that the first Russian society with a consciously expressed concern for fellow Slavs was founded —the Moscow Slavic Benevolent Committee. In January, 1858, a group of thirty-one Muscovites headed ostensibly by A. N. Bakhmetev, Superintendent of the Moscow School District (and hence the ranking representative of the Ministry of Education in Moscow), submitted a petition to Prince Gorchakov, the Foreign Minister, requesting permission to establish an organization for extending philanthropic aid to the Orthodox and other Slavs in Russia and abroad. Three aims were outlined in the petition: "(1) To send funds to the Slavs for the benefit of churches, schools, and other truly beneficial institutions such as the Society of Bulgarian Literature in Constantinople, as well as public libraries; (2) to send them aid in books, supplies, and all that is necessary for the support of Orthodox churches and schools; (3) to aid young Slavs in Moscow who have come for an education." The founders begged permission to collect and to transmit contributions to both Russian and foreign Slavs, and expressed a desire that the Foreign Ministry and the Postal Administration facilitate their establishing relations with such foreign persons and societies.[8]

The petition of the Moscow Slavic Benevolent Committee was granted on January 23, 1858. Gorchakov noted at the time: "Completely convinced of the necessity of giving aid to Orthodox churches and schools in the Turkish provinces, which find themselves in the most wretched condition, and having in mind the inadequacy of our government's means, for my part I see no obstacle which would stand in the way of voluntary collections in Moscow for the benefit of Southern Slavs."[9]

[7] Nil Popov, *Ocherki religioznoi i natsional'noi blagotvoritel'nosti na vostokie i sredi Slavian* (St. Petersburg, 1871), pp. 123-24.

[8] *Ibid.*, p. 127.

[9] K. A. Pushkarevich, "Balkanskie slaviane i russkie 'osvoboditeli,'" *Trudy Instituta slavianovedeniia Akademii nauk SSSR* (Leningrad, 1934), II, 189.

It is difficult to ascertain what persons were chiefly responsible for founding the Moscow Slavic Benevolent Committee, but there is no doubt that the core of the organization was formed by the Slavophile circle. However, over half of the thirty-one charter members were not Slavophiles. It is also noteworthy that, with the possible exception of Khomiakov, the most renowned Slavophile leaders in the Committee were participants more than organizers. Unpublished documents in the Pogodin archives of the Moscow Lenin Library would point to A. V. Rachinskii as the first active organizer of the Committee.[10] Rachinskii had taken part in the Danubian campaign during the Crimean War. He was later Russian consul at Varna. Thus he had both a personal interest in the Balkan Slavs and an official connection with them. While the list of the thirty-one charter members who signed the petition which was sent to Foreign Minister Gorchakov does not in any way indicate the relative role of each member, it does at least provide a definite clue as to the various interests represented in the Committee.

There were, first of all, the Slavophiles—Iurii F. Samarin, statesman and writer; Alexander I. Koshelëv, publisher and editor since 1856 of the *Russkaia Besieda*; Alexis S. Khomiakov, Slavophile philosopher and lay theologian; and Constantine S. Aksakov, Slavophile theoretician and writer. Ivan S. Aksakov, absent from Moscow at the time, was not among the charter members. None of the Slavophile leaders was actively engaged in the work of the Committee, with the exception of Ivan S. Aksakov, who was always more of a publicist than a theoretician. Of the others, Khomiakov probably showed the most interest and support. Samarin's official duties left him little time for Panslavic interests. Constantine Aksakov's interest in the other Slavs was theoretical rather than practical, and illness deprived him of opportunity for any activity. Koshelëv's visits to the Slavic lands of Austria and his resulting friendships with Slavic figures abroad offered proof of his interest, but he was not very active in the work of the Committee.

A second, and numerically the strongest, group among the

[10] Nikitin, "Vozniknovenie Moskovskogo slavianskogo komiteta," *Voprosy Istorii*, No. 8 (August, 1947), p. 61, footnote.

charter members were some ten professors of the University of Moscow, roughly half of whom were connected with Slavic studies. Among them, Michael P. Pogodin stood out almost as an institution by himself. Though definitely influenced by the Slavophile outlook, Pogodin was a vigorous man of action whose many trips to foreign Slavic lands and whose many memoranda to the government indicated a passionate interest in the Slavic cause. Others included Osip M. Bodianskii, professor of Slavic linguistics and author of many learned works on the Slavs; Sergiei M. Soloviëv, famed Russian historian who, though basically a Westernizer in outlook, had never forgotten his earlier allegiance to the Slavophiles; Apollon A. Maikov, Bodianskii's distinguished pupil and himself the author of a monograph on the history of the Serbian language; Fëdor I. Buslaev, student of Slavic languages and a close collaborator of the Slavophiles; and finally Pogodin's great friend and associate, Michael A. Maksimovich, who began his career as a biologist but who had been prevailed upon by Uvarov to teach Russian literature. His special interests were in folklore and the Ukrainian language.

Of the other professors, none had any scholarly interest in the Slavs. Fëdor I. Inozemtsov, professor of therapeutic medicine and founder of the Russian Society of Physicians, was not even of Slavic origin but the son of a Persian brought to Russia by Count P. A. Buturlin. Professor Modest Ia. Kittari taught engineering and was interested chiefly in industry. Alexander N. Drashusov taught astronomy. I. M. Sokolov was professor of anatomy. Count Alexis S. Uvarov, son of Nicholas's famous Minister of Education, was a noted archaeologist.

Yet another group of charter members included a category which Russians designate as "publicists," editors, publishers, and authors. Old Sergiei T. Aksakov, the father of Ivan and Constantine, was the only distinguished novelist among them. Of the others, the most important and influential was Michael N. Katkov, editor since 1851 of *Moskovskiia Viedomosti* (Moscow News) and publisher since 1856 of *Russkii Viestnik* (Russian Herald). As a student in Moscow, Katkov had been a Westernizer and had been close to Bielinskii and Bakunin. In 1840 he made a pilgrimage to

Berlin and attended Schelling's lectures on philosophy. In 1845 he defended at the University of Moscow a thesis on "The Elements and Forms of the Slavic Russian Tongue" and was made an assistant in that university's philosophy department. He taught there for five years and was known as a rather uninspiring lecturer. In 1850, as the result of the scare of 1848, the government discontinued the chair of philosophy, thus releasing Katkov and driving his students into classes on theology. It was then that he was appointed editor of the liberal (in the English nineteenth-century sense) but increasingly conservative *Moskovskiia Viedomosti*. From this time on, Katkov was despised by the radical Westernizers as a reactionary supporter of the regime, while the reactionaries as well as the Slavophiles distrusted him as an admirer of English parliamentary institutions. He fancied himself to be, in the 1860's, a distant follower of Slavophilism. Actually Katkov was, like Pogodin in some respects, an institution in his own right, an eclectic whose one constant base was a strong Russian nationalism. It was this nationalism that attracted Katkov to both Slavophilism and Panslavism.

Two other publicists in the group were closely associated with Katkov. Paul M. Leontiev had been known till 1856 largely as a professor of Latin literature and the ancient world at the University of Moscow. With the founding of Katkov's *Russkii Viestnik* in that year, he became a steady contributor to the journal as well as with Katkov coeditor of *Moskovskiia Viedomosti*. The other writer, Nicholas F. Pavlov, was known especially for his articles in the Katkov press.

Peter I. Bartenev, editor of the scholarly Russian historical journal, *Russkii Arkhiv* (Russian Archive), was a close friend of the Slavophiles and had in fact founded his journal under the influence of Khomiakov's ideas. Finally there was Alexander N. Karamzin, poet and writer, and son of the famous historian of the Russian state.

A fourth group among the thirty-one charter members consisted of public officials, either active or retired. Prince Irodion A. Obolenskii, State Councilor and Master of the Court, had been head of the translation section of the Foreign Ministry in 1854.

He left this post upon being appointed Kammer-junker of the Court. Above all he was a zealous philanthropist who favored all sorts of public causes. He was closely associated with Ivan S. Aksakov, under whom he had served in the revision of the court system in Astrakhan. He was also interested in the question of land reform. S. M. Sukhotin, another charter member, was also a State Councilor. Nicholas von Kruse had been a censor on the Moscow Board until 1858, when he was retired because of his liberal attitude. His retirement provided the occasion for an address of thanks signed by fifty-three of Russia's most distinguished writers including Goncharov, Chernyshevskii, Dobroliubov, Nekrasov, Saltykov, Kavelin, and several Slavophiles. Other officials among the charter members were A. I. Rachinskii, of the Foreign Ministry, and A. N. Bakhmetev, ranking member of the Ministry of Public Education in the Moscow province.[11]

The first president and, in the beginning, the only officer of the Committee was A. N. Bakhmetev, who owed this post largely to his official connections. With his death in 1861, the augmented membership of the now officially recognized Moscow Slavic Benevolent Committee met on May 19, 1861, to elect a regular slate of officers. Count D. N. Bludov, then president of the Council of State, was elected honorary president, which post he held until his death in 1875. Ivan S. Aksakov was made secretary-treasurer. On his suggestion, a standing committee of three was elected to help the officers of the Committee: P. I. Bartenev, P. A. Bezsonov, and Ia. O. Orël-Oshmiantsev.[12] In 1862 Aksakov asked to be relieved of office because of the pressure of his duties as editor of *Den'* (Day). Reluctant to lose the services of its moving spirit, the Committee prevailed upon Aksakov to remain as treasurer, using the practical argument that the public was accustomed to sending him money, and that his name was well known. Orël-Oshmiantsev was unanimously elected secretary.[13] In 1868 Nil A.

[11] A complete list of the thirty-one charter members of the Moscow Slavic Benevolent Committee may be found in Nil Popov, *Kratkii otchët o desiatiletnei dieiatel'nosti Slavianskago blagotvoritel'nago komiteta v Moskvie* (Moscow, 1868), pp. 1-2.

[12] N. P. Barsukov, *Zhizn' i trudy M. P. Pogodina*, XIX (St. Petersburg, 1905), 90-91.

[13] Popov, *Kratkii otchët*, p. 17.

Popov, Slavic historian at the University of Moscow, was elected secretary.[14] On Pogodin's death in 1875 he was succeeded by Ivan Aksakov, who remained president until the society's formal dissolution in 1878.

The Moscow Committee never had a formal constitution. In 1861 it drew up a set of rather rudimentary by-laws which stated that anyone who contributed to the Committee was to be considered a member. The amount of the contribution was left to the discretion of the donor. The rules suggested five rubles a year as an acceptable though not obligatory minimum.[15] This stipulation encouraged many to join. In its first year the Committee claimed 326 members, among them 55 women.[16] Various official accounts of the Committee's activities are generally silent on the question of membership figures for other years, largely because the number of members was never as important to the Committee as the size of their contributions. Besides, the membership at large did not generally participate in the actual work of the Committee. Rather striking proof of this was offered by the Committee's first session in 1872. President Pogodin concluded his opening statement to the meeting with the following bitter comment: "In delivering these words I ask you to observe, to the comfort of Austrian and Turkish alarmists over Panslavism, that at this first annual meeting of the Slavic Committee, a total of nine members, including three officers, have gathered! Is it not true that our Committee is very powerful, and that it conceals no trifling threat to two empires!"[17]

As the number of contributors grew, the membership at large became more and more heterogeneous. Four years after the founding of the Moscow Slavic Benevolent Committee, an official report for the years 1858 to 1862 stated with regard to the membership, "Its composition at the present time is completely alien to any exclusivism. It includes men of various literary parties, of various convictions and viewpoints, who are united only by a single com-

[14] *Ibid.*, p. 23.
[15] *Ibid.*, pp. 7-8.
[16] Josef Jirásek, *Rusko a my; dějiny vztahů československo-ruských od nejstarších dob až do roku 1914* (2d ed., Brno, 1946), I, 57.
[17] M. P. Pogodin, *Sobranie statei, pisem i riechei po povodu Slavianskago voprosa* (Moscow, 1878), p. 136.

mon idea: to be useful morally and materially to our native
brethren, the Slavs, to collaborate in the free development of their
national spirit, and to work together for their enlightenment."[18]
It is true that the Committee attracted a wide variety of people
who contributed to it for various reasons—not only out of sympathy for the Slavic cause, however one might interpret that vague
phrase, but also out of Orthodox piety, philanthropy, social ambition, or just personal friendship for Committee members. Yet
nobody knew better than the author of that official report, Ivan
Aksakov, that the underlying ideology which inspired the leaders
of the Committee was Panslavism.

Since many records of the various Slavic Benevolent Committees
in Russia—those of Moscow, St. Petersburg, Odessa, and Kiev—
have not been published, it is difficult to ascertain the degree to
which the Russian government was implicated in the work of these
committees. Even published material leaves no doubt, however,
that the Moscow Committee and its sister organizations enjoyed
official patronage, protection, and guidance. From its inception the
Moscow Committee was required to submit reports on its activities
to the Asiatic Department of the Foreign Ministry, which, despite
its name, also dealt with Balkan affairs. The first report was submitted to Egor P. Kovalevskii, the departmental chief, by Bakhmetev in 1859. Kovalevskii replied as follows:

The Minister for Foreign Affairs hastened to submit to the Sovereign
Emperor for his inspection the financial report of sums contributed by
the Benevolent Society during the last year to South Slavic churches
and schools, which report Your Excellency was pleased to send me
with your most esteemed letter of March 30. Though its financial
means are not large, the Society's activities are encouraging; even more
encouraging is the news which you report regarding the significant
increase in contributions during the present year.

There can be no doubt that, with the active and beneficial cooperation of Your Excellency, the Society's scope of activities will grow.
The beginning may be difficult, all the more inasmuch as our public
unfortunately knows little as yet about our Slav coreligionists and
their needs. Acquaintance with them will, however, be made wide-

[18] "Otchët Slavianskago obshchestva ili blagotvoritel'nago komiteta," *Den'*,
No. 17 (February 3, 1862), pp. 13-14.

spread as a result of the Society's activities as directed by you, and with this will also increase the material means for this activity, and it will undoubtedly yield a harvest in the future.[19]

While Egor Kovalevskii supervised the activities of the Moscow Committee insofar as they dealt with foreign affairs, his brother, Evgraf, supervised the philanthropic activities of the Committee, not only in his capacity as Minister of Public Education but as an elected trustee of the Committee. The financial records of the Committee show that it regularly received funds from the Ministry of Public Education, largely for the purpose of supporting Bulgarian and Serbian students in Russia. The Ministry was the Committee's most generous single donor.

The Court showed its solicitude through the personal interest which the Empress took in the work of the Moscow Committee. That society's financial records for the 1860's show that she regularly contributed 300 rubles a year to its education fund.[20] The Empress, the Heir Apparent, and other members of the Imperial family (though never the Emperor himself) also contributed both funds and supplies to the St. Petersburg Committee after its founding in 1867.[21]

The Moscow Committee maintained close relations with the Russian Orthodox Church, both through the Ober-Procurator of the Most Holy Governing Synod, Akhmatov, and directly with the hierarchy. Official reports indicate that the Church helped to collect contributions for the Committee. The Holy Synod was also useful as a channel for disbursing gifts to Balkan religious institutions. The Metropolitan Archbishop of Moscow, Philaret, was a warm supporter and generous patron of the Moscow Committee.

III

The so-called Saint Petersburg Section of the Moscow Slavic

[19] Cited by Nil Popov, *Iz istorii Slavianskago blagotvoritel'nago komiteta v Moskvie; pervoe piatilietie, 1858-1862* (Moscow, 1871), p. 45.

[20] Popov, *Kratkii otchet, passim.*

[21] *Pervyia 15 liet sushchestvovaniia S.-Peterburgskago Slavianskago blagotvoritel'nago obshchestva* (St. Petersburg, 1883), pp. 160, 216, 266, 271, and elsewhere.

Benevolent Committee—which designation it kept until 1877, when it was incorporated as a separate society—arose directly out of a committee organized in 1867 to arrange a welcome for the foreign Slavs who participated in the Moscow Slav Congress. This *ad hoc* committee was organized largely by three men: Professor Vladimir Lamanskii, Vice-Admiral A. V. Freigang, and Colonel of the General Staff M. F. Mirkovich. At least the first two, and possibly the third, were adherents of Slavophilism.[22]

It was Lamanskii's idea that the reception committee organized in 1867 be transformed into the St. Petersburg Section of the Moscow Committee. The first formal meeting of the Section took place on May 7, 1868, when about a dozen members gathered to commemorate the anniversary of the Moscow Slav Congress and to pay homage to Saints Cyril and Methodius, whose feast day is on May 11. At first the organization of the St. Petersburg Section was very informal, since it regarded itself as only a part of the Moscow Committee and therefore subject to the latter's rules and procedures, which were in turn quite informal. From its first meeting in May, 1868, to January, 1869, the Section was presided over by various members. On January 26, 1869, the Section unanimously elected Alexander Hilferding its president, which post he held until June 20, 1872.[23]

In his inaugural address of May 11, 1869, Hilferding outlined the aims of the St. Petersburg Section in the following terms:

Our aim has been and, I trust, will always be primarily to support, insofar as our means permit, the spiritual needs of the Slavic peoples across the border—their churches, schools, and literary undertakings as well as those of their young men whom they may send to us for an education; in the second place, to bring about a mutual rapprochement and to acquaint Russian society with the Slavs. No more and no less. . . . With regard to the Slavic peoples abroad, anything that lies outside of our purely spiritual and social program is alien and unknown to us. We therefore always stop where the realm of politics begins, and we avoid it. We do not do this for appearance's sake or out of calcu-

---

[22] F. M. Istomin, *Kratkii ocherk dieiatel'nosti S.-Peterburgskago Slavianskago Blagotvoritel'nago Obshchestva za 25 liet ego sushchestvovaniia, 1868-1893* (St. Petersburg, 1893), p. 12.

[23] *Pervyia 15 liet*, p. 86.

lation, but because such is the very essence of our Committee, which is a *benevolent society*.[24]

There can be no doubt that the interests and hopes of the Panslavic leaders, including Hilferding himself, went far beyond disbursing charity to other Slavs. Yet it may be said that in the period of 1870, the St. Petersburg Section as well as its sister organizations adhered, as organizations, to the aims of philanthropy, even though their very interest in the foreign Slavs inevitably bore political implications.

Like the Moscow Committee, the St. Petersburg Section sought and attracted a rather heterogeneous following—not only Slavophiles, but Orthodox zealots, Slavic scholars, professional soldiers, government officials, society ladies, publicists, and philanthropists.

Naturally the Slavophile element was less influential in the northern capital than it was on its home ground in Moscow. Nevertheless the Slavophiles and their outlook influenced the work of the Section more than any other single element. The famous poet Fëdor Tiutchev was the dean of the St. Petersburg Slavophilism of the old school. Iurii Samarin, whose official duties necessitated long stays in St. Petersburg, also represented the old guard. A more recent set of Slavophile disciples who were, at the same time, ardent Panslavists in the more political meaning of that term, included notably Hilferding, Lamanskii, Budilovich, and Miller—all of them also Slavic scholars. A closely allied ideological grouping centered about Nicholas Danilevskii and included especially N. N. Strakhov, the littérateur, and Professor K. N. Bestuzhev-Riumin.

The most distinguished Orthodox zealot in the Section was Fëdor M. Dostoievskii, the famous writer. The most active supporters of Orthodoxy abroad were the three titled ladies mentioned earlier—Countess N. D. Protasova, Princess T. V. Vasil'chikova, and Countess Antonina Bludova—whose own philanthropic circle became the kernel of a very thriving ladies' auxiliary of the St. Petersburg Section. The Section also included clerics of the Orthodox Church.

The Slavic scholars of the St. Petersburg Section included,

[24] *Ibid.*, p. 18.

besides Hilferding and Lamanskii, Orest F. Miller, mildly Slavophile and zealously Panslavist professor of history at the University
of St. Petersburg; Anton S. Budilovich, then professor of Russian
and Church Slavonic at Niezhin and also an ardent Panslavist;
K. N. Bestuzhev-Riumin; Fëdor M. Istomin, ethnographer and
folklorist; Michael I. Koialovich, professor of history at the
St. Petersburg Theological Academy and expert on church history
in the Western Provinces; and that distinguished pioneer of Slavic
studies in Russia, I. I. Sreznevskii.

The St. Petersburg Section included an important element which
was not in evidence in the Moscow Committee—the professional
military men. Among the original members, A. V. Freigang was a
vice-admiral; M. F. Mirkovich was a colonel on the General Staff;
A. B. Ivanitskii was a retired major general and army engineer;
A. I. Petrov was a high-ranking naval officer; S. A. Khrulëv was
a lieutenant general who fought under Paskevich in the Hungarian
campaign of 1849, a hero of Sevastopol during the Crimean War,
and a veteran of the Central Asian campaigns; and Major General
Michael G. Cherniaev was a hero of the Central Asian campaigns
and was destined to lead Serbia's army against the Turks in 1876.
The author of the sensational Panslavist tract *Opinion on the
Eastern Question*, General Rostislav A. Fadieev, was an important
addition to this group.

Among the most distinguished government officials in the Section
there were Iurii Samarin and Prince Alexander I. Vasil'chikov, a
close associate of Samarin's in the work of land reform, though by
no means a Slavophile himself. The latter was to preside over the
Section during its most active and difficult period, from 1876 to
1878, during the Balkan crisis and the Russo-Turkish War. Among
the officials there was also Count Nicholas Ignatiev, Russian ambassador to the Porte from 1864 to 1877, whose absence from Russia
prevented him from taking an active part in the work of the Section
in those years.

The two most noteworthy publicists in the St. Petersburg Section
were Nicholas N. Strakhov, best known for his anti-Western essays
in *Bor'ba s zapadom* (Struggle with the West), and Andrew A.
Kraevskii, publisher of the famous journal of the Westernizers,

Otechestvennyia Zapiski (Notes of the Fatherland), and editor of the *S.-Peterburgskiia Viedomosti* (St. Petersburg News) to 1862, and thereafter editor of the progressive *Golos* (Voice). As a rich man, Kraevskii was well known for his philanthropy. He was especially interested in supporting public education.

Having started with about a dozen members, the St. Petersburg Section counted 233 members by January 1, 1872, and in that single year raised the membership to almost 700.[25]

IV

A Slavic Benevolent Committee was founded in Kiev late in 1869, thanks especially to encouragement from the president of the Moscow Committee, M. P. Pogodin. In October of that year Pogodin made a visit to Kiev. An organizing meeting of interested citizens was held on October 1, on the fiftieth anniversary of the opening of the Kiev Theological Academy, and a formal letter was handed to Pogodin asking that the Moscow Committee accept the Kievan group as an affiliate. The request was signed by some of the leading figures of Kievan society, including Princess N. A. Dondukov-Korsakov, wife of the Governor-General of Kiev, Volhynia, and Podolia; P. A. Antonovich, Superintendent of the Kiev School District and ranking local official of the Ministry of Public Education; and P. D. Seletskii, head of the provincial nobility.[26] Pogodin's colleague and a charter member of the Moscow Slavic Benevolent Committee, Professor Michael A. Maksimovich, was also present at the meeting.

Acting for the Kiev group, the Moscow Committee transmitted formal requests to Count D. A. Tolstoi, Minister of Public Education, and to P. N. Stremoukhov, chief of the Foreign Ministry's Asiatic Department, for authorization to establish a Kiev Section.[27] With the approval of both officials, the Kiev Section of the Moscow

[25] Istomin, *Kratkii ocherk*, pp. 18-19.

[26] Popov, *Ocherki*, pp. 139-40. For Pogodin's part in the first meeting of the Kiev group, see M. P. Pogodin, "V predvaritel'nom sobranii Kievskago otdieleniia Slavianskago komiteta 1-go oktiabria, 1869," *Riechi proiznesenyia M. P. Pogodinym v torzhestvennykh i prochikh sobraniiakh, 1830-1872* (Moscow, 1872), p. 593.

[27] Popov, *Ocherki*, p. 140.

Slavic Benevolent Committee was legally established on December 21, 1869.[28] The first president of the Section was Bishop Porfirii (Uspenskii). Its first vice-president was Gregory P. Galagan, scion of an old Russian noble family, a high government official with a special interest in land reform in the Southeastern Provinces, and an amateur of Ukrainian folklore.[29] One of the most active members of the Kiev Section was V. A. Bil'basov. Once called by Pogodin "the soul of the Kiev Slavic Benevolent Committee," Bil'basov was for twelve years coeditor of the *Golos* with his father-in-law, A. A. Kraevskii, and author of historical works on Saints Cyril and Methodius and Jan Hus.

The Odessa Slavic Benevolent Society of Saints Cyril and Methodius was founded on May 11, 1870, on the feast of the Protopraeceptors of the Slavs and the thousand-year anniversary of the Bulgarian Orthodox Church.[30] Its most active founders were two professors of Slavic studies at the University of Novorossiisk in Odessa, Grigorovich and Bogišić.

Victor Ivanovich Grigorovich, first secretary of the Society, was a pioneer of Slavic studies in Russia. He was the author of a history of Slavic literature which Kotliarevskii called "the first learned work in Russia on Slavic literature from the standpoint of Slavic mutual relations."[31] As a member of the Odessa Society, A. Kochubinskii, declared, "Our Society was not only the offspring of Grigorovich's cherished thoughts; it existed within him even before its realization. . . . An enthusiast, a poet in politics, somewhat of a dreamer, he was nevertheless far from resorting to journalistic pathos or memorized phrases—in Slavic reciprocity he was a realist."[32]

Valtazar (Baldo) Bogišić was a native of Cavtat (Ragusa Vecchia), just outside of Dubrovnik, a Serb who became an authority on the history of Slavic jurisprudence, especially the common law. In 1868, thanks partly to the efforts of Father Raevskii in Vienna,

[28] *Pervyia 15 liet*, p. 39, minutes for January 4, 1870, citing a report in the *Pravitel'stvennyi Viestnik*, No. 280, 1869.

[29] *Ibid.*, p. 154, minutes for March 14, 1871.

[30] Popov, *Ocherki*, p. 140.

[31] *Novyi Entsiklopedicheskii Slovar'*, XV (St. Petersburg, n.d.), 22-23.

[32] A. Kochubinskii, *My i oni (1711-1878); ocherki istorii i politiki slavian* (Odessa, 1878), p. 224.

Bogišić was invited to Russia to lecture at the University of St. Petersburg. In 1870 he was appointed professor of Slavic law at the University of Novorossiisk (previously the Richelieu Lycée).[33]

The constitution of the Odessa Slavic Benevolent Society of Saints Cyril and Methodius was officially confirmed by the Minister of the Interior on April 8, 1870. The first two articles of the constitution outlined the following aims:

Art. I. The Odessa Slavic Benevolent Society has as its aim to extend help to needy Slavs and to encourage beneficial work in the field of Slavic learning and art.

Art. II. In accord with this aim and commensurate with the expansion of the Society's means, its activity may include the following:

1. To give material aid to the really needy;
2. To aid those young Slavs who may come to Russia to receive an education; and
3. To enable Slavs arriving in Odessa to find means of support through applications on their behalf to the local authorities, social institutions, or private persons.[34]

The Odessa Slavic Benevolent Society was apparently not subordinated to the Moscow Slavic Benevolent Committee, which was not mentioned in the constitution of the Odessa Society.

In the period 1856 to 1870, the committees of Moscow, St. Petersburg, Kiev, and Odessa were the only Panslavic organizations in the Russian Empire. They had only a small membership, of which number the really active Panslavists comprised but a handful. In these years the Russian Panslavic movement certainly could not be described as something powerful or nation-wide in its influence.

V

A review of the activities of the Russian Slavic Benevolent Committees shows the modesty of their effort. Up to the Balkan crisis of 1875, these organizations devoted themselves exclusively to cultural and philanthropic enterprises—scholarships for foreign

---

[33] V. N. Korablev, "Baltasar Bogishioh i akademik Lamanskii," *Trudy Instituta slavianovedeniia Akademii nauk SSSR*, II (Leningrad, 1934), 163.

[34] *Pravitel'stvennyi Viestnik*, No. 92, May 2/14, 1870, p. 1.

Slavs studying in Russia, aid to Orthodox churches and schools abroad, the dissemination of the Russian language and literature among other Slavs, support of Slavic learned and literary societies abroad, and the like.

The financial records of the Moscow and St. Petersburg Committees (records are not available for the organizations in Kiev and Odessa) indicate that their largest single expenditure went for the support of Bulgarian and Serbian students. In the first decade of its existence the Moscow Slavic Benevolent Committee contributed to the support of some forty-six Bulgarian and Serbian students for varying periods of time. Thirty-one of these students attended the University of Moscow; eight were theological students; three were enrolled in military academies; three were art students (of whom one specialized in iconography); and one student was assigned to a monastery.[35] Statistics are not available for the number of foreign Slavic students supported by the St. Petersburg Section. Its expenditures for scholarships indicate, however, that the Section regarded the education of foreign Slavs in Russia as its prime and most regular commitment.[36] Inasmuch as the St. Petersburg Section devoted its attention to a wider variety of projects than did its Moscow counterpart, its expenditures for scholarships accounted for a lower percentage of total disbursements than was the case with the Moscow Committee. The declared intent of the St. Petersburg Section as of 1870 was to allot 25 percent of its future annual budgets to the education of foreign Slavs in Russia, this item being one of eight categories of expenditures.[37] The overwhelming majority of scholarship students were Orthodox Bulgars and Serbs.

The number of Balkan students educated by the Moscow and St. Petersburg Committees was not impressive. It must be noted, however, that some of these stipendiaries became prominent national leaders among their own people. Probably the most brilliant example among them was Liuben Karavelov, who was to become one of the most outstanding leaders of the Bulgarian liberation movement. Enrolled in the history and philosophy faculty of the

[35] Popov, *Kratkii otchët*, pp. 26-27.

[36] See *Pervyia 15 liet*, Appendix VI, for the financial records of the St. Petersburg Section.

[37] *Ibid.*, pp. 98 ff., especially minutes for the meeting of Nov. 14, 1870.

University of Moscow from 1857, Karavelov spent nine years in Russia gaining a conservative formal education and a liberal informal one.[38] Among the Bulgarian stipendiaries there was also Constantine Miladinov, who came to Moscow in 1858 to study philology. He died only four years later in Istanbul, but his collection of Bulgarian folk poetry, published in Zagreb, was a great contribution to his people's cultural awakening. There was also the young Macedonian, Xenofont Raiko Zhinzifov, who became one of Bulgaria's greatest revolutionary poets. A fourth stipendiary was Marin Drinov, student in both the Kiev Theological Academy and the history faculty of the University of Moscow. He subsequently became professor of Slavic history at the University of Kharkov, and gained repute as a historian of the Bulgarian people and its church. After 1878 he held an official post in the Russian administration of Bulgaria. Other important Bulgarian stipendiaries of the Moscow Committee included Khristo K. Daskalov, V. Popovich, G. Teokharov, P. Todorovich, who translated Hilferding's history of the Serbs and Bulgars, and K. Viazanko, who translated Samarin's work on the Jesuits into Bulgarian.[39]

The second most important activity of the Slavic Committees, as measured by the amount of money spent, was aid to schools and churches, predominantly in the Orthodox Slavic provinces of the Ottoman Empire—Bulgaria, Macedonia, Bosnia and Hercegovina in particular—and in the partly Orthodox provinces of Austria-Hungary, especially Galicia, Carpatho-Russia, and Bukovina. The records of the Moscow and St. Petersburg Committees include, for example, items such as the following: 48 rubles from Prince Vasil'chikov for the Bulgarian monastery of St. John of Rila; 260 rubles for vestments and religious articles for various Bulgarian churches; 107 rubles for religious and school books for Bulgarian schools; funds for the completion of the Serbian cathedral in Mostar, Hercegovina; 225 rubles for an Orthodox monastic school in Dalmatia; funds for a girls' school at Sarajevo; 66 rubles for the monastery of Žitomislić in Hercegovina; books for a public school

---

[38] Georgi Konstantinov, *Vodji bugarskog narodnog pokreta* (Belgrade, 1939), pp. 115 ff.

[39] Popov, *Ocherki*, pp. 135-36.

in Brčan, Hercegovina; bells for the Orthodox convent of Kazanlik, Bulgaria; 17 rubles for the Bulgarian school in Istanbul.[40]

Churches and schools in Serbia and Montenegro also received support. When the head of the Serbian Church, Metropolitan Michael, visited Russia in 1869, he attended a meeting of the Moscow Committee on October 13 and a meeting of the St. Petersburg Section on October 26 to thank both groups for their aid.[41] Following his visit to Russia, Prince Nicholas I of Montenegro also sent to the Moscow Committee his personal thanks for aid, in April, 1870.[42]

That the Slavs of Austria-Hungary were not entirely neglected is shown by items such as the following: 125 rubles for Russian historical and literary works sent to Galicia, Bohemia, and Slovakia; 120 rubles to the Society of St. John the Baptist in Prešov (Priashev) for the education of Carpatho-Russian youths; 50 rubles' worth of books on Russian history and religion to various Slavic centers, plus a personal donation of ten crates of books by Michael Pogodin; 55 rubles' worth of Russian books for schools in Lwów (Lvov), Prešov, Prague, Zagreb, and Belgrade; 100 gulden to K. A. Dieditskii for a Russian cultural center in Lwów.[43]

One of the more important cultural activities of the Slavic Benevolent Committees in Russia was the maintenance of relations with various learned and national societies in the Slavic lands abroad. The significance of these societies in the national awakening of the Slavic peoples outside Russia was enormous. By 1869 there were nine such societies in the non-Russian Slavic world, eight of them in Austria-Hungary.[44] A report of the Moscow

---

[40] These items were selected at random from Popov, *Kratkii otchët*, for the Moscow Committee, and *Pervyia 15 liet* for the St. Petersburg Section.

[41] For a description of Metropolitan Michael's visit to the Moscow Committee, see Popov, *Ocherki*, pp. 136-37; for the Serbian prelate's visit to the St. Petersburg Section, see *Pervyia 15 liet*, pp. 30 ff.

[42] Popov, *Ocherki*, p. 138.

[43] See footnote 40 above.

[44] Most of these societies bore the Slavic name *matica* (from the root *mat'* or "mother"), after the first such organization, the Serbian Matica in Budapest, which was founded in 1826. In Serbian the word *matica* signifies the queen bee. The nine Slavic learned societies mentioned above included the following: the Serbian Matica of Budapest, which was removed to Novi Sad; the Czech Matica; the Lusatian Serbian Matica in Bautzen (Budyšin); the Galician Matica in Lwów; the Society of Saints Cyril and Methodius, which later became the Moravian

Slavic Benevolent Committee for 1869 states: "The Moscow Committee maintained relations with the most important of the Slavic learned and literary societies and served as an intermediary between them and Russian societies and scholars, predominantly those of Moscow, in the matter of the mutual exchange of their publications. Through its mediation fourteen editorial offices of Russian newspapers and journals sent their publications to the Slavic lands free of charge."[45] In 1871 the St. Petersburg Section formally resolved to become a member of the nine Slavic literary centers abroad. By November of that year it was enrolled in all except the Galician and Serbian societies in Lwów and Novi Sad, whose constitutions forbade the inclusion of non-Austrian subjects in their organizations, but the St. Petersburg Section nevertheless contributed to these two societies.[46]

Relations between the Moscow and St. Petersburg Committees and the Slavic societies abroad were facilitated by the fact that many distinguished members of the Russian groups were honorary and corresponding members of the foreign Slavic societies. Pogodin, Sreznevskii, Hilferding, Soloviëv, and Buslaev were members of Czech societies. Bludov, Protasov, Bodianskii, Lamanskii, Bezsonov, Maikov, and Ivan Aksakov belonged to the Serbian Matica. Pogodin and Sreznevskii were both enrolled in Croatian societies. Raevskii and Lamanskii belonged to the Slovak Matica.[47] Through these men the Slavic Benevolent Committees were able to reach the most active leaders of the various Slavic national movements.

The St. Petersburg Section fulfilled one of the functions of a learned society by supporting the publication of monographs on Slavic history and culture. This activity of the Section was super-

---

Matica in Brno; the Illyrian Matica of Zagreb; the Slovak Matica, then in Bistrica; the Dalmatian Matica in Zara (Zadar); and the Slovenian Matica in Ljubljana. In addition to these national literary organizations, there were also such learned societies as the Serbian Learned Society of Belgrade, the Yugoslav Academy of Zagreb, and the Learned Society of Cracow. See A. S. Budilovich, "Slavianskiia matitsy i uchenyia druzhstva," *Zhurnal Ministerstva Narodnago Prosvieshcheniia,* CXLI (1869), 460-61.

[45] Cited by Popov, *Ocherki,* pp. 137-38.

[46] *Pervyia 15 liet,* p. 162, minutes for May 2, 1871; p. 168, minutes for October 3, 1871; and p. 204, minutes for April 2, 1872.

[47] Budilovich, "Slavianskiia matitsy i uchenyia druzhstva," *Zhurnal Ministerstva Narodnago Prosvieshcheniia,* CXLI, 455-56.

vised by a special publications board which was established in April, 1869, at the suggestion of Hilferding. The board, which originally consisted of eight members, declared that its aim was "(1) to acquaint Russia with the Slavic world, and (2) to acquaint the Slavic world with Russia." A separate fund was set aside for publications.[48] The Moscow Committee also supported the publication of learned works, though on a more modest scale.[49]

Apart from supporting foreign Slavic students in Russia, subsidizing Slavic churches and schools outside Russia, encouraging the spread of Russian culture among the other Slavs, and publishing learned works, the Slavic Benevolent Committees in Russia engaged in a wide miscellany of activities. For example, the Moscow Committee sponsored the erection of a Serbian hostel and chapel in Moscow, proceeds from which were to go to the Serbian Church in Belgrade.[50] The St. Petersburg Section sent subsidies to teachers of the Russian language in the Slavic lands. All four committees encouraged the cult of Saints Cyril and Methodius by holding annual commemoration services on May 11. They also sponsored lectures on the Slavs, designed to enlighten the Russian public. Probably the most unusual venture of the Slavic Benevolent Committees was their support of a project to attract Czech colonists to the Caucasus and the Amur valley. The idea never attracted more than a very few Czech families.[51]

[48] *Pervyia 15 liet*, Appendix II, pp. 830-35, contains a short sketch of the activities of the St. Petersburg Section's publications board. Most of the monographs published under this program were marked by the Panslavic tendencies of both their authors and their sponsors. The first work to appear under these auspices was a composite volume by A. S. Budilovich and A. P. Naranovich in 1871 entitled *Chekhiia i Moraviia* (Bohemia and Moravia). The same year saw the publication of Hilferding's curious work, *Obshcheslavianskaia azbuka* (All-Slavic Alphabet), which proposed the adoption by all the Slavs of the Russian Cyrillic alphabet modified according to local need by diacritical marks. The St. Petersburg Section also set aside a fund for prizes which were awarded for monographs in certain fields of Slavic history. The John Hus Prize and the Cyril and Methodius Prize reflected the interest which Russian Panslavism had in encouraging a *los von Rom* movement among the Western Slavs.

[49] For example, in 1861 the Moscow Slavic Benevolent Committee awarded its stipendiary, Liuben Karavelov, 170 rubles for the publication of his study *Pamiatniki narodnago byta Bolgar* (Monuments of the Bulgars' Way of Life). *Ibid.*

[50] I. V. Koz'menko, "Kommentarii," *Slavianskii Sbornik; Slavianskii vopros i russkoe obshchestvo v 1867-1878 godakh* (Moscow, 1948), p. 192.

[51] *Pervyia 15 liet*, p. 2, minutes for October 7, 1868, and *passim*.

VI

A review of the history of the Slavic Benevolent Committees in Russia from 1858 to 1870 indicates that these organizations were not inspired by aggressive imperialistic designs but were concerned with the more immediate problem of establishing relations on a nonpolitical plane with the Slavs of Central and Southern Europe. In this way, certain Russian Panslavists hoped, there would eventually be created a buffer of friends between a militarily beaten and diplomatically isolated Russia and a West which they believed to be unalterably hostile to their own world. However political this aim might have been, the Slavic Committees did not engage in any direct intervention in the political affairs of neighboring states until well into 1875, at the time of the Balkan crisis, and then only over the protests of some of their leading members as well as of the Russian government itself.

It is true that the Slavic Benevolent Committee in Moscow and its sister organizations were established with the sanction of the Russian government. It is also true that they received funds from the Asiatic Department of the Foreign Ministry, from the Ministry of Public Education, the Synod of the Russian Orthodox Church, and members of the Imperial family, notably the Empress. Yet official sanction was given only with misgiving on the part of Gorchakov himself and over the opposition of various official circles which continued to regard the Panslavists as dangerous and irresponsible fanatics. The Foreign Ministry might have found it useful to support a private organization whose aim was to gain Russia a reservoir of moral support which might prove useful in a crisis or even as a good talking point in negotiations with the Austrians or the Turks. Yet there is no indication that the Russian government seriously shared Panslavic hopes of a political federation of the Slavs.

What gave political significance to the activities of the Slavic Committees was the fact that Austria-Hungary and the Ottoman Empire were subject to strong internal stresses which would have arisen had there been no Russian Panslavic activity whatever. It cannot be seriously argued that the Russian Panslavists inspired the subject Slavic nationalities to hate the governments of Turkey or Austria-Hungary. That hatred was already there. It is true that the Slavic Committees of Russia encouraged the non-Russian Slavs to look upon Russia as the leader and protector of the Slavic race. Austria-Hungary and Turkey had reason to be troubled by the activities of the Russian Panslavists. Yet these two governments had even more reason to fear a Russia whose very existence as a mighty state seemed to inspire the subject Slavic nationalities to assert their own national dignity and to seek national independence.

6

LINGUISTIC PANSLAVISM IN RUSSIA

And the Slavonic tongue and the Russian are one.

THE RUSSIAN PRIMARY CHRONICLE

ONE OF THE MORE CONCRETE aspects of Russian Panslavism in the reign of Alexander II took the form of a program for the cultural rapprochement of the Slavic peoples. Slavic unity could not rest simply on some supposed atavistic call of the blood. Before any racial affinity could become the basis for a conscious program of political unification, it was first necessary to stimulate cultural intercourse among the various Slavic nationalities, and this, in turn, required the creation or adoption of a single Slavic language, to be used by all literate Slavs.

Panslavists, both Russian and non-Russian, have generally proposed that Slavic linguistic rapprochement be achieved in one of three ways: through the adoption by all Slavs of a single Slavic tongue native to none; by making a living Slavic language the medium for higher learning, literature, and diplomacy; or through a reduction in the number of Slavic dialects and establishing a minimum number of regional literary languages.[1]

The first course involved the adoption of either Church Slavonic or some artificially contrived Slavic tongue. The only common written language ever possessed by the great majority of Slavs, Church Slavonic was hailed by Panslavists and Slavic philologists alike as proof of a proto-Slavic unity. Moreover, it was a bond between the Orthodox Slavs of Russia and the Balkans. Church Slavonic offered a tie even with Roman Catholic Slavs. The found-

---

[1] A. N. Pypin, "Teoriia obshcheslavianskago iazyka," *Viestnik Evropy*, I (1892), 793.

ers of the first Slavic written language, Saints Cyril and Methodius, were honored by Slavs of both the Greek and the Latin rites. Church Slavonic, written in the Glagolitic alphabet, was still in use by a few Roman Catholic Croatian parishes in Dalmatia and by a few monastic outposts such as the Benedictine monastery of Emmäus just outside Prague. In addition, of course, millions of Uniats or Greek Catholics in White Russia, the Ukraine Bukovina, and elsewhere in Central Europe used Church Slavonic in their services just as did their Orthodox brethren.

Despite these advantages, Church Slavonic had little appeal for many Panslavists. The stiff, complex structure and limited vocabulary of a medieval sacred language fell short of the demands of a modern political creed. Its association with a particular church— the Eastern Orthodox—and a particular script—the Cyrillic— rendered Church Slavonic unacceptable to Roman Catholic and Protestant Slavs alike. Some of its proponents, nearly all non-Russians, had hoped that the revival of a classical tongue that was the heritage of no single Slavic group would obviate the danger of arousing national jealousies. The very remoteness of Church Slavonic from daily life, however, repelled all but a very few rather obscure champions.

The conception of an alternative—a contrived *lingua slavica*— was the product of the seventeenth century. It found its most noteworthy proponent in the Croatian Roman Catholic priest Juraj Križanić. This remarkable precursor of Panslavism developed a Slavic language of his own creation during his sojourn in Muscovy in the reign of Tsar Alexis. This hybrid language was largely a mixture of his native Croatian dialect (Kajkavian), Russian, and Church Slavonic written in a modified Latin alphabet. Križanić formulated his Panslavic tongue in a grammar entitled *Objasnênje vivódno o pismĕ slovĕnskom* (Introductory Explanation of Slavic Grammar). Designed as a counterpart to the Latin of Western European society in a century of cosmopolitanism, Križanić's artificial language failed to attract more than the academic interest of nineteenth-century Slavic scholars.[2]

---

[2] See M. B. Petrovich, "Juraj Križanić; a Precursor of Pan-Slavism," *American Slavic and East European Review*, VI (1947), 75-92.

II

Many Russian Panslavists of the nineteenth century, especially such professors of Slavic studies as Lamanskii, Hilferding, and Budilovich, and publicists like Ivan Aksakov, Katkov, and Danilevskii, held that the Slavs should be linked together by one literary language, and that Russian was the only reasonable choice. Their arguments reflect the doctrine and the program of Russian Panslavism.

Many influential Panslavists in Russia, though not all, were Slavophiles, whose outlook was permeated by the distinction they saw between Romano-Germanic Europe and Greco-Slavic Europe. Themselves the pupils of Romanticism and German Idealism, these Panslavists regarded the spoken word as a true reflection of a culture and as the manifestation of its unique if not imperishable soul. The remarkable homogeneity which the Slavic vernaculars had preserved through a thousand years of diverse destinies marked, for the Russian Panslavist, the primary bond which identified all Slavdom as one. "Language was our first tie," Pogodin proclaimed to the Moscow Slav Congress in 1867.[3] And on another occasion he asserted, "All of us have a hopeful point of unification. This is language. . . . Language—this is our treasure, our strength, our honor and glory, the staff of our nationality, the anchor of our salvation, the pledge of our success."[4]

Apollon A. Maikov, a charter member of the Moscow Slavic Benevolent Committee, regarded Slavic linguistic unity as proof of an original community of Slavic peoples, which, having become separated, had each lost something of the common Slavic spirit and way of life, some more than others. Each had also preserved a portion of the common heritage. Only by mutual cultural intercourse facilitated by a common literary language could the whole be restored, Maikov declared, and the Slavs become themselves again in their own truly autochtonous culture.[5]

---

[3] *Slavianskii s"iezd v Pragie i godovshchina s"iezda v Moskvie* (Moscow, 1868), p. 18.

[4] M. P. Pogodin, "Okruzhnoe poslanie k Slavianam," *Sobranie statei, pisem i riechei po povodu Slavianskago voprosa* (Moscow, 1878), p. 15; originally written on March 25, 1862.

[5] F. M. Istomin, *Kratkii ocherk dieiatel'nosti S.-Peterburgskago Slavianskago*

Katkov propagated the same view, though in somewhat more practical language. "It is necessary for the Slavs to be able to understand one another more directly, easily, and fully," he wrote in his *Moskovskiia Viedomosti* (Moscow News) in 1867, "that is, they must have a single common language equally understood by all." Unity of spirit, fraternity, natural ties, and the like were all fine, he averred, but language was a positive test. Danes, Germans, the Dutch, the English are all related, he declared, but they are foreign to one another, and their kinship is of no interest to anyone except the ethnographers. The Slavs were different, Katkov insisted. Despite their various conditions of life, they remained Slavs.[6] He deplored the linguistic fragmentation of the Slavs and warned that it courted their complete assimilation by aggressive Western cultures, especially the German. "It is high time," Katkov proclaimed in an editorial, "to put an end to this business which has led not to unity and strength but to disunity and weakness." The Austrian Slavs especially, he complained, were nothing but loose grains of sand (*arena sine calce*, to use his expression) which needed the cement of Slavic consciousness. Katkov warned that only a single Panslavic language could lead to this consciousness.[7]

Professor Vladimir Lamanskii could hardly have emphasized the importance of the linguistic question more strongly than when he charged, "We see that the present servile status and spiritual subjection of the Saxon, Prussian, Austrian, and Turkish Slavs to other nations rests very little, if at all (we do not speak of the Turks here), on any external circumstances, but arises principally and even entirely from the linguistic autonomy of all the Slavic dialects and branches." He concluded in italics: *"Only the abolition of this autonomy among the Slavs by their recognition of the hegemony of one of the Slavic dialects can put an end to their servile position and spiritual slavery."*[8]

---

blagotvoritel'nago obshchestva za 25 liet ego sushchestvovaniia, 1868-1893 (St. Petersburg, 1893), p. 6; from an address delivered in 1867.

[6] M. N. Katkov, "Moskva, 22-go maia," *Moskovskiia Viedomosti*, No. 112 (1867), p. 264.

[7] M. N. Katkov, "Moskva, 12-go iiunia," *Moskovskiia Viedomosti*, No. 128 (1867), pp. 297-301 *passim*.

[8] V. I. Lamanskii, *Natsional'nost' ital'ianskaia i slavianskaia v politicheskom i literaturnom otnosheniiakh* (St. Petersburg, 1865), p. 17.

The expression "linguistic hegemony" became a watchword for Lamanskii and other Russian Panslavists, and one which they made no effort to conceal. On the contrary, they were quite outspoken in their abhorrence of linguistic diversity within a racial group and condemned it as reactionary. Lamanskii drew a contemptuous comparison between the linguistic patchwork of aboriginal Africa, Asia, and America—where one village could not understand the next—and the Slavic scene. "Such is the ideal," he charged, "which is being proposed to us in the form of a Slavic federation in which every people, every microscopic folk, is to have its own literature without recognizing the hegemony of any other Slavic language. Meanwhile, until such a federation is established, the Slavs are living under the rule of the Germans and the Turks, and are being subjected to the hegemony of other languages: German, Italian, Greek, and even Hungarian and Rumanian."[9]

Lamanskii insisted that there was, as he expressed it, an "aristocracy among languages." He viewed as both natural and desirable the process that compelled dialects within any given linguistic family to make way for the primacy of that dialect which was strong enough to establish itself as the medium of a higher culture. In this sense, Lamanskii argued, hegemony was a blessing, for if all languages, dialects, sub-dialects, and speeches could lay claim to equality and autonomy, there would be no science and learning.

Another Panslavist, P. Shchebal'skii, assailed Slavic linguistic fragmentation as a historically reactionary tendency characteristic of feudal times. He likened the opponents of Slavic linguistic unification to the nobles who fought the "progressive" tendencies of such monarchs as Louis XI of France or Ivan IV of Muscovy. "Our [Slavic] friends abroad," he declared ex cathedra, "are experiencing the feudal or appanage period of their intellectual history." As long as the non-Russian Slavs insisted on their own local speeches, he warned, Western Europe would hold them in contempt, and history would condemn them. Centripetal and not centrifugal forces, Shchebal'skii declared, created and molded the mighty leaders of modern universal civilization such as England or France. He urged the Slavs to follow the same course. It was

[9] *Ibid.*, p. 18.

clear to him that the Slavs would have to give up their linguistic particularism and to accept what he believed to be a Slavic counterpart of Dante's Tuscan and Luther's Saxon.[10]

But would the Pole or Czech or Serb be willing to sacrifice his own language to a Panslavic literary language? As one reply to this objection Hilferding and Lamanskii pointed to the Italian and German movements for unification. The former observed that the Germans had several times as many political divisions as the Slavs and a multitude of dialects which differed from one another more than the most diverse Slavic languages differed among themselves. Yet the Germans had reason to boast of a rich literature, while the Austrian Slavs alone insisted on some seven or eight separate languages.[11] His colleague, Lamanskii, assured his fellow Slavs that the Venetians, Genoese, and Neapolitans also gloried in their own dialects, history, and tradition. By accepting Tuscan as the language of their literature and government, he pointed out, they had not lost their own characteristics and individualities but had only gained in the preservation of their common culture. In Naples in the autumn of 1864, profoundly distressed by news of the Polish insurrection, Lamanskii wrote:

At a time when the Germans are creating theory after theory and thinking up *Verein* after *Verein* for the realization of German unity, and when the Italians are exposing themselves to worthy and vain sacrifices and efforts for the unification of Italy, the Slavic world in the south is being deprived of the most elementary rights, and in the north and west it presents a sorry picture of savage, cruel enmity between Polish and Russian brethren. Czechs are at odds with Slovaks, and Croats with Serbs. Upon looking deeper into the contemporary difference between the Slavs and the Italians and Germans, the observer will note that it consists mainly of the fact that the Slavs, unlike the latter, do not possess their own individual culture and are deprived of that agency or medium without which no national culture can exist. In other words, the Italians and the Germans have their own common literary languages, while the Slavs have not.[12]

[10] P. Shchebal'skii, "Prezhnii i nynieshnii panslavizm," *Russkii Viestnik*, LXVIII (April, 1867), 830-41 *passim*.
[11] A. Hilferding, *Sobranie sochineniia*, Vol. II: *Stat'i po sovremennym voprosam slavianskim* (St. Petersburg, 1868), pp. 85-86.
[12] Lamanskii, *Natsional'nost' ital'ianskaia i slavianskaia*, p. 15.

To be sure, the analogy which these Russian Panslavists made between German and Italian unification on the one hand and the Slavs on the other was an imperfect one in many ways. The Poles, Czechs, Serbs, and the rest could hardly regard the language of their national literatures as comparable to Plattdeutsch or Sicilian. Yet this is exactly the view which Hilferding and Lamanskii urged upon their proud non-Russian kinsmen.

One of the most frequently advanced reasons for proposing a Panslavic literary language was that the Slavs were ignorant of one another as the result of their long historic separation and linguistic differentiation. After a lengthy tour through the Slav lands outside Russia, Professor Lamanskii wrote in 1864 that he could never have imagined that his own country was so little known among the other Slavs. Their ignorance was the more curious, he reported, since so many of them were genuinely interested in the Russian people. "In general," Lamanskii admitted ruefully, "Russian history, statistics, Russian law, the Russian Church, the Russian way of life, and Russian literature are so little known to the Western Slavs that not only is it much easier to discuss Russia with a German, but even with an Englishman and a Frenchman, for with the Slav one is always obliged to start explaining *ab ovo*."[13] He reported that so few of the non-Russian Slavs read the Russian language that he found masses of Russian books in their libraries with pages still uncut![14]

The Russian Panslavists also lamented over Russians' ignorance of their Slavic brethren. "In recent times," complained an anonymous contributor to Aksakov's *Den'* (Day) in 1862, "books, journals, and newspapers have greatly multiplied among us. And what is there that we do not talk about here! We have become zealous publicists, all-knowing politicians. We have analyzed the Italian question through and through, and have attributed all blunders to Cavour's 'blockhead' policies. We are very taken up with the issue

[13] Cited by A. N. Pypin, "Literaturnyi panslavizm," *Viestnik Evropy* (September, 1879), pp. 325-26.
[14] The present writer had a similar, though less drastic, experience during his stay in Prague in 1949, nearly a century later, when he was forced to cut the pages of the original 1868 edition of Hilferding's collected articles in the Slavic Library of Charles University.

of the North American question. As to what is going on among our coracialists, the Slavs, we know nothing and care nothing."[15]

Hilferding offered some reasons to explain Russian ignorance of the other Slavs. Not having states of their own, the non-Russian Slavs did not figure in European politics sufficiently to attract the attention of the Russian public. More important to Hilferding was the habit of many Russians to look at the world through the spectacles of the German, French, or English press. "The foreigners," he charged, "make certain to speak as little as possible about the Slavs so as to conceal them, if possible, from our own eyes and the eyes of all mankind. This is to their profit, especially to the profit of the Germans, and it is very easy to understand this business."[16]

"Just ask the majority of the professors of world history in our Russian universities whether they are acquainted with the history not only of distant Slavic peoples but of those closest to us, such as the Poles," Ivan Aksakov challenged in an editorial in the first issue of *Den'*. "Every one of them will admit as a conscientious man that he knows nothing at all about it. And indeed, how would he know! The Germans (with the exception of Ranke) never wrote about it."[17]

Believing that the Slavs clearly needed a common literary language, the Russian Panslavists were unanimous in their conviction that Great Russian should be that language. Of all the Slavic languages, Lamanskii insisted, only Great Russian could pretend to a "universal-historical significance." It was the literary language of some sixty million Slavs in the Empire, and the second language of another ten to fifteen million non-Russian subjects of the Tsar, while all other Slavic languages combined could claim no more than half that number.[18] Think of what it would mean, wrote

[15] A. Ts. "Mysl' o soborie po dielu Bolgarskomu," *Den'*, No. 13 (January 13, 1862), p. 5.
[16] A. Hilferding, "Slavianskie narody v Avstrii i Turtsii," *Stat'i po sovremennym voprosam slavianskim,* in *Sobranie sochineniia,* II, 4.
[17] Ivan S. Aksakov, *Sochineniia,* Vol. I: *Slavianskii vopros, 1860-1886* (Moscow, 1886), p. 7. Aksakov made an exception of Ranke for the latter's *Die serbische Revolution,* first published in Hamburg in 1829 and republished several times.
[18] The St. Petersburg Section of the Moscow Slavic Benevolent Committee pub-

Pogodin, if all non-Russian Slavs adopted Russian as a Panslavic literary language. Each of their authors would then be writing for a public of a hundred million fellow Slavs instead of for his own small national group.[19] While Pogodin ignored the fact that the great majority of his own compatriots could not be included in the "reading public," his argument was impressive.

The "quasi-literary" languages of the non-Russian Slavs suffered even more by comparison with Great Russian, Professor Budilovich pointed out, when one considered that almost all of these languages were still doing battle with dialects which aspired to a literary status. Furthermore, Budilovich observed, each of these languages was being constantly undermined and polluted by non-Slavic influences. He found it difficult to imagine how any of the minor Slavic languages could long survive when the Czech, Serbian, Croatian, and other Slavic intelligentsia habitually used German, Italian, Magyar, and other non-Slavic languages as their medium of culture and administration.[20]

Russian, on the other hand, was the official language of the most powerful Slavic state in existence, a vast empire which covered one sixth of the world's surface. Out of every twenty-four hours

---

lished the following figures in 1875 on the number of speakers of the non-Russian Slavic languages:

Serbo-Croatian	5,940,000
Bulgarian	5,123,000
Czech	4,851,000
Slovak	2,223,000
Slovene	1,287,000
Kashub	111,000
Upper Lusatian	96,000
Lower Lusatian	40,000

Highly indicative of the Section's policy is the fact that not only did these statistics omit the Ukrainians and White Russians as separate linguistic categories, but even the Poles. The languages of these peoples were simply included in the statistics given for the Russian Empire. These statistics were compiled by Anton Budilovich, a Panslavist, and may be found in his article, "O literaturnom edinstvie narodov Slavianskago plemeni," *Slavianskii Sbornik*, II (St. Petersburg, 1877), 3. This article is a summary of an address which Budilovich delivered before the St. Petersburg Section on May 11, 1875.

[19] M. P. Pogodin, "Godovshchina Slavianskago s"iezda v Moskvie," *Sobranie statei, pisem i riechei po povodu Slavianskago voprosa* (Moscow, 1878), p. 74.

[20] Budilovich, "O literaturnom edinstvie narodov Slavianskago plemeni," *Slavianskii Sbornik*, II, 3.

in which the sun traveled its course about the earth, Pogodin observed with more national pride than fidelity to science, twenty hours belonged to Russia![21] Great Russian was the language of a world-renowned literature which was being translated into the other major languages.

Various Russian Panslavists invoked the tradition of Saints Cyril and Methodius on behalf of the claim of Russian to become the Panslavic literary tongue. Lamanskii called it "the direct and only lawful successor to the Old Slavonic written language."[22] Why try to transform Church Slavonic into a modern literary language, Pogodin objected, when Russian was but the enriched modern version of the same language? To those who, like himself, desired a common Panslavic tongue, Pogodin advised, "Take one for yourselves not from the grave but from life. Take life, not death—that is, *write in Russian!*"[23] He asserted that the Great Russian language contained so many characteristics which were common to all the other Slavic languages that it could justly be considered a true representative of them all. "God has foreordained a wondrous destiny for it," he predicted, "by having put it in the mouths of that people which has been consecrated to primacy over all the peoples of the Slavic, and perhaps of the European, world!"[24]

The same strong strain of Messianism is to be found in a letter from Ivan Aksakov to the Czech leader, František Rieger. Claiming that the Russian nation had been "anointed to primacy," Aksakov argued that the Russian language properly merited a corresponding preeminence.[25]

Lamanskii did not conceal his hope that "the spread of the Russian language beyond Russia's borders means the dissemination of Russian ideas, Russian influence."[26] On the other hand, he fore-

---

[21] Pogodin, "Godovshchina Slavianskago s"iezda v Moskvie," *Sobranie statei*, p. 75.

[22] V. I. Lamanskii, *Ob istoricheskom izuchenii Greko-Slavianskago mira v Evropie* (St. Petersburg, 1870), p. 49. See also Budilovich, "O literaturnom edinstvie narodov Slavianskago plemeni," *Slavianskii Sbornik*, II, 2.

[23] M. P. Pogodin, "O drevnom iazykie russkom," *Moskvitianin*, I, No. 2 (1856), 139.

[24] *Ibid.*, p. 138.

[25] Aksakov, *Sochineniia*, Vol. I: *Slavianskii vopros, 1860-1886*, p. 312.

[26] V. I. Lamanskii, "Izuchenie Slavianstva i russkoe narodnoe samosoznanie," *Zhurnal Ministerstva Narodnago Prosvieshcheniia* (January, 1867), p. 152.

saw that Russia would thereby become more conscious of its Slavic mission and, as the guardian of the destiny of the Slavic peoples, would be delivered from the vice of accepting Western culture wholesale.

The adoption of Great Russian by the other Slavs would, in Pogodin's view, enrich the Russian language and culture. He envisaged that non-Russian Slavic authors, scientists, historians, and other representatives of the arts and sciences would contribute much of their own learning and folk-genius to Russian education. Indeed, during the Moscow Slav Congress of 1867, compliments were cast in the direction of the Czechs, intimating that they would replace the influence of German scientists in Russia.[27]

While Ivan Aksakov heartily agreed with these arguments for the adoption of Great Russian as a Panslavic literary language, he warned his fellow Panslavists that the mere act of its adoption was not enough. If the other Slavs adopted Russian merely for practical, external reasons, merely because they saw in Russia a mighty state capable of liberating them from political oppression, then the central point was lost. Only if the Slavic brethren accepted Russian because they recognized its historic right as the carrier of a special heritage and mission would there be any true meaning to Slavic linguistic unification. Aksakov insisted that the Russian language should have an "intrinsic attraction" for the other Slavs.

But where was this intrinsic attraction to be found? What could the Slavic brethren find in Russia to attract them? It was with this question that Aksakov leveled a barrage of criticism against Russian society, in the best Slavophile tradition. What would the other Slavs think, he asked, of a Russian Academy of Sciences which still published all its findings in French and German? Indeed, Aksakov warned, the Western Slavs could well surpass Russia with their independent press, scientific traditions, and learning. Were Slavic linguistic unification and cultural collaboration really achieved, he observed caustically, the great Russian colossus might well become a Belgium to a Slavic France![28]

---

[27] Josef V. Frič, *Rub a líc tě slovanské výpravy na Rus* (Prague, 1867), p. 13.
[28] Cited by Pypin, "Teoriia obshcheslavianskago iazyka," *Viestnik Evropy*, I, 742-47 *passim*.

III

From the vantage point of the present, it is almost incredible that the Panslavists could have built their hopes so high and could have ignored the national sentiments of their "lesser brethren." While Russian Panslavists were urging the other Slavs to adopt Russian as a Panslavic literary language, the Western and Southern Slavs were engaged in the arduous task of creating their own national literatures. In Bohemia, Poland, Slovenia, or Serbia, a poem or a story in the vernacular was not just a work of art. It was for many an act of faith inscribed in a language which had become a sacred medium for expressing love of the motherland. The Russian Panslavists apparently failed to understand the depth of this nationalism. After all, the Russians had possessed a state of their own for centuries. Indeed, they themselves had become the oppressors of other nationalities, including a goodly portion of their own Slavic brethren. Consciousness of power and prestige also lent the Russian Panslavist, however well intentioned, a curiously callous view of the other Slavs—curious because it was so obviously coupled with a sincere sympathy for the oppressed Slavs across the border. Zealously seeking recognition as autonomous ethnic entities, the non-Russian Slavs were not likely to surrender their individuality easily.

To be sure, the Russian proponents of Slavic linguistic unification strove to persuade their Slavic brethren that Russian linguistic hegemony did not signify the extinction of their own local languages. But what alternative did they offer? Although Shchebal'skii and Lamanskii insisted that the local languages would continue to be supreme in the daily life of the masses, yet, in specifying what material would continue to be written in the non-Russian Slavic vernaculars, all they could mention was prayerbooks and folk tales.[29] Apart from this, the national languages were to be reduced to the status of spoken dialects.

Various Russian Panslavists spoke of the "adoption" or the

---

[29] See Lamanskii, *Natsional'nost' ital'ianskaia i slavianskaia*, p. 23; also P. Shchebal'skii, "Prezhnii i nynieshnii panslavizm," *Russkii Viestnik*, LXVIII (April, 1867), 838.

"acceptance" of the Russian language by the other Slavs as though, in the words of an able and fair critic, Professor A. N. Pypin, "the Slavs might one fine morning reach an agreement on the necessity of adopting the Russian language, and begin using it from that moment on." Pypin was irked by the habit some of his Panslavic friends had of beginning their sentences with the phrase "The Serbs must . . ." or "The Czechs must. . . ." Just who was to make them, Pypin inquired, and how?[30]

Finally, one cannot overlook the technical difficulties of Slavic linguistic unification. How were the non-Russian Slavs to learn the Russian language at all, let alone learn it well enough to make it their literary language? The Russian Panslavists replied that if their kinsmen could learn German, Italian, Hungarian, and Greek, they could certainly learn a cognate Slavic language. This attitude was hardly a realistic one. The Austrian Slav, for example, was faced daily with the necessity of communicating with others in German. He was taught German in school. There was an abundance of grammars, newspapers, and books to instruct him and to attract his interest. A knowledge of German brought benefits of an improved social and economic status. Without the German language, his participation in science and higher learning was inconceivable.

What did Russian, the language of a foreign country and another administration, have to offer? There was no pressing daily necessity which forced the non-Russian Slav outside Russia to learn it. Knowledge of Russian brought no social prestige or economic advancement, and might well render him suspect. And where was the Austrian Slav to find teachers, grammars, or dictionaries? In 1870, when the St. Petersburg Section of the Moscow Slavic Benevolent Committee decided to encourage the study of Russian by the Western Slavs, it had to send them German-Russian and Russian-German dictionaries.[31] The adoption of Great Russian as a Panslavic literary tongue was quite impracticable for most non-Russian Slavs in the mid-nineteenth century.

Calling "completely impractical" the idea of making Russian a

[30] A. N. Pypin, "Teoriia obshcheslavianskago iazyka," *Viestnik Evropy*, II (1892), 237.

[31] *Pervyia 15 liet sushchestvovaniia S.-Peterburgskago Slavianskago blagotvoritel'nago obshchestva* (St. Petersburg, 1883), p. 98, minutes for November 1, 1870.

Panslavic literary language, Nicholas Danilevskii turned against his Slavophile colleagues one of their own most cherished arguments. "Spiritual unity is the main thing," he wrote, "the essential, higher thing, and political unification is relatively lower. This lower should be achieved before all, so that the higher could be realized." Once the Slavs were physically united in a federation, Danilevskii argued, then they would have reason to adopt Russian as a common literary language and a medium for achieving a higher unity—that of the spirit.[32]

IV

Some Russian Panslavists, notably Alexander Hilferding, Nil Popov, and Michael Pogodin, urged that all the Slavs adopt the Cyrillic alphabet for their own national tongues. This was more a corollary to the program of Slavic linguistic unification than a substitute for it.

These Russian Panslavists were not alone in holding that the Cyrillic alphabet was admirably suited to all the Slavic languages. After all, the alphabet had been specifically designed to conform to Slavic phonetics. Competent philologists have been and are generally united in their admiration of the skill with which the alphabet was devised.

In the mid-nineteenth century, as to this day, the various Slavic nationalities used either the Cyrillic or the Latin alphabet. Each alphabetical camp was in turn divided by various systems of orthography. In the Cyrillic group, the reforms of Vuk Karadžić had alienated the Serbian alphabet somewhat from the Russian and the Bulgarian. The Latin group was even more divided. Each nationality used its own system of diacritical marks and modifying combinations of letters, so that often the same words were written in various manners by various nationalities within the same alphabetical group. To complicate matters even further, some of the Western Slavs—especially the Czechs—occasionally still used the German

[32] N. Ia. Danilevskii, *Rossiia i Evropa: vzgliad na kul'turnyia i politicheskiia otnosheniia slavianskago mira k germano-romanskomu* (5th ed., St. Petersburg, 1895), p. 469.

Gothic script or the *švabách*. It is little wonder that the proponents of Slavic unification should have sought to put an end to these differences in alphabet and orthography.

The problem was far from being just a technical one; it was a cultural one as well. The Latin and the Cyrillic alphabets were closely identified with, respectively, Western and Eastern Christendom. Just as the similarity of the Slavic languages betokened to Panslavists a primary cultural unity, so the difference in alphabets symbolized the split between Eastern and Western Slavdom.

At least one Russian Panslavist, A. Hilferding, was involved in a project to introduce the Cyrillic alphabet among the Poles of the Russian Empire. As the result of an idea attributed to N. A. Miliutin, Russian administrator in Poland after the insurrection of 1863, several textbooks for Polish public schools were published in 1865 in Polish, but printed in the Cyrillic alphabet. These textbooks were written by S. P. Mikucki and Hilferding. The latter boasted that at least one of the books had not been without success —a primer for village children which had three editions within five years after it was published. Of course, he admitted, the Poles were making difficulties, but this had nothing to do with the excellence of the alphabet itself![33]

The most noteworthy Russian contribution to the campaign in support of Cyrillic as a Panslavic alphabet was undoubtedly Hilferding's work, *Obshcheslavianskaia azbuka* (All-Slavic Alphabet), published in 1871 by the St. Petersburg Section of the Moscow Slavic Benevolent Committee. The book contended that the Russian alphabet had "the best right" to be adopted as a Panslavic alphabet inasmuch as it differed least from the original alphabet which bore the name of its alleged founder, Saint Cyril. Hilferding's alphabet included no less than sixty-one symbols— essentially the Russian alphabet, but with many of the letters modified by diacritical marks in order to stand for sounds peculiar to the non-Russian Slavic languages. The author claimed that no one Slavic language needed more than thirty-three of these letters. He devoted the bulk of his book to New Testament texts in the vernac-

---

[33] A. Hilferding, *Obshcheslavianskaia azbuka s prilozheniem obraztsov slavianskikh nariechei* (St. Petersburg, 1871), p. 3.

ular Slavic languages, these texts being arranged in parallel columns —one for the original alphabet, and one for his own Cyrillic system.

Apart from its obvious implication of Russian hegemony, two features of Hilferding's proposal deserve attention: his classification of the Slavic languages, and his attitude toward the Serbian alphabet of Vuk Karadžić.

Hilferding's classification revolved about three ranks in the linguistic hierarchy: language (*iazyk*), dialect (*nariechie*), and speech (*govor*). He distinguished these three terms thus:

Under the designation *dialect* we mean not those numerous *speeches* which exist in nearly all Slavic lands and whose peculiarities consist not of syntax but only of more or less significant shades of pronunciation (as, for example, our White Russian *speech*, erroneously recognized as a separate *dialect*, but which comprises only a *speech* of the Great Russian *language*). . . . We speak of separate *dialects* in the particular sense of that word, that is, those which have a special phonetic and grammatical structure.[34]

Hilferding clarified his meaning by constructing the following table of Slavic languages:[35]

    I. Russian language
        1. Great Russian language (with White Russian speech)
        2. Little Russian dialect
   II. Bulgarian language
        3. Old Bulgarian language (or Church Slavonic)
        4. Modern Bulgarian language
        5. Macedonian dialect
  III. Serbo-Croatian language
        6. Serbian language
        7. Littoral Croatian dialect
        8. Sloveno-Croatian dialect
  IV. Slovenian language
        9. Slovenian language
      10. Ugro-Slovenian dialect
   V. Czecho-Slovak language
      11. Slovak dialect

---

[34] *Ibid.*, p. cxxvii.
[35] *Ibid.*, p. cxxviii.

12. Czech language
VI. Lusatian Serbian language
    13. Upper Lusatian dialect
    14. Lower Lusatian dialect
VII. Polish-Pomeranian (or Liakh) language
    15. Dialect of the Baltic Slavs (now extinct)
    16. Kashub dialect
    17. Mazovian (Mazur) dialect
    18. Polish language

Apart from the philological questions which this classification raises, Hilferding's list contains several peculiarities which reflect the outlook of the Russian Panslavist rather than the professional linguist. Russian, for example, stands at the head, presumably as the language of the most numerous Slavic group. Yet Polish, the language of the second most numerous Slavic people, stands at the foot. "Little Russian," as he calls Ukrainian, is relegated to the status of a dialect, while White Russian does not receive even that consideration. Slovak is designated merely as a dialect of "Czecho-Slovak." Finally, Hilferding left four "dialects" unrepresented in his illustrative texts from the New Testament—"Little Russian," Macedonian, Mazovian, and Kashub—on the grounds that he was opposed to any further fragmentation of the Slavic linguistic family.[36]

Hilferding's opposition to the Serbian Cyrillic alphabet as reformed by Vuk Karadžić demonstrates that he was interested not so much in propagating the Cyrillic alphabet, in whatever form, as he was in propagating the Russian version of Cyrillic. Hilferding opposed Vuk's reforms on the grounds that any departure from the Church Slavonic and Russian influence on the Serbian language and alphabet would tend to alienate the Serbs from Russia. He regarded Vuk as a "centrifugal" force, and heaped upon him all of the abuse which the Serbian conservative party was able to fabricate. This party ascribed Vuk Karadžić's changes to pressure from Vienna and the Vatican. When his Serbian vernacular version of the New Testament appeared in 1847, his opponents charged that the Roman Propaganda Fide had paid for it, a libel which Hilfer-

[36] *Ibid.*, p. cxxvii.

ding was to repeat.[37] Hilferding also maligned the Slovene Jernej Kopitar, Karadžić's influential friend in Vienna, as the instigator of this plot and charged him with being an Austrian "agent." Hilferding found special reason to dislike Kopitar because of the latter's efforts to show that the Glagolitic and not the Cyrillic alphabet was the first truly Slavic alphabet. The Glagolitic alphabet was almost totally different from both the Latin and the Cyrillic alphabets. It had been used till recent times as a hieratic script by the Roman Catholic Croats in a few places along the Dalmatian coast. Because its use had been sanctioned by the Roman Catholic Church, the Glagolitic alphabet was regarded by Hilferding as "inimical to the Slavic spirit and the Eastern Church."[38]

Of all the Panslavic figures in Russia, only Pogodin showed a conciliatory attitude toward Karadžić's reforms. When Vladimir Lamanskii delivered his inaugural lecture at the University of St. Petersburg in 1865, he took advantage of the occasion to criticize Karadžić. When the address was published in Ivan Aksakov's *Den'*, it bore a footnote by Michael Pogodin which defended the Serbian reformer. Pogodin pointed out that Karadžić had been and still was Russia's true friend, and that he used the Russian language himself in his correspondence with other Slavs. Furthermore, wrote Pogodin, the great Serb had helped make his own people more conscious of their nationality, which was of paramount importance as a unifying factor in their national struggle. Finally, Pogodin expressed the view that Vuk's reforms would not prevent the Serbs from adopting Russian as a Panslavic literary language in the future.[39]

It must not be thought that Panslavists such as Hilferding, Lamanskii, Pogodin, or Popov represented Russian scholarship when they urged the Cyrillic alphabet on the non-Orthodox Slavs.[40]

[37] Hilferding, *Sobranie sochineniia*, II, 81.

[38] *Ibid.*, pp. 79-80.

[39] See the footnote to Vladimir I. Lamanskii's article, "Vstupitel'noe chtenie Dotsenta Peterburgskago universiteta V. I. Lamanskago," *Den'*, No. 52 (December 18, 1865), p. 1241.

[40] Nil Popov's proposal in favor of Cyrillic as a Panslavic alphabet appeared in *Sovremennaia Lietopis'*, No. 39 (1865). This article was not available to the present writer except for excerpts in Czech published by F. A. Urbánek, *Otázka o pismu všeslovanském (Vopros ob obshcheslavianskom pismie)* (Prague, 1866). For Pogo-

It is true that many scholars of Slavic linguistics were impressed by the technical perfection of the Cyrillic alphabet as a medium for denoting Slavic phonetics. Yet men like Pypin, Makushev, Baudouin de Courtenay, and others criticized the entire Panslavic campaign for linguistic or alphabetic unification on both technical and ideological grounds.[41]

Apart from a few curious attempts by a handful of Russian (and non-Russian) Panslavists, the effort to establish Russian as a Panslavic literary language or the Russian Cyrillic alphabet as a Panslavic alphabet came to naught. Nevertheless, their efforts were indicative of the basic Russian Panslavic attitude that Russia was the leader, the arbiter, and the model for all the other Slavic nations.

---

din's proposal, see *Slavianskii s"iezd v Pragie i godovshchina s"iezda v Moskvie* (Moscow, 1868), p. 49.

[41] See, for example, A. Pypin, "Literaturnyi panslavizm," *Viestnik Evropy,* CCLIII (September, 1879), p. 310; I. A. Boduen-de-Kurtene (Baudouin de Courtenay), "Nieskol'ko slov po povodu *Obshcheslavianskoi azbuki*," *Zhurnal Ministerstva Narodnago Prosvieshcheniia* (May, 1871), pp. 149-95.

7

RUSSIAN PANSLAVISTS AND THE POLISH QUESTION

Poland is a sharp wedge which Romanism has thrust into the very heart of the Slavic world with the aim of shattering it into bits.   IURII SAMARIN

THERE COULD HARDLY have been a more natural test of Russia's desire for Slavic solidarity than its treatment of the non-Russian Slavs within its own borders. Yet nothing in the grim world of reality contrasted more with the Panslavic dream than Great Russian subjugation of the Polish people. The Polish Question— the "fatal question," as it came to be called in the Russian press— confronted Russian Panslavists with a serious dilemma.

On the one hand, if Russian Panslavists supported any Russian rule of force in Poland, they would be discredited in the sight of the other Slavs.[1] Men who preached Slavic brotherhood could scarcely condone Slavic fratricide. Men who professed the free development of all members of the Slavic family could hardly justify their own country's oppression of a kindred people.

On the other hand, in their eyes Poland stood for practically everything that was abhorrent to Panslavic doctrine. For them Poland was the creation of a Westernized gentry, a liberal intelligentsia, and a Latin clergy. This Poland was the renegade vanguard

---

[1] For Serbian reactions to the Polish revolt see especially Jovan Skerlić, *Omladina i njena književnost* (Belgrade, 1925), pp. 149-50. For Czech reactions see Josef Jirásek, *Rusko a my* (Brno, 1946), II, 31-52. Russian Panslavist fears of losing the sympathies of the non-Russian Slavs are reflected in the following articles: A. Hilferding, "Pis'mo k g. Rigeru v Pragu o Russko-Pol'skikh dielakh," *Den'*, No. 18 (May 4, 1863), p. 14; and Ivan S. Aksakov, "Suzhdenie g. Palatskago o Pol'skom voprosie," *Den'*, No. 24 (June 15, 1863), p. 14.

of a hostile Romano-Germanic world.[2] Moreover, Polish Messianism was a rival of Russian Panslavism in the bid for primacy in the Slavic family. As the most numerous non-Russian Slavic people with a strong national consciousness, the Poles were potentially able to exert a moral leadership which the Roman Catholic Slavs, at least, might well prefer to the hegemony of Orthodox Tsarist Russia.

Some Russian Panslavists saw in Poland an even more specific threat to Russia's position in Eastern Europe. They were convinced that Poland provided a direct obstacle in the way of Russia's "mission" in the Balkans. "The Polish Question is not at all a diversion or even a side issue of the Eastern Question," wrote Professor Peter Bezsonov. "It is one and the same Eastern Question, in its extension, in its new decisive phase, translated exclusively to a Slavic base."[3] Ivan Aksakov wrote, "We are also convinced that a correct solution of the Eastern Question is dependent on a correct solution of the Polish Question as well, and *vice versa*." The editor of *Den'* (Day) based this conviction on five theses which he formulated thus: (1) The Polish Question forced on Russia an involuntary solidarity with Austrian policy; (2) Russian solidarity with Austria was contrary to Russia's "historic calling" in the Balkans; (3) Russia should therefore free itself from dependence on Austrian policy; (4) this could be accomplished only by devising a new Russian policy for Poland, one which would not condemn Russia to cooperation with Austria and Prussia; (5) any basis for such a new policy must resolve the "inner contradictions" inherent in the Polish Question before Russia could settle the Eastern Question.[4] In plain terms, Russia could not be oppressor and liberator at the same time.

The Polish crisis of 1863 also touched off a domestic issue which profoundly stirred the national spirit of Russian Panslavists. This

---

[2] Note Iurii F. Samarin's words at the head of this chapter, which are from his article, "Sovremennyi ob"em Pol'skago voprosa," *Sochineniia*, I (Moscow, 1877), 327. Originally published in *Den'*, No. 38 (September 21, 1863).

[3] P. A. Bezsonov, "V pamiat' Pervouchitelei Slavianstva," *Den'*, No. 27 (July 6, 1863), p. 6.

[4] Ivan S. Aksakov, "Moskva, 28 marta," *Den'*, No. 13 (March 28, 1864), p. 1.

was the question of the so-called Western Provinces—the Ukraine and White Russian. Here Russian Panslavists were confronted not only by the claims of Polish nationalism but by White Russian and especially Ukrainian desires at least for cultural autonomy.

Such, then, was the dilemma which the Polish uprising of 1863 presented to the Russian Panslavists. How were they to reconcile the forcible domination of one Slavic people by another with the Panslavic vision of Mother Russia as the champion and the liberator of oppressed Slavdom?

II

While other Russians had their eyes on the immediate circumstances leading to the Polish rebellion, Ivan Aksakov looked for deeper causes. What he saw was no mere mutiny against a levy of recruits, nor even rebellion against an oppressive Russian administration. Instead, he saw a struggle between two divergent cultures. Aksakov tersely summarized the differences between them thus:

Poland is a Catholic country; Russia is an Orthodox country. Catholicism and Orthodoxy are distinguished not only by two separate rites but by two separate cultural principles, two different historical ideas. Poland has lived and still lives through its aristocratic and feudal element: in Russia, the source of life and strength is in the people, the land. Poland considers itself in the advanced company of the West, betraying the Slavic brotherhood: we belong completely to the Slavic world. In other words, our historic paths are completely different, and if a close union is at all possible between us, it is only when Russia becomes completely *Rus'*, and when Poland returns to Slavic principles.[5]

It was also in terms of this "two worlds" concept that Alexander Hilferding sought to explain the "inner reasons" for the conflict, which he traced to the Middle Ages, when the Slavs, newly entered into the circle of historical activity, faced a choice, as he put it, of becoming a part of the older Romano-Germanic culture or

[5] Ivan S. Aksakov, "Moskva, 4-go maia 1863 g.," *Pol'skii vopros i zapadno-russkoe dielo; Evreiskii vopros, 1860-1886,* in *Sochineniia,* III (St. Petersburg, 1900), 49. Originally published in *Den'.*

developing independently. The Poles chose the first path: the Russians, the second.

The Polish people entered with all its organism into the frame of the Western European world. The religious principles of Catholicism, the social principles of chivalry, an urban life wholly translated from Germany, an education based on the traditions of Roman classicism— in a word, all was accepted and organically adopted from the West by Poland. While remaining Slavic, Poland completely became a member of the Latino-Germanic family of nations, the only Slavic country to have entered that family wholeheartedly and freely.[6]

The results of that fateful "choice," Hilferding reminded his readers, had bloodied the pages of a thousand-year history of Russo-Polish relations. Since Poland was militantly opposed to the Russian path of development, Hilferding concluded that Russia was forced by historical necessity to fight back in defense of the basic principles of its civilization![7]

Hilferding pictured Poland as a country whose main strength resided in a belligerent aristocracy which was obsessed by ambition and a belief in its own superiority. He described Russia, on the other hand, as a vast and mighty land whose strength lay in its humble folk. Hilferding reduced Russo-Polish troubles to the proposition that aristocratic Poland could not endure being subject to plebeian Russia.[8]

Whatever one may think of them, these and similar analyses of the Polish uprising regarded basic cultural considerations as more important than political differences. This approach led Aksakov, for example, to appraise the full seriousness of the uprising with greater realism than those Russians who persisted in viewing the revolt as the conspiracy of a Polish clique. "The present movement deserves our most serious attention," declared Aksakov in the first days of the revolt, "as having within itself all of the elements of a national uprising. This is not just a rebellion or a mutiny."[9] Russia was not being confronted merely by a disgruntled Polish

[6] A. Hilferding, "Pol'skii vopros," *Stat'i po sovremennym voprosam slavianskim,* in *Sobranie sochinenii,* II (St. Petersburg, 1868), 295.
[7] *Ibid.,* p. 312.
[8] *Ibid.,* p. 335.
[9] Aksakov, "Moskva, 2-go fevralia 1863 g.," *Sochineniia,* III, 18.

aristocracy, or a liberal bourgeoisie, or a group of émigrés and some secret committees whose declarations, Aksakov asserted, made no sense anyway. All of Poland, with its millions of people of all classes, was involved in a national movement for independence.

Without quarreling with this interpretation, Iurii Samarin believed, nevertheless, that the best way to solve the Polish Question was to break the Polish people into social classes and to implement a different policy for each class. In a series of articles in Aksakov's *Den'* during 1863, Iurii Samarin argued that the Polish Question involved three components: (1) the Polish people as a national concept; (2) the Polish state as a political concept; and (3) "Polonism" as a cultural concept.[10] He admitted that these three elements were not distinct. Indeed, he attributed most of the strength of the Polish cause precisely to the identification of people, state, and culture. By the same token, Samarin urged, Russian policy should find its main strength in separating these three concepts and treating each in a specific manner.

First, regarding the Poles as a people, Samarin made it quite clear that the Poles unquestionably constituted a separate and independent branch of the Slavic race. He stressed that the Polish people possessed all of the attributes of national individuality—their own language, literature, history, and living traditions. True to his Slavophile philosophy, Samarin concluded that Russians must therefore recognize the right of the Polish people to the untrammeled freedom of their national life in all of its cultural manifestations. He specified particularly freedom of religion, official use of the popular tongue in the affairs of internal administration, and the preservation by the Poles of their own civic institutions and traditions.

As for the Polish state, this was another matter. Samarin explained that nationality and state, though often closely bound, were not necessarily mutually dependent. Government was only one manifestation of nationality, and not always necessary to it. Basing himself on this view, Samarin concluded that Russia could not permit the existence of a separate Polish state, since, for a variety of reasons, that state had been and would continue to be a threat to

---

[10] Samarin, "Sovremennyi ob"em Pol'skago voprosa," *Sochineniia*, I, 319–43 *passim*.

Russian security. No more convincing proof of this could be offered, Samarin held, than the Polish claims to Russian lands under the guise of reviving "historic Poland," and the proclaimed desire of Polish leaders to reduce Russia to the confines of medieval Muscovy. "We are not savage Muscovites," wrote Samarin, "nor are we crafty Germans. We intend to subject nobody, but, on the contrary, we intend to allow full freedom of development to all without discrimination."[11] But as long as Polish honor found it impossible to accept the Ukrainians and the White Russians as equals, as long as the Jesuit-dominated Roman Catholic Church of Poland could not reconcile itself to the existence of the Orthodox Church, he concluded, Russia could not afford to permit the restoration of a Polish state on its borders.

It was the third element inherent in the Polish Question—"Polonism"—that troubled Samarin the most. For him, Poland was not just like any other Slavic nation. It claimed to be a Slavic center with a mission which extended beyond Polish ethnic frontiers. This mission was, according to Samarin, to act as the vanguard of Western Europe among the Slavs. The most inimical aspect of Polonism, Samarin contended, was Romanism (*Latinstvo*). He made clear that by this term he did not mean any single institution such as the Papacy, or the Roman Catholic Church as an ecclesiastical body. "By this word we understand," he wrote, "not only those dogmatic and hierarchic peculiarities which distinguish Western Catholicism; we also understand by it all which grew out of the seeds of Romanism, the whole aggregation of moral concepts and relations in the mode of living which is conditioned by the Roman Catholic view."[12] The great tragedy of Polish history, as Samarin saw it, was the irreconcilable struggle between Romanism and Slavism within Poland itself, "like two souls imprisoned in one body."[13]

Ivan Aksakov ably seconded Samarin's emphasis on Polonism as Russia's chief problem in Poland. In his flaming editorials in *Den'*, Aksakov tried to convince his countrymen that pacification of the

[11] *Ibid.*, p. 324.
[12] *Ibid.*, p. 330.
[13] *Ibid.*, p. 335.

armed uprising in Poland would only lead to an even more difficult period in which Russia would be confronted, not by armed Poles, but by Polonism. Russian might could presumably be counted on to crush the first enemy whenever he appeared in the open. Polonism, however, was not to be vanquished by force of arms, patriotic banquets, and newspaper editorials.[14]

Aksakov, Samarin, Pogodin, and other Panslavists regarded as their chief enemy in Poland not the Polish "people"—that is, the peasantry—but Polish "society." In their terminology "society" was synonymous with officialdom, the nobility, the professions, the intelligentsia, and the urban middle class. These were the real renegades who had created a cultural schism within the Polish spirit. Professor Pogodin so despised the Polish nobility that he could not bring himself to believe that they, too, could be Slavs! He wrote in deadly earnest, "I have long been convinced in the Western, Celtic, or Latin origin [of the Polish nobility], but now I have become convinced in this, too: these newcomers to Poland never united with the natives as they did, more or less, in other lands—but the nobility and the people there constitute to this day two completely different societies. I cannot otherwise explain to myself recent events."[15]

Aksakov railed not only at the nobility but at all of Polish "society," which he considered nothing less than a pathological element. If pathology were a science applicable to whole nations, he once suggested in a *Den'* editorial, then it would be "extraordinarily curious" to observe Poland in this light. "In this regard," he continued, "there appears, for example, *falsehood*, which has so glutted the entire organism of contemporary Polish society that it has ceased to reflect the action of a conscious will, but has become a natural, completely sincere organic part of the Polish nature (we speak not of the common Polish people, but of Polish society)."[16]

However erroneous their philosophy, data, or conclusions, these Russian Panslavists gave serious consideration to the Polish Ques-

[14] Aksakov, "Moskva, 21-go sentiabria 1863 g.," *Sochineniia*, III, 154.

[15] M. P. Pogodin, "Pol'skii vopros," *Stat'i politicheskiia i Pol'skii vopros, 1856-1867* (Moscow, 1876), p. 330.

[16] Aksakov, "Moskva, 10-go avgusta 1863 g.," *Sochineniia*, III, 108.

tion not as a political problem but as a cultural dilemma involving a whole social order. It was logical for them to insist, therefore, that the only real and lasting solution to the Polish Question had to be of necessity a social and not a military or a political solution.

III

A crucial issue in the Russian Panslavic appraisal of the Polish Question was the problem of the "Western Provinces." Such was the term which the Russians applied to those *gubernias* that lay between Great Russia and Poland—Podolia, Volhynia, Minsk, Mogilev, Vitebsk, Kovno, Vilna, Smolensk, and Chernigov. By Russian calculations, these provinces were at the time inhabited by some nine million Ukrainians and White Russians, and about one million Poles, as well as a considerable number of non-Slavs, notably Lithuanians and Jews. Subjects of the Polish Commonwealth for centuries, most of these Ukrainians and White Russians were not a part of the Russian Empire until the partitions of Poland in the last quarter of the eighteenth century. Russian Panslavists, as indeed many Russians, came to regard the question of these Western Provinces as an integral part of the Polish Question, especially since the Polish uprising of 1863 was coupled with renewed Polish demands for the restoration of "historic Poland" (as distinct from ethnic Poland).

Aksakov's attitude toward Poland was colored by pangs of conscience over Russia's historic policy toward the Poles. However much he tried to justify his own country, Aksakov did not approve of the partitions of Poland. He took the line that it was not Catherine but Frederick of Prussia that had initiated the idea, and that Catherine might have taken only the Russian-inhabited lands of Poland had not Prussia and Austria threatened to absorb all the rest of the Polish Commonwealth. "If our fault is to be sought anywhere," conceded Aksakov in an editorial in *Den'*, "it is perhaps in our indulgence of the ambitious pretensions of our neighbors and our sanctioning the subjection of a free Slavic people to a foreign rule. Speaking generally, Russia was less unjust than Prussia or Austria in the partitioning and the destruction of Poland, but being a moral power, Russia feels the injustice in this affair all the more heavily."[17]

Aksakov's Russian conscience found less grudging expression in a private letter to Countess Antonina Bludova, lady of the Imperial Court, in which he confessed the following:

As far as the Polish Kingdom is concerned, I believe that we are not in the right, that we are besmirching the Russian name by keeping Poland (pure, real Poland) by force, that we should quit Poland and stand on the borders of our Russian provinces (including a part of Lithuania), and if they poke into our side, to give them a thrashing with the greatest of pleasure. Within three years the Poles would themselves ask for unification with us. One cannot at one and the same time sympathize with the movement of the Ruthenes against the Austrians in Galicia, which Austria obtained as legally, or rather as illegally, as we obtained the Polish Kingdom, and yet consider as wrong the desire of the Poles to liberate themselves from their dependence on us. I do not love Poles, and have excoriated them for their pretensions to Kiev. But I cannot rail at them for their pretensions to Warsaw, Poznań, and Cracow.[18]

With the first news of disorder in Warsaw in February, 1861, such distinguished Panslavic leaders in Russia as Pogodin, Aksakov, and Samarin joined liberal Russians in their feelings of sympathy for the Poles. Ivan Aksakov was of the opinion that the Poles should enjoy full freedom within the borders of the Polish Kingdom and that Russian troops should be withdrawn. Samarin concurred in the view that the Poles should be granted full autonomy and freedom, both in their private and social life.[19]

As the events of 1861 progressed, however, and the resolution of the Poles grew with every public demonstration, these Russian Panslavists became correspondingly disheartened and hostile. It was the issue of the Western Provinces that became decisive for their views. Polish claims to these lands found spectacular expression in

---

[17] Aksakov, "Moskva, 18-go noiabria 1861 g.," *Sochineniia*, III, 7.

[18] Cited by N. P. Barsukov, *Zhizn' i trudy M. P. Pogodina*, XVII (St. Petersburg, 1905), 121.

[19] A. A. Kornilov, *Obshchestvennoe dvizhenie pri Aleksandrie II, 1855-1881* (Moscow, 1909), pp. 134-35.

a mass demonstration in October, 1861, at Horodlo, in the Lublin district on the Bug River. Called to commemorate the Polish-Lithuanian Union contracted there in 1413, some twenty thousand Poles met in an open field, heard Mass, sang national hymns, built a hillock of earth surmounted by a Cross, and cheered a protocol of commemoration which included the names of the territories involved in the original Union. Unlike the Polish provinces, the names of the Western Provinces appeared in italics. The protocol ended with "a demand for the restoration of Poland in its ancient regions."[20]

Aksakov's indignation was boundless. *"Kiev, Volhynia, Chernigov, Smolensk!"* he repeated in anguish. "Insane Poles! How you make haste to forfeit your own cause! How you rush to smother every spark of sympathy which your love for your homeland might ignite in your racial brethren! . . . Unhappy, unhappy, defeated Poles—maddened as though through God's punishment."[21] Stung by this defiant Polish gesture, Aksakov, Hilferding, Pogodin, and other Panslavists launched a crusade in the Russian press—especially in *Den'*—for the Russification of the Western Provinces. By their insistence on the restitution of "historic Poland," which included vast areas with a predominantly White Russian and Ukrainian population, the Polish leader presented the Russians with an argument which they exploited amply. A number of Panslavists set about writing open letters on this theme to influential figures abroad, hoping thus to gain or to keep friends for the Russian cause. Hilferding's letters to Bohemia found fruit especially in various articles and statements by Rieger and Palacký which reproved the Poles for their pretensions. Pogodin wrote one open letter after another—to Garibaldi, Guizot, French journalists, and even to the Poles themselves—all in an emotional and grandiloquent style.[22] All of these letters uniformly emphasized the Russian nature of the Western Provinces.

[20] Barsukov, *Zhizn' i trudy M. P. Pogodina*, XVII, 117.

[21] *Ibid.*, pp. 117-18.

[22] Pogodin, *Stat'i politicheskiia i Pol'skii vopros, 1856-1867*; see especially the following articles: "Pis'mo k Gizo o Pol'skom voprose," "Otpoved' frantsuzskomu zhurnalistu," and "Pis'mo k Garibaldi."

IV

What were Russian Panslavic attitudes toward various government policies and acts during the Polish crisis of 1863?

At the time of the January insurrection in 1863, Russia's policy in Poland was generally based on the "Wielopolski System." Alexander Wielopolski, Marquis of Gonzaga-Myszkowski, had first gained the attention of the Russian government during the ill-fated Polish revolt in Austrian Galicia in 1846 by his sensational "Letter of a Polish Nobleman to Count Metternich," in which he put his people under the protection of Tsar Nicholas I as "the most generous of our enemies."[23] As a subject of the Tsar, the Marquis made repeated declarations of loyalty to the Imperial government and of good will toward the Russian people. Consequently when in March, 1861, Alexander II approved Polish demands for a Council of State and broader home rule, Wielopolski was chosen, as the most trustworthy Polish candidate, to head the administration. In briefest outline, his plan was to restore Poland's constitutional status of 1815 and to undertake a reorganization of Polish society. The latter was to be accomplished through supporting the growth and prosperity of the Polish middle class, and by improving the lot of the peasantry. Another important and especially successful part of Wielopolski's program was the re-Polonization of education and administration within the Polish Kingdom.[24]

It would seem that there was much about Wielopolski and his "system" that the Panslavic mentality would have found commendable. Here was a Pole who professed loyalty to the Tsar and admiration for the Russian people—a rare bird, indeed. Here was an administrator who recognized that the crux of any solution of the Polish Question lay in the social reorganization of Poland. True, his concern over middle-class prosperity would not in itself gladden Panslavic hearts, but the measure would have served to check the influence of the landed gentry, whom the Panslavists abhorred.

[23] J. Feldman, "The Polish Provinces of Austria and Prussia after 1815; the 'Springtime of Nations,'" in *Cambridge History of Poland*, ed. by W. F. Reddaway *et al.* (Cambridge University Press, 1941), II, 354.

[24] A. P. Coleman, "Poland under Alexander II: The Insurrection of 1863," in *ibid.*, p. 374.

Most acceptable of all, however, should have been Wielopolski's program on behalf of the peasantry. Yet, for a variety of reasons, leading Russian Panslavic publicists were not in favor of the Wielopolski System.

Pogodin conceded that the Wielopolski policy was in itself a good one. After all, as far back as in 1839, Pogodin had himself urged upon the Russian government measures which were quite similar. Again in 1856, after the Crimean debacle, Pogodin had advised more leniency and freedom in the administration of Poland. What, then, did he find to criticize in the policy of 1863?

Precisely its timing. The administrators of the Wielopolski System, he charged, had made the mistake of supporting for too long a policy which had ended in failure—nay, in revolt. The idea of seeking reconciliation between Poles and Russians by such a policy was altogether laudable before the insurrection, Pogodin asserted, despite errors in its execution. But surely it should have been apparent, if not before, then certainly by January 11, 1863, that indulgence was no way to check a seething revolt. And when the Poles rejected the Emperor's amnesty of May 1, he insisted, that was definitely their last chance. "A carbuncle cannot be cured by gentle methods," Pogodin warned in ominous metaphor, "nor can it be allowed on the body to which it threatens mortal danger. A surgical operation is indispensable."[25]

Pogodin also felt that a Russian policy of forbearance toward the Poles would have reflected more to Russia's credit had it been administered by a Russian—someone like General Paskevich or Prince Gorchakov—rather than by a Pole who had every reason to be tender toward his own compatriots.[26] As it was, Pogodin remarked with some bitterness, Russians ought to demand that Marquis Wielopolski publish all the laws issued during his reign of gentleness, for the edification of the Western Powers which sympathized with the Poles.[27] It was naive of the system's supporters, he held, to think that it would save Russia from the threat of an attack by the Western Powers. Were these countries ready

[25] Pogodin, "O knige g. Shedo-Ferroti," *Stat'i politicheskiia i Pol'skii vopros, 1856-1867,* p. 482.
[26] *Ibid.,* p. 477.
[27] Pogodin, "O sistemie Markiza Velepol'skago," *ibid.,* p. 453.

for war, they would easily enough find an excuse for attack. As for the argument that Wielopolski had after all achieved a measure of success, Pogodin countered that the weakness of the administration only contributed to the violence of the insurrection. Thanks to the fact that the Polish administration had been riddled with officials sympathetic to the insurrection, the rebels knew all the government's most secret plans. In Warsaw an underground Polish government gathered taxes, printed decrees, and issued passports under Wielopolski's nose! A tolerant policy with respect to religion and education only permitted the schools of Poland to become nests of mutiny and the monasteries to serve as arsenals. From the Russian standpoint, Pogodin concluded, it was absurd in 1863 to call the Wielopolski System a success. What it had done was to lead directly to insurrection.

This was precisely the line of argument that dominated the editorial policy of Aksakov's *Den'*. In a running controversy with Katkov's *Moskovskiia Viedomosti* (Moscow News) throughout 1863, Aksakov insisted again and again that *Den'* was opposed to the Wielopolski System and any other liberal policy as being impossible at the time. "There is no need to deceive ourselves," Aksakov wrote, "Poland is now an *enemy country* for us, and we cannot trust the Poles any more than any other enemy."[28] He declared that the Wielopolski regime was doomed to failure simply because it was impossible to satisfy Polish demands when these demands exceeded by far the best that the most liberal Russian administration could offer. What the Poles really wanted was complete independence. If Russia could not grant this demand, then it would have to give up any hope of reconciling Poland to its position as a part of the Russian Empire. If this were so, the editor of *Den'* concluded with brutal logic, then any liberal administration such as Wielopolski's was out of the question, and only a military dictatorship could pacify the Poles.

Vladimir Lamanskii, a leader of the St. Petersburg Panslavists, also held that it would be an unpardonable error on the part of the Russian administration to return to the Wielopolski System after

[28] Ivan S. Aksakov, "Moskva, 7 sentiabria," *Den'*, No. 36 (September 7, 1863), p. 2.

the suppression of the Polish rebellion. He advised the Russian government not to close the Russian intermediate and high schools in Poland and not to reintroduce the Polish language into the administration and the court system. "On the other hand," he wrote, "we desire no limitations on the use of Polish in churches, theaters, the press, and literature—in all forms of social life. . . . We desire every possible freedom and every possible development of Polish literature and nationality."[29]

Thus were leading Russian proponents of Slavic brotherhood and unification placed in the position of excoriating their own government for what they held to be a liberal Polish policy! Yet while Panslavic disapproval of the liberal Wielopolski System is no doubt a valid test of their hostility to the Polish uprising itself, it is not to be taken as an indication of basic Panslavic policy for a lasting solution. When Ivan Aksakov or Michael Pogodin bespoke the need for the forcible pacification of Poland in 1863, they did so only out of what they reluctantly regarded—despite the passion of the moment—as a temporary necessity. Only pacification could lead to a permanent solution, and only force could bring about pacification. Therefore, they concluded, the Wielopolski System was impractical.

With respect to the Russian government's other acts during the Polish crisis of 1863, Panslavists were in far greater accord. When, in celebration of the Orthodox Easter, Alexander II signed an amnesty on March 31 for all Poles who would lay down their arms by May 1, *Den'* extolled the amnesty as yet another sign of Russian generosity. "Only might has the right to forgive thus," Aksakov reflected with unconcealed satisfaction, "might which is fully conscious of itself and certain in the final victory."[30] At the same time, however, Aksakov warned that even the generosity of might had its limits, and to go beyond the reasonable limits of mercy would constitute a shameful weakness which might unduly deceive Poland and all Europe.

In June, 1863, the Russian government undertook two impor-

[29] Cited by G. Kniazev, "Slavianskii 'vostochnyi' vopros v opredielenii V. I. Lamanskago," *Zhurnal Ministerstva Narodnago Prosvieshcheniia* (November, 1916), p. 25.

[30] Aksakov, "Moskva, 10 apriela 1863 g.," *Sochineniia*, III 38.

tant acts, both of which were approved by various leading Panslavists. It rejected a note by Great Britain, France, and Austria urging reforms in Poland. Pogodin and Aksakov enthusiastically applauded this rejection because they regarded the Russo-Polish conflict as a family affair in which no foreign interference could be permitted.[31] The other measure which the Russian government undertook in June, 1863, was to send General Michael Muraviev to quell the disorders in the northwestern provinces of the Empire among the Poles and Lithuanians of the Baltic region. Muraviev's brutal measures won for him the title of "Hangman." Yet upon his return from his bloody work in 1865, Muraviev received the plaudits of both Moscow and St. Petersburg Panslavists.

Aksakov lauded Muraviev editorially for having defended Russian interests in the Vilno region—"that theater of struggle between the Polish and the Russian nationalities."[32] Where harsh measures were necessary, the editor of *Den'* assured his readers, false humanitarianism and delicacy of feeling were out of place; General Muraviev deserved gratitude for suppressing the rebellion and for striking "a salutary fear" into Polish hearts. The Panslavic circle of St. Petersburg conferred high praise upon Muraviev at his homecoming in the spring of 1865. Countess Antonina Bludova, lady-in-waiting to the Empress, organized a festive welcome for the general. Her committee collected money for a costly icon of St. Michael the Archangel, Muraviev's patron saint, which was presented at the railway station to "the restorer of Orthodoxy in our western frontier land."[33] The great poet Tiutchev—the foreign minister of the Slavophiles, as someone once dubbed him—contributed his talents with an ode to the "great missionary." The Poles had bitter reason to compare this encomium with a poem of Tiutchev's younger years when he wrote to the Polish people in 1831:

[31] Pogodin, "Po povodu otvietov kniaza Gorchakova," *Stat'i politicheskiia i Pol'skii vopros, 1856-1867*, p. 438, originally published on July 12, 1863; and Ivan S. Aksakov, "Moskva, 13-go iiuliia 1863 g.," *Sochineniia*, III, 82 ff.

[32] Aksakov, "Moskva, 1 maia 1865 g.," *Sochineniia*, III, 272.

[33] Stephen Graham, *Tsar of Freedom: The Life and Reign of Alexander II* (New Haven, 1935), p. 238.

Believe the word of the Russian nation.
We shall sacredly preserve your ashes,
And our common freedom as a Phoenix
Will find its birth in them.[34]

Vladimir Lamanskii, professor of Slavic philology at the University of St. Petersburg and a leader of the capital's Panslavic circle, wrote a series of panegyrics in honor of the returning general.[35]

While supporting Muraviev's military dictatorship in Poland, Aksakov favored a benevolent program of agrarian reform. Upon the first news of the Polish rebellion Aksakov urged in *Den'* that the first step, after the suppression of the insurrection, must be to institute democracy in Poland by granting political rights to the Polish peasantry, "a healthy element," thus weakening the nobility.[36] In the summer of 1863 the Tsar sent Nicholas Miliutin to the Polish Kingdom to effect reforms which would make it difficult for the Polish landed gentry to rely on peasant support in the event of future troubles. The results were recorded in the historic decrees of February 19, 1864, which awarded the peasants of Poland both personal freedom and land ownership on terms far more generous than those which had been extended to the Russian peasant in 1861.[37]

Aksakov lauded the decrees in *Den'*. They introduced "a new historical idea, a new element into the political and social life of Poland which has not been active in her history until now—the element of the common people or the peasantry."[38] He rejected charges that the Russian government was seeking to destroy the Polish nation by setting one class against another. One class was indeed being set against the other, he admitted, but not for Poland's destruction. The charges stemmed from the classic misconception, he wrote, that the Polish gentry and the Polish nation were identi-

[34] Cited by W. Lednicki, "Panslavism," in *European Ideologies*, ed. by Feliks Gross (New York, 1948), p. 850.
[35] Graham, *Tsar of Freedom*, p. 238.
[36] Aksakov, "Moskva, 2-go fevralia 1863 g.," *Sochineniia*, III, 20.
[37] Coleman, "Poland under Alexander II," in *Cambridge History of Poland*, II, 383.
[38] Aksakov, "Moskva, 5-go marta 1864 g.," *Sochineniia*, III, 219.

cal. "It seems hardly possible," he asserted, "to deny in our time that the blame for Poland's destruction lies in the incorrect development of its social organism and in its deviation from the basic Slavic way of life and spiritual principles."[39] If the weakening of the Polish nobility was useful to Russia, which Aksakov did not doubt, he maintained that it was even more useful to the true Poland and to the cause of Polish nationality.

V

In advancing their own solutions of the Polish Question, the Panslavists insisted on certain basic principles. For example, Aksakov demanded that in its dealing with Poland Russia be entirely free from any foreign interference, either military or diplomatic, which might give the Poles false hopes and offend Russian patriotism.[40] However, Pogodin offered to submit at least one question to the judgment of other parties—the issue of the Western Provinces. Once he proposed, "We will offer our works to the judgment of the Czechs, Moravians, Slovaks, Serbs, Bulgars, Croats, and let brethren judge us with the Poles before the face of all Europe."[41] He went even further. "We will take our quarrel to any court you please," he challenged in an epistle to the Poles, "not only a fraternal Slavic one, but any foreign court."[42] *Den'* likewise demanded that the Poles repudiate all claim to the Ukraine and White Russia. The Poles had to be convinced, Aksakov insisted, that they could not expect freedom for their own nation as long as they insisted on reestablishing a "historic Poland" which included Russian ethnic territories.

Any lasting solution, Aksakov also felt, must be one which satisfied the Poles; otherwise, Russia faced a perpetual threat on its borders, a threat that could be held in check only by military dictatorship. Although Aksakov had approved such a regimen in his desire to see the revolt of 1863 quelled, he never accepted the

[39] *Ibid.*, p. 220.
[40] Aksakov, "Moskva, 21 dekabria 1863 g.," *ibid.*, p. 194.
[41] Pogodin, "Poslanie k Poliakam," *Stat'i politicheskiia i Pol'skii vopros, 1856-1867*, p. 363.
[42] *Ibid.*, p. 354.

rule of force as more than a temporary necessity. To satisfy the Poles, Aksakov pointed out, it was necessary to discover what the Poles really wanted, and this required freedom of speech and press.[43] The free interchange and expression of ideas had long been a favorite demand of his, and the bitterness engendered by the Polish insurrection of 1863 did not cause Aksakov to change this view.[44]

Any real solution of the Polish Question, Aksakov insisted, must be based on the fullest respect for the freedom of Polish national life, that is, for Polish religion, language, traditions, and institutions. Here, too, was a cardinal principle of the Slavophiles. As he wrote in 1863,

If one admits as a truth that every nationality which is conscious of itself, which feels within itself the ability and the force to live its own individual life and to contribute a deposit of its own spiritual personality to the universal-historical development of mankind, has the right to exist and to live and to develop freely (particularly a people which has already declared itself a natural entity in history)—this right, without a doubt, belongs to the Polish people as well.

Aksakov agreed with Samarin, however, that state independence was not necessarily a prerequisite for the free development of nationality.[45]

Among proposals for the settlement of the Polish Question which various Panslavists considered and rejected were: Poland's complete separation from the Russian Empire; Poland's complete absorption into the Russian state; the Russification of ethnic Poland; and the establishment of a constitutional Poland within a Russian federation. The leading Panslavists thus found themselves in opposition both to the jingoist nationalism of official circles and of public figures of the Katkov stripe as well as to the liberals and the radicals, who supported either Polish independence or the federalization of the Russian Empire.

Pogodin's views on Polish independence had run a wide gamut. In 1854, during the Crimean War, Pogodin proposed nothing less

---

[43] Aksakov, "Moskva, 18 go noiabria 1861 g.," *Sochineniia*, III, 7-8.
[44] Aksakov, "Moskva, 20-go iiunia 1863 g.," *ibid.*, p. 97.
[45] Aksakov, "Moskva, 8-go fevralia 1863 g.," *ibid.*, p. 23.

than the full liberation of the Polish-speaking lands.[46] In 1856, at the end of the war, he had tempered this to autonomy.[47] By 1863 he offered Poland liberation not as a promise but as a threat! In his epistle of March 2, 1863, to the Poles, Pogodin warned them to consider that Russian soldiers could burn and slay as well as Polish rebels. "Yet there is another punishment," he threatened, "which is more terrible than this temporary one: that is to give the Polish Kingdom to the Prussians and the Austrians. The Germans would love to suck Slavic blood."[48] Pogodin meant by "giving" Poland away to its German neighbors the simple withdrawal of Russian troops—"to abandon you," as he put it to the Poles, "and to leave you to your own devices while we stand fully armed on the banks of the Niemen and the Bug, three hundred thousand strong; have you ever thought of this, Poles?"[49] If the Russian army left Poland, he prophesied, the Polish leaders would soon be begging the Russian Tsar to take Poland back again!

Ivan Aksakov, too, spoke of the possibility of Poland's liberation, but only as an alternative to something far worse, namely, a permanent military dictatorship. He observed in *Den'*, "It is better to exclude Poland completely from the Slavic family, to leave it to its own devices in the struggle against Germanism, than to hold it in a forcible union with us."[50] But when he was assailed by Katkov's *Moskovskiia Viedomosti* for even suggesting such a possibility, Aksakov apologized for the "untimeliness" of his remarks and reassured his nationalist colleague, "We never proposed, nor do we now propose, the possibility of immediately realizing the idea of Polish independence. All of this is too soon." However, Aksakov did declare that Polish political independence was possible at some future date, even though not in 1863.

While recognizing the necessity for pacifying the revolt at the present time [he wrote], and while admitting the necessity of a dictatorship,

[46] M. P. Pogodin, *Sobranie sochinenii*, Vol. III: *Istoriko-politicheskiia pis'ma i zapiski vprodolzhenii krymskoi voiny 1853-1856 M. P. Pogodina* (Moscow, 1874), pp. 127-28.

[47] *Ibid.*, p. 338.

[48] Pogodin, "Pol'skii vopros," *Stat'i politicheskiia i Pol'skii vopros, 1856-1867*, p. 381.

[49] *Ibid.*, p. 382.

[50] Aksakov, "Moskva, 6-go iiuliia, 1863 g.," *Sochineniia*, III, 80.

we maintain the view that, upon delivering the country from the terror, and after returning to it freedom of opinion and expression, and after introducing into Poland's civil life a new element—the Polish peasantry—with full rights, it would be beneficial to allow Poland complete political independence. It can be separate from Russia or in union with it, but only in voluntary union, if Poland itself—realizing the full danger, the full impossibility of its political existence without Russia—desires to be in union with Russia.[51]

While it is difficult to gauge how far Pogodin or Aksakov were willing to go in satisfying Polish demands, it seems reasonable to conclude that in admitting the possibility of Polish political independence, they regarded it as neither essential in their theory nor desirable in practice. The conditions which they posed permitted them to avoid stating unequivocally that they were for Polish independence. Either the Polish "people" had to be protected from Western influences, or all of Poland had to be protected from its German neighbors—or else they assumed that a "truly Slavic Poland," once established, would never wish to cut itself off completely from Russia.

On the other hand, Aksakov opposed Poland's complete political absorption into the Russian Empire. The Poles would not be willing partners in the total obliteration of their political identity, and Poland's political amalgamation with Russia would have a deleterious influence on Russian national institutions. To erase the administrative border that separated Poland from Russia would mean to invite into Slavic Holy Russia the influence of "Polonism" and all the Western evils which that term denoted to him. "Is there a stomach capable of digesting such a mass of hostile elements?"[52] Russian society was already too riddled with Westernism to suit him. The accommodations which the Russian way of life would have to make in a direct political merger with Poland, that is, a Poland not administratively separate from Russia proper, Aksakov feared, would weaken rather than strengthen the Russian nationality.[53]

[51] Aksakov, "Moskva, 7-go sentiabria, 1863 g.," *ibid.*, p. 142.
[52] Aksakov, "Moskva, 21-go noiabria 1864 g.," *ibid.*, p. 266.
[53] Aksakov, "Moskva, 4-go maia 1863 g.," *ibid.*, p. 45.

Because his Slavophile philosophy supported the free development of every historic nationality, Aksakov rejected any proposal
for the Russification of ethnic Poland with almost the same vehe-
mence with which he supported the Russification of the Russian-
inhabited Western Provinces. His theoretical arguments need no
repetition here. Two practical difficulties which he raised, however, are especially noteworthy: a political consideration and a
cultural one.

Ivan Aksakov advanced the political argument against Russification in Poland in a polemic with the Russian nationalists. If there
were no longer a "Polish Kingdom" as such within the Russian
Empire, but only Russian provinces in Poland, if there were no
longer Poles but "Russians," that is, Poles whom the law regarded
as Russians, Aksakov argued, then the government could not undertake any special measures with respect to the Poles alone.[54] His
cultural argument against Russification in Poland was aimed at
Russian "society"—that is, Russian officialdom, the nobility, the
intelligentsia, the professions, and generally the upper middle class.
How could Russians Russify another people, Aksakov demanded,
when Russian society itself had so little confidence in the culture
of the Russian people and was itself so susceptible to Western
influences![55]

A final proposal which several leading Panslavists rejected was
Russian federalism and constitutionalism. Some Western-minded
nationalists, especially in the bureaucracy, believed that Russia
ought to follow the example of Austria and to transform itself into
an imperial federation of provinces. If the Russian state were a
common fatherland based on a common citizenship and loyalty to
the ruling house, the Polish Question would then be solved. As
Iurii Samarin described the proposal, "The state would know
neither a Western nor an Eastern region, neither Russians nor
Poles, Orthodox or Catholics. It would recognize only the subjects
of one sovereign—landlords in possession of the land, peasants
squatting on another's soil and working off their obligations to the

[54] Aksakov, "Moskva, 21-go noiabria 1864 g.," *ibid.*, p. 270.
[55] *Ibid.*, p. 271.

landlord, clergy who prayed for the Tsar, whatever church they might serve, officials serving the Tsar: all these it would regard with the same benevolence and impartiality."[56]

Pogodin was furious at the proponents of this idea. "No, my dear sirs, . . ." he exclaimed in high indignation, "Russia is Russia and not Liflandia or Mingrelia or Dauria. The Russian Sovereign is mighty because he is the Russian Sovereign, the Sovereign of a people sixty million strong, of one faith, one language, and comprising with him a single, indestructible whole. The root of his might is in Holy Russia. His honor and glory are bound to the Russian name, to Russian history, and to no other." Pogodin insisted that he had nothing against non-Russians in the Empire and thought that they should have all the political, civil, and economic advantages which Russians enjoyed. "But for us to stay in the background, to efface ourselves before the Russian Sovereign as being no different from them, and to see in the Sovereign not a Russian, but a collective man composed of all the nationalities living in Russia," the Panslavist asserted, "this is such stupidity that no real Russian could listen to it without indignation."[57]

Ivan Aksakov also lashed out against the Russian federalists. He made clear that he was for civil equality and freedom of worship as much as the proponents of federalism, but he could not relinquish the Russian character of his sovereign and his country to a "St. Petersburg centralism."[58]

Alexander Hilferding held that while a parliament for Great, Little, and White Russia was conceivably feasible, the inclusion of the Poles on an equal basis could only end in failure. They could never assume the role of "His Majesty's Loyal Opposition," Hilferding asserted, since the Poles were opposed not only to state policy but to the state itself.[59]

[56] Iurii F. Samarin, "Po povodu zashchity Kievskoi administratsii," *Sochineniia,* I (Moscow, 1877), 311.
[57] Pogodin, "O knige g. Shedo-Ferroti," *Stat'i politicheskiia i Pol'skii vopros, 1856-1867,* pp. 486-87.
[58] Aksakov, "Moskva, 31 avgusta 1863 g.," *Sochineniia,* III, 137.
[59] A. Hilferding, "V chem iskat' razriesheniia Pol'skomu voprosu," *Stat'i po sovremennym voprosam slavianskim,* in *Sobranie sochinenii,* II, 316-17.

VI

The positive measures which the Russian Panslavists proposed in
1863 for the final settlement of the Polish Question were both
political and social in character. Ivan Aksakov, for example, urged
the necessity of home rule and civil liberties for Poland. The only
way to distinguish between the desires of the Polish people and
the demands of a small privileged class, he insisted, was to enfran-
chise the Polish people at large and to grant Poland a parliament,
not the Polish Sejm of the gentry which had brought disaster to
Poland, but a truly representative body—like the old Russian
zemskii sobor, Aksakov added, with characteristic Slavophile nos-
talgia for seventeenth-century Muscovy. A truly popular Sejm
could be assured complete autonomy in domestic affairs, Aksakov
proposed, and Russia would then stand in honorable relations with
Poland and lift from its own conscience a heavy yoke. Aksakov
believed that with the participation of the Polish peasantry—which
he maintained had ample cause to feel grateful for their liberation
from serfdom—and with assurances of home rule, a democratic
Polish Sejm would decide to cast in its lot with Russia.[60]

But what about that main stumbling block in Russo-Polish relations—the question of the Western Provinces? If only this question
could be settled, wrote Hilferding, "then the Poles would assume
their natural place in the Slavic world, a place in the same order
with all the other Slavic peoples, a place in accord with their
numbers and actual importance, their geographic position and
national character. There would be no Polish Question, but Poland
would be spoken of as part of one general Slavic Question."[61]
But that great day would come only when the Russian state and
Russian society transformed the Western Provinces into, not only
an administrative, but a social and cultural, part of Russia.

Iurii Samarin proposed specifically support of the White Russian and Ukrainian peasantry, whom he called simply "Russian,"

[60] Aksakov, "Moskva, 2-go fevralia 1863 g.," *Sochineniia*, III, 20-21.
[61] Hilferding, "V chem iskat' razriesheniia Pol'skomu voprosu," *Sobranie
sochinenii*, II, 332.

by ensuring "the full independence of their economic way of life." This would be accomplished by establishing fair courts in which peasants could lodge complaints against landlords, by curtailing the privileges of the gentry—largely Polish—in the judiciary and the administration, and by employing Russian officials in their place.[62] Pogodin proposed, far more drastically, that all Poles in the Western Provinces—gentry, officials, and priests—be evicted with all their movable property from "the Russia of our blood."[63]

Aksakov and Samarin repeatedly stressed, however, that no punitive measures should be taken against Poles in the Western Provinces. Aksakov criticized Russian officials who punished Polish political crimes while taking no action at all to counter Polish cultural influence in the Western Provinces, and he frankly advocated the active propagation of Russian culture to offset centuries of Polonization. According to Samarin,

In the Western region two orders are in conflict: the Russian Orthodox and the Latino-Polish. The former of these is basic: the latter—superimposed. The interests of the Russian state and the Russian nation are bound up with the triumph of the former over the latter. The Russian order is personified in the masses of the rural population, in the common people, and in the Orthodox clergy. The Polish—in the landed gentry and the Latin clergy. On our side, that is, on the side of the state and Russia, is the strength of numbers and the power of popular historic instincts: against us is the strength of wealth and education, the might of corporate organization and political experience, the power of property and the social hegemony founded upon it.[64]

Samarin was certain that if the region were left to itself, the forces of wealth, education, and property would prevail, even though Russia gained the political and the military victory. Since Romanism was regarded as the main enemy, Samarin proposed that the education of the common people in the Western Provinces be entrusted to the Orthodox clergy "as the only reliable transmitters

---

[62] Samarin, "Po povodu zashchity Kievskoi administratsii," *Sochineniia*, I, 311.
[63] Pogodin, "Nieskol'ko slov o zapadnykh guberniiakh," *Stat'i politicheskiia i Pol'skii vopros, 1856-1867*, pp. 388-94 *passim*; also in the same volume, "O sistemie Markiza Velepol'skago," p. 454.
[64] Samarin, "Po povodu zashchity Kievskoi administratsii," *Sochineniia*, I, 309.

of Russian and Orthodox culture rather than some sort of colorless and juiceless culture which every man could take as he pleased."[65]

In sum, the program proposed by Aksakov, Samarin, Pogodin, Hilferding, and other Panslavists envisioned political home rule, civil liberties, and cultural freedoms for Poland. They urged support of the Polish peasantry as the one truly Slavic element in Poland and as the true embodiment of Polish nationalism. The Western Provinces, however, were to be Russified by all of the means and agencies at the disposal of the Russian government and of Russian society.

However one chooses to evaluate the statements of the Panslavists regarding Poland, it must be recognized that these men showed a real sympathy for the vast majority of the Polish population, and that they recognized Poland as a historic entity with a natural right to develop its own national way of life. It must also be remembered that these Russian Panslavists expressed such views at a most tense moment in Russo-Polish relations and under an extremely sensitive censorship. As Professor A. N. Pypin, a contemporary observer of Panslavism though not a Panslavist himself, pointed out, "It is not to be doubted that in more peaceful times and under a greater freedom of the press these sympathies would have been proclaimed even more loudly and forcefully."[66] It is, of course, incorrect to portray the Russian Panslavists as admirers and benefactors of the Poles. Yet surely men who spoke up for certain rights of Polish nationality, who urged liberties for the Poles which they themselves did not enjoy in their own empire, who wished to grant Poland home rule and a democratic parliament, cannot be dismissed as Polonophobes.

Basic to the whole Panslavic viewpoint in Russia was the deep conviction that sooner or later Poland and Russia would find themselves side by side in a larger union of all the Slavs. "When Poland's internal social strength is restored and matures, when the black cloud from the West which hangs over it is dispelled one

---

[65] *Ibid.*, p. 311.

[66] A. N. Pypin, "Die polnische Frage in der Literatur der russischen Slavophilen," *Russische Revue*, XVII (St. Petersburg, 1880), 224.

way or another, when the dream of political Panslavism in this or that form is realized, then, it seems to us," Budilovich declared, "Poland, too, will find itself an honored place and independent position in a united Slavdom."[67]

[67] Anton Budilovich, "Nieskol'ko zamiechanii o pol'skom voprosie s tochki zrieniia vseslavianstva," *Besieda,* VI (1871), 163.

8

THE MOSCOW SLAV CONGRESS OF 1867

Wir wollen sein ein einig Volk von Brüdern.
FRIEDRICH SCHILLER, *Wilhelm Tell*
And there shall be one fold, and one shepherd.
ST. JOHN 10:16

THE FIRST CONGRESS of the representatives of the Slavic peoples, held in Prague in the turbulent year 1848, was not in reality an "all-Slav" gathering. The Russian people, which in numbers and in might exceeded the other Slavic peoples combined, was not represented. The only native of the Russian Empire to attend was Michael Bakunin; his personal involvement in the revolutions then sweeping over Western Europe and his enforced lack of contact with his homeland hardly qualified him as a representative of his own country. Indeed, Bakunin advised the delegates in Prague that Russia was nothing but a vast graveyard and that the non-Russian Slavs should expect nothing from autocratic Russia.[1] It is known that Václav Hanka, Czech Slavist, had sent invitations in the name of his colleagues not only to such academic figures in Russia as Sreznevskii, Pogodin, Bodianskii, and Grigorovich—but even to Count Uvarov, the Minister of Public Education.[2] Russian participation in any liberal movement, however, even a Slavic one, was inadmissible under the regime of Nicholas I.

It was in the sixties of the nineteenth century that a whole complex of political purposes and cultural trends brought together representatives not only of the Western and Southern Slavs but, for the first time, representatives of the Russian people in a Slav

---

[1] František Roubík, *Český rok 1848* (Prague, 1948), p. 213. See also E. H. Carr, *Michael Bakunin* (London, 1937), p. 159.

[2] Václav Žáček, "Přípravy k sjezdu průběh szjezdových jednání," *Slovanský sjezd v Praze 1848*, ed. by Václav Čejchan et al. (Prague, 1948), p. 55.

congress held in Russia. Convened at the peak of a whole era of Slavic fellowship, the Moscow Slav Congress of 1867, such as it was, represented the most significant manifestation of Slavic solidarity in the latter half of the nineteenth century.

The Moscow Slav Congress was not initiated by the Russian government but by certain members and friends of the Moscow Slavic Benevolent Committee—and then not as a separate project. On December 9, 1864, a newly founded learned society at the University of Moscow, the Society of the Friends of Natural Science, resolved to sponsor an ethnographic exhibition devoted largely to the peoples of the Russian Empire. This scientific enterprise was to be modeled on the anthropological section of the Sydenham Crystal Palace Exhibition in London. The Emperor himself agreed to open the exhibition in the fall of 1867.[3] It was not until late in 1865 that any Panslavic theme was introduced into the plans.

In view of fragmentary evidence, it is not clear at what point Russian Panslavic circles first became interested in the exhibition as a vehicle for their particular interest. A recent Soviet work based on archival material has brought out a letter from Professor Vladimir I. Lamanskii in St. Petersburg to Professor Nil Popov in Moscow dated October 23, 1865, in which the former writes:

You know what should be done by you there in Moscow on the occasion of the Ethnographic Exhibition in 1867. First, organize several public lectures on the Slavs. You could give two or three lectures, I would also not refuse, and it might be possible to invite Lavrovskii and others. Second, organize at the same time the first Slavic congress in Moscow.[4]

Ten years later, in a commemorative address before the St. Petersburg Section of the Slavic Benevolent Committee, Lamanskii disclaimed any personal credit for originating the idea. It was Popov who, said Lamanskii, "undertook this task so energetically that to

[3] *Vserossiiskaia efnograficheskaia vystavka i Slavianskii s"iezd v maie 1867 goda* (Moscow, 1867), pp. 2-3. Hereafter referred to as *Vserossiiskaia.*

[4] A. 3. Nikitin, "Slavianskie s"ezdy shestideslatykh godov XIX veka," *Slavianskii Sbornik: Slavianskii vopros i russkoe obshchestvo v 1867-1878 godakh* (Moscow, 1948), p. 18.

him undoubtedly belongs the main honor of organizing the Slavic ethnographic exhibit and the glory of being the author of the Slav Congress in Moscow."[5] Other evidence suggests that this was no mere modesty on Lamanskii's part. A historian at the University of Moscow, Popov had made an extensive tour of the Slavic lands of Eastern Europe in 1863 and 1864. He returned full of enthusiasm both for Slavic studies and for the Slavic cause, as his many articles in the Russian journals of his day testify. It was he who proposed to the Society of Friends of Natural Science at its session of November 24, 1865, that it include a Slavic section in the Moscow Ethnographic Exhibition.[6] The Society accepted the proposal and invited Popov on December 30, 1865, to carry it out.

Professor Popov began immediately to issue invitations to various Slavic organizations and scholars abroad, and was helped in this task by Lamanskii and Pogodin, whose many personal ties with the Western and Southern Slavs made their services invaluable. Popov's most active assistant proved to be the Very Reverend M. F. Raevskii, dean of the Russian Embassy church in Vienna, who had cultivated the friendship of many prominent Austrian Slavs during his many years of service in the Hapsburg capital.[7] Popov and his colleagues in Russia themselves negotiated with the Balkan Slavs, though they were greatly helped in this task by Russian diplomatic personnel on the spot. All in all, over three hundred invitations were sent. There is no evidence that any were sent in the name of the Moscow Slavic Benevolent Committee.

Almost overnight, what had begun as a purely academic project of a learned society swelled into a public cause supported by all the influence which the Panslavists could muster. The project found its two most vociferous champions in Michael N. Katkov, editor of *Moskovskiia Viedomosti* (Moscow News), and Ivan S.

---

[5] *Pervyia 15 liet sushchestvovaniia S.-Peterburgskago Slavianskago blagotvoritel'nago obshchestva; po protokolam obshchikh sobranii ego chlenov, sostoiavshimsia v 1868-1883 gg.* (St. Petersburg, 1883), p. 452, minutes of the meeting of May 11, 1877.

[6] *Vserossiiskaia*, p. 23.

[7] To stimulate interest among the Slavs of Austria, Prussia, and Saxony, Raevskii published an unsigned brochure in Vienna in 1866, *Die russische Ethnographische Ausstellung in Moskau*. Once again practical necessity overruled the call of blood; the pamphlet was written in German.

Aksakov, then editor of *Moskva* (Moscow). In a passionate editorial, Aksakov proclaimed on March 28, 1867:

There have been Slavic meetings before, especially in 1848 in Prague—but they were of no import. *We* were not there. There were no representatives of that Slavic people which, by the grace of God, alone has kept its freedom, established the most powerful state in the world, and to which God has assigned a lofty task: to serve the liberation and rebirth of its enslaved and oppressed brethren. There is in Russia no desire for usurpation, no thought of political domination. It desires but the freedom of spirit and life for those Slavic peoples which have remained faithful to the Slavic confraternity.[8]

Usually apathetic toward the Slavic cause, Russian society responded with a surprising generosity. The Municipal Duma of Moscow voted ten thousand rubles to provide a suitable welcome. Russian railways offered the free use of their services to the visiting Slavs for all travel within Russia's borders. A prominent hotel owner contributed rooms free of charge. Funds were raised with even greater success in that den of Westernism, St. Petersburg. Panslavists like Lamanskii organized a committee of welcome in the northern capital, which later formed the nucleus for the St. Petersburg Section of the Moscow Slavic Benevolent Committee.

Though this public display of sympathy for the oppressed Slavs of the neighboring empires would have been unthinkable only a decade before, the Russian government did not intervene, despite the direct control exercised over the Moscow Slavic Benevolent Committee by the Ministry of Foreign Affairs. Indeed, even an official source, *Correspondance russe*, which was published by Valuev's Ministry of the Interior in French for the benefit of foreigners in Russia, echoed the Moscow press. An editorial proclaimed:

We will have our guests know that they come to a nation from which they have everything to gain without having anything to fear. We will listen to their troubles, for a recital of their ills cannot but make stronger the ties which bind us to them. If they should be of a mind to make a comparison between their political system and ours, we will

[8] Ivan S. Aksakov, "Moskva, 28-go marta," *Slavianskii vopros, 1860-1886,* in *Sochineniia,* I (Moscow, 1886), 148.

not be so foolish as to prove to them that they are living under conditions which are more favorable to the development of the Slavs. These conditions, we believe to the contrary, are bad, we have said so a hundred times, and we would certainly say so again.[9]

The fact that the Emperor did not withdraw his assent to open the Ethnographic Exhibition in person, even after the obviously nonscientific interest which that exhibition had evoked at home and abroad, also served to indicate the government's interest in the affair.

II

With the exception of the Poles, the response of the Slavs of Eastern Europe indicated that they considered the Russian invitation to be an opportune one. All in all, eighty-one Slavs from abroad, the majority from the Hapsburg Empire, attended the Moscow Slav Congress. Among sixty-three Austro-Hungarian Slavs were twenty-seven Czechs and Moravians, sixteen Serbs, ten Croats, four Ukrainians, three Slovaks, and three Slovenes. In addition, twelve Serbs represented the Principality of Serbia, and two the Principality of Montenegro. A single Bulgar came from the Ottoman Empire. The vanishing Slavs of the Germanies were represented by a single Kashub from Prussia and two Lusatian Serbs from Saxony.[10]

For the Serbians it was an opportune time to strengthen ties with Russia. The evacuation of the Turkish garrison from Belgrade was only the most recent in a series of difficulties with the Porte. As always, the Serbian government needed money, and it had appointed Milan Petronijević, Assistant Minister of Justice, to negotiate a loan from the Russian government.[11] As though to emphasize the importance which it attached to the Serbian delegation, the Belgrade government ordered Petronijević to go with the group as both delegate to the Moscow Exhibition and diplomatic

[9] Cited by Julian Klaczko, "Le Congrès de Moscou et la propagande panslaviste," *Revue des deux mondes*, XXXVII (September, 1867), 11.

[10] *Vserossiiskaia*, pp. 111-51 *passim*.

[11] Nikitin, "Slavianskie s"ezdy shestidesiatykh godov XIX veka," *Slavianskii Sbornik*, p. 30.

emissary of Prince Michael. Officially, however, it was Milan Milićević who led the delegation, both as chief delegate of the Serbian Learned Society (Srpsko učeno društvo) and by virtue of his fluency in the Russian language. Next in importance was Janko Šafarik, secretary-treasurer of the Society, historian, archivist, a founder of the Belgrade Museum, and nephew of the famed Czech Slavist, Pavel Josef Šafařík. The third delegate of the Society was Steva Todorović, professor of geometry and patron of Serbian music. In addition to these official delegates the Serbian group included, among others, the Russophile publicist, Milorad Medaković, and the twenty-three-year-old Vladan Djordjević, then known as a founder of the patriotic *Omladina* (Youth) and one day to be prime minister of Serbia.

As for the only other independent Slavic state in the Balkans, rockbound Montenegro, Prince Nicholas was at first content to send a lavish array of folk costumes and other articles to the Ethnographic Exhibition itself. After the other Slavic delegates had arrived in Russia, however, and the political value of the congress had become apparent, the wily mountain chieftain changed his mind. He quickly dispatched two of his most distinguished and colorful warriors to "Mother Russia": his father-in-law, Petar Vukotić, and Ilija Plamenac—both senators and *vojvodas* (military commanders).

Except for a Bulgarian geographer, M. D. Bogorov, a former student in Odessa, the Ottoman Slavs were unrepresented, probably for fear of reprisals from the Turkish government.

The isolated Slavic enclaves of the Germanies were represented by a Kashub from Prussia, Dr. Florjan Cenôva, an authority on the history and ethnography of his people, and two Lusatian Serbs from Saxony: the Slavic scholar and publicist, Jan Arnošt Smoleŕ (or Schmaler, as he signed himself in German), and a young doctor from Budyšin (Bautzen) called, ironically enough, Pětr Dučman (Dutchman).

It was without a doubt the Slavs of the Austro-Hungarian Empire, and among them particularly the Czechs, who made the most of the Russian invitation. The call from the Slavic colossus of the East came at the very height of their despair under the rigors of the Beust regime in Vienna. Having been drubbed by Bismarck's legions of blood and iron in the Seven Weeks War, the shaky Austrian government resolved to preserve the Empire by sharing its administration with the Magyars to the detriment of the Slavic plurality. What lay in store for the Austrian Slavs was made graphically clear in the dictum attributed to Baron Beust: "Man muss die Slawen an die Mauer drücken" ("The Slavs must be pressed against the wall").

"No people in the realm was as hard hit by the agreement of 1867 as were the Czechs," wrote Ernest Denis, distinguished French historian of the Czech nation. "Every article of the agreement touched them in their most tender spot."[12] In 1848 František Palacký, famed Czech historian and public leader, had made famous the opinion that if Austria did not exist, she would have had to be invented. Nearly two decades later he warned, "The day Dualism is proclaimed will, by an invincible necessity, likewise be the day when Panslavism will be born in its least desirable form."[13] In 1867 both the Old Czech and the Young Czech parties were ready to patch up their quarrel over the Polish uprising and to make good that threat—or at least to give Vienna a good fright. *Národní Listy* (National Press), organ of the Young Czech party in Prague, openly recognized in these words the political character of the trip to Moscow:

We do not intend to conceal the fact that the Moscow Exhibition bears a truly profound political significance for those of us who are not going for the sake of mere philology or ethnography. It is not we who have lent it this significance. Those who inaugurated Dualism in Austria . . . have transformed a simple ethnographic exhibition into a Slavic congress with an undeniable political significance. . . . The Slavs of all lands are going there not "to coquet with a distant state in the East" but to greet a people close to them by blood and kinship, and to establish a foundation for the reciprocity of all the Slavic stock which will procure protection especially for the Austrian Slavs against

[12] Arnošt (Ernest) Denis, *Čechy po Bílé Hoře,* II, Book III (Prague, 1911), 117.
[13] František Palacký, "Idea státu rakouského," *Národ* (April-May, 1865), cited by Milan Prelog, *Pout' Slovanů do Moskvy roku 1867,* trans. Milada Paulová (Prague, 1931), p. 35.

all kinds of future storms which threaten that national development they so vainly seek here at home.[14]

Such were the sentiments not only of the politically astute and aggressive Czechs but also of the Slovaks, Serbs, Croats, Slovenes, and the so-called Ruthenes of the Austrian Empire. It was no accident that less than two weeks after Francis Joseph had been crowned Rex Hungariae under the terms of the Ausgleich, sixty-three of his Slavic subjects set off to Moscow to seek solace. They went, as Rieger made clear, not to conspire but to demonstrate their dissatisfaction by using Russia as a public forum.[15]

The Czech delegation was a most impressive one. The venerable Palacký and his distinguished son-in-law, František Rieger, publicist and fiery champion of Czech national rights, stood out among all the Slavic delegations from abroad. With them were other active members of the Old Czech party: František Brauner, lawyer, economist, and member of parliament who had made a name for himself in the days of 1848; František Skrejšovský, leading Old Czech journalist whose ideals included the establishment of an all-Slavic church and the recognition of Russian as an all-Slavic tongue; Dr. Karel Mattuš, Russophile Czech lawyer; Antonín Vrťátko, philosopher and librarian of the Czech Museum; Antonín Patera, Slavic philologist; Professor Josef Kolář, expert in the Russian language; Josef Hamerník, renowned professor of medicine and member of parliament; and Tomáš Černý, the Sokol leader. The Young Czech party was represented by Dr. Julius Grégr, editor of *Národní Listy*, whose trip to Russia was a great surprise in view of his pro-Polish and anti-Russian stand in 1863; Emmanuel Vávra, publicist, collaborator on *Národní Listy*, and translator of Russian literature, especially Turgenev; and Baron Karel Dragutin Maria Villáni, noble landowner and author. Other participants included the poet and historian Karel Jaromír Erben, translator into Czech of the *Tale of the Host of Igor* and the Russian Primary

[14] Cited by Zdeněk Tobolka, *Politické dějiny československého národa od r. 1848 až do dnešní doby*, II (Prague, 1932-36), 153-54.
[15] Cited by Prelog, *Pout' Slovanů*, p. 37.

Chronicle; Dr. Karel Jičínský, lawyer; and a dozen others including architects, factory owners, merchants, and local officials.[16]

The Slovaks sent three representatives. Ondrej Radlinský was a Roman Catholic priest of Polish ancestry, a grammarian, and author of religious tracts, including sermons in Russian, who had gained notice for advocating a Slavic church union.[17] Ján Jesenský and Pavel Mudroň were both prominent lawyers from Turčiansky sv. Martin, the cradle of Slovak Protestant nationalism.

The Austrian Serbs demonstrated their religious solidarity with Russia by sending four Orthodox priests of whom the ranking cleric was Archimandrite Kovačević, member of the Dalmatian Diet. Officials included Dr. Jovan Subotić, judge of the Supreme Court and man of letters, and Aleksandar Vukašinović and Dr. Mihajlo Polit-Desančić, both members of the Croatian Parliament. Among the prominent literary figures of the Serbian delegation from Austria were Count Ilija Dede-Janković, Dalmatian publicist, and Dr. Laza Kostić, then professor at the Gymnasium of Novi Sad and fiery poet of Serbian nationalism.

Chief of the three Slovene delegates was the littérateur and philologist Matija-Ziljski Majar, who had only recently published an all-Slavic grammar as part of his campaign for a single Slavic literary language. He was accompanied by Ivan Vilhar, journalist and brother of the nationalist poet and editor Miroslav Vilhar, and Dr. Hudec, a pedagogue.[18]

The Croats appear to have taken the Russian invitation in a non-political spirit. Their delegation did not include any distinguished figure with the exception of Ljudevit Gaj, whose earlier zeal as a Panslavist and leader of the Illyrian movement in the 1830's had won him much acclaim in the Slavic world.[19] In his later years, however, he had been suspected of being an Austrian agent and

---

[16] Josef Jirásek, *Rusko a my; dějiny vztahů československo-ruských od nejstarších dob až do roku 1914* (Brno, 1945), III, 10 ff.

[17] Albert Pražák, *České obrození* (Prague, 1948), p. 170.

[18] Ivan Prijatelj, *Kulturna in politična zgodovina Slovencev, 1848-1895*, IV (Ljubljana, 1939), 105.

[19] Philip E. Mosely, "Pan-Slavist Memorandum of Ljudevit Gaj in 1838," *American Historical Review*, XL (July, 1935), 704-16.

was practically ignored throughout his stay in Russia.[20] The real leader of the Croatian group of ten was Dr. Petar Matković, who was so obviously engrossed in the scientific aspects of the Moscow Ethnographic Exhibition that he was given official leave of absence from his teaching post at the Zagreb Gymnasium to represent the Society of Yugoslav History and Antiquity (Društvo za jugoslavensku povijest i starine). Two Roman Catholic prelates, Juraj Strossmayer and Franjo Rački—both ardent Croatian nationalists and supporters of the Yugoslav movement—had promised their support and were expected in Moscow, but neither came. As the Croatian correspondent of the Czech newspaper *Národní Noviny* (National News) reported at the time, many prominent Croats might have gone to Moscow had there not been a session of Parliament and had they not been in fear of losing their seats.[21]

The Ukrainian subjects of the Austro-Hungarian Empire were represented by four delegates, all of them characteristically noted simply as "Russians" in the roster included in the proceedings published in Moscow.[22] By far the most noteworthy of them was the Slavist, linguist, and historian, Iakiv F. Holovackij (known in Russian as Iakov Fëdorovich Golovatskii), professor at the University of Lwów (Lvov), who had been pensioned and placed under surveillance by the Vienna government for his Russophile leanings. His three companions included Iosif N. Livchak, young Galician author; Evhenii Osipovich Pavlevich, a lawyer from Lwów; and the Reverend M. B. Molchan, Consistorial Notary of the Greek Catholic Uniat diocese of Prešov.

It is more difficult to enumerate the Russian delegates to the Moscow Slav Congress, since there was in fact no congress in any formal sense of the term. Indeed, the designation "congress" (*siezd*) was employed throughout by its participants in its simple generic meaning of "get-together." The Moscow Slav Congress of 1867

[20] See V. N. Korablev's article, "Liudevit Gai; k 60-letiiu so dnia ego smerti," *Trudy Instituta slavianovedeniia Akademii nauk SSSR*, II (Leningrad, 1934), 254 ff.

[21] Prelog, *Pout' Slovanů*, pp. 41-42.

[22] The entire roster of all the Slavic guests may be found in *Vserossiiskaia*, pp. 111-51. The list of "Russians" from Austria is on pp. 113-21.

was really a tour or a "pilgrimage," as certain German observers maliciously observed, marked by an unending series of banquets, both public and private, attended by passionate oratory in which Russians and their guests declaimed on their love for one another and their common hatred of their Western enemies. The ostensible purpose which had brought them together—the Moscow Ethnographic Exhibition—occupied their attention for only part of one afternoon! From the day the Slavic guests crossed the Russian border on May 4, until their departure on June 3, the Slav Congress of 1867 consisted of one prolonged love feast and public demonstration of political sympathy and cultural solidarity.

It is obvious that under these conditions one could hardly consider the architects of the Ethnographic Exhibition as the hosts. It might be more appropriate to regard the Moscow Slavic Benevolent Committee as such. Yet at no point did it act in an official capacity. Nevertheless an examination of the detailed Russian record of the Congress, published in 1867, shows that the Russians who participated most actively in welcoming the Slavic guests were members of the Panslavic circles in Moscow and St. Petersburg. Among them were representatives of various backgrounds. There were Slavophiles of the old school—Iurii Samarin, Ivan Aksakov, A. I. Koshelev, and the great poet Fëdor Tiutchev. There was also the academic group—M. P. Pogodin, V. I. Lamanskii, O. M. Bodianskii, A. A. Maikov, N. A. Popov, O. F. Miller, and other professors of Slavic studies. The nationalist element was represented by such conservatives as M. N. Katkov, P. M. Leontiev, D. I. Ilovaiskii, and others. Professors S. M. Soloviëv and F. I. Buslaev constituted a moderate liberal element.

In actual fact, the Slavic delegates from abroad were greeted by most segments of Russian society from the peasant elder or *starosta*, who was brought forward to offer them bread and salt on their entry into ethnic Russia proper, to Alexander II at Tsarskoe Selo. They were welcomed by prominent public officials such as the Foreign Minister, Prince Gorchakov. They enjoyed the hospitality of wealthy noblemen such as Count Kushelev-Bezborodko. They worshipped in Count Sheremetiev's fabulous palace chapel in St. Petersburg and in St. Isaac's Cathedral. They were dined and wined in Moscow at the swank English Club and the Clubs of the Merchants and the Nobility. They were blessed by the most venerable prelates of the Russian Orthodox Church. They were entertained by Russia's greatest musicians. They heard lectures by members of the Academy of Sciences and by spokesmen of eighteen learned societies. They were honored by the naval base at Kronstadt. They were cheered and tossed into the air by mobs of people on several occasions. In short, the Slavic guests were fêted with all the exhausting enthusiasm of which guests in Russia have happily complained down the ages.

III

Most of the delegates gathered first in Vienna and on May 3 entrained for Warsaw by way of Přerov, where a party of Czechs joined them. On May 4 they arrived at the Russian border, whence a special train took them to Warsaw.[23]

From the very first an ominous cloud was to hang over the visitors throughout their stay within the Russian Empire—the Polish Question. The Polish press in Austria and Germany had dire messages for the Moscow-bound Slavs. Said one dramatic editorial:

You wish to go to Moscow. You aspire to greet there the only independent Slavic power capable of reuniting you, of assuring you your national development! Behold, then, the national development which this power has assured an ancient and glorious people, united a century ago under the scepter of the Tsar! You hold dear your language, your traditions and customs? Ask, then, what Russia has done with the language, the traditions and customs of Poland! You guard with a touching piety the monuments of your literature and the ruins of your antiquity? Ask, then, what has become of the Załuski and Czącki libraries, our art collections, and the Crown jewels of our Jagiellons! You are attached to your clergy, you cherish your wives and children, you take pride in your prosperity? See our exiled bishops, our priests hanging from infamous gallows, our wives and children driven like a vile herd to the polar regions, and our fortunes exposed to the most

---

[23] Unless otherwise indicated, general descriptions of the journey and the sojourn in Moscow are from *Vserossiiskaia*.

despicable and systematic spoliation! . . . Traverse . . . this red sea, this sea of Polish blood across which they would show you the promised land. Carefully observe our hell; it leads to your paradise.[24]

Assuredly such a Godspeed was not a pleasant one. Its solemn impact grew as the party made its way across Russian Poland and observed the more obvious results of Russification in that country.[25] Palacký and Rieger did not join the party until it had reached Vilna. The two Czech leaders had thought it necessary to go to Paris for two reasons: first, to justify their Moscow trip before the French and, if possible, to interest the French Court in the Czech cause after the Ausgleich; and second, to reach some understanding with the Polish émigrés. They failed on both counts. As far as Napoleon III was concerned, the Czechs were not to have their Biarritz or Plombières. As for the Poles, a Czartoryski or a Zamojski living in exile could hardly have regarded the Czech visit to Moscow as anything but treason to all of European civilization. On May 1 a special delegation of Polish exiles visited Palacký and Rieger and presented their Czech brethren with a bitter manifesto denouncing the Russians and the aims of the Moscow Slav Congress.[26] Palacký and Rieger assured the Poles that they would not hesitate to speak their minds in Moscow. To another delegation Palacký put the question, "Do you wish to be Germanized or Russified?" The answer he received was disturbing in its simplicity: neither! It was with this answer still ringing in their ears that the two Czech leaders joined their fellow wayfarers in Vilna on May 7.

That same night the Slav delegates entrained for the last stage of their journey to Russia proper. The next morning found them in Ostrov, the first station in ethnic Russia. They were welcomed by a peasant *starosta* or elder with the traditional bread and salt, which Palacký received for the entire group. At the Pskov station a similar scene was enacted—only with more pomp and music.

[24] Cited by Klaczko, "Le Congrès de Moscou et la propagande panslaviste," *Revue des deux mondes*, XXXVII (September, 1867), 19.

[25] For some of the delegates' unfavorable reactions to Russification in Poland, see especially M. Polit-Desančić, *Putne uspomene* (Novi Sad, 1896), pp. 59 ff.; Prelog, *Pout' Slovanů*, p. 71; Klaczko, "Le Congrès de Moscou et la propagande panslaviste," *Revue des deux mondes*, XXXVII (September, 1867), 19 ff.

[26] *Vserossiiskaia*, p. 106, cites an excerpt from this memorandum.

Holovackij received the bread and salt this time. By three o'clock that afternoon the train arrived in Gatchina, some thirty miles from St. Petersburg. There was a committee of welcome from the local Duma, a band played, and greetings were delivered by students. Professor Lamanskii joined the party here to ride with the delegates to the capital. For most of the Slavic guests this was not the German-named *Sankt-Peterburg.* "Petrohrad. . . . To je Petrograd!" they shouted excitedly in their own tongues. Their Russian hosts were not to call their own capital by its Slavic name until the First World War!

IV

The Slavic guests spent their first day in the Russian capital by taking a tour of the city which included the great public library and the cathedrals of St. Isaac and Our Lady of Kazan. Their debut in Russian society took place that evening when they attended the Mariinskii Theater for a performance of Glinka's *A Life for the Tsar*. The very choice of the opera was a sublime example of Russian tactlessness. Based on the Polish invasion of Muscovy during the Time of Troubles in the first years of the seventeenth century, the opera brought out in all its ferocity the enmity between aristocratic, feudal, Romanized Poland and Holy Russia. After the opera ballet consisting of folk dances was presented. Despite the excellence of the two principal danseuses, the excited public catcalled and hooted down the Polish mazurka while the Russian dance earned phrenetic applause.

News of the mazurka incident reached even Herzen's ears in London. *Kolokol* (The Bell) condemned the "cruel lack of tact." Commenting on the fact that there were no Poles among the Slavic guests in Russia, Herzen remarked with masterful irony that there were indeed Polish "guests" in Russia, only they were not in the Mariinskii Theater but in Siberia, and instead of wearing the Tsar's cross on a ribbon around their necks, they were carrying it on their backs![27]

[27] Alexander Herzen, *Polnoe sobranie sochinenii i pisem,* ed. M. K. Lemke (St. Petersburg, 1922), XIX, 352-55.

On May 10, after a tour of the Hermitage Museum, several groups among the Slavic guests made separate visits to two significant figures—the Russian Foreign Minister, Prince Gorchakov, and the Austrian Ambassador, Reverter.

The Austrian Slavs were the first group to visit Gorchakov. They first held a council as to what line to adopt in the conversation. Little did they know that this particular matter as well as their entire trip would be reported to the Austrian police in Prague. Emmanuel Vávra, the Czech publicist, had promised his father-in-law, Karel Sabina—the writer known for, among other works, his delightful libretto for Smetana's opera *The Bartered Bride*—to send letters from Russia which Sabina said he wished to use purely as background material for some articles in the *Kölnische Zeitung*. Relying on his father-in-law's discretion, Vávra peppered his private letters with a mass of piquant details which he never dreamed would find their way to the police section of the Austrian Council of Ministers![28] Among his reports was a revealing description of the audience with Gorchakov and of its preliminaries.

Before going to Gorchakov, the Austrian Slavs weighed the advisability of introducing any politics whatsoever into the conversation. According to Vávra's report:

Rieger advised that all political observations be avoided and that the emphasis be placed on literary reciprocity and academic solidarity. All agreed to this, but Palacký wished nevertheless to include at least that our position with respect to the Germans inspired hopes in our hearts that Russia would not allow the extinction of the most threatened Slav people in the West. . . . The Croats, Serbs, and Slovaks voted for this; ours did, too, and so it was that this passage was included.[29]

To Vávra, Gorchakov's welcome seemed rather officious. Rieger delivered in Czech an address agreed upon by the delegation, and Gorchakov replied in Russian. Then both settled on French. The Foreign Minister praised the Czechs for being good Slavs and remarked that it was the Tsar's desire to be kindly remembered

---

[28] Karel Kazbunda, *Pouť Čechů do Moskvy 1867 a rakouská diplomacie* (Prague, 1924), p. 118, Appendix X, Publications of the Archive of the Ministry of Foreign Affairs, No. 1.
[29] *Ibid.*

by the Slavs. The deputation took up the cue by asking the old statesman if they might not thank the Tsar personally. Gorchakov replied warily, with an eye to protocol, that they ought to apply through their own ambassador.

On the same day the delegation of the Principality of Serbia gained an audience with Gorchakov through the Director of the Asiatic Department of the Russian Foreign Ministry ("for here Serbia is reckoned among the Asiatic countries!" Milićević exclaimed in his memoirs). The Serbs thanked the Foreign Minister for the hospitality which they encountered everywhere in Russia. Gorchakov diplomatically indicated that his government was in no way officially involved. "Our Russian people are receiving you with such enthusiasm," he declared, "that the Imperial Government had nothing to do." The Serbs begged leave to present themselves to the Tsar. "Good," he replied, "I am going to see the Emperor today at Tsarskoe Selo and will inform him of your desire." He emphasized again, however, that any Austrian subjects should apply for an audience through the Austrian ambassador.[30]

Meanwhile the Austrian Slavs paid a reluctant courtesy call on their ambassador. Count Friedrich Reverter de Salandra received his august master's wayward subjects with studied coldness. This attitude hardly typified his dispatches to Vienna, however.

When he had first gotten wind in mid-April of the proposed visit by the Austrian Slavs to Moscow, Reverter hurried off to Gorchakov for an explanation. His subsequent report to Baron Beust in Vienna described the stand of the Russian government as follows:

Gorchakov's reply was very evasive. As far as Petersburg was concerned, the Petersburg committee for the Exhibition had been reminded that it was not to allow the welcome of the Slavic deputies to assume any political coloration. He denied the possibility of reaching Moscow on this subject, where the government's influence stopped in such affairs. The only medium was, in his opinion, a reminder which the Minister of the Interior would *probably* send directly to the Moscow committee.[31]

[30] M. Milićević, *Etnografska izložba i slovenski sastanak u Moskvi, 1867* (Belgrade, 1884), pp. 18-20.

[31] Kazbunda, *Pouť Čechů*, p. 35, Reverter to Beust, April 27/15, 1867.

Reverter was naturally disturbed by this reply. The expression *probablement*, which the Austrian ambassador had doubly underscored in his dispatch, appeared to testify to the intentional passivity of the Russian government in the whole affair. Reverter informed Gorchakov with acid irony that his government could not quite comprehend how the authority and the responsibility of the Russian government could possibly cease at the city limits of St. Petersburg.

Some ten days later Reverter again wrote to Beust on the matter, pointing out the danger involved for Austria in Russian Panslavism. "The Slavophile faction, to which the [Russian] government is often inclined," he reported, "though it has every interest in keeping it in check, would be capable—given the opportunity—of bringing Russia into an open break with the whole world."[32]

Beust replied that nothing could be less opportune than an official Austrian objection to the proposed Slavic gathering in Russia. "Unconvinced that St. Petersburg has chosen the right path in permitting an exhibition which is for the glorification of a so-called single Slavic nationality which, despite being a Utopia, is no less a cause for concern," Baron Beust wrote, "we do not have, for the present at least, any motive in making out of this the subject of any observation, for we would not dream of placing the slightest obstacle in the way of this entertaining and instructive journey to Russia which has been proposed to our nationals." Taking into account the probability that the Russian government would deny responsibility for the affair, Beust added, "We also restrict ourselves to taking note of the incident in question and to express the hope that in this event the Russian government would not express surprise if we, following its example, should declare our incompetence to intervene should hypothetical manifestations analogous to those in Moscow take place by chance in Galicia with the participation of the subjects of His Majesty, the Emperor of Russia." Beust concluded with the advice that Reverter communicate all this to Gorchakov "in an easy manner and one more friendly than official."[33]

[32] *Ibid.*, pp. 50-51, Reverter to Beust, May 8/April 26, 1867.
[33] *Ibid.*, pp. 83-84, Beust to Reverter, May 3, 1867.

In accordance with his chief's instructions, Reverter had another interview with Prince Gorchakov on May 6. His report to Baron Beust indicated clearly that the Russian government was washing its hands of the Slavic congress. According to Reverter, Gorchakov declared that the Russian government was entirely alien to the glorification of any single Slavic nationality. Furthermore, the Russian Foreign Minister assured Reverter that this whole movement had as its adherents in Russia but a handful of men known for their eccentricity and only a fraction of the Moscow press. It was true that the Imperial Court had lent its patronage to the Ethnographic Exhibition, Gorchakov admitted, but that Exhibition had nothing to do with the utopian ideas of the Moscow Panslavists. Finally Gorchakov denied in advance his government's responsibility for any declarations or speeches which the Slavic visitors or their Russian hosts might make. As for the Austrian suggestion concerning a hypothetical manifestation of an analogous nature in Austrian Galicia, the veteran Russian diplomat assured Reverter that few indeed would be found in all Russia to attend such a meeting!

None of the concern expressed in these diplomatic exchanges was apparent in the suave ambassador's reception of Palacký, Rieger, and their party. As His Apostolic Majesty's disgruntled but still correct subjects, the Austrian Slavs requested their ambassador to arrange for them an audience with the Tsar. Wishing to avoid giving recognition to these Austrian Slavs as a deputation, Reverter dismissed them with the advice that they could themselves individually apply to the Russian Foreign Ministry for such an audience. Later Reverter was visited by another group of Austrian Slavs, probably most of them Serbs, who exhibited somewhat less concern over protocol and frankly presented themselves as a deputation. The ambassador disclaimed any knowledge of a deputation. When his Slavic compatriots innocently explained about the Moscow Ethnographic Exhibition, he remarked sardonically, "Oh, so you are students." The sobered visitors replied with aplomb that they were "spectators." The interview ended abruptly with the same suggestion which Reverter had given to the earlier party—that they themselves arranged directly with the Russians for an audience with the Tsar.[34]

While these arrangements were being made, the Slavic guests spent the next three days seeing the sights and being entertained by capital society. As the Austrian ambassador reported to Baron Beust, "These gentlemen are for the moment the lions of St. Petersburg. They are being dragged from one feast to another, and in the streets people run after their carriages in order to see 'the Slavs.' One would suppose that they had never seen any before, as though one had just discovered a new archipelago in Polynesia. It is impossible for serious minds not to be struck by the ridiculousness which attends this national farce."[35]

May 11 was the feast of Saints Cyril and Methodius. Various Russian scholars had only recently unearthed from medieval service books the long-neglected services to these remarkable Greek missionaries to the Slavs. The Slavic guests were given places of honor in the Cathedral of St. Isaac during the Holy Liturgy. The text of the sermon was: "And there shall be one fold, and one shepherd." Later in the day the guests attended a session of the Russian Academy of Sciences, regularly held on that feast day for the section on Russian language and literature.

The evening of May 11 was devoted to a banquet at the Hall of the Nobility. The Slavic brethren from abroad were confronted by the Imperial Russian coat-of-arms with both heads of the eagle brooding over the escutcheons of all the Slavic lands. Above there was emblazoned a curious bit of linguistic information: "The Slavic language and the Russian are one." The religious theme of the day was illustrated by an icon of Saints Cyril and Methodius, "the preceptors of Slavdom." Even the menu bore a message of unity, probably the least assuming statement of all: "One sun warms us all." There was a gala supper and a concert of Slavic music which included the Serbian march, *Rado ide Srbin u vojnike* (Joyfully the Serb Goes Off to War). Few Russians there could have guessed that they would hear this song many times just ten years hence. Tchaikowsky was to popularize it by including it in his *Marche*

---

[34] *Ibid.*, pp. 60-61.
[35] *Ibid.*, p. 62.

slave, which he composed for benefit concerts given on behalf of the Serbs during the Serbo-Turkish War in 1877. An ode of welcome penned for the occasion by Tiutchev assured the delegates that they were not mere guests in Russia.

> You are at home here, more at home
> Than yonder on your native soil,
> For here the lordship is unknown
> Of rulers of another tongue.
>
> .   .   .   .
>
> Even though we were divided
> By an evil destiny,
> Yet we all are of one people,
> Of one mother are we sons.[36]

The public greeted the poem with an ovation for the distinguished old author.

One of the leading representatives of Panslavism in St. Petersburg, Professor Vladimir Lamanskii, began his address by citing the words with which František Palacký had opened the Slav Congress of 1848 in Prague:

That which our fathers never hoped for, that which in our youth stirred our hearts as precious dreams, that of which we dared not even speak not so long ago, is now occurring before our eyes. Slavic brethren from various ends of the vast fatherland have gathered together, have come to confess themselves the sons of one great family and to give one another their hands in an eternal alliance of fraternity and love.

Lamanskii followed this stirring quotation with a curious anticlimax that was to find unpleasant reverberation in the Slavic press outside Russia. "Our gathering is founded on the same Slavic idea," he continued, "but not on that aim and inspiration. At that time the Western Slavs gathered to save their common fatherland and to discuss political questions. We do not trouble ourselves about the salvation of others. We do not wish to save, and we cast out politics from our friendly words."[37]

It was becoming obvious that the Russian hosts had been cau-

---

[36] *Vserossiiskaia,* pp. 199-201.
[37] *Ibid.,* p. 203.

tioned by their own government to avoid politics. The result was
an anomalous situation. The Russians, who were suspected by all
of Europe for their imperialistic designs on the Slavic peoples,
were carefully sidestepping political issues. The visiting Slavs, however, were bitterly disappointed. Most of them had come to Russia
precisely with the aim of scaring Vienna into compromise by con-
sorting with bogeys. Their strategy was doomed to failure if Russia
was going to insist on being such a cautious and prim bogey!

Both Lamanskii and his Panslavist colleague, Professor Orest
Miller, interjected another jarring note into the proceedings—the
religious question. The former closed his address at the banquet of
May 11 with the following finale:

On this feast of the Slavic Church [*sic*], it is necessary to remind ourselves that spiritual unity is possible for us, that there is a common
banner for us all . . . the banner of the Slavic protopraeceptors who
gathered us into one Slavic Church and united us through a Slavic
scrip and a common written language.[38]

Lamanskii did not explain what he meant by the "Slavic Church."
Miller took up the same theme in even more outspoken measures.
He began by paying his respects to the memory of Saints Cyril
and Methodius, "those wise brothers of Salonika whose eloquent
lips confessed in the ninth century the equal right of all peoples,
without exception, to receive the word of God in their own tongue,
an equality which was even then disputed by the West." Not content with using these two Orthodox (and, let it be said, Roman
Catholic) saints in his frontal attack on Romanism, Miller brought
up a Protestant reserve—Master John Hus.

Let us remember him who dared in the fifteenth century, in the midst
of the Romanism then reigning over the Western part of the Slavs, to
call to mind the forgotten rights of the popular tongue, the right of
the laity to receive the cup in the communion—a privilege usurped by
the clergy; let us not forget the ancient fellowship of the Slavic community, the conciliar principle of the Church which was suppressed
by the autocracy of Rome.[39]

[38] *Ibid.*, p. 206.
[39] *Ibid.*, pp. 213-14.

Despite such speeches, it must be observed that the Russian Panslavists never urged openly at the Moscow Slav Congress that the Slavs unite under the Orthodox Church itself. It is quite probable that many Panslavists would have been gratified if the Roman Catholic Slavs had at least held out for certain reforms within their own church, such as the establishment of national Catholic churches, and especially the use of Church Slavonic in the services.

The next two days in St. Petersburg were spent in more sightseeing and in farewell visits. Before leaving their hotel for the railroad station, the Slavic guests signed their names in a special guest book, and many added impressions of their stay in the northern capital. When this album was sent to the philanthropic Princess Trubetskaia as a keepsake, that worthy patroness of the Slavs must have been troubled by at least one Slav's summation of his experience in St. Petersburg. Written in English there was a sentiment by the Serbian poet Laza Kostić: "Words, words, words, instead of swords, swords, swords!"[40]

V

At ten o'clock on the morning of May 14 the visitors entrained for Tsarskoe Selo, the Russian Versailles, where they were to be presented to His Imperial Majesty, Alexander II, the Tsar-Liberator. Imperial coaches awaited at the station and drove the guests directly to the Court chapel for the Sunday morning services. After the Holy Liturgy, a select group was conducted to the Gold Room.[41] Alexander II entered, dressed in an Uhlan uniform, and was followed by the Empress, their children, and retinue. Count Lieven, Master of Ceremonies, first introduced the Serbians of the Principality. Being the eldest, Šafarik addressed the Tsar. He thanked His Imperial Majesty for having deigned to allow the Slavs present to look upon his Most August presence, and prayed

[40] *Ibid.*, p. 227.
[41] Neither the list in *Vserossiiskaia* nor Milićević's list (*Etnografska izložba*, p. 31) are correct. The former places the number of the group at twenty-three though it lists only twenty-one names, and places the Croat Matković among the Austrian Serbs. The latter lists twenty-one names but omits even the heading "Croats" and puts Matković among the Slovaks!

that God might grant the Tsar many years, not only for the happiness of the great Russian people, but to "the joy and comfort of all the Slavic peoples."[42]

The tall, spare Emperor leaned on his sword the while, and then replied in Russian, "I thank you for your good wishes. We have always considered the Serbs our native brethren, and I hope that God will soon prepare a better future for you. God grant that all your desires may soon be fulfilled." The Emperor remarked to Petronijević that he remembered him from five years ago when Prince Michael Obrenović had visited Russia. After a few words about the inclement weather, the Tsar moved on to Milićević. After asking him where he had learned Russian, the Tsar asked if the Turks had yet evacuated the Belgrade fortress. Upon receiving the affirmative reply he had expected, Alexander added, "It is good that the matter is finally settled."

When he came to the Austrian Slavs, Alexander asked Palacký whether they had not seen each other before. Was it in Prague? Palacký replied that it had been in Rome during Alexander's European tour as Heir Apparent. Having thus chatted with each of the twenty-one picked representatives, the Tsar passed on to the next room where all the other Slavic visitors were eagerly awaiting to greet him. To their cries of *živeo* (hail) and *slava* (glory) he replied: "Greetings, gentlemen. I am happy to see you Slavic brethren on native Slavic soil. I hope that you will be content with our reception, both here and especially in Moscow. Until we meet again." With that he left.

Meanwhile the Empress and the Imperial family chatted with the group still in the Gold Room. The Empress spoke especially with Palacký, whom she had met in Prague. She praised him for his contributions to Czech culture. Her Imperial Majesty expressed her regret that all the Slavic peoples did not possess a single alphabet and orthography. It is noteworthy that she expressed these regrets in German!

After lunch and a tour of the palace at Tsarskoe Selo, the

[42] Milićević, *Etnografska izložba*, claims on p. 32 that in a last-minute switch, Petronijević was placed first so that Šafarik never got to deliver this speech. *Vserossiiskaia* does not mention this but quotes the speech in full on p. 230.

travelers returned to St. Petersburg for their last day in the capital before going on to Moscow. Back in the Bellevue Hotel, they began to send telegrams to Prague, Zagreb, Belgrade, and other native cities describing the audience for their newspapers. The Tsar's reference to "Slavic brethren on native soil" produced an especially powerful effect on them. Indeed, a remarkable departure from protocol had been made which was bound to be interpreted as a sign that the Russian government had taken a step toward espousing the Slavic cause. As the Austrian Serb Polit-Desančić observed in his memoirs, "It was difficult to imagine that the Russian Tsar would receive at the Russian Court the Slavic guests, who were foreign subjects, without their being introduced by the ambassadors of those states. But Russian public opinion was engaged on behalf of the Slavic guests, and Tsar Alexander II held it necessary to make this concession to his people."[43] Every gesture and expression of the Tsar's was plumbed for special meanings. A Czech recalled later that the Serbs were particularly enthusiastic because the Emperor had spoken with them at great length.[44] A. A. Kirieev, zealous young Russian Panslavist, wrote in his diary opposite the date May 14 that even the Tsar's "till me meet again" had an "enormous effect" on the Slavic visitors. Some felt that this meant "till we meet again in Vienna or in Constantinople"![45] In a private letter to Iurii Samarin, Tiutchev wrote, "I still have not learned what happened yesterday at Tsarskoe. I only know that the Sovereign spoke to them in Russian, and this is the main thing. Petersburg has met its task well, and now it is Moscow's turn."[46]

Before relinquishing its guests to the hospitality of Moscow, the northern capital gave them a gala farewell luncheon at the Bellevue Hotel on May 15. The affair was not without an incident. Seized by a fit of good fellowship, a certain Russian, General Ivanitskii, mounted a chair and shouted, "One sun warms us all; we should

[43] Polit-Densančić, *Putne uspomene,* p. 71.

[44] V. V., *Pouł Slovanů do Ruska 1867 a jejì význam* (Prague, 1867), p. 43.

[45] Nikitin, "Slavianskie s"ezdy shestidesiatykh godov XIX veka," *Slavianskii Sbornik,* p. 40. Actually the Russian *do svidaniia,* like the French *au revoir* or the German *auf Wiedersehen,* is the common formal expression for taking leave of anyone.

[46] K. Pigarev, "F. I. Tiutchev i problemy vneshnei politiki tsarskoi Rossii," *Literaturnoe Nasledstvo,* XX (1935), 236.

all speak one tongue!" The Serbian representative, Milićević, recalled in his memoirs, "Many guests did not understand the meaning of these words, but for those of us who did, the food stuck in our throats!" These guests were not entirely mollified by the personal assurances of Russian friends that this was simply the outburst of an overzealous Russian nationalist who had had a little too much to drink.[47] Just three days later they were to hear the same theme in Moscow, and spoken by perfectly sober and responsible Russians.

VI

The party reached Moscow Tuesday morning, May 16, in a thick fog. A crowd far too large for the station to hold greeted the visitors with enthusiasm. Moscow had prepared herself well for her guests. Spurred on by the solicitations of the Panslavists as well as by the example of St. Petersburg, the Municipal Duma was eager to outdo the upstart city on the Neva. Moscow was still in a festive mood as the result of two recent visits. There was the American naval mission and then the Imperial family's visit on April 24, when the Tsar had formally opened the Moscow Ethnographic Exhibition at the Manège.[48]

It appeared, however, that not all official quarters in the administration were as pleased by the arrival of the foreign Slavs as they had been by the two previous visits. At first some of the authorities affected to regard it as a rather insignificant event. At the same time they were disturbed by the fear of some excessive demonstration of Slavic solidarity which might embarrass the government. The Governor General, Prince Dolgorukov, was especially fearful that the arrival of the "Slavic riffraff" (*svoloch*) might overexcite the citizenry of Moscow. When that citizenry learned through its newspapers of the magnificent reception in St. Petersburg, they reacted with an enthusiasm which confounded their officials. The Governor General relented by granting a long-sought concession: he permitted a dinner to be held in the pavilion at Sokolniki Park.

[47] Milićević, *Etnografska izložba*, p. 38.
[48] For a description of the welcome accorded to the American naval mission, see Thomas Bailey, *America Faces Russia* (Cornell University Press, 1950), pp. 96-98.

A kind of benevolent air of fellowship began to pervade Moscow, an eyewitness recalled. "One should not go against the very nature of things," this Muscovite decided. "The Slavic wave has caught us up, and great, portentous events are to be expected."[49]

Meanwhile the Slavic Benevolent Committee of Moscow was making its own plans and deciding on its strategy. While gratified by the press reports from the northern capital, some Panslavic leaders of Moscow were unpleasantly aware that many Russians viewed the whole affair pretty much as a lark, another occasion for festivities and good cheer. The Russian government presumably regarded the congress as a temporary embarrassment which might have its future uses. What the Panslavists hoped to do was defined with precision by that "Foreign Minister of Slavophilism," Tiutchev, in a letter to Iurii Samarin written on the day the Slavic guests left St. Petersburg for Moscow:

The more I think of it, the more I arrive at the conviction that, aside from the question of details and their execution, there is a single viewpoint, a single *Grundansicht* which should be stressed both in official speeches and private talks. And though, taken abstractly, this point of view seems only commonplace, nonetheless it contains the key to the problem. All depends on how the Slavs understand and feel their relations to be with Russia. In actual fact, if they see in Russia—and this they are very disposed to do, some of them—only a friendly, allied, helpful, so to speak, foreign power, nothing will have been accomplished and we will be far from our goal. This goal will be reached only when they sincerely realize that they are one with Russia, when they feel that they are bound to it with a dependence, an organic communality, which binds together all the component parts of an entity into something really living. Alas, how many misfortunes they must pass through before they accept this point of view entirely and with all of its consequences. Just the same, a clear and precise declaration of this truth in the form of a philosophical formula would, in my opinion, be quite to the point at the present time.[50]

The Slavic brethren had to be made to see that a united Slavdom

[49] S. M. Sukhotin, "Iz pamiatnykh tetradei S. M. Sukhotina, 1867-i god," *Russkii Arkhiv*, I (1894), 602.

[50] Pigarev, "F. I. Tiutchev i problemy vneshnei politiki tsarskoi Rossii," *Literaturnoe Nasledstvo*, XX (1935), 236.

would not be founded on external alliances or on relations based on the political exigencies of the moment. Slavic unification could not be like one of those magnanimous formal marriages which Westernized Russian students contracted with progressive girls just to emancipate them from parental authority.

Mother Moscow! Moscow the White-stoned! This was the capital of Ivan, the first caesar of Muscovy. This was the Third Rome, the shrine of Holy Russia. For Alexander Herzen (and Chaadaev before him) it was a city whose particular claim to fame was its possession of a monster bell which did not ring and a monster cannon which could not shoot. For the Slavic visitors it was Mecca. They devoted their first full day to a tour of the wondrous city, especially its Kremlin and golden-domed churches. They called on the highest government official, Governor General Prince V. A. Dolgorukov, and on the highest ecclesiastic, the venerable Metropolitan Philaret. The Orthodox among them prayed before the much-venerated icon of the Iberian Mother of God. Others climbed the bell-tower of Ivan the Great for the best view of Moscow.

At 3:00 P.M. the entire party gathered to consummate the ostensible purpose of their trip to Russia. They visited the Moscow Ethnographic Exhibition. Out of some 473 pages devoted to *The All-Russian Ethnographic Exhibition and the Slavic Congress in May, 1867*, published anonymously in the same year as a record of the visit, only a single paragraph dealt with this visit. The majority of the Slavic guests devoted but the latter part of a single afternoon to an exhibition to which they had been specifically invited out of ostensibly scientific interests!

On Thursday, May 18, the Slavic visitors attended the combined session of eighteen learned and professional societies at the University of Moscow. A representative of each society welcomed the guests and elaborated on some appropriate bond between his society and the foreign Slavs. On the following day the faculty of the University of Moscow held a dinner for the Slavic visitors. The rector of the University, S. I. Barshev, alluded in his address to the modern trend of "once disunited nationalities to restore their destroyed unity." He was referring especially to the unification of

Italy and of Germany. As this tendency had met with the seeming approval of the European Powers, he continued, the Slavs could also regard their own unification as a fully valid venture.[51]

The advocates of a single Slavic literary language received a setback with Rieger's restatement of the traditional Czechoslovak ideal—reciprocity. The Slavic languages were so close to one another, Rieger stated, that had it not been for a thousand years of separation from one another, the various Slavic peoples might well have developed as a single nation. But destiny had willed it otherwise. Therefore, said Rieger, two paths lay before the Slavs: either complete unification or diversity in harmony. "Many would perhaps prefer a confluence into a single whole, body and soul," he observed, "but the history of a millennium cannot disappear without a trace. . . . I hold this view, gentlemen: that diversity of parts does not exclude unity; unity must be sought in the harmony of these parts. An indivisible unity can lead to uniformity and lifelessness, just as dismemberment and lack of a guiding spirit can lead to weakness and destruction."[52]

Sunday, May 21, was undoubtedly the highlight of the Slavic meeting in Moscow. The occasion was a banquet held in Sokolniki —Moscow's Hyde Park. The pavilion used for the event was a recent structure built in honor of the Empress when Alexander II brought her as a young bride to present her to Moscow. It was at Sokolniki that both the Russian hosts and their Slavic guests not only made significant declarations of their unity but gave rather frank expression to the sources of their disunity.

The opening salvo was fired by Professor M. P. Pogodin—always an outspoken partisan of Slavic unity and, in his advancing years, an especially emotional one. Standing dramatically next to a banner of Saints Cyril and Methodius, Pogodin began with a declaration of Slavic equality with the rest of Europe—a prevalent compulsion with the self-conscious Russian Panslavists. Let the West know, he thundered, that the day of oppression was over, and that the Slavs were determined to share the rights which were the proper due of every citizen in nineteenth-century Europe. In this desire all

[51] *Vserossiiskaia*, pp. 291-92.
[52] *Ibid.*, pp. 299-303.

Slavs were united, he proclaimed, and then proceeded to enumerate the Slavs in a rather curious fashion for a Slavicist: Czechs and Serbs, Croats and Bulgars, Slavonians and Styrians, Bosnians and Montenegrins, Slovaks and Moravians, Lusatians and Dalmatians, Russian Galicians and Poles.

"I mentioned the name of the Poles," he suddenly interjected, as though by way of an afterthought. "But where are they? I see none here." Pogodin paused for effect and was rewarded with shouts from the audience: there aren't any! "Alas," cried the veteran Panslavist, "they alone of the Slavs stand off and cast reproachful glances at us. There is no need for that. God be with them! We do not exclude them from our family." Then in the midst of this seemingly charitable mood, he denounced the treacherous Poles for allying themselves with such ancient foes of Slavdom as the Turks. His address ended with a pious hope:

Oh, if they [the Poles] would only—let us pray, brethren—forget the past, leave off their enmity, and be convinced of the kindness of our beloved and noble Sovereign who bears the name of their first benefactor, Alexander, then our Russian and Slavic joy would be complete.[53]

It was for Rieger, the practical and enlightened Czech politician, to present a different view of the Polish Question.

I observe with sadness, gentlemen [Rieger declared], that only the Poles have absented themselves from this fraternal gathering. . . . I think that such a remarkable act could not have occurred without some cause. When your last war raged among you, a fratricidal war, unfortunately, then one of your compatriots made an appeal to the unbiased opinion of the Czechs, for at that time all Europe had risen up against the Russians. At a time when all Europe, all the peoples of the West had raised their voices against Russia, gentlemen, my friend and father-in-law, Palacký, and I boldly declared that we considered the action of the Poles unfortunate, and that what they were writing against the Russian people itself we considered to be a gross injustice perpetrated against their own brethren. Gentlemen, as the brethren of both the Poles and the Russians, we Czechs stood aside and wished to judge the case justly for both our brothers. We knew from history

[53] *Ibid.*, pp. 337-38.

what great injustices the gentry and the Polish government had committed against the Russian people, estranging from the Russian people their Little Russian branch, introducing among its inhabitants the so-called Unia by unpraiseworthy means. We recognized this injustice sincerely and openly. We considered just your desire to restore to your realm this region which had been forcibly wrested from you. We declared that this branch of the Russian people had the right to be restored to you for, in the judgment of learning, they are one people with you. But we cannot conceal within ourselves the thought that the Poles have a right to their own national existence as a branch of the Western Slavs which is distinct from the Russian people in language and in history.[54]

There was no mistaking that there were many in the audience who were not pleased at all with Rieger's frank words. Indeed his address was frequently interrupted with demonstrations of disapproval by some, as well as of approval by others. The Czech promise to the Parisian Poles to speak out frankly at the Moscow gathering had been kept. The Russians had been squarely thrust on the defensive, and the burden of proving their sincerity now lay all the more heavily on their shoulders.

The reply to Rieger was made by Prince V. A. Cherkasskii, Russian statesman who, together with Miliutin and Samarin, had distinguished himself in the reorganization of the Polish Kingdom after 1863. Panslavist though he was, Cherkasskii was not of the philosophical Slavophile type so much as the practical administrator. Granting that Slavic unity had to be founded on justice and on equality for all members, he embarked on a review of Russo-Polish relations to show that Russia had given the Poles many privileges in both their public and private lives. Speaking of the Polish Kingdom's position within the Russian Empire after the Congress of Vienna, Cherkasskii declared proudly, "Without blushing before either Europe or the Slavic world in general, or before any particular branch of the Slavic world, we can declare loudly here and everywhere that these relations were not only equitable but preferential to a high degree." In other words, Poland enjoyed rights within the Russian Empire which not even Russians possessed. If the Poles lost some of their politicial rights, the speaker

[54] *Ibid.*, pp. 342-48.

explained, they had only themselves to blame for their rashness in 1830 and 1863. Despite these two revolts, Cherkasskii stated, the Poles still enjoyed a good court system with fair and speedy trials, their own system of education, the lowest taxes in Europe, and other privileges in the domain of private law of which no people ruled by another people could boast. "I turn to all our Slavic guests," the statesman challenged, "and I submit that they would all, from first to last, without enumerating specific peoples and territories, be satisfied if in all their own relations they had the unconditional benefit of all those rights which the rulers of their own governments enjoy."

Here was the neatest thrust of all! Who among the foreign Slavs present did not know the meaning of oppression and the price of rebellion? Let Poland's children voluntarily return to the Slavic common homestead in the raiment of sincere penance like the prodigal son, and, Prince Cherkasskii promised, there would be no calf fat enough for the Russians to prepare for such a joyous feast! He hoped that Poland's well-wishers among the guests would express these sentiments to the Poles for the good of all Slavdom. The speaker then turned to the offensive—by describing the plight of the Western Provinces of Russia under Polish rule. As he spoke, opposite him Holovackij, the Ukrainian, bent his head and silently wept in the presence of the company. Cherkasskii had made his point, but the cause of Slavic unity seemed dimmer than before.[55]

Many of the guests present indicated their desire to speak after Cherkasskii, but the toastmaster insisted on maintaining the original program. If he had hoped thereby to avoid further controversy, he was mistaken.

The following speaker, Dr. Vladan Djordjević, opposed the suggestion that all the Slavs adopt Russian as the language of their common literature and learning. A leading representative of the nationalistic trend in Serbian literature, Djordjević was naturally jealous for his mother tongue. A thousand years of separation, he argued, had endowed each branch of the Slavic family with an individuality of its own. Any attempt to injure that individuality would mar the cause of Slavic unity. What would men of letters

[55] *Ibid.,* pp. 356-63.

gain by adopting a common literary language such as Russian? They would only set themselves up as a caste among their own people and thus create a barrier between the masses and their literature. What would scientists gain thereby? Unlike literature, Djordjević declared, science had no nationality but was universal. The fact that European science had made such rapid strides forward after abandoning Latin as a common language seemed to the speaker to constitute proof that science was not served by linguistic conformity. Instead, he urged that the learned societies of all the Slavic lands maintain close relations with one another.[56] Again the cause of reciprocity against uniformity!

It must have been with some relief that the audience heard the next speaker, František Brauner. Instead of continuing the controversy, the Czech lawyer confined himself to a eulogy of Little Mother Moscow. Meanwhile the crowds that were milling about the pavilion were becoming increasingly impatient to get a closer look at the foreign guests. About nine o'clock in the evening they began to clamor so vociferously that the toastmaster was forced to interrupt the proceedings. The Slavic guests filed out to the portico of the pavilion in a processional with an Orthodox priest bearing aloft the banner of Saints Cyril and Methodius. The throng cheered and caps flew into the air. Mothers lifted their children to see especially those Slavic guests who came dressed in their national costumes.[57]

When the Slavic guests returned to their places inside the pavilion, they heard a short address by a Russian priest, and then a reading of F. I. Tiutchev's poem "To the Austrian Slavs," which he had penned especially for the occasion. It was based on the notorious dictum attributed to Baron Beust: "Man muss die Slawen an die Mauer drücken." Tiutchev's point was that there was indeed a wall toward which the Germans were driving the Slavs. That wall was Russia—a formidable battlement that encompassed one sixth of the globe. This wall would ever stand as a rampart against the Teuton, the poem promised, and as a shelter for the Slavs now beyond its pale. The audience was so taken by the poem that it

---

[56] *Ibid.*, pp. 365-66.
[57] Milićević, *Etnografska izložba*, pp. 61-62.

demanded two readings—one by S. M. Sukhotin, and the other by Ivan Aksakov.[58]

In the uproar that followed, a young Bulgarian student from the University of Moscow called Zhinzifov—the world was to hear more of him in years to come—impetuously jumped up on a table and shouted, "O Slavic world, I beg a word!" He then proceeded to remind his audience that though they belonged to all the Slavs, Saints Cyril and Methodius had been born in Bulgaria "or in Slavic Macedonia, which is all the same." He begged all to remember that Bulgaria was still under an Asiatic yoke, and that it needed Russia's helping hand. Few might have guessed that this appeal would find response in exactly ten years. Zhinzifov ended his impassioned address with an ode to Slavdom in the Bulgarian language. With that the program ended, though the festivities lasted until midnight.

VII

After a week of official festivities, the Slavic guests spent their remaining week in Moscow becoming acquainted with the city and its society. Many were invited to soirées or dinners. Various memoirs left by the guests reveal that such occasions were not always completely happy ones. The Serbian Milićević recalled with particular regret a dinner in the home of Prince Nicholas Meshcherskii at which the non-Russian Slavs were again urged to adopt Russian as their literary language.[59] Palacký, too, had occasion to meet this issue during a visit by a group of university students. The Czech historian declared that the Slavs hardly had need of a common literary language because they understood one another already.

It was at a dinner that Rieger was again fated to confront the Polish Question. Prince Cherkasskii had invited a large party. Among the Russians present were Aksakov, Samarin, Pogodin, and Lamanskii. As Cherkasskii and Rieger had been the principal protagonists at the Sokolniki banquet, it was inevitable that they should continue their discussion of the Polish Question on a more private

[58] *Vserossiiskaia*, p. 370.
[59] Milićević, *Etnografska izložba*, pp. 62–63.

basis here. Rieger restated his basic thesis of the previous Sunday and asked whether the Russians would make peace with the Poles and give them their national rights if the Poles definitely relinquished their pretensions to the Western Provinces. Rieger was in fact angling for a Russian commitment which he could transmit to his Polish friends. The Russians present, however, gave him no satisfaction whatsoever. Cherkasskii and Samarin both maintained that it was useless even to discuss the prospect inasmuch as it would be impossible to show proof of Polish sincerity in this matter.[60]

On Friday, May 26, an event occurred which had a profound effect on both hosts and guests. News arrived that the Tsar, who was then visiting Paris, had barely escaped an assassin's bullet. An émigré Pole had sought success where the Russian revolutionary Karakozov had failed just a year before. A thanksgiving service for the Tsar's deliverance was immediately held in the Merchants Club, where the Slavic guests were having dinner. The entire company sent congratulations by wire to Paris. The message was written by Palacký in Czech, translated by Milićević and Šafarik into Russian, and finally rendered into French for the telegraph office by Petronijević.

Despite the joy of the occasion, many minds were troubled by the fact that the would-be assassin's nationality made any reconciliation between Poles and Russians even more remote. Indeed, while it had been most difficult to discuss the Polish Question at all at the Slavic gathering in Moscow, it now became impossible. Rieger's position became especially unpleasant. He was to pay with a decided decline in popularity for his championship of the Poles—a most thankless role in this case, since both the Poles and the Russians spurned the compromise which he proposed.

Saturday, May 27, marked the end of the Slavic gathering in Moscow. In the morning all went to the Kremlin to attend a thanksgiving service for the Tsar's salvation. The Kremlin square outside the church was filled with kneeling worshippers. Afterward the Slavic guests and their Muscovite hosts returned to the Kokorev Hotel for a luncheon and a short prayer service. By 6:00 P.M. most of the guests had boarded the St. Petersburg night express, and

[60] *Vserossiiskaia*, p. 395.

soon the golden domes of Moscow faded into the realm of memory.

The Moscow Slav Congress had been no congress in the formal sense of the word. However, toward the end of their stay, some of the Slavic guests, chiefly the publicists among them, and some of the Panslavic professors of the University of Moscow had drafted a plan for future congresses. The text, which was signed by over two thirds of the Slavic visitors to the Moscow Congress, read as follows:

In realization of the necessity of working together for the intercourse and the unification of the Slavs in word and in deed, we at the first Slavic Congress in Moscow propose the following:

1) To meet at least once every two years in an all-Slavic congress in a place to be arranged;

2) To submit for free discussion at these congresses various questions concerning the academic, literary, artistic, and general moral rapprochement of the Slavs;

3) Such questions and particular consideration of them may be determined at local Slavic congresses;

4) The period for holding such all-Slavic congresses will be between August 1 and September 1.[61]

There is no evidence that any concrete program of Slavic political unification was discussed at the Moscow Slav Congress, either by the Russians or by their guests. The closest that the Russian Panslavists came to an expression of their political ambitions was the publication in Russian of a treatise entitled *Slavianstvo i mir budushchago* (Slavdom and the World of the Future) by the Slovak author L'udovít Štúr.[62] Written in German shortly before his death in 1856, and never published in any language until 1867, this work called upon the Slavs to unite with the Russians in a federation, to accept the Orthodox faith, and to adopt Russian as

---

[61] *Ibid.*, pp. 410-11. The first provision remained a dead letter for some forty years; the next Slav congress met in Prague in 1908.

[62] L'udovít Štúr (Liudovit Shtur), "Slavianstvo i mir budushchago; Poslanie Slavianam s beregov Dunaia," translated from the German MS by V. I. Lamanskii, in *Chteniia Imperatorskago Obshchestva Istorii i Drevnostei Rossiisskikh pri Moskovskom Universitetie*, III, Materialy slavianskie, Books 1-3 (Moscow, 1867), pp. 1-191. For a more complete discussion of Štúr's treatise and its place in the history of Russian Panslavism, see Michael B. Petrovich, "L'udovít Štúr and Russian Panslavism," *Journal of Central European Affairs*, XII (April, 1952), 1-19.

their common literary language. It was no accident that this treatise was published in time for the Moscow Congress. Štúr's program was practically identical with the Russian Panslavic ideology. Since the Russian government had forbidden the Russian participants in the Moscow Congress from engaging in political discussions involving Slavic unification, Štúr's testament served as a godsend. What better way was there to let the other Slavic delegates know what kind of Panslavic unity the Russian Panslavists favored? What more effective means of combating Austro-Slavism, Polish Messianism, Kollár's idea of "reciprocity," and Yugoslav Illyrianism than to confront the adherents of these regional tendencies with a frank appeal for Russian leadership written by a non-Russian Slav? As Lamanskii observed in his translator's preface, "Though written eleven to twelve years ago, Štúr's work *Slavdom and the World of the Future* could hardly be more to the point than now."[63] If the Slavic visitors in Moscow got the point, there is ample evidence that not all were pleased by it.

VIII

The express from Moscow arrived in St. Petersburg Sunday morning, May 28. While some of the travelers stayed in the capital just long enough to board a train for Warsaw, others remained for another week of festivities and sightseeing. The Municipal Duma had voted 4,500 rubles and a special collection had been raised to make possible this extended stay of eight days.

Friday, June 2, was for most of the remaining guests their last full day in Russia. Since it was Palacký's sixty-ninth birthday, a luncheon was held in his honor. After lunch Palacký, Rieger, Erben, Vrťátko, Subotić, Milićević, Šafarik, and Holovackij framed a farewell address. Their formal statement was delivered the following morning during a late breakfast at the Bellevue Hotel. The text read in part as follows:

On the occasion of our meeting there was felt and recognized the need, in order to keep the Slavic peoples from drifting farther apart

[63] L'udovít Štúr (Liudovit Shtur), "Slavianstvo i mir budushchago," in *Chteniia Imperatorskago*, III, p. ii.

from one another, to come closer to one another at least in science and in the academic field through the lively exchange of ideas and of works as well as through reciprocal aid in fostering a general store of native Slavic learning.

In all of this there is no political tendency whatsoever. These aims are not and should not be a threat to other peoples. Universal learning can only gain if young nations in the fullness of their strength and flaming inspiration take their place in the effort for the common cause, awakening one another, and thus join the crowned veterans of human learning in the serried ranks of a new, zealous, glorious war for freedom, humanity, and enlightenment.

By their national character the Slavs have not been accustomed to perpetrating wrongs and injuries on others. They always joyfully and gratefully repay love and the preservation of their rights with love and respect for the rights of others. Knowing, nevertheless, from experience how few friends we have in Europe, we feel the need all the more for loving one another, for supporting one another as true brethren, and for not forgetting one another in time of danger.[64]

The final Russian address was delivered by Professor Vladimir Lamanskii. His parting advice to the Slavic guests was that they remember that Slavdom had its own tasks and aims apart from those of Europe, and that they should not confuse such diverse interests.

Thus these two final addresses exemplified a divergence of position between the Slavic guests and their Russian hosts which their meeting in Russia failed to reconcile. The Western and Southern Slavs present desired recognition of their right to participate as free and respected partners in European civilization; Russian Panslavism insisted that the Slavs could gain freedom and respect only by cutting themselves off from Western Europe.

IX

Contemporary opinions—both Russian and foreign—of the Moscow Slavic Congress of 1867 were very mixed.

The Russian organizers of the Slavic gathering hailed it as a

[64] *Vserossiiskaia,* pp. 464-65.

conspicuous success. In the view of Ivan Aksakov, writing in his newspaper *Moskva* on July 1, 1867, the principal result of the Slav Congress was to be sought in Russia itself. "The greatest, the best result of the Slav visit," he wrote, "is that the Slavic Question has penetrated the mind and the consciousness of Russian society. It has passed from abstraction to active reality; it has passed from the realm of books into life." The editor of *Moskva* concluded hopefully, "As soon as all Russia is filled with a consciousness of its Slavic calling, the Slavic Question will be solved. This is not yet, but a beginning has been made, and the beginning is the job half done, says the proverb."[65]

Half a year later Ivan Aksakov summarized the achievements of the Slav Congress of 1867 rather more modestly:

There was no political program established, no course of action agreed upon, no political advice or instructions given. No Russian said anything or thought to incite the Slavic guests to insubordination against their governments. There was never expressed any intention or even suggestion of Russia's absorbing the Slavs, nor even of the political unification of the Slavic peoples under Russia's leadership. There was expressed only this: our joy on meeting, the happiness of becoming acquainted with our brethren . . . and a sincere warm desire that all the Slavic peoples might secure life, liberty, and an independent development.[66]

In November, 1867, writing in his *Moskovskiia Viedomosti*, Michael Katkov insisted that the Moscow Slav Congress had been no more entertaining spectacle but a far-reaching event of real substance. He prophesied that the warmth of the family reunion which had taken place in Russia would course throughout the Slavic world. Whatever its future success, he wrote, the idea of Slavic unity had finally emerged from dark places, and Russia now understood that Panslavism concealed nothing dangerous or terrible. "The Slavic idea," he declared, "has evidently shown itself to be

[65] Aksakov, "Moskva, 1-go iiulia," *Slavianskii vopros, 1860-1886,* in *Sochineniia,* I, 150-52.

[66] Aksakov, "Moskva, 11-go ianvaria," *ibid.,* pp. 193-94, originally published in *Moskvich,* January 11, 1868.

the most desirable and the most benevolent of all possible Russian ideas."[67]

The rest of the Russian press was generally confused in its re-action to the congress. The initial burst of enthusiasm which the visit of the foreign Slavs engendered made it difficult to gauge the event without falling into some extreme. The conservative press was especially divided at first. *Golos* (The Voice) admitted, "The congress was not a political demonstration in the full sense of that word, but it has a full right to be considered as a political event of enormous significance for the effect it is going to have on the task of Slavic unification as well as for its having stirred up our public opinion and for having brought our public to make state-ments which, only a short time ago, it seems, would not have been dreamed of."[68]

The ultraconservative *Viest'* (News), which was at the time calling for an alliance with Germany, chose to belittle the entire affair. "A few Slavs, both known and unknown, elected inci-dentally by nobody and empowered to do nothing, came to Moscow to an ethnographic exhibition. Many words were spoken, quite poetic. Much champagne was drunk. Several street urchins shouted *živio* and *slava*."[69]

The staid *Sankt-Peterburgskiia Viedomosti* (St. Petersburg News) at first adopted a would-be practical view, probably in an attempt to reflect the momentary attitude of the government. "We are necessary to the Slavs," it stated in an editorial on May 30, 1867. "In turn, the Slavs are necessary to us. Our commerce and our importance as a state necessitate a free exit through the Bosporus and amicable relations with the Danubian countries. We can achieve all this through a close alliance with the Southern and the Western Slavs." As the pendulum of official policy swung toward collaboration with Germany, however, this newspaper declared in a facile turnabout, "The kissing and hugging of the

[67] M. N. Katkov, "Moskva 9-go noiabria," *Sobranie peredovykh statei Moskov-skikh Viedomostei, 1867 god* (Moscow, 1897), p. 644, originally published in *Moskovskiia Viedomosti*, No. 247, November 9, 1867.

[68] *Golos*, No. 153, June 4/16, 1867, cited by Nikitin, "Slavianskie s"ezdy shesti-desiatykh godov XIX veka," *Slavianskii Sbornik*, p. 86.

[69] Cited by Nikitin, "Slavianskie s"ezdy shestidesiatykh godov XIX veka," *Slavianskii Sbornik*, p. 82.

brother Slavs, with endless shouts of *živio*, *zdravo*, and *slava* and the like has been evaluated by all thinking men on its merits, as the empty amusement of children, as intolerable though innocent non-sense of no consequence and with no significance." The capital newspaper expressed surprise that the Germans should have ever mistaken those children with their cardboard swords for real knights of the Panslavic Order.[70]

The liberal Russian press, which was basically pro-Western in the sense of admiring Western democratic institutions, was rather aloof and, at best, distantly friendly. Its standard-bearer, the sensible *Viestnik Evropy* (Herald of Europe), took the position that Russia would do better to look to its own internal development. A Russia whose power lay in an enlightened government, a prosperous nation, and a fully developed culture could attract the Slavs beyond its borders with the natural might of a magnet. Regarding a Slavic federation, however, the *Viestnik Evropy* evidently had misgivings. "We are Slavs, and Slavs we were born," it pointed out, "but we made ourselves into Russians after great efforts and trials through the ages; this is why we should not be required in our politics to be Slavs first and Russians second."[71]

As for the radical press, such as there was of it in Russia in 1867, its line had already been established long before by such leaders as Herzen and Chernyshevskii, who had repeatedly in the past warned their Slavic brethren against official, autocratic Russia. Bakunin indicated the same view during the Slavic Congress when he wrote to Herzen and Ogarëv, "All this official flirting with the Slavs is repulsive."[72] In Russia itself the editor of *Iskra* (The Spark) declared with heavy sarcasm just after the congress:

The Slavs are probably quite pleased with us. Unfortunately I cannot say the same for ourselves. . . . We had hoped to see our humiliated and injured brethren come to us to be instructed in mind and reason, to admire our greatness and power. . . . We saw not wise men who loved order, but wild men who loved independence. We said to them: come, let us form one flock. And they gave us as their reply: we

[70] *Ibid.*, p. 85.
[71] *Ibid.*
[72] *Pis'ma M. A. Bakunina* (St. Petersburg, 1906), p. 303.

humbly thank you—but we do not wish to be members of a flock. . . .
And our own knew us not.[73]

On one point all were fairly unanimous: that the Moscow Slav
Congress of 1867 had evoked much public enthusiasm. While some
opponents of Panslavism tried to explain away this phenomenon,
none could ignore it. Yet various contemporaries, Panslavists as
well as non-Panslavists, are agreed that very soon after the congress, public enthusiasm in general subsided as quickly as it had
flared up.[74]

The anti-Russian press abroad, especially in Austria-Hungary,
took the opportunity to engage in a virulent campaign against "the
Slavic Peril" and Russia's imperialistic designs, which did not abate
until after the Berlin meeting of the Three Emperors and their
alliance in 1872.[75] This hostile press campaign did much to transform the rather nebulous Panslavic movement into one of the most
discussed and least understood bogeys of European politics.

The pilgrimage of the Austrian and Balkan Slavs to Russia in
1867 brought them momentary consolation. Most of them had
journeyed to Moscow as members of oppressed minorities. They
returned with the sense of belonging to the great Slavic family of
peoples, the most numerous in all Europe, and with the conviction
that they possessed at least the moral support of the largest state
in Europe. "This trip has given the world proof," wrote one of
the Czech group on his return to Prague, "that the lesser Slavic
peoples are not so isolated as to allow German arrogance to scoff
at their national development or to hinder their glorious and certain future."[76] Some of Austria's Slavic subjects were to pay dearly
for this whistling in the dark. The Austrian Serb Polit-Desančić
was deprived of the right to practice law. His colleague Subotić
lost his position in the Croatian courts and was denied a pension
because he had gone to Russia. The Slovenian Roman Catholic

[73] *Iskra*, No. 21, June 11, 1867, p. 255, cited by Nikitin, "Slavianskie s"ezdy
shestidesiatykh godov XIX veka," *Slavianskii Sbornik*, p. 84.

[74] See, for example, P. D. Boborykin, "Na Slavianskom rasput'ie," *Otechestvennyia Zapiski* (1878), No. IV, p. 194; also "W," "Nieskol'ko slov o slavianskom
voprosie," *Besieda*, No. 1 (1871), p. 254.

[75] For a review of Austro-Hungarian and German press opinions regarding the
Moscow Slav Congress, see *Vserossiiskaia*, pp. 99 ff.

[76] *Pouł Slovanů do ruska 1867 a její význam*, p. vii.

priest Matija Majar was forced by the Bishop of Klagenfurt to pay a fine.[77] If the Hapsburg monarchy was supposed to be frightened by the Moscow Slav Congress, it gave little sign of it.

Undoubtedly the most authoritative statement to be made by a Slavic guest in Russia after the Moscow Slav Congress came from Palacký himself.

> There exist various opinions in Europe and in Russia [he explained] as to the nature of Russia's relations with the other Slavs. Some Russians see in these relations proof of a certain platonic love among the Slavic peoples; others suppose that the Slavs should merge with the Russians. . . . The latter claim that all Slavs should become Russians. Their Panslavism is, consequently, Panrussianism.
>
> I reply to each and to all thus: for over a thousand years the Czechs fought for their national individuality and preserved it at the cost of countless sacrifices. They will not desire to surrender it in exchange for any dubious promises. The same applies to all the other Slavs, particularly those of the South.[78]

Palacký was not speaking in vain when he said that he spoke for the Southern Slavs as well. Commenting on the Czech historian's statement, the Belgrade *Vidovdan* (St. Vitus Day) wrote on November 12, 1872, "The voice of Palacký is the voice of the whole Czech nation; and what the Czechs condemn as dangerous no other Slavic people will accept."[79] So jealous were the Serbs of their national pride that Prince Michael's government actually deprived young Vladan Djordjević of a stipend because his Russophile speeches in Russia "lowered the dignity of the Serbian government."[80]

It is little wonder that the Moscow Slav Congress produced such a variety of opinions. It was a rather strange phenomenon. Although the Russian government was made to bear responsibility for it, official Russia had not in fact initiated the Slavic gathering. True, the government tacitly permitted it to take place. The Emperor

---

[77] *Vserossiiskaia*, p. 470.

[78] Cited by A. N. Pypin, *Panslavizm v proshlom i nastoiashchem* (St. Petersburg, 1913), p. 153.

[79] Cited by E. L. Mijatovics, "Panslavism; Its Rise and Decline," *Fortnightly Review*, XIV, New Series (1873), 111.

[80] *Vserossiiskaia*, p. 470.

and Prince Gorchakov even gave the affair some sanction by receiving the foreign participants of the congress, although what was said at these audiences could scarcely have had less substance. In the last analysis, Bakunin's phrase, "official flirting," aptly described the Russian government's attitude.

The Moscow Slav Congress achieved very little. The foreign Slavs did not agree to adopt Russian as a common literary language; indeed, many were shocked at the suggestion. There was no serious talk of conversion to Orthodoxy. Political federation was not even discussed. The Ukrainian Question was ignored. It might have been better for Russian Panslavism if the Polish Question had been ignored as well. The Slavic visitors were not convinced that Western civilization as such was an evil. Russian hospitality had indeed created good will, but beneath this friendly feeling lay an undertow of suspicion engendered by Russian Panslavic dogmatism. As a meeting of men, the Moscow Slav Congress certainly yielded no concrete results. Yet it constituted Russia's greatest moral contribution to the advancement of the Panslavic idea in the third quarter of the nineteenth century.

9

THE POLITICAL PROGRAM
OF RUSSIAN PANSLAVISM

*From the Nile to the Neva, the Elbe to
  Cathay,
From the Volga to the Euphrates,
The Ganges to the Danube,
There is the Russian realm.*

TIUTCHEV

*Let us restore Athens to the Athenians,
And the city of Constantine—to Constantine!* DERZHAVIN

RUSSIAN PANSLAVISM WAS NOT so much an organized policy as it
was a set of attitudes and opinions. There was no single political
program to which all Panslavists formally adhered. Thanks to
government supervision, the Slavic Benevolent Committees duti-
fully avoided stating political aims. To determine the political program of Russian Panslavism in this period, one must look largely
to the writings of a handful of leading Panslavists who wrote on
political subjects as private individuals.

The movement of Russian Panslavism which developed uninter-
ruptedly between the Crimean War and the Russo-Turkish War
gravitated around two general viewpoints concerning the prospect
of Slavic political unification. An earlier viewpoint held that a
Slavic political union would come about after the cultural rapprochement of the Slavs. Its exponents emphasized cultural objectives—a Panslavic literary language, a "Slavic Church," mutual
cultural relations among the Slavs, and propagation of the Russian
Panslavic cosmology, especially the Russian Panslavist dogma of
the incompatibility between the Romano-Germanic and the Slavic
world. A second viewpoint, which began to assert itself about

1867, turned the earlier proposition upside down by maintaining that only through political unification could the Slavs effectively "restore" the unity of their culture. The proponents of this view, including converts from the earlier trend, subordinated cultural objectives to political objectives and favored direct political action.

II

In the decade following the Crimean War the chief concern of the Russian Panslavists was to define the sources of Slavic unity, to endow the Slavic movement with an ideological direction, to propagate the Slavic cause, and to win friends for their ideology. The meager resources of the Slavic Benevolent Committees were devoted exclusively to philanthropic projects and the maintenance of cultural relations with the other Slavs. During this first decade, the Russian Panslavic movement was dominated largely by latter-day Slavophiles such as Ivan Aksakov, Samarin, Khomiakov, and Koshelëv, or else by scholars of Slavic studies—Pogodin, Hilferding, Lamanskii, Popov, and others—most of whom were Slavophile disciples. Their discussion of political problems tended to be vague and eventually turned about spiritual or intellectual solutions which often bore little relation to real life. Most of them saw as their main problem the need to convince all the Slavs that a unification of the flesh was in vain without a unification of the spirit. Politics was a secondary interest.

Hilferding begged his readers not to be alarmed by the word "Panslavism"; Panslavism would not "bring the Russian eagles down upon the shores of the Adriatic and the Elbe," for it was a peaceful cultural movement.[1] Even that most politically-minded of the earlier Panslavists, Professor Pogodin, denied repeatedly that Russian Panslavism contemplated any political objectives. He protested that a Panslavic political union existed only in the minds of German publicists or in the dreams of non-Russian Slavs such as the Slovak publicist L'udovít Štúr, for whose opinions Russians

[1] A. Hilferding, *Sobranie sochinenii*, Vol. II: *Stat'i po sovremennym voprosam slavianskim* (St. Petersburg, 1868), p. 73.

were not responsible.[2] Pogodin chided the *Sanktpeterburgskiia Viedomosti* (St. Petersburg News), a newspaper which frequently reflected official opinion, for speaking of Panslavism as "the wish of a supposed party to unite all the Slavic peoples under a single state . . . and of our plots to help them, in case of necessity, by force of arms." Pogodin challenged the newspaper to cite Panslavist writings which expressed any such views. All the Panslavists wanted, he insisted, was a moral, spiritual, intellectual, literary rapprochement of all the Slavic peoples.[3] As president of the Moscow Slavic Benevolent Committee, Pogodin proclaimed before its members, "Neither we as private persons, nor the alleged Old-Russian or Muscovite party, which is nowhere to be seen, nor (still less) the government have ever had or now have any Panslavic aims and tendencies in a political sense, in the sense of Russia's ruling over the Slavic peoples."[4] As late as 1867, just after the close of the Moscow Slav Congress, Pogodin announced, "I have long ago abandoned any Panslavic dreams, and have long since stopped thinking about any unification."[5] And this from the man who in 1854 secretly proposed to the Russian government the establishment of a Panslavic union under Russian hegemony![6] Certainly one cannot exclude the possibility that his denials were at least partly prompted by a politic desire to allay suspicions and fear. Though hardly accurate, Pogodin's disavowals were certainly in tune with the spirit which dominated Russian Panslavism before the mid-1860's.

One looks in vain through the Russian Panslavic literature in the decade following the Crimean War for any definite schemes of Slavic political unification, for any specific description of the form which an eventual Slavic union would take. To begin with, the Russian government would not have approved the publication of any such program. Yet this was not the only reason early Pan-

[2] M. P. Pogodin, "Peterburgskomu opponentu," *Sobranie statei, pisem i riechei po povodu Slavianskago voprosa* (Moscow, 1878), p. 139.

[3] Pogodin, "Zamietka (Pis'mo k redaktoru)," *ibid.*, pp. 99-100.

[4] Pogodin, "Riech 16 maia," *ibid.*, p. 109.

[5] Pogodin, "Nieskol'ko zamietok," *ibid.*, p. 50.

[6] N. P. Barsukov, *Zhizn' i trudy M. P. Pogodina*, XIII (St Petersburg, 1905), 100 f.

slavists were reticent about spelling out their views on Slavic political unification. They had their eyes fixed on a New Jerusalem whose radiance shimmered above a distant horizon. Their hour of triumph, the consummation of Russia's "Slavic vocation," was a vision of the future, not a five-year plan. And yet, Pogodin's disavowals notwithstanding, various Russian Panslavists did lay the groundwork, even before the mid-1860's, for a Russian Panslavist political program.

However vaguely they phrased their ambitions, some Russian Panslavists made a notable contribution to the formulation of a political program for their movement simply by daring to proclaim openly before Russian public opinion what Professor Pogodin had found more convenient to suggest to the Russian government in secret memoranda during the Crimean War—that it was Russia's mission to liberate the non-Russian Slavs and to unite them under the protection of the Russian Empire.

Probably the first such statement to appear in the Panslavic press came from the pen of Prince Vladimir A. Cherkasskii. A somewhat distant follower of Slavophilism, Cherkasskii was first and foremost a statesman, an administrator with the practical outlook of a realist.[7] His article "Two Words regarding the Eastern Question," published in *Russkaia Besieda* (Russian Discourse), was that publication's first attempt to present a political discussion concerning the contemporary Slavs.[8] Cherkasskii addressed himself to the Eastern Question, which he described as "the struggle between Russia and the West on the soil of the Orthodox Greco-Slavic world."[9] The author commiserated with the Balkan Christians; not only were they oppressed by the Turks, but they were kept in that state of oppression by the Concert of Europe "as the first victims of the final crusade of the Western states against Russia."[10] He claimed for Russia the right to raise its voice anew on behalf of its coreligionists despite the "tacit plot of Western European poli-

[7] A. Leroy-Beaulieu, *Un homme d'état russe (Nicolas Milutine) d'après sa correspondance inédite* (Paris, 1884), p. 248.

[8] V. A. Cherkasskii, "Dva slova po povodu Vostochnago Voprosa," *Russkaia Besieda*, IV (1858), 65-92.

[9] *Ibid.*, p. 67.

[10] *Ibid.*, p. 69.

tics against the renascence and future of the Greco-Slavic peoples."[11] Regretfully taking note of the rivalry between Balkan Slavs and Greeks, he proclaimed that it was Russia's prerogative as an Orthodox state and as "the eldest sister in the numerous family of Slavic peoples" to act as mediator. Cherkasskii concluded that "the liberation of the Greco-Slavic world in the East is Russia's legitimate task."[12] To this end he advised, "Henceforth Russia must have a definite program of political activity in the East, based on the recognition of nationalities and on our declaration of complete material unselfishness."[13] He did not elaborate on the definite program which he urged.

There was little of anything new in Cherkasskii's article, with one exception: it was essentially a restatement of Catherine II's aims, but with the addition of the Panslavic theme. It was precisely this coupling of Russian traditional aims in the Balkans with Panslavic aspirations which gave Cherkasskii's statement importance so soon after the close of the reign of Nicholas I. Although there were many non-Slavs in the Balkans, leading Russian Panslavists chose to regard the Eastern Question and the Slavic Question as essentially the same problem.[14]

Despite his emphasis on the Eastern Question and his preoccupation with the plight of the Balkan Slavs under Turkish rule, Ivan Aksakov, for example, by no means regarded the Turks as the main enemy. For him, too, the Ottoman Empire was but a "sick man." The real villains were the Western Powers, and especially Austria.[15] Here was the main oppressor of Slavdom and the chief obstacle in the path of Russia's historic task. Here was the spearhead of a possible Western crusade against Russia.

[11] *Ibid.*, p. 84.
[12] *Ibid.*, p. 91.
[13] *Ibid.*, p. 92.
[14] This identification of the Slavic Question and the Eastern Question is especially evident in the writings of Ivan Aksakov. See his *Sochineniia*, Vol. I: *Slavianskii vopros, 1860-1886* (Moscow, 1886), *passim*. Note also R. Fadieev's statement, "The Eastern Question cannot be solved in the Balkans, the Polish Question cannot be unraveled in Warsaw, and the Black Sea Question does not end at the Bosphorus. All three difficulties are tied up in a common knot, which lies on the Middle Danube." *Mnienie o vostochnom voprosie* (St. Petersburg, 1870), p. 80.
[15] Aksakov, *Sochineniia*, I, 29.

One of the basic arguments of Russian Panslavism after the Crimean War was that a diplomatically isolated Russia could attract the non-Russian Slavs as allies against a hostile West. It will be remembered that this was the leitmotif of Pogodin's Panslavic memoranda to Nicholas during the Crimean War. It was a theme he did not abandon, even when he later alleged that he had given up any idea of a Panslavic union. "We shall raise up the spirits of the [non-Russian] Slavs, of which there are about thirty millions in Europe," he wrote just before the Moscow Slav Congress of 1867. "Here are our faithful and ardent allies, ready to a man to go to war."[16] Ivan Aksakov proclaimed at the same time in his *Den'* (Day), "Russia is *not alone*; her policy in the East will be supported not only by the most sincere sympathy, the most lively cooperation, of the Russian people itself, but by all of the moral and material strength of the Greco-Slavic world."[17] Soon after, he wrote, "All the strength of the [non-Russian] Slavs is in Russia; all of Russia's strength is in Slavdom."[18] Hilferding evidently shared this view in a quite literal way. He was especially impressed by the number of Slavic soldiers in the Austrian army. Not citing any source for his statistics, Hilferding claimed that Austria's peacetime standing army just before the Italian campaign of 1859 included 333,400 Slavs as opposed to 313,000 non-Slavs. He added that Austria's Military Marches in the Balkans contained a total population of some 310,000 Serbs and 550,000 Croats who could recruit about 100,000 soldiers at any time. It would be well, he suggested, to have so many proven fighters on Russia's side in the event of hostilities.[19]

In the decade after the Crimean War, Russian Panslavist writings betrayed a certain reluctance to discuss Slavic political unification openly and directly. On occasion, Panslavists availed themselves of quite circuitous means to present their views. In 1859,

---

[16] M. P. Pogodin, *Russkii*, Nos. 1-2, March 13, 1867, p. 11.

[17] Aksakov, *Sochineniia*, I, 142. Originally published in the *Den'* on February 21, 1867.

[18] *Ibid.*, p. 153. Originally published in the *Moskva* on July 1, 1867.

[19] Hilferding, "Slavianskie narody v Avstrii i Turtsii," *Sobranie sochinenii*, II, 12-13. Originally published in 1860, Hilferding's suggestion was not put to the test until the first World War, when it was proved that his expectations were not altogether unfounded.

for example, *Russkaia Besieda* published excerpts from Pogodin's memoranda of 1839 and 1842 to the Minister of Public Education concerning Slavic affairs.[20] The editor, Koshelëv, explained in a footnote that because of their timeliness the excerpts were being published then, some twenty years later. In his memorandum of 1838, Pogodin had reported, following a tour of the Slavic lands outside Russia, that the non-Russian Slavs dreamed of "a Slavic state with Russia at its head—from the Pacific Ocean to the Adriatic Sea, a state that has no parallel in history." It is noteworthy that Pogodin did not claim the idea as his own. Even more noteworthy was the following comment which the editor of *Russkaia Besieda* felt called upon to make two decades later with reference to this passage:

A dream which, fortunately, is impracticable. Such a political unification would smother the spiritual independence of each separate nationality. No! Russia's standard should be, in our opinion, not Panslavism in the political sense, not centralization, but the recognition of the right of each nationality to its own independent existence.

However, the editor added, without any elaboration, the following alternative:

Or else: a free union of independent, separate Slavic peoples whose protection and preservation would be Russia's natural right.[21]

During the same year, another circuitous attempt was made to publicize the idea that Russia had a historic mission to liberate and to unite the Slavs. P. A. Bezsonov, a member of the Moscow Slavic Benevolent Committee and a Slavic scholar, resurrected and published Juraj Križanić's seventeenth-century manuscript, *Razgovory ob vladatelstvu* (Discourses on Government).[22] Here was a plea by a Croatian Slav (Bezsonov mistakenly thought him to be a Serb)

[20] M. P. Pogodin, "Otryvki iz pisem o polozhenii Slavian v Evropie, M. P. Pogodina k Ministru Narodnago Prosvieshcheniia po vozvrashchenii iz puteshestviia v 1839 i 1842 gg.," *Russkaia Besieda*, IV (1859), Smies', pp. 53-88.
[21] *Ibid.*, editor's footnote, p. 61.
[22] For a fuller discussion of Križanić's treatise, see Chapter I of the present work as well as my article, "Juraj Križanić: a Precursor of Pan-Slavism," *American Slavic and East European Review*, VI (1947), 75-92. Križanić's treatise is included in P. A. Bezsonov's edition, *Russkoe gosudarstvo v polovinie XVII vieka* (Moscow, 1859), Vol. I.

who called upon Russia to unite all the Slavs under the aegis of the Tsar.

Eight years later, at the time of the Moscow Slav Congress, another Russian Panslavist, V. I. Lamanskii, published a nineteenth-century Slovak appeal for Slavic unification under the protection of Russia—L'udovit Štúr's *Das Slawenthum und die Welt der Zukunft* (Slavdom and the World of the Future). Lamanskii's Russian edition marked the first time this work had ever been published in any language.[23] Štúr called upon his Slavic brethren to realize that without the Russian Empire they had no future, and that only in a federation under Russia's leadership could they preserve their national identities and Slavic way of life.[24]

It is not difficult to see why Russian Panslavists were partial to Križanić and Štúr.[25] Both offered proposals for a Slavic union such as no Russian Panslavist had dared make public before this time. There was also a strategic advantage in being able to tell both the Russian government and the non-Russian Slavs that their proposals did not emanate from Russian Panslavists but from non-Russians.

In the ten years following the end of the Crimean War, no Russian Panslavist was as forthright about Russia's mission to liberate and to unite Slavdom as Ivan Aksakov. In the opening issue of his first newspaper, *Den*, Aksakov declared his stand as a Panslavist. Russia was the only completely independent Slavic nation; everywhere else, he wrote, the entire "Slavic nationality" was being oppressed by the Germans or the Turks. Meanwhile, as Russia was growing in might, Slavs everywhere, Aksakov said, expected their racial elder to deliver them from a shameful yoke. Aksakov then added in italics:

[23] L'udovít Štúr (Liudovit Shtur), "Slavianstvo i mir budushchago; Poslanie Slavianam s beregov Dunaia," translated from the German MS by V. I. Lamanskii, in *Chteniia Imperatorskago Obshchestva Istorii i Drevnostei Rossiiskikh pri Moskovskom Universitetie*, III, Materialy slavianskie, Books 1-3 (Moscow, 1867), pp. 1-191.

[24] *Ibid.*, pp. 159 ff. For a discussion of Štúr's work, see Michael B. Petrovich, "L'udovit Štúr and Russian Panslavism," *Journal of Central European Affairs*, XII (April, 1952), 1-19.

[25] See Bezsonov's preface to his edition of Križanić's works; also V. I. Lamanskii's preface to his edition of Štúr's treatise, cited above. Also A. S. Budilovich, "Nieskol'ko zamiechanii ob izuchenii slavianskago mira," *Slavianskii Sbornik*, II (1878), 15.

To liberate the Slavic peoples from physical and spiritual oppression and to grant them the gift of an independent spiritual and, if you please, political existence under the shade of the mighty wings of the Russian eagle—here is Russia's political calling, its moral right, and its obligation.[26]

The editor of *Den'* did not explain to his readers by what means Russia was to liberate its Slavic brethren, nor did he describe the kind of political existence the non-Russian Slavs could expect under the mighty wings of the Russian eagle. In a private letter to V. I. Lamanskii, Ivan Aksakov wrote in 1858, "God preserve me from any thought of *annexing* the Slavs to Russia; we would only spoil them. No, let all the Slavic peoples, as many of them as there are, comprise a confederative union, while remaining free, each preserving its own national independence."[27]

Though the early Russian Panslavists were vague about the political forms Slavic unification would take, some of them were quite definite about rejecting any kind of Slavic union which excluded the Russians. Regarding this issue, Lamanskii's correspondance with Ivan Aksakov in 1858 is especially interesting. In October of that year Lamanskii sent Aksakov an article praising the proposal of the Czech national leader, František Palacký, for an Austrian Confederation in which the Austrian Slavs would enjoy equality with non-Slavic subjects. "I do not know, Ivan Sergieevich," Lamanskii wrote, "whether you will approve of my views. Slavic equality—they say—is an illusion, a pure impossibility. Who knows? First it must be tried. . . . As well-wishers of the non-Russian Slavs, we Russians should wish them that which they wish for themselves."[28]

Aksakov categorically rejected Austro-Slavism. "I do not share at all in your views and Palacký's regarding the possibility of a Slavic Austria," he wrote. "How can you imagine possible the unification of the Slavic nationality under a German emperor? Under

---

[26] Aksakov, *Sochineniia*, I, 5-6. Originally published in *Den'*, No. 1, October, 1861, Slavianskii obzor.

[27] O. V. Pokrovskaia-Lamanskaia, "Perepiska dvukh slavianofilov," *Russkaia Mysl'* (September, 1916), p. 11, Ivan Aksakov's letter of October 27, 1858, to V. I. Lamanskii.

[28] *Ibid.*, p. 5, V. I. Lamanskii's letter of October 17, 1858, to Ivan Aksakov.

the banner of the German nationality? You say that then all will be equal, both Slavs and Germans. But *external, formal* equality is not enough. . . . Grant equality—and in ten years all the Slavs [in an Austrian Confederation] will be Germans. Posen serves as the best proof."[29]

Lamanskii was hurt by Aksakov's blunt reply and accused him of showing no faith in the ability of the Austrian Slavs to withstand assimilation by the Germans.[30] Nevertheless, Lamanskii eventually adopted Aksakov's viewpoint. When, in late 1865, Lamanskii delivered his inaugural lecture as an instructor at the University of St. Petersburg, he specifically condemned all forms of Slavic unification—Ukrainian federalism, South Slav Illyrianism, Polish Messianism, and Czech Austro-Slavism—which excluded Russia.[31]

The idea of Austro-Slavism was also assailed by Hilferding. In a historical review of the events of 1848 in Central Europe, the Panslavist described as unrealistic the hopes of Austrian Slavs for equality with their German and Hungarian rulers. Such equality would have been impossible even had the Austrian Slavs constituted a single people, he observed, rather than seven or eight scattered national groups. While the Austrian Slavs had fought for the Hapsburg Crown in 1848, they had done so, not because they loved it, but because of "an instinctive and irresistible feeling of their own weakness, their disunity and inability to create a new order of things by their own efforts."[32] They sought a center outside of themselves, one which would stand above their own internal disputes. Hilferding argued that Slavic Russia was in a far better position than a moribund Austrian monarchy to fill this role.

A year after Austria declared a policy of federalism on October 20, 1860, Hilferding warned especially the Czechs against placing

[29] *Ibid.*, p. 11, Ivan Aksakov's letter of October 27, 1858, to V. I. Lamanskii. Aksakov denounced Austro-Slavism in his public writings as well, calling the term a *contradictio in adjecto*. See, for example, his editorial of November 13, 1865, in *Den'*, also published in his *Sochineniia*, I, 45.

[30] Pokrovskaia-Lamanskaia, "Perepiska dvukh slavianofilov," *Russkaia Mysl'* (September, 1916), p. 14, Lamanskii's letter of November 1, 1858, to Ivan Aksakov.

[31] V. I. Lamanskii, "Vstupitel'noe chtenie Dotsenta Peterburgskago universiteta V. I. Lamanskago," *Den'*, No. 52, December 18, 1865, pp. 1239-40.

[32] Hilferding, "Razvitie narodnosti u zapadnykh Slavian," *Sobranie sochinenii*, II, 90. Originally published in 1856 in *Russkaia Besieda*.

their trust in this change. "There can be no doubt," he conceded, "that the present move will bring to the Austrian Slavs great benefits in that it will strengthen, disseminate, and evoke national consciousness within them. But their position is a sad one, and before them stand many false hopes, many sore trials; a bright, comfortable future is still distant. When will it be brought about? We do not know; we know only one thing: *the future of the Slavic world is insoluble without the participation of the Russian people.*"[33] He described Russia as "that only vital support of the Slavic world, that only defender of Slavic principles—Russia, without which the Slav peoples would be in the East what the Celts are in the West, material to serve for the formation of other peoples, and surviving here and there in sorry remnants."[34]

"If there were no Russia," Ivan Aksakov declared in 1863, "or if Russia ceased to be a Slavic state, the [non-Russian] Slavs would have to abandon any thought of a future in history. This is what should be understood, and what is so imperfectly understood by the Western Slavs, and what is not understood at all by the Poles."[35] Four years later he wrote of his country's role in Slavdom, "To it alone belongs the solution of the Eastern Question and of the Slavic Question generally: without it any solution is unthinkable, or is thinkable only as political and spiritual death—for Russia as well as for the whole Slavic world."[36]

Russia was the God-given leader of the Slavs, another Panslavist —N. Barsov—proclaimed. "In the mighty future we can see a single Slavic world in the universal history of mankind . . . and among the Slavic peoples, our great fatherland has been ordained to assume first place."[37]

How did Russian Panslavists envisage, in the decade following

---

[33] Hilferding, "Slavianskiia narodnosti i Pol'skaia partiia v Avstrii," *ibid.*, p. 262. Originally dated October 31, 1861. The italics are Hilferding's.

[34] *Ibid.*, p. 261.

[35] Ivan Aksakov, *Sochineniia*, Vol. III: *Pol'skii vopros i zapadno-russkoe dielo; Evreiskii vopros, 1860-1886* (St. Petersburg, 1900), p. 92. Originally published in *Den'*, July 20, 1863.

[36] Ivan Aksakov, *Sochineniia*, Vol. VII. *Obshcheevropeiskaia polhika, 1860-1886* (Moscow, 1887), p. 90. His article "Rossiia—vsia eshche v budushchem" was first printed in *Den'*, January 13, 1867.

[37] N. Barsov, *Slavianskii vopros* (Vilna, 1867), p. 16.

the Crimean War, the achieving of Slavic liberation and unification by Russia? Although Panslavist writings frequently alluded to the prospect of a Western crusade against Russia, with the single exception of Count N. P. Ignatiev, whose secret diplomatic dispatches in 1866 are in a separate category, it is impossible to find any suggestion by an early Panslavist that Russia should make war on the West. Indeed, even in the excitement of 1867, Pogodin wrote just before the Moscow Slav Congress, "Believe that we will receive all that we have coming to us even without a war!"[38] As will be seen, this attitude of pacifism was hardly characteristic of later Panslavic writings.

Ivan Aksakov insisted on two basic prerequisites for a Slavic union: (1) the Slavs must not be united by conquest or coercion of any kind; and (2) a physical unification could take place only after the Slavs had become morally united by a common awareness of and return to "Slavic principles." Russia must not desecrate its sacred calling, he warned, by forcibly absorbing the non-Russian Slavs into its own empire; rather it must draw the Slavs together by offering them a strong "unifying principle" as reflected in its own Slavic way of life. It was Russia's task to persuade its Slavic brethren by virtue of its own example to renounce their "petty egoistic notions, their personal political desires," and to become conscious of "the higher good of unity."[39] Aksakov insisted that Russia's main task was, therefore, to remain true to the Slavic way of life. "Russia's vocation is clear," he wrote. "It is the only representative of these ancient principles of the Slavs, and it must bear high and in strict purity the political and spiritual standard of Slavdom—not with any selfish designs, but as a symbol which will show the way, which will lend strength and encourage the hopes of our suffering Slavic brethren."[40]

When Hilferding spoke of the salvation of the Slavs by Russia, he was not thinking of Russia as a political entity. "Some sort of intervention by the state did not even occur to me," he protested

---

[38] M. P. Pogodin, *Russkii*, Nos. 1-2, March 13, 1867, p. 11.
[39] Aksakov, "Germanskomu mogushchestvu my dolzhny protivopostavit' nashe mogushchestvo, germanskomu edinstvu—nashe edinstvo," *Sochineniia*, VII, 94. Originally published in *Den'*, February 16, 1867.
[40] Aksakov, *Sochineniia*, I, 50. Originally published in *Den'*, November 13, 1865.

when a Slovak newspaper, the *Peštbudimské Vedomosti* (Budapest News), translated an article of his so as to suggest that he was alluding to Russian political or military intervention on behalf of the non-Russian Slavs. "Whoever translated my article," Hilferding complained, "had me speaking of politics. He transported my thoughts from the social sphere to that of the state." Hilferding cited this as but an example of the tendency of many Western Slavs to regard their own cause strictly in terms of political liberation, whereas their primary problem was a spiritual and cultural one. He advised the Western Slavs to study "Slavic principles" as understood in Russia and to seek salvation in "a living intercourse with a living Slavic organism." He concluded, "It is not politics, no matter what kind, whether Slavic or any other, that can save the Slavic peoples!"[41]

There was little agreement as to just which "Slavic principles" were those decisive ones which the Slavs had to adopt before a physical union was possible. As a direct heir of the Slavophiles, Ivan Aksakov stressed unity in the Orthodox faith.[42] As a philologist, Lamanskii made the adoption of Russian as a Panslavic language the most important prerequisite. "All talk of a Slavic federation without a previous solution of the question regarding a common Slavic language," he wrote in 1864, "is the greatest nonsense."[43] There was little discussion as to just when the Slavs might achieve this spiritual or cultural unity, the general assumption being that the process would take a long time.

In the decade following the Crimean War Russian Panslavism was in a dilemma. It both espoused the cause of Slavic political unification and clung to a set of principles borrowed from a romantic, pietistic Slavophilism which subordinated political objectives to cultural aims and made political unification dependent on a prior cultural integration. What if there was no time to achieve cultural unification first? What if the opportunity presented itself for a

[41] Hilferding, "Vzgliad zapadnykh Slavian na Rossiiu," *Sobranie sochinenii*, II, 265-76 *passim*.
[42] Aksakov, *Sochineniia*, I, 49-50. Originally published in *Den'*, November 13, 1865.
[43] V. I. Lamanskii, *Natsional'nost' italianskaia i slavianskaia v politicheskom i literaturnom otnosheniiakh* (St. Petersburg, 1865), p. 92.

physical unification even before the cultural prerequisites had been achieved? What, indeed, if the whole theory which insisted on the previous satisfaction of cultural aims were fallacious to begin with? It was when Panslavists began asking themselves these questions that their political speculations took a path which gave others abroad a cause to fear the consequences.

III

By 1866, and especially by 1867, Russian Panslavists were becoming aware of a different world. They had caught up, so to speak, with a general change in the intellectual climate as well as with certain specific political shifts in the European scene. Throughout Europe this was a time of reaction against democracy in politics, against romanticism in literature, and against sentiment and idealism. Philosophy was being pushed into the background by science and by pseudo science. "It seemed that the course of politics was determined by material forces and interests rather than by ideal principles or ethical truth."[44]

Certain political events especially impressed themselves upon Russian Panslavists: the unification of Italy, the Cretan uprising, the Serbo-Turkish crisis which ended in the withdrawal of the Turkish garrison from Belgrade, and, above all, Prussia's victory over Austria at Königgrätz in 1866. This last event led not only to the establishment of a North German Confederation but to the Ausgleich of 1867, by which the Austrians shared power with the Magyars in a dual monarchy at the expense of the Slavic and other subject nationalities. The war of 1866 marked a definite divide in the history of nineteenth-century Europe.[45]

It was also a turning point in the history of Russian Panslavism. On February 16, 1867, in the midst of portentous events in Europe, Ivan Aksakov proclaimed in an editorial in his *Moskva* (Moscow), "If the proximity of mighty Prussia threatens us with danger, so also does the proximity of mighty Russia threaten Prussia with

[44] Robert C. Binkley, *Realism and Nationalism, 1852-1871* (New York, 1935), pp. xvii-xviii.

[45] Hans Kohn, *Pan-Slavism: Its History and Ideology* (Notre Dame, 1953), pp. 146 f.

danger. We must counter its might with our might, German unity with our unity. Parallel with its vocation—to gather the scattered parts of the German world into a whole—we can and must emerge with our own vocation—the unification of the Slavic world."[46] Aksakov also called attention to a recent Address from the Throne in which Napoleon III recalled the first Napoleon's words spoken on St. Helena: "One of my most majestic ideas was to gather together racially akin populations scattered and divided by historic revolutions and politics. This unification will come to pass sooner or later in the very nature of things." Evidently, Aksakov pointed out, Napoleon III was dreaming of a Latin Confederation. The Italians were energetically consolidating their new state, and Germany was being united by blood and iron. Did not all this mean, Aksakov asked, that Europe would be forced—"in the very nature of things"—to recognize also the right of the Slavs to unite?[47]

Another Russian Panslavist, N. Barsov, posed the same question, again in 1867. "In our time there reigns the law of national unity. Among the historic peoples of Europe we see a tendency toward the unification of the Latin and the Germanic peoples," he wrote. "Why should the Slavs in this case remain behind them?"[48]

It was natural—given the intellectual climate of the time—that in wishing to emulate the aims of the *Risorgimento* and of the *Reichsgründung*, Russian Panslavists should have fallen into the pattern of thinking which is so graphically expressed in Bismarck's phrase, "blood and iron." Whereas the Slavophile theorist and academician were the typical representatives of Russian Panslavism in the decade after 1856, a crowd of rather more worldly types characterized the movement in its later phase. One thinks first of generals such as Rostislav Fadieev or Michael G. Cherniaev, of scientists such as Nicholas Danilevskii, who wrote *Rossiia i Evropa* (Russia and Europe) between two state ichthyological expeditions, and of *Realpolitiker* such as Ambassador Nicholas P. Ignatiev and his corps of consuls throughout the Balkans. Still one cannot say that the difference between the earlier and the later phases of

[46] Aksakov, "Germanskomu mogushchestvu my dolzhny protivopostavit' nashe mogushchestvo, germanskomu edinstvu—nashe edinstvo," *Sochineniia*, VII, 93.
[47] *Ibid.*, pp. 93-94.
[48] Barsov, *Slavianskii vopros*, p. 16.

Russian Panslavism was one of two generations. The earlier Panslavists were still on the scene after 1867, but the same transformation which changed the movement as a whole took place in the minds of many of them. The movement did not abandon its cultural ideals in the later phase, just as most earlier Panslavists had not ignored political aims. Nevertheless, many Panslavic leaders came to feel the need to subordinate their cultural ideals to a program of political and military action.

Aksakov's own long career as an active Panslavist perhaps best personifies the gamut which Russian Panslavism spanned in the course of one lifetime. Beginning in the mid-1840's as an orthodox Slavophile who upheld the primacy of the spirit and decried violence as a cardinal sin, Aksakov was beating the drums of war in 1868 and shouting from his editorial pages that Russia could settle the Eastern Question and the Slavic Question "by no other means than those by which the Gordian knot was unloosed."[49] By 1875 Aksakov was expediting Russian volunteers and weapons to Balkan battlefields. And he was abetted in this pursuit by the very government which had jailed him in 1848 for intimating in private letters to his family that he had Slavic sympathies![50]

As of 1867, leading Russian Panslavists were no longer willing to limit their activities to propaganda, philanthropy, and cultural relations with the other Slavs. Especially men such as Fadieev and Danilevskii found such a policy too ethereal and ineffective. They belonged to a world which apotheosized force. "As long as our resources . . . are limited to those of the present Slavic Committee, which lacks the means to realize a tenth of its desires," Fadieev drily observed, "success for us is hardly likely."[51]

Danilevskii professed to agree with the earlier Panslavist view that a spiritual union was a loftier aim than a union of the flesh, but precisely because the former aim was loftier, he argued, the Panslavic movement ought to concentrate, as a preliminary step,

---

[49] Aksakov, *Sochineniia*, I, 201. Editorial published in *Moskva* on February 14, 1868.

[50] For Aksakov's activities 1875 to 1878, see S. A. Nikitin, "Vvedenie," *Slavianskii Sbornik: Slavianskii vopros i russkoe obshchestvo v 1867-1878 godakh* (Moscow, 1948), p. 10. Also Aksakov, *Sochineniia*, I, 213 ff.

[51] R. A. Fadieev, *Mnienie o vostochnom voprosie* (St. Petersburg, 1870), pp. 83-84.

on the realization of the more mundane political unification of the Slavs. In other words, while upholding the primacy of the Slavic spirit, Danilevskii in fact urged the physical unification of the Slavic peoples as the primary task of the Russian Panslavic movement. He argued frankly that the movement's concern with the "cultural preparation" of the Slavs for eventual unification was impractical. Danilevskii openly asserted that Russia was losing its Kulturkampf with the West for the minds of the non-Russian Slavs. He offered as proof the progressive Westernization of even the Balkan Slavs. "To think that the pedagogical role of history—for the Western Slavs as well as for us—can be replaced by oral or written propaganda," he proclaimed rather sententiously, "means not to understand in true measure one's own strength and the strength of one's opponent, and to undertake the struggle (which is to decide our fate) on a theater of operations which will be least favorable for us."[52] Russia's best and only course was an armed conflict with the West, a struggle whose magnitude would bring into full play the racial and religious sympathies of the Slavs. "A struggle with the West," Danilevskii declared, "is the only saving means, both for curing our own Russian cultural ailments and for developing Panslavic sympathies which would swallow up the petty quarrels among the various Slavic peoples and factions. The already ripening Eastern Question is making this struggle inevitable in the more or less near future, despite anyone's wishes."[53]

General Fadieev stripped this theme of its ideological trappings and presented it in all its nakedness, brandishing it as he would a sword. "This great question can be settled only by force," he assured his readers, "and at first by Russian force alone."[54] Fadieev did not doubt that Russia would find a propitious opportunity to use force. "The nineteenth century," he observed cynically, "is hardly an age of peace and tranquil prosperity in Europe."[55] He had little patience with the idea of a Slavic cultural rapprochement

[52] N. Ia. Danilevskii, *Rossiia i Evropa; vzgliad na kul'turnyia i politicheskiia otnosheniia slavianskago mira k germano-romanskomu* (5th ed., St. Petersburg, 1895), p. 471.
[53] *Ibid.*, pp. 472-73.
[54] Fadieev, *Mnienie*, p. 95.
[55] *Ibid.*

sponsored by what Hilferding had called the "social sphere" in
Russia. "When the idea of Panslavism becomes a state idea,"
Fadieev proclaimed, "it will dazzle all like lightning."[56]

There was something ironically symbolic about the fact that in
this change of emphasis from spiritual right to political might,
Russian Panslavism transferred its center of gravity from Moscow
to St. Petersburg—a shift which was to receive official recognition
when the St. Petersburg Section of the Moscow Slavic Benevolent
Committee became a society in its own right in 1877. In many ways
this change reflected the very difference in outlook which, according to the Slavophiles, divided West from East, St. Petersburg from
their beloved Moscow the White-stoned, the real capital of Holy
Russia. To them Moscow had always stood for the Russian spirit,
while the city of Peter and his imperial successors represented the
very incarnation of force as a way of life. It was in the latter milieu,
under the leaden skies of the northern capital, that the political
program of Russian Panslavism was developed.

IV

Count Nicholas Pavlovich Ignatiev (1832–1908) holds a place
somewhat apart in the emergence of Russian Panslavism. He was
neither a publicist nor a Slavic scholar, but a career diplomat.
Indeed, no Panslavist of his time held a higher post in the Foreign
Ministry. An exceptionally capable and energetic man, Ignatiev
entered the diplomatic service in 1856, and by 1860—at the age of
twenty-eight—he had already made a name for himself by securing
for Russia the Treaty of Peking.[57] From 1861 to 1864 he served as
Director of the Asiatic Department of the Ministry of Foreign
Affairs, a section which included the Balkans in its purview. From
1864 to 1877 he was Russia's envoy in Constantinople.[58] It was
largely Ignatiev's renown as a champion of Slavdom which led
some alarmed Western Europeans to regard Panslavism as the

---

[56] *Ibid.*, p. 97.
[57] "Zapiski Grafa N. P. Ignatieva (1864-1874)," *Izviestiia Ministerstva inostrannykh diel*, 1914, Book I (St. Petersburg, 1914), note by P. Voeikov, pp. 93-94.
[58] "Zapiski Grafa N. P. Ignatieva," *Istoricheskii Viestnik*, CXXXV (1914), 49,
footnote.

mainspring of Russian foreign policy in the 1870's. While he belongs chiefly to the later history of Russian Panslavism, Ignatiev did make a noteworthy contribution to the Panslavist political program before 1870.

The circumstances of Ignatiev's first adherence to Panslavism are obscure. There is nothing in his views to suggest that he came to Panslavism by way of Slavophilism.[59] It is known that in 1858, during a trip abroad, he became acquainted with Palacký, Rieger, Brauner, and other Slav nationalist leaders in Austria.[60] Whatever his early interests in the Panslavic movement might have been, his absence from Russia in the period 1864 to 1877 prevented his taking an active part in the work of Russian Panslavist organizations, although he was made an honorary member of the St. Petersburg Section of the Slavic Benevolent Committee in 1874.[61] His views on Panslavism were not a matter of public record in the 1860's. Indeed, his memoirs—which were based on his memoranda—were not published until the years of the First World War.[62] Nevertheless, these memoirs reveal that even before the 1870's Count Ignatiev was an active exponent of Panslavism in the Russian Foreign Ministry.[63]

Ignatiev began his memoirs with a statement of the views which he had held in 1864 as Director of the Asiatic Department. He was then convinced that Russian foreign policy should focus on three aims: (1) "destruction" of the Treaty of Paris; (2) Russian control

[59] As B. H. Sumner observed, "The fundamental difference between the panslavism of Ignatyev and his like and the philosophical and religious slavophilism of the older type is equally well illustrated by Ignatyev's frank repudiation of any pretence at idealism in his championship of the Slavs." See B. H. Sumner, *Russia and the Balkans, 1870-1880* (Oxford, 1937), p. 35.

[60] "Zapiski Grafa N. P. Ignatieva (1864-1874)," *Izviestiia Ministerstva inostrannykh diel*, 1914, Book I, note by P. Voeikov, p. 94.

[61] *Pervyia 15 liet sushchestvovaniia S.-Peterburgskago Slavianskago Blagotvoritel'nago Obshchestva* (St. Petersburg, 1883), Appendix III, p. 836.

[62] Ignatiev's memoirs appeared posthumously, in Russian, in the *Istoricheskii Viestnik*, Vols. CXXXV, CXXXVI, and CXXXVII (1914); an additional section entitled "Posle San Stefano" appeared in Vols. CXLIII and CXLIV (1916). The part covering his activities from 1864 to 1874 is also found, in French, in the *Izviestiia Ministerstva inostrannykh diel*, 1914, Books I-VI, and 1915, Books I-IV.

[63] Two excellent summaries of Ignatiev's memoirs may be found in Alexander Onou, "The Memoirs of Count N. Ignatyev," *Slavonic Review*, X (December, 1931), 386-407; and B. H. Sumner, "Ignatyev at Constantinople, 1864-1874," *Slavonic Review*, XI (January, 1933), 341-53, and XI (April, 1933), 556-71.

over Constantinople and the Straits; and (3) establishment of a Russian-led united front of all the Slavs.[64] Though all three aims were connected, it is particularly the last which is of interest here.

Count Ignatiev professed the belief that the Slavs, unlike the Germans, possessed a natural racial tendency to strive for the national independence of each Slavic group rather than for political unification as a race. Nevertheless, he maintained that their common enemies would force the Slavs to unite in a defensive alliance and to submit to "a common diplomatic and economic direction."[65] A common literary language, he added, would facilitate this union, but this involved "a slow process." According to Ignatiev, three difficulties militated against a Slavic federation: the particularism of the Slavs in general, the hostility of the Poles in particular, and the enmity of Austria-Hungary. "If only Austria could cease to be the instrument of Roman propaganda, German politics and Germanization, and the denationalization of the Slavs," he wrote, "if only the Magyars were not predominant in Vienna, and among the Slavs—the Poles, then it would be easy for us to reach an understanding and take common action with the government of a country in which the great majority of the population consists of peoples of one blood with us."[66] Ignatiev averred that a centralistic "Old Austria" could have been Russia's ally, but not a dualistic Austria which trained its sights on the Aegean Sea and dreamed of an Eastern Hapsburg Empire in which the victims would be especially the Slavs. This second Austria, Ignatiev declared, was Russia's "natural rival and enemy with whom sooner or later we will have to fight to the death for supremacy in the East, for Russia's unity and integrity, and for the possibility of maintaining and developing the historical position prepared by the labor of centuries and foreordained by the Almighty for Russia—to be the representative of Orthodoxy and of the most numerous and mighty race of Slavs."[67]

How was Russia to achieve its God-given mission? Ignatiev offered a simple formula. The Austrian and the Ottoman Slavs

[64] "Zapiski Grafa N. P. Ignatieva," *Istoricheskii Viestnik*, CXXXV (1914), 50-54 *passim*.
[65] *Ibid*., p. 54.
[66] *Ibid*.
[67] *Ibid*.

were to become Russia's allies and "instruments of our policy against the Germans." To obtain the help of the non-Russian Slavs, Russia had to "make sacrifices" for the liberation of the Slavs. However, Ignatiev emphatically opposed liberating the Slavs and then allowing them to go their own ways, perhaps even to turn against Russia. For Russia to content itself with a policy of humanitarianism, he asserted, would be "unreasonable and criminal."[68]

Ignatiev admitted that these views clashed directly with those of his chief, Prince Alexander M. Gorchakov, and the latter's principal advisers—Baron Alexander Jomini, and the erstwhile Panslavist, Eugene P. Novikov. These men believed that Russian interests would not suffer if, for example, Austria took Bosnia and Hercegovina from the Turks. Sooner or later, Gorchakov predicted, such a gift would serve Austria as fatally as the robe of Nessus served poor Hercules. The Slavic majority in Austria would eventually rise up against its master.

Ignatiev was not content with this optimistic view. His aim was not merely the liberation of the non-Russian Slavs but their subordination to Russian policy. He feared that a Catholic Slavic federation built on Austria's ruins would become a threat to Russia by acting as a magnet on Russian Poland, the Baltic states, and even White Russia and the Ukraine. "It has always seemed to me," he wrote, "that it was Russia's historic mission to gather together the Slavs and to keep them for herself, not relinquishing voluntarily a single foot of Slavic soil to anyone."[69] The Slavic standard should be borne exclusively by the Tsar, and no other state was to be allowed to play any role among the Slavs, particularly the Slavs of the Balkans. Ignatiev urged the view that it was far better for Russia to postpone indefinitely any attempt to solve the Balkan Question than to surrender any rights in this area, particularly to Austria.

Ignatiev's memoirs made much of his efforts while envoy in Constantinople to realize his Panslavic program. As he wrote with utter candor, and even pride:

[68] *Ibid.*
[69] *Ibid.*, p. 55.

I undertook negotiations with all the Slavic peoples, preparing them for independence. The work of undermining the Treaty of Paris and of countering Western and all foreign influences on the Bosporus, especially those of Turkey itself and of Austria-Hungary, had to be continued until the development of Russia's strength and until propitious events in Europe would permit us to effect an independent solution of the Eastern Question in the Russian sense, that is, by forming territories [*oblastii*] of coracialists and coreligionists bound to Russia by indissoluble bonds, while leaving the Straits to our disposition.[70]

When in 1866 Prussia attacked Austria, Ignatiev believed that the "propitious events in Europe" which he anticipated had arrived. At the same time, an insurrection on the island of Crete inspired Ignatiev all the more to urge upon the Russian Foreign Ministry a more active policy in the Balkans. He kept in close touch with secret revolutionary committees throughout the Balkans. "I tried to utilize the general turbulence of the Eastern peoples by drawing them closer together," he recalled, "by smoothing over their mutual misunderstandings and quarrels, and by preparing a defensive-offensive alliance between Serbia, Greece, Montenegro, and the Bulgars."[71] In a confidential letter of December 27, 1866, Ignatiev advised Gorchakov to take action in the Balkans. He admitted that Russia's precarious state of finances, lack of strategic railways, and involvement in an unfinished program of domestic reforms were possible reasons for not taking action. "But events do not await our military and economic preparedness," he warned. "Arising independently of our will, they oblige us to adapt ourselves to them, in order to gain benefits for Russia."[72] If the Balkan peoples were to succeed in a general insurrection against the Turks without Russia, Ignatiev reminded his chief, then they might fall under Western influence and be used against Russia, a result which would be worse than the present status. He advised Russia to step in now, in 1866, while the Balkan Slavs were aroused and while a

[70] *Ibid.*, p. 56.
[71] *Ibid.*, p. 58.
[72] *Ibid.*, p. 59.

Serbo-Bulgarian confederation under Prince Michael of Serbia, Russia's friend, was in the making.[73]

Ignatiev's goal in the Balkans was "an Eastern union similar to the North German Confederation brought into being by Prince Bismarck."[74] Russia would take part in this Balkan Confederation (though Ignatiev did not define the exact nature of Russia's participation). Constantinople, the proposed capital of the Confederation, was to be declared a free city with an international garrison which would include a Russian detachment. The Free City of Constantinople, which was to include outlying districts as well, was to be a monarchy governed by some member of the Russian Imperial family. Such an arrangement was to last, Ignatiev suggested, until "the first propitious occasion for annexing this truly important political, spiritual, and commercial center."[75]

Such was the Panslavist program which Ignatiev urged on Gorchakov in 1866. His failure to win the approval of the Russian Foreign Ministry—indeed, the hostility which Ignatiev's plans and activities aroused in Gorchakov, Shuvalov, Novikov, Grand Duke Nicholas, and others—offers but further proof that Panslavism was hardly a basis of Russian foreign policy in the 1860's. Official St. Petersburg chose not to take advantage of Austria's weakness as the result of its defeat by Prussia. It chose to ignore the Cretan uprising. Prince Michael's death disrupted all of Ignatiev's efforts to help create a Serbo-Bulgarian union, and Russia could no longer count on Serbia. Ignatiev was thwarted on all sides until 1870, when the Russian government took advantage of France's defeat by Germany and disavowed the Paris Treaty of 1856. With this act a new chapter in Russia's Balkan policy was opened, and Russian Panslavism sought another opportunity to exert its influence. Though Ignatiev's plans came to nought in the 1860's, they do illustrate the aggressively political trend which Russian Panslavism was taking in this period.

[73] On Ignatiev's participation in plans for a Balkan alliance, see B. H. Sumner, "Ignatyev at Constantinople, 1864-1874," *Slavonic Review*, XI (January, 1933), 351.
[74] "Zapiski Grafa N. P. Ignatieva," *Istoricheskii Viestnik*, CXXXV (1914), 66.
[75] *Ibid.*, p. 67.

V

The political program of Russian Panslavism received no more definite expression than in the works of two authors: Nicholas Iakovlevich Danilevskii (1822-85) and General Rostislav Fadieev (1824-83). Both were members of the St. Petersburg Section of the Moscow Slavic Benevolent Committee. Danilevskii's *Rossiia i Evropa*, which was published in Strakhov's journal, *Zaria* (Dawn), in serial form in 1869 and as a separate volume in 1871, was beyond any doubt the most significant statement of both the general ideology and the specific political aims of Russian Panslavism ever published.[76] Fadieev's plain-spoken advocacy of political Panslavism had greater immediate resonance.

Major General Rostislav Andreievich Fadieev was the scion of a family of provincial gentry. His father rose to be governor of Saratov; his mother was a Dolgorukii, one of the most prominent princely families in Russian history. As a military man Fadieev had served for twenty years in the Caucasus and was known as an ardent supporter of Russia's expansion into Central Asia. He was closely associated with Prince Bariatinskii, the "Pacifier of the Caucasus" and Shamyl's nemesis. In 1867, inspired by the retired Prince, Fadieev joined in the attack of the Old Guard on D. A. Miliutin's army reforms by writing a series of articles in *Russkii Viestnik* (Russian Herald) in which he criticized severely the Minister's innovations. A revised version of these articles appeared in book form in Moscow in 1868 under the title *Vooruzhennyia sily Rossii* (The Armed Forces of Russia). For his pains, Fadieev was immediately retired from active military duty.[77] He thereupon joined forces with another of Miliutin's victims, Major General Michael Grigorievich Cherniaev, the famed "Lion of Central Asia."

[76] Danilevskii also wrote a whole series of political articles, largely for *Zaria* and General M. G. Cherniaev's *Russkii Mir* (Russian World), especially during the Balkan crisis of 1876 and the ensuing Russo-Turkish War. These were later republished in 1890 in St. Petersburg in a single volume entitled *Sbornik politicheskikh i ekonomicheskikh statei* (Collection of Political and Economic Articles). These articles fall outside the scope of the present study.

[77] B. H. Sumner, "Russia and Panslavism in the Eighteen-Seventies," *Transactions of the Royal Historical Society*, Fourth Series, XVIII (1935), 40.

Both became active supporters of the St. Petersburg Section of the Moscow Slavic Benevolent Committee.

Fadieev's book, devoted largely to technical matters, did suggest in its conclusion that Russia take advantage of the fact that it had millions of potential natural allies in the Eastern European Slavs, and he proposed that Russia become "the center of the Slavic and the Orthodox world."[78] Only an incidental part of his book, this view attracted attention and created a rather wide difference of opinion in the Russian press. Fadieev then decided to write a sequel in order "to define more clearly those aspects of the question which have given rise to a misunderstanding," in the hope that "every idea, insofar as it is in itself sound, has all the greater chance of being in time converted into action."[79] This sequel was the famous *Mnienie o vostochnom voprosie* (Opinion on the Eastern Question), which appeared in 1870 as a book after having been published in serial form in the St. Petersburg *Birzhevyia Viedomosti* (Stock Exchange News).[80] Whereas his first book had been almost entirely a military one, its sequel was boldly political and frankly proclaimed as its aim the establishment by Russia of a Panslavic confederation of states.

The public, both at home and abroad, was quick in grasping the significance of Fadieev's book. Only a comparatively few Russians had plowed through Danilevskii's ponderous and highly intellectual disquisitions in the still little-known *Zaria* in 1868, and even when *Rossiia i Evropa* was published as a separate volume in 1871, only twelve hundred copies were sold. Fadieev's brochure of ninety-eight hard-hitting pages, however, reflected both the direct simplicity of a military man and the zeal of a Panslavist. It no sooner appeared than it was translated into Czech, Serbian, and English.[81] In fact, there was a second English edition in 1876 at the height of the Balkan crisis—in the same year in which English passions were

---

[78] R. A. Fadieev, *Vooruzhennyia sily Rossii* (Moscow, 1868), p. 268.

[79] Fadieev, *Mnienie*, pp. 3-4.

[80] Alfred Fischel, *Der Panslawismus bis zum Weltkrieg* (Stuttgart and Berlin, 1919), p. 400.

[81] *O zaležitostech vychodní a slovanské* (Prague, 1870); *O istočnom pitanju* (Belgrade, 1870); *Opinion on the Eastern Question*, trans. T. Michell (1st ed., London, 1871, 2d ed., London, 1876).

so successfully inflamed by Gladstone's famous brochure, *Bulgarian Horrors and the Question of the East.* The very fact that Fadieev's work had been permitted to see print in Russia appeared to enhance its significance. Russian Panslavism had come a long way since the 1840's, when the government had regarded it as subversive and revolutionary.

To be sure, Danilevskii and Fadieev were not the only Panslavists in this period to give expression to the political tendencies of their creed. Especially noteworthy were Ivan Aksakov, Hilferding, La- manskii, and Budilovich. Yet none of these came out with any clear-cut political program. Rather, their statements and prophecies served more to buttress the general plan outlined by these two men.

A dominant theme in their writings continued to be Russia's need for allies against a hostile West. "Russia has no reliable allies in Europe beyond the members of its own family—the Slavs and the Orthodox," Fadieev wrote. "As soon as that family is thoroughly imbued with confidence in Russia, it will then be necessary at the first favorable opportunity to assist it in rising, that is, it will be necessary to reach that family by a victory at the outset. . . . If the Slavs of the Balkans and of the Danube cannot do anything without Russia, Russia likewise cannot do very much without them. Against us we have Europe."[82]

Danilevskii proclaimed that just as in the cultural field Russia "would be deprived of every cultural-historical significance" unless it included the whole Slavic world within its own cultural unit, so in the political field Russia was too weak by itself. Its European treaties and alliances had only served to tie its hands. By its very existence, Danilevskii argued, vast Russia threw the European sys- tem of states out of balance. On the other hand, he found Russia's isolation from Europe unthinkable. In his opinion Russia was bound to Europe by "the most obvious rights, wholesome interests, natu- ral sympathies, and sacred obligations."[83] "Therefore, nothing is left for it but to assume its own real role—predetermined by ethno- graphic and historical circumstances—and to serve as a counter- weight not to this or that European state, but to Europe as a whole,

[82] Fadieev, *Mnienie,* pp. 79-80.
[83] Danilevskii, *Rossiia i Evropa,* p. 436.

in its entirety and generality."[84] To assume this role, however, Russia needed the other Slavs. "Being alien to the European world by its internal order," he wrote, "and moreover, being too strong and mighty to assume the position of being just another member of the European family, to be just another Great Power in Europe, Russia cannot assume a place in history worthy of itself and of Slavdom without placing itself at the head of a distinct independent political system of states and serving as a counterbalance to Europe."[85] What had Russia to gain thereby? For Danilevskii the answer was clear: the aggrandizement of its external might so that Russia would be in a position to protect itself and its confederates from attack by a hostile West and thus be able to devote itself to its own internal moral and material welfare.[86]

Especially in the light of the present tension which exists between Russia and the United States, it is impossible not to observe parenthetically that Danilevskii and Fadieev regarded the United States as Russia's only real friend in an otherwise uniformly inimical West. Danilevskii enumerated Russia, the United States, and Western Europe as the three chief protagonists in contemporary world history, and he linked the first two countries by maintaining that both shared the same function—that of providing counterweights to the third protagonist—and both shared a great future.[87] Fadieev went even further when he stated, "Speaking *en passant*, the only possible ally in the world which is not inimical to Russia's historic tasks is America. But an American alliance, however immeasurably important to us as a counterpoise to the naval force of the Western Powers, cannot help us on land."[88]

Russian Panslavists were a much more outspoken and ambitious lot after 1866 and 1867 than in the previous decade. General Fadieev reflected well their prevailing mood when he declared:

I shall speak my mind frankly: contemporary Russia has already outgrown those national limits which gave legality and stability to the existence of a state, while it has not yet attained that higher legality—

[84] *Ibid.*
[85] *Ibid.,* p. 437.
[86] *Ibid.,* p. 445.
[87] *Ibid.,* p. 463.
[88] Fadieev, *Mnienie,* p. 42.

that of becoming the center of its own special Slavic and Orthodox world. Russia cannot consolidate itself in its present state; political, like natural, history does not lend eternity to undefined, unfinished forms. All depends now on the solution of the Slavic Question. Russia must either extend its primacy to the Adriatic Sea or withdraw again beyond the Dnieper.[89]

While Fadieev and Danilevskii appeared to be speaking in the terms of an ideology which had been established a decade earlier, they were actually saying something far different. Whereas just after 1856, following Russia's defeat in the Crimea, Pogodin and Aksakov were truly concerned with Russia's immediate defense, some ten years later Danilevskii and Fadieev proclaimed that the best defense was the offense. Earlier, Russian Panslavism had held that the only way to deter Europe from making war on Russia was to make allies of the non-Russian Slavs. Later Panslavism, however, expounded the view that the only way to win the other Slavs was through a general war with Europe, and only then could Russia establish a Slavic union. Just as Fadieev and Danilevskii reversed the Panslavic philosophy by claiming that a physical Slavic union was not the ultimate aim of a cultural unification but a prerequisite for the latter, so they reversed Panslavic political policy by maintaining not that Slavic solidarity was the best way of avoiding war but that war was the only way of obtaining Slavic solidarity. It is in the light of this significant change that other Panslavic arguments for a Slavic federation must be examined.

A basic political argument which various Russian Panslavists advanced, especially after 1867, in favor of a Slavic confederation was that the Ottoman and Hapsburg empires were in the last stages of dissolution, and that sooner or later Russia would be forced to fill the political vacuum left by their demise. This was the long famous Sick-Man-of-Europe argument, only now refurbished to apply not only to Turkey but to Austria as well. Russian Panslavists were positively macabre in their "somewhat exaggerated" reports of the death of these two empires.

"At the present time," Ivan Aksakov wrote with supreme confidence in 1868, less than a year after the Ausgleich, "Austria is no

[89] *Ibid.*, pp. 86-87.

more than a political prejudice which still beclouds the consciousness." Though its peoples were very much alive as "organic forces," he maintained, the Austrian Empire itself was really quite dead. He diagnosed the cause of death as paralysis induced by the fact that the nationally ambitious Hungarians had made centralism impossible, while the numerically preponderant Slavs within the Empire made dualism impossible.[90] Danilevskii suggested three years later that Austria could no longer be seriously regarded as a political entity but only as a political symbol.[91] For Fadieev, Austria's importance lay only in the melancholy circumstance that it lay between Russia and Russia's destiny in the Balkans.[92]

Fadieev reminded his readers that in 1870 one could no longer discuss the Eastern Question in the same terms as in the time of Lord Chatham. "To Europe, which does not desire the independence of the Slavs," he wrote, "the Eastern Question may continue to exist in its previous form . . . as an unfinished question involving the dissolution of Turkey; but we Russians have no reason to close our eyes to reality. We must see in this notorious question that which it really is—our own Slavic Question, which is depicted on the map of Europe in two different colors, but which is in reality indivisible and insoluble except in its entirety; for that both its parts are reciprocal is now an indisputable fact which cannot be altered by any eventualities."[93] Danilevskii, too, regarded the "ever nearer and nearer, riper and riper" Eastern Question as a final obstacle to a Slavic confederation, and he saw in the imminent settlement of the question "the triumph of Slavdom and the establishment of its independence and autochthony."[94]

VI

No other Russian Panslavist formulated such precise plans for a Slavic union as did Nicholas Danilevskii in his work *Rossiia i*

[90] Aksakov, "Vsiakoe sblizhenie s Avstrieiu . . . ," *Sochineniia*, VII, 202-3. Originally published in *Moskva*, September 19, 1868.

[91] N. Ia. Danilevskii, "Rossiia i Franko-Germanskaia voina," *Sbornik politicheskikh i ekonomicheskikh statei* (St. Petersburg, 1890), p. 18.

[92] Fadieev, *Mnienie*, p. 21.

[93] *Ibid.*, pp. 29-30.

[94] Danilevskii, *Rossiia i Evropa*, p. 468.

Evropa. Danilevskii envisaged the Panslavic union as a federation of the following eight units:

1. The Russian Empire (including Galicia, Carpatho-Russia, [most of] Bessarabia, and Dobrudja);

2. The Czech-Moravian-Slovak Kingdom, 9,000,000 inhabitants and 1,800 square kilometers;

3. The Kingdom of the Serbs-Croats-Slovenes (including Serbia, Montenegro, Bosnia, Hercegovina, Old Serbia, northern Albania, Vojvodina, Banat, Croatia, Slavonia, Dalmatia, the Military Marches, Carniola, Gorizia, Gradisca, Istria, Trieste, two thirds of Carinthia, and one fifth of Styria along the Drava), 8,000,000 inhabitants and 4,500 square kilometers;

4. The Bulgarian Kingdom (including the greater part of Rumelia, and Macedonia), 6,000,000 or 7,000,000 inhabitants and over 3,000 square kilometers;

5. The Rumanian Kingdom (including Wallachia, Moldavia, part of Bukovina, half of Transylvania up to approximately the Maros River, and the western portion of Bessarabia), about 7,000,000 inhabitants and over 3,000 square kilometers;

6. The Hellenic Kingdom (including Thessaly, Epirus, southwestern Macedonia, and all the islands of the Archipelago, Rhodes, Crete, Cyprus, and the islands along the coast of Asia Minor), over 4,000,000 inhabitants and from 2,800 to 3,000 square kilometers;

7. The Magyar Kingdom (that is, Hungary minus areas with a Russian Czechoslovak, Serbian, and Rumanian population, and Transylvania, minus the half given to Rumania), nearly 7,000,000 inhabitants and about 3,000 square kilometers;

8. The District of Constantinople (including adjacent parts of Rumelia and Asia Minor surrounding the Bosporus, the Sea of Marmara, the Dardanelles, the peninsula of Gallipoli, and the island of Tenedos).[95]

Using Danilevskii's own estimates for the year 1869, his federation was to include a total population of about 125 million people. Of this total some 82 million were to belong directly to Russia, and over 43 million inhabitants were to be divided among the other seven constituent units.

It is obvious that such a scheme entailed serious difficulties. In this supposedly Slavic union no less than half of the constituent

[95] *Ibid.*, pp. 423-24.

units—Rumania, Greece, Hungary, and the District of Constantinople—were non-Slavic, and their population amounted to roughly
half that of the non-Russian part of the union. It will also be noted
that Danilevskii denied to the Albanians a separate national status,
apparently regarding them as a sub-national ethnic entity. It goes
without saying that the non-Slavic Finns, Latvians, Estonians, Lithuanians, and the other non-Russian groups in the Russian Empire
were accorded the same treatment. Danilevskii's plan likewise
denied a separate status to the Ukranians and the White Russians.
He omitted the Poles from his list of constituent units because, as
will be seen, he believed that Poland should not be admitted into
the federation as a separate unit until it had demonstrated its willingness to cooperate. Far from being willing to sacrifice any ethni-
cally non-Russian parts of the Russian Empire to other members of
a federation which Russia would control anyway, Danilevskii required the addition of four provinces to Russian territory as well
as the inclusion in it of all Poles not already subjects of the Tsar.
Finally, the non-Russian states in the federation were outnumbered
two to one by Russia in size of population, and were so surpassed
by Russia in area, resources, political importance, and military
might as to render equality within the federation impossible.

Danilevskii made no attempt to conceal the fact that his federation was mainly for the benefit of the Slavs. He claimed that union
with Russia would offer the other Slavs liberation from the Germans, Turks, and Magyars, the consolidation of their historic lands,
political home rule in their domestic affairs, cultural autonomy,
protection from Western imperialism, and protection from one
another through Russia's mediation.

The Bulgars, he argued, had special reason to join. "Of all the
Slavic peoples, they find themselves under the worst oppression,
for they live in closest contact with their oppressors," Danilevskii
observed. Moreover, he believed that the Bulgars were on such a
low level of culture that they could scarcely pass from a "tribal"
to a national political existence without the support of some outside agency such as a Slavic federation. Indeed, he actually proposed an initial Russian trusteeship over Bulgaria as an administratively autonomous province of Russia until such time as the Bulgars

were deemed able to assume full political independence. Danilevskii also suggested that Bulgaria needed protection from the ambitions of its more highly developed Serbian neighbor.[96]

"For Serbia itself," he proposed, "close ties with Russia and all of Slavdom are no less useful—to check its bad glory-seeking instincts and to direct them into proper channels, not toward Bulgaria, but toward the emigrated Serbs and their kinsmen, the Croatian and the Slovenian peoples, who find themselves under the rule of Austria."[97] Like Khomiakov in his "Epistle from Moscow to the Serbs," published a decade earlier, Danilevskii warned the Serbs against emulating the vainglorious Poles in their xenomania. "Only in a political union with all of Slavdom, under Russia's leadership," Danilevskii declared, "can the Serbian people find the necessary strength and hope for success in their struggle against the Italianization, Magyarization, and Germanization of their land."[98]

As for the Czechs, Danilevskii felt that this "apple of discord between Slavdom and Germandom" could make secure its position against the Germans both without and within its borders only by joining forces with Slavdom in a mighty union.[99] The same applied to the Slovaks in their struggle against Magyarization.

It was in the Polish Question that Danilevskii encountered his major stumbling block. Poland—ethnic Poland, he made clear—could adopt any one of four possible courses. First, it could insist on complete independence, but Russia would never agree to this for reasons of security. Danilevskii categorically rejected any possibility that a free Poland might be friendly to Russia; the Rzecz Pospolita (Polish Commonwealth) had had its chance to be friendly in the seventeenth century when it was at the pinnacle of its power, and did not seize it. What reason was there to suppose, he asked, that a free Poland would be friendly to Russia, now that it could add the desire for revenge to its old pretensions? Poland's second choice was to remain within the Russian Empire, but to offer stubborn passive resistance. Danilevskii predicted that this would be most unfortunate, because the Russians would then be forced to

[96] *Ibid.*, pp. 439-41 *passim.*
[97] *Ibid.*, pp. 441-42.
[98] *Ibid.*, p. 442.
[99] *Ibid.*

repress Poland all the more. Danilevskii presented as a third possibility the Russification of the Poles. In the light of charges that the Russian Panslavists were Russifiers, it is noteworthy that even as extreme a Panslavist as Danilevskii rejected the Russification of Poland as being undesirable even if it were possible. The Russians did not need more Russians, he pointed out; they needed friends. It was the fourth choice which Danilevskii supported—an autonomous Poland as a separate member of a Slavic federation. "Poland can find a pleasant way out of its long languor," he promised, "only in the bosom of a Panslavic union, in close unity and friendship with Russia."[100] However, Poland could not be included in such a federation as a separate member until it demonstrated its readiness to cooperate sincerely. Danilevskii did not say when this might be expected to occur or how one would judge that it had occurred.

What was to be the position of the non-Slavs in the Slavic union? Apart from the Asiatic subject peoples of the Russian Empire, there were in Eastern Europe the Finns, Lithuanians, Latvians, Estonians, Magyars, Rumanians, Albanians, and Greeks. Russian Panslavists who wrote on this problem were generally agreed that all these peoples simply had to share the destiny of their more numerous Slavic neighbors. "All these peoples are inseparably bound to the Slavic world," wrote Hilferding just four years after the Crimean defeat. "Ordained by the very nature of things, this bond has penetrated their entire past history, which has revolved completely within the confines of the Slavic world. No power can break that bond." For these peoples to be hostile to the Slavic world, Hilferding argued, would be senseless. Surely these small peoples did not possess the material strength necessary to wage a constant struggle with the Slavs. More important, thought Hilferding, they did not possess sufficient spiritual strength to support competition with the Slavs. "What original vital principles," he demanded without pausing for an answer, "can the Lithuanians, Rumanians, Albanians, or Magyars contribute to the advancement of mankind?" Especially now that the Slavic world was on the point of fulfilling its mission in universal history, he said, the non-Slavs of Eastern Europe had all the more reason to hitch their

[100] *Ibid.*

wagons to the Slavic star. "We would like to say to these peoples, and particularly to the Magyars," Hilferding declared, " 'Unite your hearts to the Slavs. Unite your labors to theirs. Room was found in the Slavic world for your valiant and distinct people: room will also be found for your valiant, distinct labor in the great role which is to be played by the Slavic world for the benefit of all mankind.' "[101]

General Fadieev wrote somewhat similarly, "In speaking of the Slavs, I mean the whole group of nations which are bound to Russia by historical destiny, by blood, and by religion. One cannot pass over the Greeks and the Rumanians in this great question; especially the latter have grown into the compact body of Slavdom and must involuntarily share its fate."[102]

So, too, Danilevskii declared, "All these non-Slavic peoples (Greeks, Rumanians, Magyars) which historic destiny has, for better or worse, inseparably bound to us, wedging them into the Slavic mass, must willy-nilly also join the Panslavic federation." He did not make quite clear whether the willy-nilliness was to proceed from some abstract necessity such as the logic of history or from some more material force.

While Fadieev and Danilevskii were far from satisfied with either the Rumanians or the Greeks, they were more tolerantly inclined toward these two Orthodox peoples than toward any other non-Slavs in Eastern Europe. They believed that within a Slavic union both peoples would find ample benefits to justify their cooperation. "The only nation which has any reasonable cause to desire the independence of the Rumanians," Fadieev observed, "the only nation which has created and supported that independence is the Russian nation. Not only are the Rumanian people unable by their own efforts to gather together their scattered branches, which, like the Slavs, are being trampled under foot by foreigners, but they cannot even maintain their own position as a free nation except with the aid of Russia. . . . In case of a new struggle over the Eastern Question, or rather over the new Slavic Question, which has taken the place of the former, the existence of the Rumanians,

[101] Hilferding, "Vengriia i Slaviane," *Sobranie sochinenii*, II, 142-43.
[102] Fadieev, *Mnienie*, p. 52.

not only as a people, but as men and citizens, will depend exclusively on Russia's victory."[103]

Danilevskii also pointed out that only with the consent and participation of Russia could the Rumanians hope to gain their ethnic territories in Transylvania, Bukovina, and western (but not eastern) Bessarabia. Only with Russia's support could the Rumanians successfully withstand Magyar pressure. "Only by leaning on the . . . Slavs," he declared, "could they cope with corrosive Gallomania and the tendency of their sorry intelligentsia to copy others."[104]

As for the Greeks, Danilevskii argued that history and geography had made them not a farming or an industrial people but primarily traders. To protect themselves from British and German imperialism and to maintain their trade in the face of their Western competitors, the Greeks needed the backing of a friendly Great Power such as Russia. "Where indeed," he demanded, "will Greece obtain a sufficiently mighty fleet for its own trade, one which would give that trade a world-wide character?" His reply was that only a mighty Greco-Slavic union—"this unique form in which the Eastern Roman Empire can be born anew"—could make of Greece the great sea power it once was.[105] Fadieev warned the Greeks that their "Great Idea" of a resurrected Byzantine Empire which they themselves would dominate was but a "senseless chimera which Russia cannot permit to be realized, and which is only the fruit of the archaeological fancies of the Greek learned party." He assured the Greeks, however, that "the only people that sincerely desires their liberation, and is ready to shed its blood for them, is the Russian people, and none other."[106]

Of all the non-Slavic peoples of Eastern Europe, it was the Magyars that Hilferding and Danilevskii least admired. There was practically nothing about the Magyars that merited grace, in the light of the Panslavist doctrine. Not only were the Magyars non-Slavs; they were not even Indo-Europeans. These Panslavists frankly regarded them as Asiatic interlopers whose usurpation of

[103] *Ibid.*, pp. 52-53.
[104] Danilevskii, *Rossiia i Evropa*, p. 442.
[105] *Ibid.*, p. 439.
[106] Fadieev, *Mnienie*, p. 52.

the Pannonian Plain had resulted in the separation of the Slavic peoples from one another. This was a historic crime for which the progeny of the Arpads now had to pay a price. Moreover, Hungary had been a bastion of Romanism and of feudalism for a millennium. Its culture and its orientation were Western. Its greatness had been achieved at the expense of several oppressed Slavic peoples. Thus Hungary was nothing less than an enemy in the camp.

Hilferding warned that, despite its geographic position, Hungary would find it impossible to stand in the way of Slavic unification. "God preserve the Magyars from the fruitless role of being a Chinese Wall in the midst of the Slavs, who have become conscious of their brotherhood and who aspire to unification!" he exclaimed. "If they [the Magyars] are not blind, then they must see that at the present time history is bringing with it the rebirth of the Slavic race in all its branches. . . . Woe to the Magyars, should they wish to interfere. The march of history has crushed better peoples."[107]

Danilevskii, too, offered the Magyars little encouragement. "Only for Hungary," he admitted without any qualms, "the prospect of a union which would put an end to its ambitious and highly presumptuous plans cannot be presented in a cheerful light; but even it can hope for the satisfaction of all of its valid claims. Only it would have to abandon its iniquitous lust for power."[108]

What was to be Russia's position in the Slavic union? Budilovich observed that a federation of states equal in power was "a fairly unwieldy form of political balance" which in any case did not correspond to the racial character of the Slavs.[109] Just as the ideal Slavic complex family centered its authority in the *starosta* or the paterfamilias, he contended, so the Slavic family of nations would be based on the patriarchal principle.

It is obvious that Russia's overwhelming preponderance over the other member states of the union in physical vastness, size of population, national wealth, political prestige, and military might would

[107] Hilferding, "Vengriia i Slaviane," *Sobranie sochinenii*, II, 142-43.
[108] Danilevskii, *Rossiia i Evropa*, p. 442.
[109] A. S. Budilovich, "Nieskol'ko zamiechanii o pol'skom voprosie s tochki zrieniia vseslavianstva," *Besieda*, VI (1871), 155.

have naturally militated against any real equality of power. Instead of attempting to conceal this fact, Danilevskii went rather out of his way to insist on Russian hegemony as a basic principle. "The position of the Slavs face to face with a West which is hostile to them," he declared, "is what makes us wish for them a very close federal tie under Russia's political leadership and hegemony, to which Russia has the most valid rights, both by its relative strength . . . and by its experience of many centuries."[110] The fact that of all the Slavic peoples, the Russians alone had been able to maintain their national independence and to establish "the mightiest state in the world," he argued, certainly gave Russia a clear claim to primacy within the Slavic family. He deplored the fact that "even many leading Slavic thinkers, men who are dedicated heart and soul to the Slavic cause, fear . . . Russia's ambition." Danilevskii chose to attribute this fear to two sources: ignorance of Russia and Polish libel.[111] What would Russia gain by seeking to destroy the autonomy of its confederates and by their annexation to the Russian Empire? "Instead of some forty million faithful, amicably disposed allies," Danilevskii pointed out, "it would gain forty million dissatisfied subjects."[112] Danilevskii offered the Russian past as the best guaranty that Russia would respect the integrity of its sister nations! He pointed to Russia's magnanimous treatment of Finland as proof, adding that Poland would have preserved the same privileges as Finland if it had not twice embarked on rebellion against Russia.[113] Danilevskii insisted that Russia's leadership would be not a threat but a source of material benefit to Russia's confederates. He described Russia's part in his proposed federation as being one of "nonintervention in the internal affairs of its associates, and an unbiased conciliatory influence in their own reciprocal relations in cases of disputes, claims, and ambitious inclinations."[114]

How was the Slavic federation as a whole to be organized, and what was to be the role of each member within it? General Fadieev

[110] Danilevskii, *Rossiia i Evropa*, p. 420.
[111] *Ibid.*, p. 443.
[112] *Ibid.*, p. 445.
[113] *Ibid.*, p. 448.
[114] *Ibid.*, p. 445.

wrote, "The independence of each member of the liberated family in its internal affairs, a separate ruler and separate political institutions, as may be most convenient to each—all this is already settled by history. But independence in international and military affairs is quite another matter. It is not enough to free oneself; one must remain free. In the present state of Europe there is no room for a heap of small folklings who dispose of their own small armies, declare war, make peace and alliances—each in its own name." Fadieev believed that the existence of separate, entirely independent small states in Eastern Europe would be made utterly impossible by the constant desire of their erstwhile masters to enslave them anew, and by continuing strife among them. The only solution, Fadieev warned, was a union with a common head, "the Tsar of Russia, the natural leader of all the Slavs and the Orthodox," who would be commander-in-chief of all the military forces of the union, and a common council which would conduct foreign relations.

As to the ruler of each member state, Fadieev, like Danilevskii, took for granted that each state would be a monarchy. He advised that inasmuch as personal relations between ruling families were still an important consideration in European politics, and since a variety of ruling dynasties within the union might shake its unity, each member should be ruled by a monarch to be chosen from the ruling dynasty of Russia.

He suggested further that the citizens of each member state should also enjoy all-union citizenship.[115]

No part of the Russian Panslavic scheme evoked such emotion in Fadieev, or in Danilevskii, as the claim to Constantinople or, as they called it, Tsargrad, as capital of the Slavic union. For Danilevskii there was no place on earth to equal this crossroads of the world. Thebes, Memphis, Babylon, Nineveh, Carthage—all these, he declared, were but archaeological curiosities. Even Rome, the Eternal City which twice ruled the world, Danilevskii wrote, had turned into a museum of rarities and the chief city of a mere peninsula. But Constantinople was so great a city, he boasted, as to have survived the fall of its own empire. Once known as

[115] Fadieev, *Mnienie*, pp. 92 ff.

Byzantium, Constantinople, and "momentarily" as Istanbul, Danilevskii predicted that this magnificent city would rise to a new glory as Tsargrad. Then Khomiakov's stirring prophecy would come true:

> And the domes of ancient Sophia
> In the new Byzantium
> Once more Christ's altar will enshrine!
> Fall down before it, Russian Tsar,
> And rise as Tsar of all the Slavs.[116]

In Danilevskii's federation, Constantinople and the surrounding territory were to form a district which was to be the capital of the entire union. He expressly denied any Greek claim to the city. The Eastern Roman Empire was dead—extinguished by the Goths, Lombards, Slavs, Latins, and Turks. Historic rights did not impress Danilevskii. If one took them seriously, then the Greeks could claim half the world, and the Mongols all of Russia. "All these crowns of Stephen, Jagiellon, Paleologos, are very worthy articles," he observed with callous irony, "as long as they lie in historical museums of antiquities where they can always evoke lofty thoughts concerning the deeds of the departed and the transitory nature of man's greatness." He regretted that the crowns of Suleiman and of the Hapsburgs "have not yet been laid in their graves and are still among the living, though they have long since begun to stink and to corrupt the political atmosphere with putrid miasmata. . . . Oh how the Slavic heart will leap when Russia assumes its historic mission and honorably buries these dead things."[117]

Danilevskii claimed that "in a strictly juridical sense" Constantinople was a *res nullius*, an object which belonged to no one. In a larger and loftier historical sense, he felt that the city should belong "to him who will continue to nurture within himself that idea which the Eastern Roman Empire had once served to realize." Danilevskii believed that Ivan, Peter, and Catherine were the true successors of Philip of Macedon and of Constantine the Great! Who else, he asked with sublime indifference to Turkish possession

---

[116] Cited by Danilevskii, *Rossiia i Evropa*, p. 398.
[117] *Ibid.*, p. 406.

and Greek ambition, could really claim the city? France and England had no stake in it except to keep it from Russia. He charged that this was the only reason why these two nations were supporting the Sublime Porte.[118] As another Panslavist, Michael Pogodin, had once remarked petulantly, "Russia is not to have any influence in Constantinople—that is dangerous for Europe. England —now that is a different matter, and Lord Redcliffe can dismiss and appoint ministers in Turkey, bind and loose the faithful, make loans, lay roads, and play the master."[119] To give this grandiose gift to small Greece seemed to Danilevskii like *lèse-majesté*. Constantinople in Greek hands would be but a Pandora's box of troubles, he prophesied. Like the poet Derzhavin, Danilevskii proposed:

> Let us give Athens back to the Athenians,
> And the city of Constantine—to Constantine!

Despite the poetry, Danilevskii did not seek Constantinople for sentimental value. He considered possession of the city a strategic necessity, in view of Russia's vulnerability in the south. Evidently recalling the Crimean campaign, Danilevskii complained that the city was Russia's "Achilles' heel," and only its inclusion in a Russian-led Slavic union would make Russia secure. He was also impressed by Constantinople's importance as a port—and not only out of mercantile considerations. He prophesied that with this city as a naval base, Russia would soon take its place among the greatest maritime powers in history. Finally, the city of Constantine was important to the Panslavist as the Second Rome, the home of the "Great Church," the center of Orthodox Christendom. Russian control over the Phanar, Danilevskii envisioned, would give his country vast influence in the Orthodox East and would give substance to Russia's role as the heir of the Byzantine Empire.[120]

Both Fadieev and Danilevskii agreed that Constantinople should not be annexed outright by Russia but should be the capital of the whole Slavic union. "The most positive interests of Russia render it desirable," Fadieev declared, "that that city, far more eternal than

[118] *Ibid.*

[119] M. P. Pogodin, "Vtoroe pis'mo k izdateliu gazety *Le Nord*," *Stat'i politicheskiia i Pol'skii vopros, 1856-1867* (Moscow, 1876), p. 27.

[120] Danilevskii, *Rossiia i Evropa*, pp. 409-16 *passim*.

Rome, should become the free city of a racial union."[121] Danilevskii similarly stated, "A Panslavic federation with Russia at the head, with the capital in Constantinople—this is the only reasonable, logical solution to the great historical problem which has in recent times received the name of the Eastern Question. . . . The non-inclusion of the capital on the Bosporus directly within the Russian state is dictated not only by the latter's private interests but also by fairness."[122] This was indeed a fine distinction. Certainly few Russians were aware of any such distinction when in 1877 the Pan-slavists were to make popular the slogan "Constantinople must be ours!"

VII

How was the Slavic federation to be achieved? For Danilevskii and Fadieev the answer was clear—war with the West. They did not mean a mere nonmilitary struggle for cultural supremacy, a Kulturkampf against the West, which had been the dominant theme in the late 1850's and early 1860's, but a full-fledged military encounter.

"Sooner or later, whether we like it or not," Danilevskii wrote in 1869, setting a keynote for the coming decade, "a struggle with Europe (or at least with its most significant part) over the Eastern Question, that is, over the freedom and independence of the Slavs, over the possession of Constantinople—over all that which in Europe's opinion is the object of Russia's illicit ambition, and which, for every Russian worthy of the name, is the irresistible demand of its historic calling—is inevitable."[123] Danilevskii expressly denied that the Panslavists were warmongers because they believed in the inevitability of war with the West. "Such a charge would be unjust," he protested. "We do not preach war—if for no other reason than that such preaching would be too ridiculous, coming from such weak sources; we assert, and not merely assert but demonstrate, that a struggle is inevitable, and we submit that

[121] Fadieev, *Mnienie*, p. 92.
[122] Danilevskii, *Rossiia i Evropa*, pp. 419-20.
[123] *Ibid.*, pp. 474-75.

although war is a very great evil, there is something far worse than war, something for which war can also serve as a cure, for 'man shall not live by bread alone.' "[124]

Also of the opinion that war with the West was inevitable, Fadieev found it impossible to conceive of such a war as a local one. "Not only for the professional soldier who knows his job," he asserted, "but for any man who weighs the circumstances, there can be no more obvious a truth than that the question which is usually called the Eastern Question cannot be solved by a local war limited to the Balkan Peninsula."[125] Indeed, he was convinced that the only way for Russia to reach the Balkans at all was over Austria's dead body. Thus he came to the conclusion in 1870— which was to be proved wrong seven years later—that before Russia could do anything about the Ottoman Empire, it would have to settle the problem which faced it on its own western borders. In any case, he stated, Russia would be opposed by Austria and its ally, Prussia, as well as by Britain and France.

And when Russia won this inevitable war and achieved the unification of the Slavs and the other peoples of Eastern Europe, what then? "The Panslavic union," Danilevskii prophesied, "would result not in world domination but in an equitable and just division of power and influence among those peoples or groups of peoples which can be considered the active protagonists of world history in the present period: Europe, Slavdom, and America."[126] He believed that once Slavdom was able to establish its own sphere, world peace could become a reality. A developing America and mighty Slavdom would hold in check the aggressive tendencies of Western Europe. *Et qui custodiet custodes?* Who would watch the watchers? That question never occurred to any Russian Panslavist.

[124] *Ibid.*, p. 475.
[125] *Fadieev, Mnienie,* p. 20.
[126] Danilevskii, *Rossiia i Evropa*, p. 463.

10

AN EVALUATION

A GREAT DEAL WAS MADE of the "Slavic Peril" in some segments of the Western press, particularly in Austrian and Magyar newspapers, after 1848. Confronted by the nationalist strivings of long-submerged Slavic peoples, as well as by Russian imperial ambitions, some European publicists and statesmen, who had reason to fear both phenomena, were quick to sound an alarm at any sign of what they so dreaded—an alliance between these two forces. To what extent especially Austrian and Magyar fears were genuine, and to what extent their alarms were meant to justify their own policies of repression and imperialism, is an open question. Nevertheless, there was a general tendency in Europe to overestimate the appeal of the Panslavic idea and certainly the bond between Russia and the other Slavs.

An examination of Russian Panslavism in the decade and a half following the Crimean War shows that while this movement was potentially dangerous, it was actually not a strong force in this period.

The vast majority of the Russian people consisted of a politically inert mass of recently liberated serfs. Despite any latent sympathies which they might have had for their fellow Slavs abroad, especially for their Balkan coreligionists, the Russian peasants were not asked in this period to support the Panslavic movement, nor did they volunteer any support.[1]

The Russian government was initially hostile to Panslavism, in the reign of Nicholas I. Under Alexander II a few officials, particu-

---

[1] Professor A. N. Pypin, an informed and critical observer of Russian Panslavism in this period, argued that Panslavic tendencies could not properly be attributed to the Russian peasantry, and that their sympathies for the Balkan Slavs were religious rather than ethnic in character. Thus Russian peasants sympathized with the Balkan Slavs, Pypin alleged, not because the latter were Slavs, but because they were Orthodox; the Russian peasants hated the Roman Catholic Poles even though the latter were Slavs. See A. N. Pypin, *Panslavizm v proshlom i nastoiashchem* (St. Petersburg, 1913), p. 65.

larly in the Ministries of Foreign Affairs and Public Education, began to show interest in the Panslavic idea as a possible instrument of Russian foreign policy. This was more than offset by the hostility shown to Panslavism by many other officials concerned. While some foreigners were inclined to ascribe Panslavist designs to Russian foreign policy, various Russian Panslavists found it necessary repeatedly to decry their government's reluctance to espouse the Slavic cause. In the period from 1856 to 1870, Count Ignatiev's efforts notwithstanding, Russian foreign policy was not determined by Panslavism. It continued to rely on cooperation with both Austria and Prussia and to seek a *modus vivendi* within the Concert of Europe.

The Russian bureaucracy, the intelligentsia, and the upper and middle classes in general were on the whole indifferent to the Panslavic cause, though the Panslavic press and such activities as the Moscow Slav Congress of 1867 served to keep the Slavic Question before a part of the public. Post-Crimean Russia had many other and more essential problems to think about—notably the Great Reforms. Russian nationalist aspirations found an outlet at the time in the Caucasus and in Central Asia. Russian bureaucrats and intellectuals were generally faced with the choice of conforming to the official line or else of taking up with the liberals or radicals. In any case, these camps were either not much concerned with Panslavism or else hostile to it. The Slavic Benevolent Committees had only a small membership in this period. Though they were strictly limited to philanthropic and cultural activities, their resources were still too meager to meet even this obligation.

As for the non-Russian Slavs, some were enticed by the vision of their liberation through Russian physical might. Very few, however, felt attracted to the Russian Panslavist ideology—for some compelling reasons. There was the fundamental difficulty that the modern Slavs did not belong to a cultural unit but differed from one another markedly in religion, social organization, and intellectual orientation. Russian Panslavists attached vast importance to Orthodoxy as a faith peculiarly consonant with the Slavic way of life; yet the majority of non-Russian Slavs had long historic ties and often deep emotional identification with Catholicism, Protestantism, and even Islam. Russian Panslavists urged the non-Russian Slavs to shun a "rotting West"; yet a still backward Russia could have relatively little attraction for Western-minded Slavs. This is precisely why Russian Panslavists such as Ivan Aksakov attached so much importance to Russia's own regeneration as a prerequisite to a Slavic union; they felt the need to offer the non-Russian Slavs an attraction that would compete successfully with the West.

Another obstacle to Slavic unification was Slavic particularism. Russian Panslavists took on the difficult task of asking the non-Russian Slavs to submerge their own national identities in a larger ethnic union. The non-Russian Slavs who attended the Moscow Slav Congress of 1867 showed that, all their speeches and toasts notwithstanding, each group had come largely to gain something for its own national movement, and not to give up anything.

Where the non-Russian Slavs had their own movements of unification, each differed substantially from Russian Panslavism.[2] Polish Messianism, Czech and Slovak Austro-Slavism, Yugoslav Illyrianism, and Ukrainian Slavic Federalism all excluded autocratic Russia from their plans.[3] Whereas they envisaged regional federal groupings, Russian Panslavism was based on a historic imperial idea. While the former movements were based on reciprocity and mutual equality, Russian Panslavism insisted on conformity to the Russian way of life and on Russian hegemony within the Slavic union.[4]

There was more than a streak of Great Russianism in Russian Panslavism from the beginning, and this tendency grew stronger as

---

[2] For a discussion of non-Russian Slavic movements of unification, see especially Hans Kohn, *Pan-Slavism; Its History and Ideology* (University of Notre Dame Press, 1953), and Alfred Fischel, *Der Panslawismus bis zum Weltkrieg* (Stuttgart and Berlin, 1919).

[3] As Foreign Minister Gorchakov wrote to Novikov on May 9, 1872 (according to notes made from the archives of the Imperial Russian Embassy in London by Baron A. F. Meyendorff): "Je ne vous dissimule pas qu'il m'est difficile de croire à une sympathie sincère des races Slaves pour la *Russie Autocratique*." Cited by B. H. Sumner, "Russia and Panslavism in the Eighteen Seventies," *Transactions of the Royal Historical Society*, Fourth Series, XVIII (1935), 39.

[4] Note Hugh Seton-Watson's discussion in his *The Decline of Imperial Russia, 1855-1914* (London, 1952), p. 91, of the parallel which he sees between Greater Germanism, Lesser Germanism, and Pangerman Imperialism on the one hand, and Greater Slavdom, Lesser Slavdom, and Russo-Panslav Imperialism on the other.

the movement developed.[5] The Russian Panslavist ideology held as a basic tenet that it was the special vocation of the Great Russian people to liberate the other Slavs and to unite them under the aegis of the Tsar. Though Russian Panslavists deplored the inroads of Westernism in the Russian government and higher levels of Russian society, they nevertheless maintained that, of all the Slavs, it was the Russian people which had best preserved the "Slavic way of life." Accordingly they judged the non-Russian Slavs by the degree to which the institutions of these ethnic kinsmen resembled those of the Great Russian people. In the 1850's and early 1860's Russian Panslavists emphasized Russian cultural hegemony. This emphasis was especially apparent in the proposal that the non-Russian Slavs accept the Great Russian language as an all-Slavic tongue. After 1867, and particularly with the publication of Danilevskii's and Fadieev's works, Russian Panslavism became dominated by the idea that the Great Russian people, with its dynasty, was the natural leader of a future Slavic political union.

Various Russian Panslavists denied that they wished to Russify the non-Russian Slavs (though they regarded as justified the Russification of the White Russians and the Ukrainians, whom they considered fellow nationals). It is equally true that various Russian Panslavists opposed the political absorption of the non-Russian Slavs into the Russian Empire and the annexation of their lands by Russia. One need not doubt the sincerity of these disavowals in order to conclude, nevertheless, that the realization of the Russian Panslavic cultural and political program would in fact have inevitably led to the increasing Russification of the non-Russian Slavs and, to a possibly lesser degree, of the non-Slavs within a Slavic federation as well. This was a prospect which few non-Russian Slavs could find enticing.

Though all these difficulties prevented Russian Panslavism from exhibiting much strength from 1856 to 1870, nevertheless the movement had political significance. In these years a small group of

[5] As B. H. Sumner observed, "What had begun as the religious and intellectual strivings of small coteries of Muscovite landowners ended by being transformed into crude appeals to nationalist mass-emotions." See his "Russia and Panslavism in the Eighteen-Seventies," *Transactions of the Royal Historical Society*, Fourth Series, XVIII (1935), 26.

Panslavists established a political ideology which bore great potential strength. Though its political program was very sketchy, Russian Panslavism offered a mystique which could appeal to Russian national pride—a pride that had been wounded at Crimea and exacerbated by German and Italian unification. Given the right moment, a clarion call in the name of a God-given historic mission might arouse millions of Russians. That this moment actually came in 1877 rather than in 1867 was due to the situation in Europe, not to the aspirations of the Russian Panslavists. In the period from 1856 to 1870, Panslavism was building up a program designed to take maximum advantage of just such a crisis. Meanwhile, it served as "a sounding-board of the new, restless Russian nationalism."[6] By its very existence an increasingly aggressive Russian Panslavism was bound to have political repercussions in the set of circumstances which plagued the eastern half of Europe in a generation of national awakening and unrest.

[6] *Ibid.*, p. 51.

BIBLIOGRAPHY

"A." "Vopros o natsional'nosti i panslavizmie" (The Question of Nationality and and Panslavism), *Sovremennik* (March, 1864), pp. 81-113.

Aksakov, Constantine S. "Eshche nieskol'ko slov o russkom vozzrienii" (A Few More Words on the Russian Point of View), *Russkaia Besieda*, II (1856), 139-47.

—— ("K. A.") "O russkom vozzrienii" (On the Russian Point of View), *Russkaia Besieda*, I (1856), 84-86.

—— Polnoe sobranie sochinenii (Complete Collected Works). Vol. I: Sochineniia istoricheskiia (Historical Works). Moscow, 1889.

Aksakov, Ivan S. Ivan Sergieevich Aksakov v ego pis'makh (Ivan Sergieevich Aksakov in His Letters). 4 vols. Moscow, 1892.

—— "Pis'mo k grafinie A. D. Bludovoi" (Letter to Countess A. D. Bludova), *Russkii Arkhiv*, VI (1915), 129-33.

—— "Riech' o A. F. Gil'ferdingie" (Address on A. F. Hilferding), in Sochineniia (Works), Vol. III: Obshcheevropeiskaia politika, 1860-1886 (General European Politics, 1860-1886). Moscow, 1887. Pp. 789-90.

—— Sochineniia (Works). Vol. I: Slavianskii vopros, 1860-1886 (The Slavic Question, 1860-1886). St. Petersburg, 1891.

—— Sochineniia (Works). Vol. II: Slavianofil'stvo i zapadnichestvo, 1860-1886 (Slavophilism and Westernism, 1860-1886). St. Petersburg, 1891.

—— Sochineniia (Works). Vol. III: Pol'skii vopros i zapadno russkoe dielo; Evreiskii vopros, 1860-1886 (The Polish Question and the West-Russian Cause; the Jewish Question, 1860-1886). Moscow, 1887.

—— Sochineniia (Works). Vol. VII: Obshcheevropeiskaia politika, 1860-1886 (General European Politics, 1860-1886). Moscow, 1887.

Allen, W. E. D. The Ukraine. Cambridge University Press, 1941.

Arseniev, K. "Russkie zakony o pechati" (Russian Laws on the Press), *Viestnik Evropy* (April, 1869), pp. 794-811.

"B., A." "O mierakh dlia rasprostraneniia v Rossii sviedienii o slavianstvie" (On Measures Taken to Spread Information in Russia about the Slavs), *Grazhdanin*, IV (1872), 132-36.

B—v, Il. "O perevodie evangeliia na malorossiiskoe nariechie" (On the Translation of the Gospel into the Little Russian Dialect), *Den'*, No. 52 (December 29, 1862), p. 19.

Barsov, N. Slavianskii vopros i ego otnoshenie k religii (The Slavic Question and Its Relation to Religion). Vilna, 1867.

Barsukov, N. P. Zhizn' i trudy M. P. Pogodina (The Life and Works of M. P. Pogodin). 20 vols. St. Petersburg, 1905.

Baudouin de Courtenay, I. A. "Nieskol'ko slov po povodu 'Obshcheslavianskoi azbuki'" (A Few Words regarding an "All-Slavic Alphabet"), *Zhurnal Ministerstva Narodnago Prosvieshcheniia* (May, 1871), pp. 149-95.

Beneš, Edvard. "Problemy slovanské politiky" (Problems of Slavic Policy), *Slovanský Přehled*, Vol. XVII (1929).

—— Úvahy o slovanstvi (Essays on Slavdom). London, n.d.

Bérard, Victor. L'Empire russe et le tsarisme. Paris, 1905.

Berdyaev, Nicolas. The Russian Idea. New York, 1948.

Bestuzhev-Riumin, K. N. "Slavianofil'skoe uchenie i ego sud'by v russkoi literature" (The Slavophile Teaching and Its Destinies in Russian Literature),
Otechestvennyia Zapiski (1862), Book 2, pp. 679-719; Book 3, pp. 26-58;
(1865), Book 5, pp. 1-23.

—— "Teoriia kul'turno-istoricheskikh tipov" (The Theory of Cultural-Historical
Types), in N. Ia. Danilevskii, Rossiia i Evropa. 5th ed., appendix. St. Petersburg, 1895.

Bezsonov, P. "V pamiat' Pervouchitelei Slavianstva" (To the Memory of the
Protopraeceptors of the Slavs), *Den'*, Nos. 24-27 (June and July, 1863).

Bidlo, Jaroslav. Dějiny Ruska v devetnáctém století (The History of Russia in
the Nineteenth Century). Vol. II. Prague, 1908.

Bielozerskii, N. A. I. Gertsen, slavianofily i zapadniki (A. I. Herzen, the Slavophiles, and the Westernizers). St. Petersburg, 1905.

Bobchev, Nikola. "Slavianofilskoto dvizhenie v Rusiia i novobŭlgarskoto obrazovanie," in Proslava na osvoboditelnata voina 1877-1878 g. (Anniversary of the
War of Liberation of 1877-1878). Slavianskoto Druzhestvo v Bulgariia. Sofia,
1929.

Boborykin, P. D. "Na slavianskom rasput'ie" (At the Slavic Crossroads), *Otechestvennyia Zapiski* (1878), IV, 193-222; VI, 172-205; VII, 1-24.

Bratiam slavianam; stikhotvoreniia Aksakova, Berga, kn. Viazemskago, Tiutcheva
i Khomiakova (To the Brother Slavs; the Poems of Aksakov, Berg, Prince
Viazemskii, Tiutchev, and Khomiakov). Moscow, 1867.

Braun, Jerzy. "Die slavische messianistische Philosophie als Entwicklung und
Vollendung der deutschen philosophischen Systeme Kants und seine Nach-
folger," *Germanoslavica*, III (1935), 291-315.

Brodskii, N. L. Rannie slavianofily (The Early Slavophiles). Moscow, 1910.

Budilovich, A. S. "Ian Kollar i zapadnoe slavianofil'stvo" (Ján Kollár and Western
Slavophilism), *Slavianskoe Obozrenie*, II (1894), 1-14.

—— "Mechta-li panslavizm?" (Is Panslavism a Chimera?), *Besieda*, I (1872),
195-215.

—— "Nieskol'ko zamiechanii ob izuchenii slavianskago mira" (A Few Observations on the Study of the Slavic World), *Slavianskii Sbornik*, II (1878), 1-54.

—— "Nieskol'ko zamiechanii o pol'skom voprosie s tochki zrieniia veslavianstva"
(A Few Words on the Polish Question from the Panslavic Point of View),
Besieda, VI (1871), 146-64.

—— "O literaturnom edinstvie narodov Slavianskago plemeni" (On the Literary
Unity of the Peoples of the Slavic Race), *Slavianskii Sbornik*, II (1877),
Part III, 1-15.

—— "O sovremennom polozhenii i vzaimnikh otnosheniiakh slavian zapadnykh
i iuzhnykh" (On the Contemporary Position and Mutual Relations of the
Western and Southern Slavs), *Slavianskii Sbornik*, I (1875), 585-604.

—— "Slavianskiia matitsy i uchenyia druzhstva" (Slavic Maticas and Learned
Societies), *Zhurnal Ministerstva Narodnago Prosvieshcheniia*, CXLI (1869),
459-75.

Bulgarian Academy of Sciences. Arkhiv na Naiden Gerov, 1857-1870 (The Naiden
Gerov Papers, 1857-1870). Edited by M. G. Popruzhenko and T. Panchev.
Vol. I of Dokumenti za bŭlgarskata istoriia (Documents for Bulgarian His-
tory). Sofia, 1931.

—— Arkhiv na Naiden Gerov, 1871-1876 (The Naiden Gerov Papers, 1871-1876).
Edited by M. G. Popruzhenko and T. Panchev. Vol. II of Dokumenti za
bŭlgarskata istoriia (Documents for Bulgarian History). Sofia, 1932.

Carr, E. H. Michael Bakunin. London, 1937.
Cherkasskii, V. A. "Dva slova po povodu Vostochnago Voprosa" (Two Words regarding the Eastern Question), *Russkaia Besieda*, IV (1858), 65-92.
Clementis, Vlado. "Panslavism" Past and Present. London, 1943.
Coleman, A. P. "Poland under Alexander II: The Insurrection of 1863," in Cambridge History of Poland. Edited by W. F. Reddaway, J. H. Penson, O. Halecki, and R. Dyboski. Cambridge University Press, 1941. Vol. II, pp. 365-86.
D., D. "Panslavizm i Liudevit Shtur" (Panslavism and L'udovít Štúr), *Otechestvennyia Zapiski* (1867), CLXXII, No. 11, 565-80; CLXXIII, No. 13, 49-77.
Daničić, Djuro. Sitniji spisi Dj. Daničića (The Lesser Works of Dj. Daničić). Srpska Kraljevska Akademija: Posebna izdanja, Vol. LIV (1925).
Danilevskii, N. Ia. Rossiia i Evropa; vzgliad na kul'turnyia i politicheskiia otnosheniia slavianskago mira k germano-romanskomu (Russia and Europe; a Study of the Cultural and Political Relations of the Slavic to the Germano-Roman World). 5th ed. St. Petersburg, 1895.
—— Russland und Europa; eine Untersuchung über die kulturellen und politischen Beziehungen der slawischen zur germanisch-romanischen Welt. Translated by Karl Nötzel. Stuttgart and Berlin, 1920.
Daskalov, Kh. "Vozrozhdenie Bolgar ili reaktsiia v evropeiskoi Turtsii" (The Renascence of the Bulgars or the Reaction in European Turkey), *Russkaia Besieda*, II (1858), Smies, 1-58.
Deckert, Emil. Panlatinismus, Panslawismus und Panteutonismus. Frankfurt, 1914.
Dementiev, A. G. Ocherki po istorii russkoi zhurnalistiki, 1840-1850 gg. (Outlines on the History of Russian Journalism, 1840-1850). Moscow and Leningrad, 1951.
Denis, Arnošt (Ernest). Čechy po Bilé Hoře (The Czechs after White Mountain). Vol. II. Prague, 1931.
"Die Idee des Panslavismus verwirklicht durch eine allgemeine slavische Sprache," *Magazin für die Literatur des Auslandes*, CCVII (July-December, 1867), 499-501.
Dmitriev, A. "Slavianofily i slavianofil'stvo" (Slavophiles and Slavophilism), *Istorik-Marksist*, LXXXIX (1940), 85-97.
Dmitriev-Mamonov, E. A. "Slavianofily" (The Slavophiles), *Russkii Arkhiv* (1873), pp. 2488-508.
Dorn, N. Kirieevskii; opyt kharakteristiki ucheniia i lichnosti (Kirieevskii; a Descriptive Essay on His Teachings and Personality). Paris, 1938.
Doroshenko, Dmitro. History of the Ukraine. Translated and abridged by Hanna Chikalenko-Keller. Alberta, Canada, 1939.
Dranitsyn, S. N. Pol'skoe vosstanie 1863 g. i ego klassovaia sushchnost' (The Polish Insurrection of 1863 and Its Class Content). Leningrad, 1937.
Druzhinin, N. M. (ed.) Slavianskii Sbornik; Slavianskii vopros i russkoe obshchestvo v 1867-1878 godakh (Slavic Review; the Slavic Question and Russian Society in the Years 1867-1878). Moscow, 1948.
Eckhardt, Julius von. Russia before and after the War. New York, 1880.
Fadieev, R. A. Mnienie o vostochnom voprosie (Opinion on the Eastern Question). St. Petersburg, 1870.
—— O istočnom pitanju (On the Eastern Question). Belgrade, 1870.
—— Opinion on the Eastern Question. Translated by T. Michell. London, 1871; 2d ed., London, 1876.
—— O zaležitostech vychodní a slovanské (Of Eastern and Slavic Affairs). Prague, 1870.
Fadner, Frank. "Development of Pan-Slavist Thought from Karazin to Danilevskii,

1800-1870." Unpublished Ph.D. dissertation, London School of Slavonic Studies, 1949.

Feldman, J. "The Polish Provinces of Austria and Prussia after 1815; the 'Springtime of Nations,'" in Cambridge History of Poland. Edited by W. F. Reddaway, J. H. Penson, O. Halecki, and R. Dyboski. Cambridge University Press, 1941. Vol. II, pp. 336-64.

Filevich, I. P. "I. S. Aksakov i pol'skii vopros" (I. S. Aksakov and the Polish Question), *Otchët S.-Peterburgskago Slavianskago blagotvoritel'nago obshchestva* (1887), pp. 192-97.

Fischel, Alfred. Der Panslawismus bis zum Weltkrieg. Stuttgart and Berlin, 1919.

Florovsky, Anton. "Historical Premonitions of Tyutchev," *Slavonic Review*, III (1923), 346.

Francev, V. A. "Ohlasy Kollárovy rozpravy 'O literární vzájemnosti' v ruské literatuře let třicatých a čtyřicátých" (Repercussions of Kollár's Discussion "On Literary Reciprocity" in the Russian Literature of the Thirties and the Forties), in Slovanská vzajemnost, 1836-1936. Edited by Jiří Horák. Prague, 1938.

Frič, Josef V. Rub a líc té slovanské výpravy na Rus (The Ins and Outs of That Slavic Affair in Russia). Prague, 1867.

Geisman, P. A. Slavianskii krestovyi pokhod; po sluchaiu 25-lietiia so vremeni nachala voiny 1877-1878 (The Slavic Crusade; on the Occasion of the Twenty-fifth Anniversary of the Beginning of the War of 1877-1878). St. Petersburg, 1902.

Gershenzon, M. Istoricheskie zapiski (Historical Notes). 2d ed. Berlin, 1923.

Gertsen, A. I. *See under* Herzen.

Ghikas G. Botschafter von Novikow über den Panslavismus und die Orientalische Frage. Vienna and Leipzig, 1907.

Gil'ferding, A. F. *See under* Hilferding.

Giliarov-Platonov. "Moskva, 2-go avgusta (1867)," included by error in I. S. Aksakov, Sochineniia, Vol. I. Moscow, 1886. Pp. 159-65.

Ginsburg, R. A. Jan Kollar; a Poet of Panslavism. Chicago, 1942.

Giusti, Wolfgango. Il Panslavismo. Milan, 1941.

Goriainov, Serge. La Question d'Orient à la veille du Traité de Berlin, 1870-1876. Paris, 1948.

Gradovskii, A. D. Sobranie sochinenii (Collected Works). Vol. VI. St. Petersburg, 1901.

Gradovskii, G. K. "Arkhistratig slavianskoi rati" (The Archstrategist of the Slavic War), *Obrazovanie*, I (1909), 115-25.

—— "Retsidiv slavianofil'stva" (The Return of Slavophilism), *Obrazovanie*, III (1909), 55-76.

Graham, Stephen. Tsar of Freedom; the Life and Reign of Alexander II. New Haven, 1935.

Gratieux, A. A. S. Khomiakov; la pensée. Paris, 1939.

Grekov, B. D. (ed.) Dokumenty k istorii slavianovedeniia v Rossii, 1850-1912 (Documents concerning the History of Slavic Studies in Russia, 1850-1912). Moscow and Leningrad, 1948.

Grot, K. Ia. Ob izuchenii Slavianstva (On the Study of the Slavs). St. Petersburg, 1901.

Halecki, O. A History of Poland. New York, 1943.

Haumant, Émile. La Culture française en Russie, 1700-1900. Paris, 1913.

Heidenreich, Julius (Dolanský). Ruské základy srbského realismu (The Russian Foundations of Serbian Realism). Prague, 1933.

Herceg, Jakša. Ilirizam (Illyrianism). Belgrade, 1935.

Herzen, A. I. My Past and Thoughts; the Memoirs of Alexander Herzen. Translated by Constance Garnett. New York, 1924.
—— Polnoe sobranie sochinenii i pisem (Complete Collected Works and Letters). Edited by M. K. Lemke. Vol. XVI. St. Petersburg, 1920.
Hilferding, A. F. Chiem podderzhivaetsia pravoslavnaia viera u iuzhnykh slavian? (What is Maintaining the Orthodox Faith among the South Slavs?). Moscow, 1861.
—— "Drevnieishii period istorii Slavian" (The Most Ancient Period in the History of the Slavs), *Viestnik Evropy*, IV (1868), 223-77.
—— "Narodnoe vozrozhdenie Serbov-Luzhichan v Saksonii" (The National Awakening of the Lusatian Serbs in Saxony), *Russkaia Besieda*, I (1856), Smies, 1-35.
—— Obshcheslavianskaia azbuka s prilozheniem obraztsov slavianskikh nariechii (An All-Slavic Alphabet with an Appendix of Specimens of Slavic Dialects). St. Petersburg, 1871.
—— "O vseslavianskom slovaria g. Shumavskago" (On the All-Slavic Dictionary by Mr. Shumavskii), *Russkaia Besieda*, I (1857), 94-96.
—— "Pis'mo k g. Rigeru v Pragu" (Letter to Mr. Rieger in Prague), *Den'*, No. 18 (May 4, 1863), pp. 14-17.
—— Sobranie sochinenii (Collected Works). Vol. II: Stat'i po sovremennym voprosam slavianskim (Articles on Contemporary Slavic Questions). St. Petersburg, 1868.
—— Sobranie sochinenii (Collected Works). Vol. IV: Istoriia Baltiiskikh Slavian (History of the Baltic Slavs). St. Petersburg, 1874.
—— "V chem iskat' razriesheniia Pol'skomu voprosu?" (Where Can One Find a Solution to the Polish Question?), *Den'*, No. 32 (August 10, 1863), pp. 4-10.
Horák, Jiří. Z dějin literatur slovanských (From the History of Slavic Literatures). Prague, 1948.
Ignatiev, N. P. "Zapiski Grafa N. P. Ignatieva, 1864-1874" (The Memoirs of Count N. P. Ignatiev, 1864-1874), *Izviestiia Ministerstva inostrannykh diel*, I (1914), 93-135.
Istomin, F. M. Kratkii ocherk dieiatelnosti S.-Peterburgskago Slavianskago Blagotvoritel'nago Obshchestva za 25 liet ego sushchestvovaniia, 1868-1893 (A Short Outline of the Work of the St. Petersburg Slavic Benevolent Society during Twenty-five Years of Its Existence, 1868-1893). St. Petersburg, 1893.
Iuriev, S. A. "V chem nasha zadacha?" (Wherein Lies Our Task?), *Besieda*, I (1871), 81.
Ivanov-Razumnik, R. V. Istoriia russkoi obshchestvennoi mysli (The History of Russian Social Thought). Vol. I. St. Petersburg, 1908.
"Izvlechenie iz otchetov o dieiatel'nosti Slavianskago Obshchestva v techenie pervago dvadsatipiatilietiia ego sushchestvovaniia (1868-1893 gg.)" (Extract from Reports on the Work of the Slavic Society during the First Quarter-Century of Its Existence, 1868-1893), *Otchët 1883*. Title page missing.
Jagić, V. I. (Iagich). Istoriia Slavianskoi filologii (The History of Slavic Philology). St. Petersburg, 1910.
Jirásek, Josef. Rusko a my; dějiny vztahů česko-slovensko-ruských od nejstarších dob až do roku 1914 (Russia and We; the History of Czechoslovak-Russian Relations from Earliest Times to the Year 1914). 2d ed. 4 vols. Brno, 1946.
Jovanović, Slobodan. Vlada Aleksandra Obrenovića (The Reign of Alexander Obrenović). Belgrade, 1936.
—— Vlada Miloša i Mihajla (The Reign of Miloš and Michael). Belgrade, 1933.
K., M. "K sviedieniiam ob ukraino-slavianskom obshchestvie" (Some Facts on the Ukrainian Slavic Society), *Russkii Arkhiv*, VII (1893), 399-406.

Karazin, V. N. Sochineniia, pis'ma i bumagi V. N. Karazina (The Works, Letters, and Papers of V. N. Karazin). Kharkov, 1910.

Katkov, M. N. "Moskva, 12-go maia (1867)" (Moscow, May 12, 1867), *Moskovskiia Viedomosti,* CIV (1867), 242-45.

—— "Moskva, 23-go maia (1867)" (Moscow, May 23, 1867), *Moskovskiia Viedomosti,* CXIII (1867), 265-67.

Katsainos, C. T. "The Theory and Practise of Russian Panslavism." Ph.D. dissertation submitted to Georgetown University, Washington, 1950.

Kavelin, K. D. "Moskovskie slavianofily sorokovykh godov" (The Moscow Slavophiles of the Forties), in his Sobranie sochinenii, Vol. III. St. Petersburg, 1904. Pp. 1133-166.

Kazbunda, Karel. Pout' čechů do Moskvy 1867 a rakouská diplomacie (The Pilgrimage of the Czechs to Moscow in 1867 and Austrian Diplomacy). No. 1 of the Publications of the Archives of the Foreign Office. Prague, 1924.

Khomiakov, A. S. "K Serbam poslanie iz Moskvy" (An Epistle from Moscow to the Serbs), *Russkii Arkhiv,* III (1876), 104-27.

—— "Pis'ma A. S. Khomiakova" (The Letters of A. S. Khomiakov), *Russkii Arkhiv,* XI (1879), 276-362.

—— Polnoe sobranie sochinenii (Complete Collected Works). Edited by I. S. Aksakov. Moscow, 1861.

—— Polnoe sobranie sochinenii Aleksieia Stepanovicha Khomiakova (Complete Collected Works of Aleksiei Stepanovich Khomiakov). 3d enl. ed. Moscow, 1900.

—— Srbima poslanica iz Moskve (An Epistle from Moscow to the Serbs). Srpska Kraljevska Akademija: Posebna izdanja, Vol. LIV. Sremski Karlovci, 1925. Pp. 266-89.

Kirieevskii, Ivan V. Polnoe sobranie sochinenii I. V. Kirieevskago (Complete Collected Works of I. V. Kirieevskii). 2 vols. Moscow, 1911.

Kizevetter, A. "Slovanská otázka u děkabristů" (The Slavic Question among the Decembrists), in Z dějin východní Evropy a Slovanstva; Sborník věnovaný Jaroslavu Bidlovi. Prague, 1929. Pp. 376-79.

Klaczko, J. "Le Congrès de Moscou et la propagande panslaviste," *Revue des Deux Mondes,* XXXVII (1867), reprint.

Kniazev, G. "Slavianskii 'vostochnyi' vopros v opredielenii V. I. Lamanskago" (The Slavic "Eastern" Question as Defined by V. I. Lamanskii), *Zhurnal Ministerstva Narodnago Prosvieshcheniia,* September, 1916, pp. 1-26; October, 1916, pp. 45-69; November, 1916, pp. 1-34; December, 1916, pp. 50-101.

Kochubinskii, A. My i oni (1711-1878); Ocherki istorii i politiki slavian (We and They [1711-1878]; Outlines of the History and Politics of the Slavs). Odessa, 1878.

Kohn, Hans. The Idea of Nationalism; a Study in Its Origins and Background. New York, 1944.

—— "Pan-Movements," in Encyclopaedia of the Social Sciences. Vol. XI. New York, 1933. Pp. 544-53.

—— Pan-Slavism; Its History and Ideology. University of Notre Dame Press, 1953.

—— The Twentieth Century. New York, 1949.

Koialovich, M. I. Istoriia russkago samosoznaniia (The History of Russian Self-Consciousness). St. Petersburg, 1893.

Korablev, V. N. "Liudevit Gai; k 60-letiiu so dnia ego smerti" (Ljudevit Gaj; on the Sixtieth Anniversary of His Death), *Trudy Instituta slavianovedeniia Akademii nauk SSSR,* Vol. II. Leningrad, 1934. Pp. 247-60.

—— "Valtasar Bogishich i akademik Lamanskii" (Baltazar Bogišić and Academician

Lamanskii), *Trudy Instituta slavianovedenii Akademii nauk SSSR*, Vol. II. Leningrad, 1934. Pp. 163-87.
Kornilov, A. A. Modern Russian History. Rev. ed. New York, 1943.
—— Obshchestvennoe dvizhenie pri Aleksandrie II, 1855-1881 (Social Movements under Alexander II, 1855-1881). Moscow, 1909.
Koshelëv, A. I. "Shest' nediel' v avstriiskikh slavianskikh zemliakh" (Six Weeks in the Austrian Slavic Lands), *Russkaia Besieda*, IV, Part 2 (1857), 1-18.
—— "Vospominaniia ob A. S. Khomiakove" (Reminiscences of A. S. Khomiakov), *Russkii Arkhiv*, XI (1879), 265-76.
—— Zapiski (Memoirs). Berlin, 1884.
Kostomarov, N. I. "Avtobiografiia Nikolaia Ivanovicha Kostomarova" (Autobiography of Nikolai Ivanovich Kostomarov), *Russkaia Mysl'*, V (1885), 190-223; VI (1885), 20-54.
—— "O federativnom nachalie v drevnei Rusi" (On the Federative Principle in Ancient Russia), *Osnova*, I (1861), 121-58.
—— "Otviet Moskovskim Viedomostiam" (A Reply to the Moscow News), *Den'*, No. 27 (July 6, 1863), pp. 18-19.
—— "Pravda Moskvicham o Rusi" (The Truth to the Muscovites about Russia), *Osnova*, X (1861), 1-15.
—— "Pravda Poliakam o Rusi" (The Truth to the Poles about Russia), *Osnova*, X (1861), 100-112.
Koyré, Alexandre. La Philosophie et le problème national en Russie au début du XIXe siècle. Paris, 1929.
"K prebyvaniiu kniaza Chernogorskago v Moskvie" (On the Stay of the Prince of Montenegro in Moscow), *Russkii*, No. 137 (January 31, 1869), p. 2.
Kucharzewski, Jan. The Origins of Modern Russia. New York, 1948.
Kulish, P. "Ob otnoshenii malorossiiskoi slovesnosti k obshche-russkoi" (On the Relation of Little Russian Literature to General Russian Literature), *Russkaia Besieda*, III (1857), 123-45.
Lamanskii, V. I. "Izuchenie Slavianstva i russkoe narodnoe samosoznanie" (The Study of the Slavs and Russian National Self-Realization), *Zhurnal Ministerstva Narodnago Prosvieshcheniia* (January, 1867), pp. 116-53.
—— "Natsional'naia beztaktnost' " (National Tactlessness), *Den'*, No. 2 (October 21, 1861), pp. 14-19.
—— Natsional'nost' italianskaia i slavianskaia v politicheskom i literaturnom otnosheniiakh (The Italian and the Slavic Nationalities in Their Political and Literary Relations). St. Petersburg, 1865.
—— "Nieskol'ko slov ob otnosheniiakh russkikh k Grekam" (A Few Words on Russian Relations with the Greeks), *Russkaia Besieda*, IV (1858), Smies, 103-40.
—— Ob istoricheskom izuchenii Greko-slavianskago mira v Evropie (On the Historical Study of the Greco-Slavic World in Europe). St. Petersburg, 1871.
—— "Rasprostranenie russkago iazyka u zapadnykh Slavian" (The Spread of the Russian Language among the Western Slavs), *Zhurnal Ministerstva Narodnago Prosvieshcheniia*, CXXXIX (June, 1867), 441-47. (Signed "V. L.")
—— "Rossiia uzhe tiem polezna Slavianam chto ona sushchestvuet" (Russia Is Useful to the Slavs Simply by Its Existence), in Bratskaia pomoch' postradavshim semeistvam Bosnii i Gertsegoviny. St. Petersburg, 1876. Pp. 10-33.
—— "Vstupitel'noe chtenie Dotsenta Peterburgskago universiteta V. I. Lamanskago" (Inaugural Lecture by V. I. Lamanskii, Instructor at the University of St. Petersburg), *Den'*, Nos. 50-51 (December 11 and December 18, 1865).
Lednicki, W. "Panslavism," in Feliks Gross (ed.), European Ideologies. New York, 1948. Pp. 808-912.

Lednicki, W. (*Continued*)
— "Poland and the Slavophil Idea," *Slavonic and East European Review*, VII (1928), 128-40.
Léger, Louis. "Le Panslavisme," *Scientia*, XXV (1919), 33-45.
— "Panslavisme," in La Grande Encyclopédie. Pp. 954-55.
— Le Panslavisme et l'intérêt français. Paris, 1917.
Lemke, Mikhail K. Epokha tsenzurnykh reform 1859-1865 godov (The Epoch of Censorship Reforms, 1859-1865). St. Petersburg, 1904.
— Ocherki po istorii russkoi tsenzury i zhurnalistiki XIX stolietiia (Outlines on the History of Russian Censorship and Journalism in the Nineteenth Century). St. Petersburg, 1904.
Leontiev, K. Sobranie sochinenii; Vostok, Rossiia i Slavianstvo (Collected Works; the East, Russia, and Slavdom). Vols. V, VI, and VII. Moscow, 1912-13.
Leroy-Beaulieu, Anatole. Un homme d'état russe (Nicolas Milutine) d'après sa correspondance inédite. Paris, 1884.
Levine, Louis. "Pan-Slavism and European Politics," *Political Science Quarterly*, XXIX (1914), 664-86.
Liaskovskii, Valerii N. "Aleksiei Stepanovich Khomiakov; ego biografiia i uchenie" (Alexis Stepanovich Khomiakov; His Biography and Teachings), *Russkii Arkhiv*, III (1896), 338-510.
— Bratiia Kirieevskie; zhizn' i trudy ikh (The Kirieevskii Brothers; Their Life and Works). St. Petersburg, 1899.
Littman, Mark. "The Bible of Panslavism," *Nineteenth Century*, CXXXVIII (1945), 261-63.
Maikov, A. A. "Vseslavianstvo" (Panslavism), *Besieda* (March, 1871), pp. 219-61.
Maksimovich, G. A. Uchenie pervykh slavianofilov (The Teachings of the Original Slavophiles). Kiev, 1907.
Mamontov, E. "Slavianofily: istoriko-kriticheskii etiud; po povodu stat'i g. Pypina" (The Slavophiles: A Historical Critical Study; regarding Mr. Pypin's Article), *Russkii Arkhiv*, XII (1873), 2488-508.
Masaryk, T. G. Rusko a Evropa (Russia and Europe). 2d rev. ed. Prague, 1930.
— The Spirit of Russia; Studies in History, Literature, and Philosophy. 2 vols. New York and London, 1919.
Matković, Petar. "Moskovska etnografička izložba u svibnju 1867" (The Moscow Ethnographic Exhibition in May, 1867), *Rad Jugoslavenske Akademije znanosti i umjetnosti*, I (October, 1867), 189-228.
Mezhov, V. I. Russkaia istoricheskaia bibliografiia za 1865-1876 gg. (Russian Historical Bibliography for the Years 1865-1876). Vol. VI. St. Petersburg, 1886.
Mezier, A. Chto chitat' po slavianskomu voprosu (What to Read on the Slavic Question). Petrograd, 1914.
— Russkaia slovesnost' s XI po XIX stolietie (Russian Literature from the Eleventh to the Nineteenth Century). Part II. St. Petersburg, 1902.
Mijatovics, E. L. "Panslavism; Its Rise and Decline," *Fortnightly Review*, XIV, New Series (1873), 94-112.
Milićevíc, M. Dj. Etnografska izložba i slovenski sastanak u Moskvi, 1867 (The Ethnographic Exhibition and the Slavic Meeting in Moscow, 1867). Belgrade, 1884.
Miliukov, Pavel. Ocherki po istorii russkoi kul'tury (Outlines on the History of Russian Culture). 3 vols. St. Petersburg, 1903-5.
— "Razlozhenie salvianofil'stva; Danilevskii, Leontiev, Vl. Soloviëv" (The Dissolution of Slavophilism; Danilevskii, Leontiev, Vl. Soloviëv), *Voprosy filosofii i psikhologii*, XVIII (May, 1893), 46-96.
Miller, Orest. "Osnovy ucheniia pervonachal'nykh slavianofilov" (The Founda-

tions of the Teachings of the Original Slavophiles), *Russkaia Mysl'* (1880), Book 1, pp. 77-101; Book 3, pp. 1-44.

—— Slavianstvo i Evropa; Stat'i i riechi, 1865-1877 (Slavdom and Europe; Articles and Addresses, 1865-1877). St. Petersburg, 1877.

Mordovtsev, D. L. "O masonskoi lozhie 'Soedinennykh Slavian' " (On the Masonic Lodge of the "United Slavs"), *Russkaia Starina*, XXI (1878), 187-89.

—— "Razvitie slavianskoi idei v russkom obshchestvie XVII-XIX vv." (The Development of the Slavic Idea in Russian Society in the Seventeenth to the Nineteenth Centuries), *Russkaia Starina*, XXI (1878), 65-78.

Mosely, P. E. "Pan-Slavist Memorandum of Ljudevit Gaj in 1838," *American Historical Review*, XL (July, 1935), 704-16.

Mousset, Albert. Le Monde slave. 2d ed. Paris, 1946.

Mousset, Jean. La Serbie et son église, 1830-1904. Paris, 1938.

Mráz, Andrej. L'udovít Štúr. Bratislava, 1948.

"N., A." "Budushchnost' Slavianstva" (The Future of Slavdom), *Viestnik Evropy*, VI (1877), 805-29.

Narishkin-Kurakin, Elizabeth. Under Three Tsars; the Memoirs of the Lady-in-Waiting Elizabeth Narishkin-Kurakin. Translated from the German by Julia E. Loesser. New York, 1931.

Nechkina, Militsa V. Obshchestvo Soedinennykh Slavian (The Society of United Slavs). Moscow, 1927.

Neviedienskii, S. (pseudonym for S. S. Tatishchev). Katkov i ego vremia (Katkov and His Times). St. Petersburg, 1888.

"Nieskol'ko slov po voprosu o Slavianstvie" (A Few Words on the Question of a Slavdom), *Besieda*, I (1872), 216-32.

Nikitenko, A. V. Zapiski i dnevnik, 1804-1877 gg. (Memoirs and Diary, 1804-1877). 2 vols. St. Petersburg, 1904-5.

Nikitin, S. A. "Slavianskie s"ezdy shestidesiatykh godov XIX veka" in Slavianskii Sbornik; Slavianskii vopros i russkoe obshchestvo v 1867-1878 godakh (The Slavic Review; the Slavic Question and Russian Society in the Years 1867-1878). Moscow, 1948.

—— "Vozniknovenie Moskovskogo slavianskogo komiteta; Iz istorii russko-bolgarskikh sviazei posle Krymskoi voiny" (The Rise of the Moscow Slavic Committee; from the History of Russo-Bulgarian Ties after the Crimean War), *Voprosy Istorii*, VIII (1947), 50-65.

Nol'de, B. E. Iurii Samarin i ego vremia (Iurii Samarin and His Times). Paris, 1926.

Nötzel, Karl. Die Grundlagen des geistigen Russlands. Jena, 1917.

Onou, Alexander. "The Memoirs of Count N. Ignatyev," *Slavonic Review*, X (December, 1931), 386-407.

Ovsianiko-Kulikovskii, D. N. Istoriia russkoi literatury XIX vieka (The History of Russian Literature in the Nineteenth Century). Vol. I. Moscow, 1911.

Ovsianyi, N. P. Blizhnii Vostok i Slavianstvo (The Near East and Slavdom). St. Petersburg, 1913.

Palacký, F. "Suzhdenie g. Palatskago o Pol'skom voprosie" (Mr. Palacký's Appraisal of the Polish Question), *Den'*, No. 24 (June 15, 1863), pp. 14-15.

Panov, I. "Slavianofil'stvo kak filosofskoe uchenie" (Slavophilism as a Philosophical Doctrine), *Zhurnal Ministerstva Narodnago Prosvieshcheniia*, XI (1880), 1-67.

"Panslavizm i L. Shtur (Slavianstvo i mir budushchago)" (Panslavism and L. Štúr, Slavdom and the World of the Future), *Otechestvennyia Zapiski* (1867), CLXXI, 565-80; CLXXIII, 49-77.

Pavlovitch, Michel. "Romantisme et réalisme dans l'imperialisme russe," *La Revue Politique Internationale*, II (1914), 219-45.

Pervyia 15 liet sushchestvovaniia S.-Peterburgskago Slavianskago blagotvoritel'nago obshchestva; po protokolam obshchikh sobranii ego chlenov, sostoiavshimsia v 1868-1883 gg. (The First Fifteen Years of the Existence of the St. Petersburg Slavic Benevolent Society; Based on the Minutes of General Meetings of Its Members Which Took Place in the Years 1868-1883). St. Petersburg, 1893.

Perwolf, Josef. Germanizatsiia Baltiiskikh Slavian (The Germanization of the Baltic Slavs). St. Petersburg, 1876.

—— "Slavianskaia vzaimnost' s drevnieishikh vremen do XVIII vieka" (Slavic Reciprocity from Earliest Times to the Eighteenth Century), *Zhurnal Ministerstva Narodnago Prosvieshcheniia*, Vols. CLXX-CLXXII.

—— Vývin idey vzájemnosti u národův slovanských (The Development of the Idea of Reciprocity among the Slavic Peoples). Prague, 1867.

Petrov, K. P. "Slavianofil'skoe uchenie" (The Slavophile Doctrine), *Istoricheskii Viestnik*, LXXXV (1901), 897-918.

Petrovich, Michael B. "Juraj Križanić; a Precursor of Pan-Slavism," *American Slavic and East European Review*, VI (1947), 75-92.

—— "L'udovít Štúr and Russian Panslavism," *Journal of Central European Affairs*, XII (April, 1952), 1-19.

Petrovskii, N. "Slavianstvo i mir budushchago" (Slavdom and the World of the Future), *Zhurnal Ministerstva Narodnago Prosvieshcheniia* (July, 1909), pp. 194-204.

Pigarev, K. "F. I. Tiutchev i problemy vneshnei politiki tsarskoi Rossii" (F. I. Tiutchev and Problems in the Foreign Policy of Tsarist Russia), *Literaturnoe Nasledstvo*, XX (1935), 177-218.

Pišút, Milan. "Štúrovo poňatie o slovanskej kultúry" (Štúr's Conception of a Slavic Culture), *Slovanský Sborník*, Nos. 1-2 (Matica Slovenská, 1947), pp. 34-52.

Pogodin, M. P. Istoriko-politicheskiia pis'ma i zapiski vprodolzhenii krymskoi voiny 1853-1856 M. P. Pogodina (The Historico-Political Letters and Memoranda of M. P. Pogodin during the Crimean War, 1853-1856). Moscow, 1874.

—— "Ob otnosheniakh Rossii k slavianam" (On Russia's Relations with the Slavs), *Russkii* (March 20, 1867).

—— "O drevnem iazykie russkom" (On the Ancient Russian Language), *Moskvitianin*, I (1856), No. 2, 138-39.

—— Pis'ma M. P. Pogodina iz slavianskikh zemel', 1835-1861 (The Letters of M. P. Pogodin from the Slavic Lands, 1835-1861). Edited by Nil Popov. Moscow, 1878.

—— Riechi proiznesenyia M. P. Pogodinym v torzhestvennykh i prochikh sobraniiakh, 1830-1872 (Addresses Delivered by M. P. Pogodin at Celebrations and Other Meetings, 1830-1872). Moscow, 1872.

—— Sobranie statei, pisem i riechei po povodu Slavianskago voprosa (Collected Articles, Letters, and Addresses on the Slavic Question). Moscow, 1878.

—— Stat'i politicheskiia i Pol'skii vopros, 1856-1867 (Political Articles and the Polish Question, 1856-1867). Moscow, 1876.

Pokrovskaia-Lamanskaia, O. V. "Perepiska dvukh slavianofilov" (Correspondence between Two Slavophiles), *Russkaia Mysl'* (September, 1916), pp. 1-32.

Pokrovskii, M. N. "Vostochnyi vopros ot parizhskago mira do berlinskago kongressa, 1856-1878" (The Eastern Question from the Peace of Paris to the Congress of Berlin, 1856-1878), in Istoriia Rossii v XIX viekie (The History of Russia in the Nineteenth Century). Edited by M. N. Pokrovskii *et al.* St. Petersburg, n.d. Pp. 1-68.

Polit-Desančić, M. Putne uspomene (Travel Reminiscences). Novi Sad, 1896.

—— Sve dosadanje besede Dr-a Mih. Polita-Desančića (All the Addresses up to This Time of Dr. M. Polit-Desančić). Vol. I. Novi Sad, 1899.

Popov, Nil. "Die Russischen Slawophilen im vierten bis zum sechsten Jahrzehnt dieses Jahrhunderts," *Russische Revue*, II (1873), 45-55, 160-75, 261-86.

—— Istoriia Slavianskago blagotvoritel'nago komiteta v Moskvie: Vtoroe piati-lietie, 1863-1867 (History of the Slavic Benevolent Committee in Moscow: Second Five Years, 1863-1867). Moscow, 1872.

—— Iz istorii Slavianskago blagotvoritel'nago komiteta v Moskvie: Pervoe piati-lietie, 1858-1862 (From the History of the Slavic Benevolent Committee in Moscow: First Five Years, 1858-1862). Moscow, 1871.

—— Kratkii otchët o desiatilietnei dieiatelnosti (1858-1868) Slavianskago bla-gotvoritel'nago komiteta v Moskvie (Short Outline of a Decade of Activity, 1858-1868, of the Slavic Benevolent Committee in Moscow). Moscow, 1868.

—— "Nieskol'ko slov o 'narodnykh nachalakh' i o tsivilizatsii' " (A Few Words regarding "National Principles" and "Civilization"), *Sovremennik*, CVIII (June, 1865), 143-64.

—— Ocherki religioznoi i natsional'noi blagotvoritel'nosti na vostokie i sredi Slavian (Sketches of Religious and National Benevolence in the East and among the Slavs). St. Petersburg, 1871.

—— Otázka o písmu všeslovanském (The Question of an All-Slavic Alphabet). Translated from the Russian into Czech by F. A. Urbánek. Prague, 1866.

—— "Serbiia i Porta v 1861-1867 gg." (Serbia and the Porte in the Years 1861-1867), *Viestnik Evropy* (1879), I, 505-53; II, 210-78.

—— "Serbiia poslie Parizhskago mira" (Serbia after the Peace of Paris), *Besieda*, VI (1871), 165-224.

Popović, Vasilj. Istočno pitanje (The Eastern Question). Belgrade, 1928.

Pout' Slovanův do Ruska roku 1867 a její význam (Pilgrimage of the Slavs to Russia in the Year 1867 and Its Significance). Prague, 1867.

Pražák, Albert. České obrození (The Czech Renascence). Prague, 1948.

Prelog, Milan. Pout' Slovanů do Moskvy roku 1867 (Visit of the Slavs to Moscow in the Year 1867). Translated from the Serbo-Croatian MS. into Czech by Milada Paulová. Prague, 1931.

Prijatelj, Ivan. Kulturna in politična zgodovina Slovencev, 1848-1895 (The Cul-tural and Political History of the Slovenes, 1848-1895). 4 vols. Ljubljana, 1939.

Prince, John Dyneley. "The Pan-Slavonic Ideal," *Canadian Magazine*, XLVII (1916), 15-18.

Pushkarevich, K. A. "Balkanskie slaviane i russkie 'osvoboditeli' " (The Balkan Slavs and Russian "Liberators"), *Trudy Instituta slavianovedeniia Akademii nauk SSSR*, Vol. II. Leningrad, 1934. Pp. 189-229.

—— "Zapiska uchenykh chlenov Serbo-Luzhitskoi Matitsy" (Memorandum by the Learned Members of the Lusatian-Serb Matica), *Trudy Instituta slaviano-vedeniia Akademii nauk SSSR*, Vol. II. Leningrad, 1934. Pp. 293-309.

Pypin, A. N. ("A. V–n.") "Davnost' slavianskoi idei v russkom obshchestvie" (The Antiquity of the Slavic Idea in Russian Society), *Viestnik Evropy*, LXXI (May, 1878), 283-316.

—— "Der Panslavismus," *Russische Revue*, XIV (1879), 385-415, 526-48.

—— "Die polnische Frage in der Literatur der russischen Slavophilen," *Russische Revue*, XVII (1880), 193-224.

—— "Eshche nieskol'ko slov po iuzhno-slavianskom voprosu" (A Few More Words on the South Slav Question), *Viestnik Evropy*, II (March, 1877), 357-87.

—— "Iuzhane i sieveriane" (Southerners and Northerners), *Viestnik Evropy* (April, 1886), 733-76.

Pypin, A. N. (*Continued*)
—— "Iz istorii panslavizma" (From the History of Panslavism), *Viestnik Evropy,* CLXIII (1893), 267-313.
—— "Literaturnyi panslavizm" (Literary Panslavism), *Viestnik Evropy,* CCLI (1879), 591-633; CCLII (1879), 711-48; CCLIII (1879), 307-35.
—— "M. F. Raevskii i rossiiskii panslavizm" (M. F. Raevskii and Russian Panslavism), *Viestnik Evropy* (January, 1885), 439-43.
—— "Novyia dannyia o slavianskim dielakh" (New Facts about Slavic Affairs), *Viestnik Evropy,* XCIX (1893), 712-59.
—— Obshchestvennoe dvizhenie v Rossii pri Aleksandrie I (Social Movements in Russia under Alexander I). St. Petersburg, 1900.
—— "Obzor russkikh izuchenii Slavianstva" (A Review of Russian Studies of the Slavs), *Viestnik Evropy* (April-September, 1889).
—— Panslavizm v proshlom i nastoiashchem (Panslavism Past and Present). St. Petersburg, 1913.
—— "Russkoe slavianoviedenie v XIX-m stolietii" (Russian Slavic Studies in the Nineteenth Century), *Viestnik Evropy,* IV-V (1889), Book 7, 238-74; Book 8, 683-728; Book 9, 257-305.
—— "Teoriia obshcheslavianskago iazyka" (The Theory of an All-Slavic Language), *Viestnik Evropy* (1892), Book 2.
—— "Zamietka po iuzhno-slavianskomu voprosu" (An Observation on the South Slav Question), *Viestnik Evropy,* III (June, 1877), 803-8.
Rapant, Daniel. "Štúrovci a Slovanstvo" (Štúr's Followers and Slavdom), *Slovanský Sborník,* Nos. 1-2 (Matica Slovenská, 1947), pp. 22-34.
Rapoport, Semen. "The Russian Slavophiles and the Polish Question," *Polish Review,* I (April, 1917), 141-52.
Rappoport, Angelo S. "The Slav Peril; Pangermanism versus Panslavism," *Nineteenth Century,* LXXIV (August, 1913), 283-94.
Reclus, Elisée. "Le Panslavisme et l'unité russe," *La Revue,* XLVII (1903), 273-84.
Riasanovsky, Nicholas V. Russia and the West in the Teaching of the Slavophiles. Harvard University Press, 1952.
Rieger, František. "Otviet doktora Rigera g. Gil'ferdingu" (Doctor Rieger's Reply to Mr. Hilferding), *Den',* No. 28 (July 13, 1863), pp. 11-14.
Rozenberg, Vladimir. Russkaia pechat' i tsenzura v proshlom i nastoiashchem (The Russian Press and Censorship in the Past and Present). Moscow, 1905.
Rubinshtein, Nikolai L. Russkaia istoriografiia (Russian Historiography). Moscow, 1941.
Russkii Slavianin (pseudonym). Pervyi vseslavianskii s"iezed v Rossii, ego prichiny i znachenie (The First All-Slavic Congress in Russia, Its Causes and Significance). Moscow, 1857. (This date is a typographical error and should read 1867.)
Samarin, Iurii F. "Dva Slova o narodnosti v naukie" (Two Words concerning Nationality in Learning), *Russkaia Besieda,* I (1856), 34-47.
—— Sochineniia (Works). Vol. I. Moscow, 1877.
—— Sochineniia (Works). Vol. I. 2d ed. Moscow, 1900.
—— Sochineniia (Works). Vol. XII. Moscow, 1911.
Schubart, Walter. Europa und die Seele des Ostens. Lucerne, 1938.
—— Russia and Western Man. New York, 1950.
Seligman, Raphael. "Die Grundlagen des Panslawismus," *Sozialistische Monatshefte,* Jahrg. 20, II (1914), 1246-253.
Sembratovytch, Romain. Le Tsarisme et l'Ukraine. Paris, 1907.
Semevskii, V. I. "Nikolai Ivanovich Kostomarov, 1817-1885," *Russkaia Starina* (1886), pp. 181-212.

Seton-Watson, R. W. "Pan-Slavism," *Contemporary Review*, CX (1916), 419-29.
Shchebal'skii, P. "Prezhnii i nynieshnii panslavizm" (Panslavism Before and Now), *Russkii Viestnik*, LXII (1867), 830-41.
Skabichevskii, A. M. Ocherki istorii russkoi tsenzury, 1700-1863 (Outline of the History of Russian Censorship, 1700-1863). St. Petersburg, 1892.
Skerlić, Jovan. Istorija nove srpske književnosti (The History of Modern Serbian Literature). Belgrade, 1926.
—— Omladina i njena književnost (The Omladina and Its Literature). Belgrade, 1906.
Sladkevich, N. "K voprosu o polemike N. G. Chernyshevskogo so slavianofil'skoi publitsistikoi" (On the Question of N. G. Chernyshevskii's Polemics with the Slavophile Press), *Voprosy Istorii* (June, 1948), pp. 71-79.
"Slavianskii blagotvoritel'nyi komitet" (The Slavic Benevolent Committee), *Besieda*, VIII (1872), 18-22.
Slavianskii sbornik (Slavic Review). 3 vols. St. Petersburg, 1875-77.
Slavianskii s"iezd v Pragie i godovshchina s"iezda v Moskvie (The Slavic Congress in Prague and the Anniversary of the Congress in Moscow). Moscow, 1868.
"Slovanská vzájemnost' (Panslavismus)," (Slavic Reciprocity [Panslavism]), in Ottův Slovník naučný, Vol. XXIII. Prague, 1905.
Smoliar, I. E. (Smoleŕ, Jan Arnošt). "Golos zagranichnago knigoprodavtsa ob ustroistvie russkoi knizhnoi torgovli" (The Voice of a Foreign Bookseller concerning the Establishment of a Russian Trade in Books), *Russkaia Besieda*, IV (1858), Smies, 81-102.
Sorokin, Pitirim. Social Philosophies of an Age of Crisis. Boston, 1950.
Spasovich, V. D. "Po povodu broshiury Oresta Millera: Slavianskii vopros v naukie i v zhizni" (Regarding Orest Miller's Brochure: The Slavic Question in Learning and in Life), in his Sochineniia (Works), Vol. IV. St. Petersburg, 1891. Pp. 233-44.
Stählin, Karl. "Die Entstehung des Panslavismus," *Germanoslavica*, IV (1936), 1-25, 237-62.
Steppun, F. "Niemetskii romantizm i russkoe slavianfil'stvo" (German Romanticism and Russian Slavophilism), *Russkaia Mysl'* (March, 1910), pp. 65-91.
Strakhov, N. N. Bor'ba s zapadom v nashei literaturie (The Struggle with the West in Our Literature). Vol. II. St. Petersburg, 1883.
—— "Danilevskii i slavianofil'stvo" (Danilevskii and Slavophilism), in *Otchët S.-Peterburgskago Slavianskago blagotvoritel'nago obshchestva 1886* (Report of the St. Petersburg Slavic Benevolent Society for 1886), pp. 181-83.
—— ("Russkii.") "Rokovoi vopros" (The Fatal Question), *Vremia*, IV (1863), 152-63.
—— "Zhizn' i trudy N. Ia. Danilevskago" (The Life and Works of N. Ia. Danilevskii), in Rossiia i Evropa (Russia and Europe) by N. Ia. Danilevskii. 5th ed. St. Petersburg, 1895. Pp. ix-xxxv.
Strakhovsky, Leonid I. A Handbook of Slavic Studies. Harvard University Press, 1949.
Struve, Peter. "Ivan Aksakov," *Slavonic Review*, II (March, 1924), 514-18.
Štúr, L'udovit. Das Slawenthum und die Welt der Zukunft (Slovanstvo a svět budoucností). Edited by Josef Jirásek. Bratislava, 1931.
—— (Shtur, Liudovit.) "Slavianstvo i mir budushchago; Poslanie Slavianam s beregov Dunaia" (Slavdom and the World of the Future; an Epistle to the Slavs from the Banks of the Danube), *Chteniia v Imperatorskom Obshchestvie istorii i drevnostei Rossiiskikh* (1867), Vol. III. Book One, Materialy slavianskie, 1-191.

Sukhotin, S. M. "Iz pamiatnykh tetradei S. M. Sukhotina, 1867-god" (From the Journal of S. M. Sukhotin for the Year 1867), *Russkii Arkhiv*, I (1894), 599-610.

Sumner, B. H. "Ignatyev at Constantinople, 1864-1874," *Slavonic and East European Review*, XI (January, 1933), 341-65; (April, 1933), 556-71.

—— Peter the Great and the Ottoman Empire. Oxford, 1949.

—— "Russia and Panslavism in the Eighteen-Seventies," *Transactions of the Royal Historical Society*, Fourth Series, XVIII (1935), 25-52.

—— Russia and the Balkans, 1870-1880. Oxford, 1937.

Timanskaia, L. Ia. "Gosudarstvennyi istoricheskii arkhiv Leningradskoi oblasti: Obzor dokumental'nykh materialov fonda S.-Peterburgskago slavianskogo blagotvoritel'nogo Obshchestva (1868-1921)" (State Historical Archives of the Leningrad Region: A Review of Documentary Materials in the Collection of the St. Petersburg Slavic Benevolent Society, 1868-1921), *Slavianskii Sbornik*. Moscow, 1947. Pp. 359-65.

Tiutchev, F. I. Stikhotvoreniia (Poems). Edited by K. Pigarev. Moscow, 1935.

—— Tiutcheviana. Foreword by Georgii Chulkov. Moscow, 1922.

Tobolka, Zdeněk. "Der Panslavismus," *Zeitschrift für Politik*, IV (1913), 215-35.

—— Politické dějiny československého národa od r. 1848 až do dnešní doby (The Political History of the Czechoslovak People from 1848 to the Present). Prague, 1932-36.

Trubetskaia, O. Materialy dlia biografii kn. V. A. Cherkasskago (Materials for a Biography of Prince V. A. Cherkasskii). Vol. I. Moscow, 1901.

"Ts., A." "Mysl' o soborie po dielu Bolgarskomu" (The Idea of a Council on the Bulgarian Question), *Den'*, No. 13 (January 13, 1862), pp. 4-5.

Uspenskii, F. Kak voznik i razvivalsia v Rossii vostochnyi vopros (How the Eastern Question Arose and Developed in Russia). Moscow, 1887.

Ustrialov, N. "Natsional'naia problema u pervykh slavianofilov" (The National Problem among the First Slavophiles), *Russkaia Mysl'*, X (1916), 1-22.

Vassili, Paul. Behind the Veil at the Russian Court. London, 1914.

Viazemskii, P. A. "Pis'mo kniaza P. A. Viazemskago k K. S. Aksakovu (1857)" (Letter by Prince P. A. Viazemskii to K. S. Aksakov, 1857), *Russkii Arkhiv*, XI (1879), 404-6.

Vinogradov, Paul. "The Slavophile Creed," *Hibbert Journal*, XIII (1915), 243-60.

Voroponov, F. "Sorok liet tomu nazad" (Forty Years Ago), *Viestnik Evropy*, IV (1904), Part VI, 437-66.

Voznesenskii, S. Russkaia literatura o slavianstvie (Russian Literature on the Slavs). Petrograd, 1915.

—— Slavianstvo v russkoi zhurnalistikie, 1896-1914 (The Slavs in Russian Periodicals, 1896-1914). Petrograd, 1915.

V pamiat' Iuriia Fëdorovicha Samarina; riechi proiznesenyia v Peterburgie i v Moskvie po povodu ego konchiny (To the Memory of Iurii Fëdorovich Samarin: Addresses Delivered in St. Petersburg and in Moscow on the Occasion of His Death). St. Petersburg, 1876.

Vserossiiskaia efnograficheskaia vystavka i Slavianskii s"iezd v maie 1867 goda (The All-Russian Ethnographic Exhibition and the Slavic Congress in May, 1867). Moscow, 1867.

Wallace, Mackenzie. Russia. New York, 1878.

Weingart, Miloš. Slovanská vzájemnost: Úvahy o jejích základech a osudech (Slavic Reciprocity: Essays on Its Bases and Destinies). Bratislava, 1926.

Zabolotskii, P. A. "Vozrozhdenie idei slavianskoi vzaimnosti i novyia izucheniia slavianstva" (The Birth of the Idea of Slavic Reciprocity and New Studies on the Slavs), *Sbornik Istoriko-filologicheskago obshchestva*, VIII (1912-13), 1-31.

Zaderatskii, N. P. Slavianskii ezhegodnik; Kalendar' na 1876 god (visokosnyi), (Slavic Almanac; Calendar for the Year 1876, Leap-Year). Kiev, 1876.

"Zapadnye Slaviane" (The Western Slavs), *Russkaia Besieda*, IV (1858), 1-65.

Zavitnevich, V. Z. Russkie slavianofily i ikh znachenie v dielie uiasneniia idei narodnosti i samobytnosti (The Russian Slavophiles and Their Significance in the Clarification of the Idea of Nationality and Way of Life). Kiev, 1915.

Zen'kovskii, V. V. Russkie mysliteli i Evropa; kritika evropeiskoi kultury u russkikh myslitelei (Russian Thinkers and Europe; a Critique of European Culture by Russian Thinkers). Paris, 1926.

—— (Zenkovsky, V. V.) "The Slavophil Idea Re-stated," *Slavonic Review*, VI (December, 1927), 302-10.

Zernov, Nikolai. Three Russian Prophets: Khomiakov, Dostoevsky, Soloviev. London, 1944.

Zhinzifov, Ks. R. "Pis'mo odnogo iz uchashchikhsia v Moskvie Bolgar k redaktoru" (Letter to the Editor by a Bulgarian Student in Moscow), *Den'*, No. 3 (October 28, 1861), p. 13.

INDEX

Date D